GOD AND MAMMON IN AMERICA

THE FREE PRESS
A Division of Macmillan, Inc.
NEW YORK

Maxwell Macmillan Canada
TORONTO

Maxwell Macmillan International
NEW YORK   OXFORD   SINGAPORE   SYDNEY

GOD
AND
MAMMON
IN
AMERICA

Robert Wuthnow

The Free Press
A Division of Macmillan, Inc.
866 Third Avenue, New York, N.Y. 10022

Maxwell Macmillan Canada, Inc.
1200 Eglinton Avenue East
Suite 200
Don Mills, Ontario M3C 3N1

Macmillan, Inc. is part of the Maxwell Communication Group of Companies

Printed in the United States of America

printing number
1 2 3 4 5 6 7 8 9 10

Library of Congress Cataloging-in-Publication Data

Wuthnow, Robert.
    God and Mammon in America / Robert Wuthnow.
        p.   cm.
    Includes bibliographical references and index.
    ISBN 0-02-935628-8
    1. Economics—Religious aspects.   2. United States—Religion.
    3. United States—Economic conditions.   I. Title.
    BL2525.W86   1994
    306.6'911785'0973—dc20

                                                                                94–18799
                                                                                        CIP

He owns the cattle on a thousand hills,
The wealth in every mine.
He owns the rivers and the rocks and rills,
The sun and stars that shine.
Wonderful riches more than tongues can tell,
He is my Father so they're mine as well.

—Children's chorus

Contents

Preface

Possibilities for gossip and intrigue notwithstanding, others' confessions are seldom as interesting to us as our own. It follows, I suppose, that prefaces were invented to let authors confess their foibles without readers needing to show much interest. True to the norm, therefore, let me admit that this book does have an autobiographical dimension—and that I've tried hard to stifle it. My own upbringing in largely Presbyterian and Baptist circles impressed the importance of religious questions on me at an early age. Having had the misfortune of majoring in economics and business as an undergraduate, I spent many years thereafter puzzling about how such thinking could ever be reconciled with matters of faith. Writing the present book was thus a way for me to struggle explicitly with questions that have been of personal interest for a long time.

The more important reason for writing it, though, is that the relationship between religious faith and economic behavior remains profoundly significant to the health and direction of our society. Certainly the scandals that rocked the business community in the 1980s pointed to the need to consider whether there were any sources of value and commitment that could curb overweening, greedy self-interest. Religious leaders and ethicists have also been paying greater attention to questions about work, the uses of money, and economic justice. Yet few attempts have been made to bring empirical information to bear on these discussions. Nor has much attention been devoted to applying and updating the legacy of theorizing about these issues that was initiated a century ago by Max Weber and others. As a result, the subject remains frequently alluded to but is seldom addressed systematically.

To be more specific, surveying the books most commonly used in undergraduate and graduate sociology of religion courses reveals that the topic of religion and economic behavior is virtually ignored in all of these books. A look at books used in economics courses yields even less. Despite the burgeoning of economic sociology as a new field in recent years, scholars have paid hardly any attention to religion in this work either. Yet one can scarcely read any of the classic figures in sociology—Marx, Durkheim, Weber, Troeltsch, Simmel—without being impressed by the amount of attention they devoted to this topic.

Delving into a somewhat broader array of literature nevertheless shows clearly how much the relationship between religion and economic behavior remains of interest in many quarters. Publishing houses associated with religious bodies—Catholic, mainline Protestant, evangelical, and independent alike—have been the source of numerous writings on this relationship over the past decade. Theological treatises on work and money abound, as do all varieties of how-to books dealing with career selection, job stress, workaholism, money, family budgets, materialism, and a host of related subjects, all from a religious perspective. Religious leaders and religious organizations have also been involved in numerous activities bearing directly on economic behavior. From papal pronouncements on the subject to statements by the National Conference of Catholic Bishops to policy papers by nearly all the major Protestant denominations to stockholder resolutions and boycotts—religiously motivated activism has been paying increasing attention to the economic sphere. Religious organizations are themselves economic entities taking in huge sums of money each year. And their role in sponsoring volunteer activities and in promoting charitable giving is considerable.

One of the reasons why no general overview of the subject has been written from a sociological perspective is that relatively little has yet been done in the way of empirical research. Compared with, say, the topic of religion and politics, about which so much has been written in recent years, religion and economic behavior remains an unexplored field. This is because no major movement, such as the New Religious Right in the 1980s or the New Religious Movements of the 1970s, has emerged to spark concentrated interest in the subject. There has, however, been much speculation about the social significance of such issues as overwork, materialism, greed, and economic exploitation. In fact, a considerable number of scattered studies have dealt with such topics as religion and job-related stress, religion and employment, religion and work values, and religion and charitable giving. And there remains, of course, the substantial theoretical legacy of the founding writers themselves.

Both the need and the opportunity, therefore, suggest that the time is ripe for a volume devoted specifically to the relationships between religion and economic behavior. The present volume is, however, conceived less as a survey of the existing literature than as an effort to build on previous work through the presentation of new evidence. This evidence comes primarily from a major national survey conducted as part of a five-year project on Religious and Economic Beliefs and Values, of which I was the director. The survey was conducted among a nationally representative sample of more than two thousand members of the U.S. labor force. The questionnaire, which on average took more than an hour to administer, included specific items on numerous aspects of the relationship between religion and economic behavior and values, as well as a wide range of questions about work, money, material possessions, values, and interests. The study, to my knowledge, thus provides more ample information on the relationship between religion and economic behavior than any previous research. The quantitative data were also supplemented by in-depth qualitative interviews with more than 175 people in various occupations and regions of the country. A wide range of published and unpublished material, including sermons, tracts, stewardship reports, and newspaper clippings, were consulted as well. In addition, use was made of a recent national survey that I conducted on volunteerism and charitable giving and of data made available from several recent studies conducted by Independent Sector, Inc.

Although based primarily on original research, this volume is intended for a broad, nonspecialized audience and for use in undergraduate and graduate courses on the sociology of religion, religious studies, American religion, or religion and society. The material is relatively free of jargon but makes ample references to the relevant theoretical and empirical literature. Although personal biases are inevitable, I have deliberately tried to avoid taking a single perspective on the subject matter and have tried not to present the data in such a way that favors a single theme or normative outlook. My aim is rather to pose alternative arguments wherever possible and present data that bear on these arguments. I must, therefore, apologize in advance to readers who may have expected me to take a strong position favoring or opposing certain religious teachings or economic activities. For the specialist, however, I believe there is a great deal here worth considering. Besides presenting new evidence, I have also tried to make sense of this evidence by relating it to theoretical concerns and to characteristics of contemporary society. At the end of each chapter I have provided an interpretive summary that pulls together various threads of analysis and speculates about their meaning. In Chapters 8 and 9 I have presented a synthesis of a broader sort, attempting especially to suggest why religious and economic commitments intermingle in contemporary society as they do.

I should also explain at the outset that this book does not try to address the entire range of topics that its title might conjure up. How broad changes in economic conditions over time have contributed to shifts in religious commitments has been treated so often in other contexts that I have paid relatively modest attention to it here. Topics such as the internal financing and organization of religious bodies as economic entities or the pronouncements of particular religious traditions on economic issues are also dealt with more fully in other recent studies. I have focused on topics that draw the relationship between religion and economic behavior at the individual level. Thus work, money, attitudes toward materialism, views of the poor and of economic justice, and charitable behavior merit special consideration. In addressing these topics, I of course had to situate them in a broader historical and social context as well.

Among the nations of the world, the United States has been exceptionally privileged. Its economic growth has at times been spectacular. Despite present concerns, its level of affluence remains extraordinarily high relative to that of the rest of the human population. In the midst of this affluence, many Americans still live in abject poverty, and scarcely anyone escapes feeling now and then that times are hard. Yet for most Americans, material well-being has been a fact of life.

It has thus been common for social observers interested in the connection between religion and economic life to stress the so-called gospel of wealth—how religious convictions legitimated affluence, and how the rich in turn shaped religious teachings to their own ends.

Clergy such as William Lawrence, the Episcopal bishop who came close to equating material prosperity with Christian virtue, and Russell Conwell, the Baptist minister who exhorted men and women of faith to pursue money, have provided ample grist for such reflections. Some of the individuals featured in this book are also people of enormous wealth. And some of them have found justification for their riches in religious teachings.

But my concern is more with the ways in which ordinary Americans think about their faith and work, their faith and finances. For ordinary Americans, religious convictions many times encourage them to think about the tensions involved in serving two masters. But what this means, and how it connects to their lives and to their spirituality, is generally far from simple.

The research on which this volume is based was made possible by a grant from the Lilly Endowment. I wish especially to thank Craig Dykstra and Fred Hofheinz at the Endowment for their interest and encouragement. In an early stage of the project I solicited comments from a number of scholars. I am particularly grateful to the following for their suggestions: John Boli, Neil Smelser, Nathan Hatch, Martin Marty, Mark Noll, Jeffrey Stout, and John F. Wilson. Others who merit special thanks include Harry Cotugno, Roberta Fiske Rusciano, Natalie Searl, Elaine Friedman, Timothy Clydesdale, Yvonne Veugelers, Matthew Lawson, John Schmalzbauer, and Tracy Scott.

GOD AND MAMMON IN AMERICA

Chapter One

Serving Two Masters

Most of us are working ourselves to death. At least we feel that way as we rush to our next appointment. We are consumed by our jobs, working longer hours than ever before, struggling to stay employed and to get the next promotion. Cellular phones and E-mail make it harder for us to escape. We search restlessly for the meaning of life in what we accomplish. Most of us are also caught up in a spiral of materialism and consumer spending. We want more money so we can buy more things. We may deny that our happiness depends on these purchases, but the more we have, the more we seem to want.

As a nation, we are now facing serious questions about our future: How much longer can we continue at this pace? Can we force ourselves to work even harder? Can we cut back our material desires and still be happy, especially as economic conditions yield less prosperity in the years ahead? Furthermore, given the pressures most families are now experiencing, can we still pursue the ideals that have animated us in the past—ideals of helping the poor and providing social justice for all?

At most times in our nation's history, the churches would have had much to say about these questions. They would have counseled Americans to keep work in proper perspective and to avoid pinning their hopes on material rewards. The churches would have been a force in public discussions about poverty, welfare, and social justice. And (with a few exceptions) they would have argued vehemently for spirituality in opposition to our obsession with material goods. But where are the

1

churches today? Are they still capable of making a difference in the ways Americans behave economically? Or have the churches lost their voice?

God and Mammon

Each Saturday and Sunday, some seventy-five million Americans flock to synagogues, churches, mosques, temples, meeting houses, and fellowship halls. Each week at least fifty million participate in small fellowship groups that study the Bible, pray, and discuss spiritual issues. Virtually the entire population attests to believing in God. Most pray to this God every day. Most of the rest do so when misfortune strikes. A significant majority of the public claim to be interested in nurturing their spirituality, and many think deeply and often about their relationship to God. Even those who are not formally active in religious congregations manifest an exceptional and abiding interest in the sacred. Hundreds of thousands of Bibles are purchased each year. Religious magazines, publishing houses, radio programs, and television stations spread their messages far and wide. Seminars, workshops, and the growing numbers of students enrolling in religion courses on college campuses attest to the continuing attraction of faith. We are, in short, a deeply religious people.

As a nation of believers, we would expect our religious commitments to have a decisive impact on our economic behavior. But we are also passionately committed to the almighty dollar. We devote the bulk of our waking hours to earning it and much of the rest of our time to finding ways to spend it. In our more candid moments, we admit to being thoroughly materialistic (while deploring this trait in our children). We believe in the proverbial bottom line, shoulder greater and greater personal economic obligations, and fret about how to pay our bills. These are, we tell ourselves, matters of sheer necessity. But they also enlist our hearts and minds. Gainful employment supplies us with meaning and purpose for living. Work becomes a means of self-expression. Having money makes us happy. Financial setbacks destroy our self-esteem. We associate freedom with having a shiny new automobile capable of doubling the speed limit, and with having a Rolex watch, Armani shoes, a Sony CD system, a Lexus coupe, or whatever the latest symbols of material status may be.

How is it possible for us to be both? How do we reconcile these two aspects of our national character? Jesus warned his followers of the impossibility of serving God and Mammon. Are those who claim to be his followers today, then, defying this warning by trying to be spiritual and yet being unwilling to detach from materialistic pursuits? Or perhaps we have found a way to get beyond these ancient tensions, living in material abundance and yet keeping our eyes fixed steadfastly on the sacred. Perhaps American religion even encourages us in some subtle way to amass worldly riches. Or perhaps our faith has become so narrowly defined that it seldom pricks our conscience when pocketbook issues are at stake.

These are not strictly academic questions. Of course they bear on how we understand the larger dilemmas facing our society. If we are motivated by high spiritual ideals, we may think of our society quite differently than if we are motivated by crass materialism. How we try to solve our national problems—the public policies we support and the organizations we look to for guidance—will also depend on how we answer this question. But there are disturbing personal issues here as well. How should I conduct my life? Do my commitments to the sacred have any bearing on my decisions at work? Does my faith influence the ways I spend my money? Can I be a believer and not feel a special burden for the poor? When things are rotten financially, can faith make a difference? And if so, what is that difference? A person invariably faces these questions, whether Protestant, Catholic, Jew, member of some other faith, or simply one of the many who pursue the sacred in their own individualistic way.

Religious leaders try to be helpful when these questions arise. For the most part they believe faith is still relevant to the ways in which people think about work and money. They write books and articles on the subject. Their denominations issue policy statements about economic justice. They preach sermons on stewardship. But one can easily wonder whether their preachments make any difference. Compare the weekly sermon those seventy-five million Americans hear with the daily bombardment of television commercials to which they are exposed or the "do-this-or-get-fired" pressures they experience at work. Put a few thousand dollars in their pocket and send a young couple out to make a down payment on a new car: how much is some vague religious teaching about stewardship going to matter, compared with arguments about sportiness and acceleration?

Most economists would have us believe that the spiritual and the material exist in happy and harmonious isolation from each other. After all, they would argue, economic behavior is neutral with respect to human values. A person can pursue any aims; the marketplace simply facilitates the process. Preferences may influence the kind of work a person chooses or what he or she buys. But these preferences are private, random, and rooted in personality factors. Moreover, the modern economy works effectively because religious leaders have learned to mind their own business. Nothing would be worse than preachers purporting to understand the complexities of the market. Economics and sacred tradition are simply separate spheres. Yet the economists' arguments are likely to be armchair abstractions that are not rooted in an understanding of how people actually lead their lives.

The truth is that virtually nothing is known about how Americans relate their religious convictions and their economic pursuits. We do not know, for example, whether religious values enter into people's thinking when they are trying to choose a career. We do not know whether the devout are more satisfied with their jobs than the less devout. We do not know whether those who pray regularly may be better able to withstand the pressures of their jobs than other people. We do not know whether one group behaves more ethically in the workplace than another. Nor do we know much about how faith may influence orientations toward money and material possessions. Does it encourage people to be less greedy? Does it help them think more seriously about their responsibilities to the poor? Or does it simply make them feel better about their own material passions?

This book aims to answer these questions. Its premise is that religious faith, having been relevant to the ways in which people understood their work and their money throughout most of history, remains a vital part of our cultural heritage and, for this reason, is a resource to be considered carefully as we think about the economic pressures that face our families and our nation. Spiritual conviction can guide us to live more fully than by pursuing only crass materialistic aims alone. But we must also realize that recent developments in our society make it harder to know what the relevance of faith may be. To assess the contemporary situation, I present evidence from a new survey conducted among more than two thousand randomly selected men and women in the U.S. labor force. I also draw on qualitative evidence gleaned from in-depth interviews with 175 men and women spanning all the major faith traditions and a wide variety of occupational experiences. I examine the statistical relationships between various indicators of religious commitment and a wide range of issues having to do with work, workplace ethics, money, materialism, wealth and poverty, and charitable giving. I also report how people talk about their understandings of these issues.

The Ambiguous Presence

My argument is that religious commitment still exerts a significant influence on economic behavior in the United States, but that its influence is often mixed, leading more to ambivalence than to informed ethical decisions or to distinct patterns of life. On a broad array of personal issues—career choices, job satisfaction, commitment to work, willingness or unwillingness to cut corners, honesty at work, views of money, financial worries, views of materialism and advertising, attitudes toward economic justice and the poor, and charitable giving—we are vitally affected by our religious commitments. We still believe that biblical teachings, the churches, and the clergy have an important bearing on our finances and our jobs. Many of us think about the possible relevance of our faith to our work and our attitudes toward money. We pray that things will go well for us, we hear sermons counseling us to work hard and to be good stewards, and many of us give lip service to the idea that greed is a sin or that God is concerned about the poor. For millions of us, faith nudges our attitudes and our economic behavior in one direction or another. It does so, however, in ways that are seldom as powerful as religious leaders would like and that do little to challenge the status quo.

Religion is thus an ambiguous presence in our society. It sends mixed signals about our work, telling us to work hard but not too hard. It counsels us to be diligent with our money but seldom instructs us in how to be diligent. Indeed, it raises our anxieties about money and discourages us from talking openly about them. It warns us against the excessive materialism that pervades our society but offers little to keep us from the temptations of materialism. Feeling ambivalent about the role of faith, we therefore go about our lives pretty much the same as those who have no faith at all.

When we *are* influenced by our faith, we are more likely to say we feel better about what we do than to do anything differently. We do not look to the churches to tell us what career to pursue or what purchases to make but to tell us that whatever choices we have made are OK. Our spirituality is often little more than a therapeutic device. Having a relationship to God is a way of making ourselves feel better. Faith is a way of massaging our feelings. We pray for comfort but do not expect to be challenged. We have domesticated the sacred by stripping it of authoritative wisdom and by looking to it only to make us happy.

On issue after issue, we shall see that religious teachings make some difference to the ways in which Americans think about work and money, but not a strong difference or one that could readily be anticipated from knowledge of these teachings themselves. Religious leaders want the churches to play a heroic role in our society—challenging people to make deep commitments, inspiring them to great deeds of service, encouraging them to be concerned for the poor, and liberating us from the excesses of greed and materialism. In reality, religious faith prompts few people in any of these directions. Instead, spirituality encourages us to keep our options open, to be flexible, to think positively, and to find satisfaction in small things. From time to time, it pricks our conscience but seldom slams into us with full force—at least not where our wallets are concerned.

Why? Some of the blame must be attributed to religious leaders. It can be dangerous to afflict the comfortable, especially when they are needed to balance church budgets and to finance the new wing of the Christian education building. But the deeper answer is found in the changing character of our society itself. We live in a postindustrial setting in which many of the old rules and expectations no longer make sense. Faith now influences economic behavior but in ways that are decidedly fluid, personalistic, relativistic, situational, and psychological. Our society is no longer governed in a way that allows churches to exercise direct control over the economy. Compared with the nineteenth century, we live in a time when the rules of success are less clear as well. Working longer may not be as helpful as somehow working smarter; living morally disciplined lives may not seem as important as learning to adapt and to get along with others. In keeping with these changes, our faith is now less likely to control our bodies or help us discipline our minds. Spirituality is more likely to focus on how we feel about ourselves. If it guides us at all, it helps us to fit in and to roll with the punches, rather than taking ourselves too seriously.

The way in which our faith influences our economic behavior is to an important degree a function of the economic system itself and, more broadly, a reflection of the cultural norms that govern Middle America. Thus, religious commitment often makes only a marginal difference to the economic behavior of individual believers. It does not, for example, encourage believers to choose different careers, work longer hours, or spend less money than anyone else. Spirituality makes our work and our material goods more meaningful, thereby heightening our commitment to the workforce and the marketplace but also counseling us to keep these commitments in perspective by balancing them with commitments to our families. Faith adds gravity to our economic behavior by encouraging us to perform responsibly, by telling us we have to make our own decisions, and by reassuring us that some order exists in an otherwise chaotic world. At the same time, religious belief leaves the larger assumptions governing our economic system largely unchallenged. Rather than finding themselves at odds with the economic demands of secular society, believers feel comforted, more secure in the propriety of their own decisions, and more confident about the future.

Rethinking Spirituality

Thus, prevailing understandings of how faith operates in our society need to be reexamined. Rather than asserting, as some observers do, that religion becomes increasingly irrelevant in contemporary life, we need to recognize the continuing relevance of faith. Certainly we need to acknowledge that faith makes more of a difference to the ways in which Americans think and behave than most economists admit. But we also need to go beyond the simplistic assumption that religion is a constant—or growing—influence in contemporary society. We may look at high rates of church attendance or near-universal belief in God and assume that faith is still as powerful as it ever was. But to think that nothing has changed would require an incredible leap of faith itself.

Religious organizations can still make a difference to the ways in which we work and spend our money, but only if religious leaders recognize that the rules guiding our habits regarding work and money are changing. For faith to have an impact on economic behavior, it must now come to terms with the fact that social conditions have altered the character of economic behavior itself, and thus the ways in which it might be affected by sacred tradition. Work has become more complex, requiring greater skill and more individual discretion. The contemporary labor force is composed of people who have mostly changed careers several times since they finished school, who are often learning new skills, who are rewarded for their ability to process information and make complex decisions, and who relate to an ever-changing array of specialists, clients, and co-workers. Contrary to the image of inflexible bureaucracy envisioned by nineteenth-century observers, the contemporary workplace is more like a honeycomb in which informal relationships make an enormous difference. In these circumstances implicit norms provide their own standards of ethical evaluation. Many of the issues concerning moral discipline once embraced by religious leaders have now been removed entirely from the religious arena and placed in legal and professional institutions. Much of the remaining impact of religion is thus refocused on matters of individual meaning and personal happiness.

Living as we do in an affluent society and depending on the sale of consumer goods and services, most of us also relate to the economy as importantly in our role as consumers as workers. Again, we are faced with mixed signals on every side. Many of our purchases are really fixed payments. So counsels of responsibility and personal discipline may seem irrelevant. But we are never certain whether we have made the right choices in other areas. A form of spirituality that makes us feel better about our choices is likely to be attractive indeed. Conceptions of spirituality also function in the background, remaining in a separate compartment from our thinking about work and money, and perhaps shaping how we conceive of reality, but they no longer provide tightly regulated norms of individual behavior.

Even on broader social questions, such as issues of economic justice, stewardship, and obligations to the poor, religious commitment has not by any means retreated from the field of public discussion, but faith has become imbricated in a subtle but sweeping redefinition of the field, encouraging individuals to do only what they can, given the overwhelming institutional constraints that operate in the wider society. Above all, religious commitment appears to nudge other commitments in limited ways and to inhibit them from becoming obsessions, thereby playing a role in creating the kind of protean person who can function in today's complex economic environment.

In short, I am suggesting that orientations toward such economic activities as work, making money, and purchasing goods require us to examine how economic and social conditions are currently reshaping American religion. These orientations provide such a critical connection because we can, by examining them, see what impact religious commitments have, and thus what the limitations are when traditional religious teachings are applied in these areas. A religious concept like stewardship, for example, has been around for centuries, but it has specific meanings and implications at present that it has not always had. Why it takes its present form, therefore, points our attention to the broader restraints and needs built into our society.

This book is also intended as a challenge to the faithful. Religious leaders and their followers can do something to alter the course of their ministries if they find themselves unsettled by the evidence presented here. The reason religious commitment has the consequences it does is not completely because of inexorable forces in the economy. Strong as those forces may be, religious organizations have contributed to the strength of these trends by following the path of least resistance. The implications of faith for work or for the handling of money have often been neglected entirely by religious leaders. In other cases, the clergy have discussed these issues in such generalities that believers were left to make their own decisions based on what felt most comfortable at the moment. These tactics have perhaps been in the short-term interest of religious leaders—seldom rocking the boat, seldom offending their middle-class congregants, and seldom disrupting the steady flow of charitable giving on which their salaries depended. In the process, religious leaders have nevertheless given away much of their birthright.

If faith supplies little more than a comforting pat on the back, growing numbers of people will turn to their friends, spouses, neighbors, employers, and brokers for the same assurances. And if religious teachings send mixed signals, then we need times to gather with other believers and spiritual seekers to explore the implications of these signals. Only by reckoning with the limitations of its actual message can organized religion regain its mission of challenging the comfortable materialism of its members.

Work and money are too central to our lives to be divorced from the values and assumptions of our faith. We need the guidance and the moral strength to make hard decisions—about cutting back when we find our work stealing too much of our energy, about difficult ethical questions at work, about our consumer spending, and about ways to be of service to others. We also need guidance and moral strength in thinking about the pervasive materialism of our society, the huge disparities between rich and poor, and the ministries of our churches and charitable organizations.

Chapter Two

Our Moment in History

Lindsey Rice has it all—all the pressure and anxiety that come with being a working woman, a mother, a financial success, a homeowner, and a reliable member of the community. At forty, she is as trim as she was when she graduated from college. She exudes self-confidence. But the daily stress is beginning to take its toll. For the past nine years, she's been running a management consulting firm. Every day she has reports, meetings, and phone calls she just *has* to tend to. Usually she works on projects right up to the deadline. She says her staff has gotten used to her frenetic pace: "I'm always right on the edge." At lunch, she tries to meet with clients and in the evenings she gives seminars. When she's driving somewhere, she says her mental wheels are always going at top speed. She admits she has constant anxiety. Seldom a day goes by without "something important being at risk." She prides herself on being innovative ("never the same old dog-and-pony show"), but she says she is "stressed out" most of the time.

Much of Lindsey's identity is caught up in her work. She feels as if she is putting her intellectual talents, her creativity, and her natural beauty to good use. Every day she mixes with CEOs. They trust her and treat her like family. She enjoys "the high people contact" and "learning new stuff." She admits "the money ain't bad either." But there are times when her self-confidence is just a veneer. "I take the elevator to the top floor, to the executive suite, and there's a glass conference room. It's filled with men in gray suits. I'm the only woman there. I don't like it. I'm afraid."

Divorced and raising two children with virtually no support from her ex-husband, Lindsey feels enormous financial pressures. "I need the money," she explains. "That's why I'm always pushing." It's Saturday and she is going to spend the evening writing a proposal. If she doesn't, one of her competitors will get the business. She knows, however, that she has to draw the line. She realizes that her boys are growing up rapidly and they need time with her. She knows she needs unstructured time just to relax, lie around, read, write in her journal, and be with her friends. Yet, she says, "I let work eat up too much of my time." There is always some excuse why she can't stop. "I draw the line eventually, but I'm starting to realize that I don't draw it soon enough."

Lindsey says there is constant strain between her work and her responsibilities as a mother. She sends the boys to school whether they are sick or not. "They have perfect attendance records, except for when they had chicken pox." If the school calls her office to say that one of the boys is sick, her secretary is trained to say she isn't around. Lindsey feels guilty, of course. To make up for it, she volunteers for parent-teacher activities and is a homeroom mother. Then she has even less time for herself.

When Lindsey says the money isn't bad, she means it. Right now, she's making a six-digit income—after expenses. Still, she doesn't feel entirely good about the money. She takes on a lot of boring work just because it pays well. She wishes she could refuse these projects and focus on the ones that are more interesting. She never has enough money, even as it is, to pay all the bills. It would take at least another $50,000 a year, she figures, to live comfortably. She also worries that she is becoming like her dad. He was always hustling. Money was how he kept score. "Money was too big a deal," she explains. "He sacrificed too much for it; being upper middle class and keeping up appearances just polluted all our relationships."

Lindsey wants to be different from her father, but she is deeply torn about her own habits with money. She doesn't like to think about it. She likes to write a check or buy something and not worry about each penny. Her ex-husband was more of a tightwad and they fought all the time about money. But Lindsey also says she is desperately afraid of not having money. "I can't stand the thought that I might not have money, that I might be poor, that I might have to use food stamps; I just can't handle that."

Figuring her life out has always been a struggle. As a teenager, Lindsey was a true "child of the sixties." She wanted to make the world better, developed a strong aversion to her dad's materialism, and decided to pursue a career in art. She wound up working part-time for a catering firm, putting herself through school, and then staying on to manage the business. Figuring out her life is still a challenge. "Getting in touch with my *self* is a big issue," she says. She wishes she had time to date and to remarry. She wishes she was not so caught up with her work and her material needs. Recently, she has been trying to get in touch with the religious values she learned as a child and to think more holistically about herself. She is becoming increasingly interested in spirituality. "I know that work isn't enough," she explains. "I need to feed my spirit; otherwise I will get anemic." But it is unclear whether her interests in spirituality will make a difference to the way she works or to her attitudes about money.

The Relevance of Religion

Throughout history, the great philosophers have recognized that work and money are such vital aspects of human life that they should not be separated from our fundamental beliefs, values, and assumptions about life itself. Plato, for example, wrote that motivation ("motions of the soul") comes from satisfying our desires: the desire for wisdom and knowledge, the desire for honor and power, and the "appetitive desires," which include the love of money. Money, Plato believed, helps us fulfill all our desires and is essential for life and health. He also warned, however, of the dangers of "unnecessary pleasure" in pursuing work and money to excess.[1] Aristotle recognized that people generally work in order to obtain money, an extrinsic end, but argued that work is more satisfying if it can be justified intrinsically, for example, in terms of the creativity or artistry involved. More recent thinkers have also drawn connections between money, work, and deeper dimensions of life. Freud, for example, believed that money was necessary for the support of life and yet insisted that "powerful sexual factors are involved in the value set upon it."[2] So, it is not surprising that someone like Lindsey Rice feels it is important to strike a balance between the monetary and the spiritual aspects of her life.

Sacred tradition has been a significant source of admonitions about money, advice about work, and understandings of economic behavior more broadly. The creation story in the Hebrew scriptures provides an account of how work began and of why it is often as unpleasant as it is. Other Hebrew writings describe people being led to ruin by their love of gold and offer counsel about the wisdom of seeking God rather than wealth. Virtually all major religions specify ways in which priests and religious functionaries should be supported through gifts from their followers. Rules against charging interest on loans were widely enforced by religious leaders in the West until the end of the Middle Ages. Many of the folktales and legends that emerged during the same period offer homespun advice about persisting in one's work and receiving unexpected good fortune through humility.

It is doubtful that followers of any of the world's religions ever adhered to all the injunctions promulgated in these traditions about work and money. Yet there is enough evidence to suggest that religious teachings once had a powerful impact on economic behavior. At the end of the Middle Ages, for example, the sale of indulgences was sufficient to bring in huge sums of money to the church. In the sixteenth and seventeenth centuries, many wealthy believers included the church in their wills. During the seventeenth and eighteenth centuries, religious teachings against working on the Sabbath were widely observed.

In our time, we might suppose that religious teachings should be concerned exclusively with the spiritual, that is, with the believer's relationship to God or to some other conception of the sacred. In this view, it may seem strange that religious teachings should say much about work and money at all. But this view is symptomatic of the unique times in which we live. Religious tradition has always concerned itself with the practical, day-to-day ethical and moral conduct of believers as well as their relationship to God.

One reason why religion is relevant to our work and our money is that we live in a world of inequality. Some people are rich, some are poor, and most are somewhere in between. These inequalities demand explanation. We want to know why they exist—and, for the most part, we want to believe they are legitimate (especially if we are on top). Religious teachings have often provided us with ways of understanding these inequalities.[3] For example, consider Spain during the fifteenth and sixteenth centuries—the era of transoceanic exploration. The crown's power depended greatly on wealth from its overseas explorations, and these revenues in turn necessitated a strong military force. Religion played an important role in legitimating this system of power. By defining the Spanish monarchs as "defenders of the faith," the church legitimated the military and economic activities of the monarchs.[4] Views of wealth and poverty are still connected with religious teachings. For instance, Lindsey Rice says she admires the Puritans. They worked hard, as she does, and they deserved the wealth they accumulated.

Another way in which religion has often been relevant to our work and our money is by supplying norms of daily conduct. These norms range from simple rules of etiquette, to ethical standards concerned with honesty and equitable dealing in the marketplace, to contractual obligations focusing on property, labor, marriage, or parental responsibilities. Religious teachings undergird these norms—associating them with sacred writings, reinforcing them in sermons, and perhaps including them in sacred rituals.[5] Consider ancient Israel, where such norms were set forth elaborately by the priests and prophets. Among the Ten Commandments, for example, were norms against theft and warnings against attitudes that might lead to it. Stories were also passed down among the Israelites about parents' and children's economic obligations to each other.[6] From the Middle Ages until the late eighteenth century, patron saints were often associated with craftsmen's guilds, holiday processionals showed the various guilds' role in the larger community, and the church helped enforce taboos against revealing trade secrets or neglecting the families of members who had experienced misfortune.[7] Lindsey Rice thinks her behavior is influenced by religious norms as well. For instance, she says one of her reasons for trying to be honest in her work is that she couldn't live with herself if she weren't—and she assumes this feeling is rooted in her childhood religious training.

A third way in which religion is relevant to economic matters has to do with the practical technologies on which survival depends. In any society, ways must be found to hunt game or to plant and harvest crops in order to provide food, clothing, and shelter. The knowledge needed to carve out a satisfactory relationship with nature is often encoded in religious beliefs and rituals. For example, fishing expeditions among the Trobriand Islanders are generally preceded by religious ceremonies in which the roles to be performed by the various fishermen are rehearsed.[8] In other settings, religious practices tell farmers when to plant and harvest their crops, prayers are offered for good weather, and animals are taken to the church to be blessed.[9] Most of us look to science and technology, rather than religion, for the expertise to produce our food and clothing. But we still see some connections. For instance, Lindsey Rice has experienced miracles several times in her life—times when she thought God was intervening to take care of her.

Religious teachings also come into play as ways of understanding misfortune. People die, natural catastrophes happen, and rewards go to the undeserving rather than the deserving. Ideas about evil help to explain these undesirable events, and religious rituals make it possible to confront evil and resist it or adjust to its consequences.[10] The Hebrew creation story is an explanation of this kind because it provides an account of why evil exists (the fall of Adam and Eve and their expulsion from the Garden of Eden). This story also includes specific implications for economic behavior (a divine injunction to work). In other cases, funerals and burial rites help to express grief and restore broken social relationships, but also to legitimate wills and bequests. For Lindsey Rice, seeing a neighbor's daughter die of cancer recently became an occasion to reflect more deeply about spirituality and the meaning of life. She vowed to think less about money and to spend more time with her boys.

The Question of Change

There are, then, time-honored ways of connecting religious beliefs and teachings to our work and our money. But our moment in history is also quite different from any previous time. We are now living in a *postindustrial* epoch, in which the intersection between our religious convictions and our economic practices has become significantly altered. For a growing number, our livelihood depends on higher levels of education and communication, and it is concerned more with the production of information and services than with agriculture or manufacturing. We live in a world dominated by large organizations—corporations, government agencies, and nonprofit associations—and by webs of statutes and laws governing the relationships among them. For most of us, our day-to-day experience is profoundly influenced by these organizations. Lindsey Rice is typical. Her clients are large companies and state administrative bureaus. The goods she sells are actually services. She is a producer of knowledge who depends, as she says, "on creating new ideas," and her ideas are concerned with organizations' needs for better communication.

Lindsey Rice also exemplifies the uncertainty many of us feel—whether we run our own companies or work for others. Indeed, uncertainty seems to increase in proportion to the complexity of our world and the range of options available to us. Lindsey is no bureaucrat who does the same things over and over again. She is constantly having to innovate. The rules are never quite clear, nor is it ever certain where she will find clients or what will prove to be her best ideas. This is one reason why her work generates as much anxiety as it does. Another reason is that her economic future is uncertain. Her fear of not having money is not entirely unfounded; before she started her present company, she worked for another one that went bankrupt. Her current business demonstrates how economic relationships are often structured. Large companies find it in their interest to work with small companies like hers. If she fails to produce, they simply move to another supplier.

The uncertainties of contemporary life are accentuated by our shifting values, beliefs, and lifestyles. Lindsey was in college when American soldiers were dying in Vietnam and students were being killed at Kent State University. She was deeply moved by these events. Growing up in a reasonably affluent family, she had many educational and career options. Her parents had always taught her to be tolerant and to accept diversity. As immigrants, they had been tolerant in their own way, marrying across religious and ethnic lines (her father was an Italian Catholic, her mother a Swedish Lutheran). Lindsey took their advice a step further and started dating across racial lines. Her beliefs have also been influenced by feminism and the women's liberation movement. When she is in a room of men in gray suits, she knows she is charting new—and frightening—territory.

Under such circumstances, religious teachings send us mixed signals, compete with the messages we learn from secular sources, and leave us feeling ambivalent as to their precise implications. Lindsey's parents sent her to church every week as a child, most of the time to a Methodist church within walking distance of their home. She attended Sunday school classes and learned Bible stories and hymns. But she also learned from her father to be critical of the church. One Sunday she became disgusted with her teacher, walked home, and found her parents making love. She was a bit more cynical about why they were sending her to Sunday school after that.

As an adult, Lindsey has tried out many different styles of spirituality. She has recaptured some of the Catholic heritage from her father's side of the family, attended Baptist churches, participated in feminist spirituality groups, meditated, and learned about other world religions. She still believes in religious teachings that encourage her to be honest, hardworking, and self-sufficient. Other teachings—for example, about giving money to the church—make less sense to her. Besieged by mixed signals, she is interested mostly in spirituality that makes her feel good about herself. Religious teachings do not tell her how to make decisions about her work or money, but they help relieve some of the anxiety she experiences in making these decisions.

I develop these observations about the distinctive features of postindustrial society in the chapters that follow. Invariably, it is difficult to gain perspective on our own milieu unless we distance ourselves from it.[11] To that end, I want to highlight what is different about our time by contrasting it with two previous episodes in our history—and to present a couple of historic cases that will set someone like Lindsey Rice in sharper relief.

Puritans Past

Consider the following example. In 1635 a Puritan merchant named Robert Keayne left London to take up residence in the new settlement at Boston. From humble circumstances, he had risen through hard work and careful planning to a position of some prominence. In the New World he prospered further. But four years later his ship of fortune ran aground. The elders of the First Church in Boston, of which he was a member, brought charges against him for dishonoring the name of God. Soon after, he was tried and found guilty by the General Court of the Commonwealth as well. Writing his memoirs some fourteen years later, he was still stung by the disgrace of the event. His sin was greed. He had sold his wares at a 6 percent profit, 2 percent above the maximum allowed.[12]

This episode offers an intriguing contrast between present conditions and our Colonial heritage. The recent scandals involving figures such as Michael Milken, Ivan Boesky, and Charles Keating show how much things have changed since the days of Robert Keayne. Price gouging continues to be an issue of public concern. But it is not often today that the church takes direct action against it. The case of Robert Keayne also shows that Puritan society differs even from popular ways of remembering it. We do not often think of the Puritan past as a time when governmental and ecclesiastical forces joined hands to *regulate* commerce. It is, rather, the *encouragement* of hard work, prudent planning, self-discipline, saving, and wise investments—all the ingredients of economic success—that we generally associate with the Puritan heritage. These, for instance, are what Lindsey Rice thinks of when she talks about the Puritans. But, I want to suggest, it is not only Puritanism but social conditions that we must understand if we are to appreciate how that period differs from our own.

The case of Robert Keayne shows the extent of religion's influence in economic affairs during the first years of European settlement in America. There were of course differences from one colony to the next and among Puritans, Anglicans, Quakers, and Catholics. Yet Puritan Boston provides a vivid contrast with the present. The reason First Church could exercise so much influence was twofold: Puritanism was an official religion, and being a Puritan in good standing was valuable to conducting business. Neither is any longer the case. Only a few decades after Robert Keayne, business leaders had already substantially weakened the church's control over their affairs.

At the time of Robert Keayne, Boston was ruled by an alliance of merchants and government officials. Because trade was the main source of tax revenues, officials did what they could to help merchants prosper. Merchants, in turn, looked to government for naval protection, to make favorable treaties with other nations, and to keep taxes at reasonable levels. The small number of people at the top of this alliance were relatives and friends of one another and shared common religious beliefs. Farmers, slaves, unskilled workers, and native ethnic groups were largely excluded from power and from the strictures of official religion. These groups mattered less because long-distance trade was the best way of making money.[13]

To understand the charges brought against Robert Keayne, then, we have to recognize that the church's power was reinforced by the power of the merchant and government elite and that it was important to this elite to have clear norms about acceptable profit margins. When someone violated these norms, secular and ecclesiastical authorities alike were compelled to act. Nowadays, we would say that religious teachings do not provide clear guidance as to whether 4 percent, 5 percent, or 6 percent is an acceptable rate of return on one's investment. Nothing has changed in this regard, however. Religious teachings were ambiguous then, just as they are now. But at that time it was possible for the elite who ruled Colonial Massachusetts to discuss the issue and settle on a rate that was deemed to be divinely appointed. In our time, it is no longer possible to do this.

Lindsey Rice, talking about her own views of business ethics, illustrates how things have changed. She says that in her line of work "you better not get caught being underhanded or duplicitous." The reason, she explains, is that "people talk to each other and you could lose clients quickly." Thus, she will not participate in anything that isn't completely aboveboard. She says her stance is not "value driven" but "practicality driven"—"I have my reputation to think about." In fact, to protect herself, she always writes her clients a letter summarizing what they have discussed, sends them a copy for their files, and keeps one for hers. If something unethical has been discussed, she mentions that she informed her client it seemed unethical to her. If there were ever a lawsuit, she feels she would be covered.

These comments show that ethical issues are often vague but we consider it possible to resolve them by considering how others will behave, by letting market competition drive out those who cheat, and by turning to the courts if necessary. We feel that ethical decisions are "practical," and thus need not be discussed in terms of personal values. It would not occur to us to involve the church in ethical disputes because the issues are too technical and because the disputants would likely belong to many different churches. We do not have a tight-knit ruling elite that can call on the churches the way Robert Keayne's contemporaries did.

Robert Keayne's own reflections show clearly that people then were just as capable as people now of coming up with rationalizations for their behavior. In the first place, he says, his alleged misconduct was the exception rather than the rule. His behavior, by and large, was quite responsible, rational, and disciplined—it even bore fruit—all signs that he was trying to live out his calling. Surely God did not expect more. Moreover, his behavior (in a different context) *was* actually the rule rather than the exception; that is, every other merchant was charging just as much as he. Why should he have been singled out? In addition, he argues, business is too complicated to be reduced to simple moral dicta. It would take considerable understanding to realize that he hadn't overcharged at all. Finally, he observes that his charitable behavior must be taken into account, as must the ill motives of his accusers and an antibusiness attitude among the clergy. His arguments sound strikingly modern.

We, too, are likely to tell ourselves that business is too complex to be governed by religious teachings and that we are OK as long as we try hard and do not cheat any worse than other people we know. The fact that Robert Keayne was actually accused, tried, and found guilty, therefore, depended on the social circumstances in which he lived. Had it not been for the church's position in the public life of the community, Keayne's own motives and justifications would have been much more difficult to police.

If conditions have changed, some of the Puritan legacy has nevertheless survived. Puritanism taught that life in the present world must be lived in a way that is pleasing to God. Economic activities were no exception. God required men and women to engage in useful behavior. Generally this meant hard work, although work was defined broadly enough to include service to family and community as well as to the counting house. These ideas remain familiar to us, of course. In addition, the Puritans taught that God was not capricious, so planning and rational decision making were consistent with serving God prudently. At the same time, the Puritans thought that God was close, active, and capable of intruding on the natural order in ways that humans did not always understand. There was an implicit chasm between the divine order and the natural order—one that many of us still take for granted. Indeed, Puritan thought emphasized the differences between the two orders by conceiving of one as pure, the other as corrupt or potentially corrupt. It was therefore valuable for believers to pray, seek counsel in scripture, and attempt to mold their behavior to divine principles; discipline in economic life was a way to impose divine order on a realm that could easily veer out of control. We, too, sometimes think of the natural or material realm in this way.

Even in Puritan Boston, the churches could not enforce all of these ideas. If Robert Keayne could be tried, others nevertheless fell outside the churches' control. Fur traders, for example, were seldom in town long enough for the clergy to exercise any real control over their lives. Sailors periodically got drunk, brawled, and visited prostitutes, all to the disgust of clergy, but their employers had little incentive to regulate their behavior. Rather than being the all-encompassing theocracy we sometimes think it was, Puritan society was thus less able to govern the private lives of laboring men and women than it was to influence the public lives of its merchants, aldermen, and clergy. As we think about the ways in which religion is limited in our own society, it is valuable, therefore, to remember that the churches' influence was circumscribed even in Colonial America.[14]

Industrialization

Industrial America provides a more recent contrast with our own circumstances. It thrived by adding manufacturing to the trading in raw materials and luxury commodities that characterized the Colonial period. A principal new component of industrial society is thus the recruitment, training, organization, and management of a domestic labor force. In spite of America's vast natural resources, its industrial wealth depended largely on its capacity to mobilize labor—both the heavy physical labor required in manufacturing and the supervisory and entrepreneurial talent needed in management. Whereas the long-distance trade of Puritan Boston was conducted by a small commercial elite, industrial America was a larger and more interdependent economy and thus needed careful scheduling and coordination. Households came increasingly to be linked through markets—often at the expense of traditional ethnic and religious communities or neighborhoods. Immigrants and pioneers were mobile; railroads and telephones eventually connected them. Public schooling accompanied industrialization as a way of developing requisite skills, a common language, and standards of personal discipline. In opposition to the standardizing forces of public schooling, America also became more diverse, especially in its religious and ethnic composition.

Individual moral restraint was the key to the relationships between religion and economic behavior in industrial America. During the nineteenth century, moral restraint shifted away from the government-imposed standards of Puritan Boston and became centered more on self-imposed conceptions of personal piety. Hard work, thrift, sobriety, punctuality, and the development and application of personal talents were emphasized. The proverbial Protestant work ethic encapsulates many of these ideals.

For the industrial period, the person who symbolizes American attitudes toward work and money—perhaps more than any other person of his time—is Benjamin Franklin. Although his long life overlapped with only the beginnings of industrialization, it symbolizes the changes that were to take place in the coming century. The connection between Franklin and the Puritan tradition is of course direct, for he was

born and baptized into the Puritan community in Boston and participated in it until he was fifteen. But Franklin's religious life foreshad-
ows developments that came increasingly to characterize the nation.

As did many of the young immigrants who later settled the expanding frontier, Franklin left home at an early age and in so doing severed
the ties with his parents' faith. In Philadelphia, his transient affinities
with Presbyterian, Quaker, and Episcopal churches made him an early
example of the so-called religious switching that has become so common in the twentieth century. He was, in this respect, not unlike Lindsey Rice. While retaining membership, he seldom attended religious
services (like a large number of Americans today). He chafed at the
pretensions and "emoluments" (as he described them) of the clergy,
worked to end religious tests for public office, and espoused the more
distant God of Deism in place of the more active God of his Puritan
forebears.

Franklin, as we know, epitomizes the American work ethic. His
writings show how he organized his time to squeeze full advantage
from it. He was also extremely diligent in the handling of his money,
carefully writing down even the smallest expenditures and reconciling
them with his budget. His widely read almanac was filled with homespun advice about rising early and working late, saving money, and investing wisely. The wealth that he gradually amassed from hard work
and investments testified to the wisdom of this advice.[15]

The coercive power of Puritanism in Colonial Boston could no
longer exercise control over people like Franklin. They could too easily escape it by taking their business interests to a more tolerant location. Indeed, the limited authority of religion that we see in our own
time was evident in Franklin's Philadelphia. As religious pluralism
grew, no single church was able to govern economic affairs. Instead,
the churches turned to moral persuasion. Franklin was not a regular
participant in any religious community, but he had internalized religious principles as a child. He believed that good works (including
hard work) were pleasing to God and considered God sufficiently rational that such activities would also be in his and the community's
best interests. His ability to *restrict* his work and his interests in
money—by reading, attending concerts, and devoting much of his life
to statesmanship—also reflected the moral obligations he had internalized early in life. Devotion to family, community, and the pursuit of
knowledge for its own sake helped keep work and money in their

place. Moral dicta extolling virtue—and arguing against evils such as laziness, greed, and excessive ambition—still made sense but increasingly did so as a kind of rational, self-contained picture of the universe. Personal life, especially the daily schedule, was carved up and ordered much in the same way a textile mill or bank might be organized. With natural resources and opportunities in abundance, and with labor power much in demand, the ability to discipline one's self and to impose the same sort of discipline on one's workers proved attractive.

Many of us still admire Benjamin Franklin and believe there is truth in his maxims about work and money. Lindsey Rice, for example, says it is honorable to be self-sufficient. Yet we are more ambivalent about the rules that Franklin followed—as Lindsey's criticisms of her ex-husband suggest—and we are less certain that strict moral rules about work and money are grounded in divine wisdom. We are Franklin's heirs but also the products of a distinctive culture that arose in the nineteenth century.

The question that surfaced again and again during the nineteenth century was how moral persuasion could be kept vibrant. Franklin had received religious instruction in Puritan Boston, but it was less certain that successive generations of children would have the same training. Despite his own apostasy, Franklin continued to interact with the religious life of his community, contributing to the construction of new churches and printing pamphlets on religious topics, but others might be less inclined to do so. Religious leaders thus paid increasing attention to the moral prescriptions inherent in their teachings. The churches' efforts to provide clear moral guidance were also reinforced by industrialization itself. Captains of industry, shopkeepers, mill owners, plantation holders, and farmers threw their weight behind the churches' moral crusades, benevolent associations, and temperance movements.[16]

By the end of the nineteenth century, the orderliness of Franklin's ledgers was, in one sense, everywhere—in the pervasive use of clocks and calendars, in the timetables to which trainmen adhered, in the factory whistles that told people when to rise, arrive at work, have lunch, resume work, and eat dinner, in the efficient clicking of telegraph keys, the miles of ticker tape that linked financial markets, and the rising use of assembly lines in manufacturing. The same orderliness was evident in religious teachings as well. Systematic ways of studying the Bible were being introduced in seminaries and churches, cross-referencing and concordances became increasingly popular, standardized lessons for Sunday schools were being advocated, spirituality was deemed to be reducible to propositional knowledge and was widely regarded as compatible with—if not superior to—science, and it was thought to be an effective way of disciplining the emotions, of discouraging men from drinking, and of encouraging women to be tougher and more efficient in organizing their domestic schedules. Mental discipline was required of believers, "muscular Christianity" was a popular idea, the churches adopted systematic bookkeeping procedures and started thinking of themselves as formal organizations, and Jesus became a rugged individualist who mobilized his followers as would an industrial entrepreneur.

The Legacy of Ambivalence

The churches flourished in industrial America, adapting as they did to the demands for moral discipline, but they advanced a gospel that did more than simply reinforce industrialization. Sometimes, they provided alternative visions to those set forth in economic theories and in the public speeches of wealthy industrialists. Religious leaders challenged the adventuresome to work more diligently but cautioned the hardworking to be more compassionate and devoted to their communities. Working people found religious teachings a source of criticism against dehumanizing conditions in the factory, but so did progressives and modernists in colleges and universities or muckrakers employed by newspapers. Immigrant parishes encouraged their members to organize trade unions and to be active in municipal politics. Rural preachers favored the moral obligations of small towns rather than the aggressive self-interested style of the cities. African Americans found their churches a bastion against white discrimination and oppression.

Religion may not have stood in the way of industrial progress, but it was able to disquiet the consciences of even the heartiest proponents of this progress. Andrew Carnegie, for example, worried that the pursuit of money would degrade him beyond hope, and John D. Rockefeller struggled to find ways of reconciling his simple Baptist beliefs with his enormous wealth. Modernist thinkers in the very denominations in which industrial capitalists and middle-brow entrepreneurs abounded were decrying the working class's fate and trying to envision economic alternatives both to American free enterprise and to European socialism.

The truth was that America underwent industrialization never feeling fully at ease with its social, cultural, and moral consequences. The same questions that social thinkers were asking in Europe about the collapse of community and the fragmentation of society were being asked in other languages by their American counterparts. The language of faith, of love and brotherhood, of simple moral values, and of common human decency provided a way of expressing their concerns. Seldom did this language generate overt protest. And seldom was it incorporated very clearly into the theories of academic social scientists. But it was a source of lasting ambivalence, even as America underwent the dramatic economic transformations of the twentieth century. Indeed, much of our own ambivalence about the economic implications of our religious teachings can be traced to the nineteenth century.

This ambivalence focused on the dubious gains of progress and the fear that success might be purchased at too great a cost. It was, however, ambivalence in the true sense of the word, because progress was also very much favored. What was feared to be endangered by the forces of progress, moreover, was not so much tradition, or even community, in the European sense, for such features of the social order were far less familiar in a society built on the open frontier by waves of immigrants than they were in Europe. Nor was the fear even so much the kind of class resentment against a rising elite, such as was often evident among the industrial working classes in Germany and France. Americans resented the wealthy, to be sure, but preferred to see them as corrupt individuals rather than representatives of an entire system.[17]

Americans' ambivalence toward economic progress was expressed most clearly in the language of morality. Americans opposed great wealth not because it was unjust for some to have more than others but because wealth was associated with debauchery. They battled the scourge of working-class life in the cities by waging moral crusades against taverns and in favor of child labor laws and better sanitary codes. They held to the belief that it was morally right to work hard but also believed just as firmly that it was wrong to work all the time or to be obsessed with the financial results of one's labor. They recognized the value of science, technology, and rational planning and yet regarded these with suspicion when they threatened to undo parental authority. There was thus a constant effort to reconcile the rational methods of progress with the folk wisdom on which families and communities had always based their decisions.

A century later, we still express much of our ambivalence toward economic conditions in the language of morality. On the one hand, we continue to regard hard work as a moral virtue and laziness as a vice; we consider it not only a matter of expedience but of moral duty to pass on the opportunity for economic prosperity to our children; we have spent much of this century arguing that capitalism was morally superior to communism and have viewed the collapse of communism in Eastern Europe and the Soviet Union as a moral victory. We continue to believe that moral discipline is a way of fighting drug abuse and teenage pregnancy and of ensuring that our own children will be economically successful when they grow up. On the other hand, we express our concerns about economic conditions in moral terms as well. We decry the expansion of advertising and of the mass media because it corrupts the morals of our children; we talk about the self-interestedness that markets encourage as if this were an immoral orientation and lament the ways in which economic conditions continue to undermine communities. When loopholes in our codes of professional ethics allow doctors or stockbrokers to reap huge earnings, we put these offenders on display as examples of immorality and greed.

In the nineteenth century, religion was the primary source for the language of morality. It provided the authority for warranting statements about what should and should not be done. More important, religious communities served simply as the primary locations in which authority was grounded, providing a first language of morality that became intuitive before a child was old enough to realize its power. Religious communities also provided a protected zone in which women often gained greater power, at least informally, than they experienced anywhere else and where the special concerns of mothering, of training children, and of teaching them basic moral principles could come together.[18] Some of this, of course, was a kind of middle-class morality, more common in the small towns and among shopkeepers than in working-class neighborhoods or industrial boardrooms. But in varying ways, it was a language that went well beyond the middle class. In their own languages, the Southern blacks who moved to northern cities, the Welsh miners who moved to Pennsylvania, and the German farmers who settled the Great Plains all knew it.

The language of personal morality made a great deal of sense in the nineteenth century because social conditions reinforced its authority. Individual shopkeepers and farmers were free to get ahead largely by working harder and by living more frugally than their competitors. Disciplining one's time, as Franklin did, was a way of accommodating to the schedules that became increasingly common in factories, mills, mines, and railroads. People who could discipline themselves were often more likely to succeed. But personal discipline was also a way of resolving ambiguity. Just as it did for Franklin, a well-organized daily routine made it possible to accomplish a lot and still have time left for one's family or community.

It would give a false impression, however, to suggest that the moral languages that resisted purely economic modes of calculation were very powerful. Economic necessity drove the lives of most Americans to a greater extent than any of them wished. They worked long hours because they had to, not simply because it was moral to do so. More important, the formal discourse of economists themselves, of the business elite, and of many in the colleges and universities was increasingly threatening to replace, or subsume, the moral languages found in religious communities. Economists argued that work and money were a world unto themselves, not subject to interpretation in any way but the language of economics. The business elite never deplored the conventional morality of the common American but argued simply that economic progress was the best way of achieving these moral ideals.[19] What better way of refreshing the spirit and keeping the American public in touch with the earthy roots of its rural existence, asked Henry Ford, than to provide every working family with a cheap automobile for Sunday drives to the country? Academic arguments about the links between economics and morality were perhaps not so bold. Yet much of the progressive thought of the early twentieth century was oriented toward showing that old-fashioned moral notions could be transcended when the same rational thought that was leading to economic advancement was applied to the human condition itself.

The Postindustrial Epoch

The last half of the twentieth century contrasts with most of the century preceding it in at least two important ways: we are now reaping the fruits of the earlier era, evidenced by the fact that so many Americans enjoy relatively comfortable middle-class and upper-working-class lifestyles; we are also undergoing a major transformation away from industry and manufacturing to a more highly professionalized, service-oriented economy. Both of these developments have had enormous consequences for the beliefs, behavior, and lifestyles of Americans generally, and they provide the wider context in which specific questions about the relationships between religion and contemporary economic behavior must be addressed.

Postindustrial society of course does not differ as dramatically from industrial society as the name might imply. Producing manufactured goods, applying technology to agricultural production, and organizing labor continue to be important. In many respects, postindustrial society simply extends the principles of industrial society to new areas and new levels. To public schooling, for example, it adds higher education as a way of training the workforce. Market competition—once limited to a few durable goods—now extends across longer distances and involves a greater variety of perishable goods and human services. Bureaucratic methods—once used for producing steel and automobiles—are now adapted to fast-food establishments and health-care facilities. Government continues to work closely with business leaders to encourage investment, trade, and an adequate money supply. Nevertheless, postindustrial society also differs in important ways from its predecessor.

The rising importance of advanced education and higher levels of training mean that capital adheres to a greater extent to the individual worker who sells his or her skills—we speak of "human capital"—rather than being composed of machines or raw materials. With increasing emphasis on professional services over traditional assembly-line production, greater discretion characterizes the workplace. As Labor Secretary Robert Reich suggests, our greatest asset is an "adaptable and innovative" labor pool.[20]

Another aspect of the shift toward light industry, the professions, and services is a softening of class divisions between wielders of power and the majority of the laboring population. The relatively small fraction of white-collar owners and managers who relied on masses of blue-collar workers performing physical labor has been replaced by a much larger variety of occupations performing middle-management, sales, clerical, and technical tasks. The disparity in income and wealth between the so-called ruling elite and the remainder of the population has probably not decreased substantially as a result; indeed, it has been aggravated by some features of the service economy. But the nature of work has shifted decidedly away from heavy physical labor, allowing, among other things, greater numbers of women to be included in the labor force and making for a more finely graded system of intermediate careers in terms of prestige and social desirability. Someone like Lindsey Rice is clearly an example of these changes.

In the shift toward a service economy, professionalization has extended downward and outward, encompassing a wider variety of technical and supportive occupations as well as more careers that would once have been considered entrepreneurial or managerial. Professionalization connotes an intrinsic personal commitment to a career, internalization of a set of norms that one chooses to adhere to, and a system of rewards that base rank and prestige on merit. Devotion to the workplace and discretion in making workplace decisions are thus important implications of professionalization. In addition, professional norms have made ambiguous the question of whether work should be performed strictly for money or whether other values (such as service) should prevail.

Norms of service and professional values often reflect religious teachings—for example, teachings about helping people in need or using one's talents for the good of others. Nevertheless, the growth of professionalism makes it harder to know what the distinctive contribution of faith should be. The profession itself provides one's reference group and claims the expertise necessary to give counsel about norms and values. Lindsey Rice, for instance, rather than seeking guidance from a religious group, turns to a support group consisting of other professional women when she is facing an important decision at work or just feeling depressed about her job.

The service economy has also weakened the labor movement as a distinctive force in politics, leaving an increasing share of the working class to fend for themselves by limiting their purchases or the number of children they bear, seeking education, and maintaining dual career households. The meaning of poverty has thus shifted as well, the impoverished becoming an underclass distinguished mainly by the lack of social and moral capital assumed to characterize the majority of the middle and working classes. Thus, efforts to help the poor may be limited to those who are thought to have the same moral propensities as the middle class, while others are dismissed because they supposedly created their own problems. Religious teachings that emphasize hard work and other middle-class virtues reinforce volunteer activities that may help a broad spectrum of the public but probably fall short of addressing basic economic problems.

For the middle class, personal discretion expands as its members gain distance from economic necessity (greater wealth giving wider options), but the complexity of the marketplace also requires its members to make tough choices on a more regular basis and in a wider number of areas. An individual's decision about a career, for instance, cannot be made on a one-time basis but must be considered again and again. Lindsey Rice, for example, has pursued several different lines of work and periodically considers going back to school for an M.B.A. A growing share of the labor force is paid on a salaried rather than an hourly or piece-rate basis; thus, the sheer numbers of hours worked is decoupled from the amount of money earned. In the process, competition for qualified workers comes to focus less on monetary remuneration and more on "quality-of-life" issues, such as working conditions or opportunities for personal fulfillment.

Much of contemporary life takes place in organizations that claim to represent the public, that are publicly owned, or whose operations ultimately bear responsibility to the public. These are the corporations, the government agencies, the political parties, the news organizations, the schools, and the colleges and universities that shape so much of our life. At the same time, our personal lives are largely shielded from public scrutiny and accountability. There are exceptions to this rule, for example, the scrutiny of public officials' private lives during confirmation hearings. Generally, however, we cherish our privacy and personal freedom and try hard to protect them against incursions from large public institutions.[21] In economic life, labor and employment policy, fiscal management, taxation, the money supply, and the promotion and regulation of trade have all become public issues, to be discussed by public officials and in the media, while their private counterparts—family budgets, career choices, consumer purchases—are left almost entirely up to each of us to be decided privately.

As individuals, then, we are likely to feel we have little influence over public economic matters, except indirectly through our role as citizens, and that we are responsible for maintaining the privacy and autonomy of our own economic decisions. Under these circumstances, such decisions necessarily attach themselves to definitions of the self and to questions of personal worth, freedom, meaning, and morality. Lindsey Rice says she doesn't understand the economic system very well, even though she earns her living giving advice to large corporations. She carries the weight of her own financial decisions entirely on her own shoulders, seldom discussing these concerns with even her family or her closest friends. She admits she keeps her finances to herself because "it just seems crass to talk about money"—and she doesn't want her family to ask her for loans. Her self-esteem is wrapped up in being able to provide material comforts for herself and her children. "Money is the thing that greases my way through life," she asserts. It fills her with anxiety, therefore, to think she might fail.

Many of us believe our faith should relate to how we conduct our *private* economic affairs. Many of us are less sure that faith is relevant to the more public or institutional ways in which economic affairs are conducted. For example, we may try to pay our bills on time as a matter of religious principle but consider religious teachings to be irrelevant when the national debt is being discussed. In our private lives, moreover, we may feel that faith cannot make much of a difference because the important questions about work, ethics, or money are already decided—by our employers, by politicians, or (as Lindsey Rice believes) by the market itself. Consequently, we may look to religion more to help us feel better about the fix we are in than to give us guidance.

The postindustrial economy also depends increasingly on consumer expenditures for goods and services; thus, a greater share of our decision making shifts from production to consumption. Household items, automobiles, labor-saving devices, and in recent decades a growing variety of services—from day care to lawn care—have become commodities packaged and priced as consumer products. On the production side, the service economy is thus concerned increasingly with the creation and marketing of consumer goods and services. On the consumption side, more and more people participate more frequently in the marketplace as well. The role of the consumer has become an important aspect of individual economic behavior. With it come responsibilities to buy well and wisely. Moral injunctions to save and accumulate wealth, or aspirations of attaining higher social rankings by doing so, have largely been replaced by educational attainment systems, leaving most of us with relatively fixed or secure salaries. Discretion must then be exercised by making informed consumer choices. Having money means primarily the ability to expand one's array of possibilities as a consumer. As Lindsey Rice says, having money means you "don't have to go crotzing around, hassling, and looking for bargains."

Social norms also come increasingly into play that define reasonable levels of consumer expenditure. It is expected that people will consume automobiles, clothing, housing, and other items at a level congruent with their standing in the community. "You just feel like a cheapskate," says Lindsey Rice, "if you don't have those things." Savings and charitable giving are thus likely to be defined as trade-offs in relation to consumer spending. Questions about materialism in postindustrial society also focus primarily on consumer expenditures rather than on the mechanization that prevailed in earlier stages of industrialization. Rather than feeling trapped by machines, we now feel we are victims of some gigantic economic force—"I see it not so much on an individual level but sort of on a mass cultural or nation-wide, world-wide scale" is how Lindsey Rice describes it. "Everything gets subjugated for economic advantage." One of the major dilemmas facing religion in postindustrial society, therefore, is to find ways to address the question of materialism and to avoid imbibing too deeply in the materialistic culture itself.

With these developments, the role of religion inevitably changes. Counsels of hard work, moral discipline, and personal thrift may survive but become less meaningful. Ethical guidelines may be built into career expectations and organizational norms themselves—as Lindsey Rice says, "practicalities"—rather than being considered matters of morality that depend on spiritual tutelage. The morality of work itself may diminish for those who see no clear connection between sheer exertion and material success. Or, for others, this connection may remain so strong that exertion becomes a matter of economic calculation rather than a moral principle. When the rigidity of one's personal schedule becomes a matter of choice, the only ethical imperative remaining may be to choose in a way that maximizes personal happiness. At the same time, individuals assume greater responsibility for a host of work-related and consumer-related decisions and are subjected to a widening variety of options for expressing personal tastes. Not being able to defend some of these choices on the basis of sheer economic necessity, they thus face a heightened need for legitimacy; that is, a need to feel good about their choices no matter what the specific decision may have been. In such circumstances faith is likely to shift away from providing a heuristic for making decisions and become more of a therapeutic source of reassurance. Lindsey Rice, for example, says she prays at work, not knowing if God really hears her but just to feel more confident about what she is doing.

As advertising increasingly penetrates personal life, consumer decisions may be made largely with reference to product familiarity and cost efficiency, leaving religion to play a more ambiguous role. Religion may, for example, serve more as a source of order in personal life, or even as a fundamental way of categorizing reality, than as a set of easily decipherable rules about how to spend money. With a growing share of public life subject to the impersonal processes of markets and bureaucracies, religion also becomes more relevant simply as a source of comfort, intimacy, and support in private life. But this reorientation may also shape the ways it influences attitudes toward caring, economic need, the poor, and charitable giving.

Religion in America remains capable of addressing the desires and needs that arise in the workplace and in the realm of consumption. Although its place in postindustrial society is radically different from that in the Colonial and industrial periods, it has the resources to make a difference. Denominations, a vast number of buildings and organizations, trained clergy, mechanisms for eliciting charitable donations, and numerous periodicals, publishing houses, colleges and seminaries, retreat centers, and familiar symbols of the sacred all make it a powerful factor in contemporary life. It has thus adapted to postindustrial conditions, changing qualitatively in the process but retaining its overall vitality. Having something to say about work, money, and benevolence has actually been in its interest. But there are also pressures for it to say nothing or to speak ambiguously and for its followers to ignore it.

One of the most significant problems is that the authority of religious communities has greatly diminished. Spirituality has become a matter of the heart—entirely. People may still attend services, but they may hear nothing that they consider morally binding. Having been exposed to different religious practices that seem arbitrary, they are, like Lindsey Rice, more interested in pursuing spirituality on their own than in the company of others. And they feel justified in doing so. In Lindsey's case, for instance, her father generally stood in church when he was supposed to kneel, or vice versa, just to show his disdain for the priests, and her mother told her repeatedly, "Religion isn't what you do on Sunday, it's what is in your heart." Spirituality is thus more difficult to define and harder to draw implications from that make a difference in how we use our money and our time. Lindsey Rice admits that she has "a high level of ambiguity" whenever she thinks about religion.

The ability to deal effectively with ambiguity is increasingly regarded as a sign of mental and emotional maturity. With working conditions as complex as they are, we cannot deny the reality of ambiguity. But we must also recognize that ambiguity makes it easier to rationalize our choices, rather than confronting them responsibly. This ambiguity, our ability to rationalize ethical decisions in the face of economic pressures, and the uncertain role of religion are illustrated vividly in a story Lindsey Rice recounted about one of the most profound events in her life.

It was the summer after her sophomore year in college and she was working in Boston. One day she was walking in an older part of town—not far from where Robert Keayne had lived, as it happens. She remembers vividly that it was a warm, sunny day and that she was wearing a miniskirt. As she approached the building where she was to pick up her paycheck, four sailors who had been drinking approached her and started to proposition her. She walked on, picked up her check, and retraced her steps. She was musing about her bills, realizing that her check wasn't going to cover the money she had already spent, when the sailors approached her and propositioned her again. On impulse, she blurted out, "How much?" The sailors suggested a price and, still worrying about how to pay her bills, Lindsey accepted.

As they walked to the hotel, Lindsey started to have misgivings; one of the sailors did, too, but they decided to go through with it anyway. Lindsey had sex with two of the men. Then, suddenly, she experienced a sharp pain and started bleeding profusely. She was afraid she was bleeding to death because it was not time for her period. She was "freaking out" and the sailors were scared and angry, so they paid her and fled. Lindsey made it to the hospital, where the gynecologist explained that the bleeding was from trauma, kept her under observation, and determined that there was no permanent injury.

Looking back on this episode, Lindsey asserts vehemently that it was a stupid thing to do but it taught her a valuable lesson about money. She knew she had gone too far. She also believes the bleeding was a miracle—a sign from God to warn her about the course on which she was embarking. She still receives signs from God once in a while—often enough that she worries about doing anything bad for fear she'll get caught. But most of the time God is silent. What she feels is a "personal path of empowerment" that rewards her for doing good. The power that she feels plugged into doesn't guide her any more than that. She is like many of us, feeling pressured financially, experiencing constant anxiety about our work, taking our cues mostly from people around us, and thinking that religious teachings should guide us but not knowing quite how to make them relevant.

Our moment in history, then, is a time of growing uncertainty, of great personal challenges, and of urgent need. Despite the material prosperity our nation has enjoyed, we are now at a turning point when we need to think more deeply about our priorities. We are concerned about the materialism that surrounds us and the acquisitive values that are being communicated to our children. Our attitudes toward work and money have become more ambiguous as personal commitments and the daily pressures we experience are forcing us to think harder about what we want and how to achieve our goals. Many of us realize we cannot save ourselves through better economic programs, legislation, or inventing new technologies alone. Our problems as a nation are spiritual as well as material. We must take stock of what our spiritual heritage is telling us and of how we are being instructed by its counsel.

Chapter Three

Faith and Work

Miriam Zellers grew up on a farm in western Pennsylvania. As a child, she went to a Lutheran church every Sunday where there were so many aunts and uncles and cousins that her kin took up four full rows of the church. Her father, who ran a dairy and operated a small restaurant, wanted her to go into something practical. So she majored in nutrition and home economics in college, even though she preferred psychology. After college, she earned a master's degree and got a job not far away as a hospital dietician. There she met her husband, an engineer who was a born-again Christian. In four years she gave birth to three children, and for the next eighteen years stayed at home caring for them. With kids in college, and needing the money, she decided to go back to work and got a job as the dietary supervisor for the local school system. Five years later her husband was transferred overseas, so Miriam quit her job and spent the next six years in the Middle East and Asia. For two years now, she and her husband have been back in the United States. Miriam spends much of her time doing volunteer work at a local church.

Bill Williams is a biostatistician who holds a senior management position at a large private research firm specializing in pharmaceuticals. He is very proud of his African American heritage. His living room is adorned with artifacts from Nigeria and on one wall hang large charcoal portraits of Martin Luther King, Jr., and the black writer W. E. B. DuBois. His childhood memories include reading the Bible with his grandmother and learning to recite the Twenty-third Psalm. Although his parents were Baptists, they sent him to Catholic school because they saw education as the way to escape the poverty and segregation of the rural South. After high school, he went to college in New Orleans because he wanted to experience life in a large city, and he chose to major in chemistry simply because he felt he could do well in it. At the time, he recalls, "I had no idea what I wanted to do." But with his training in chemistry, he was highly employable after graduation and landed a well-paying job in New York City. Cancer research was expanding at the time, so that's what he did. A few years later, war broke out in Vietnam and Bill was drafted. For three years he worked as a biochemist in military hospitals. On returning to civilian life, he went back to New York, worked again in research, and taught community college courses at night. From there, he went to Harvard for an M.S. and a few years later earned a Ph.D. from the University of North Carolina. Since then he has worked for government research institutes, taught at several universities, and for four years has been with his present company.

Sonny Nicos, a man in his late twenties, lifts weights every day to keep in shape. He and his wife both work. She has a job as a retail clerk selling perfume in a department store; he works as an independent contractor operating a television camera at professional athletic events. They live in a "transitional" working-class neighborhood in Chicago. Sonny was raised in a deeply religious Greek Orthodox family. His wife, Jewish by birth, converted shortly before they married. It's been hard for Sonny to get steady work. Sometimes he works four months at a time. Then he gets laid off. Right now he's doing editing instead of camera work. He says he prefers it this way. At least it pays more than the $5.50 an hour he was making at CNN. It's also a better life than his father had: he worked virtually around the clock at a restaurant until his death five years ago. Sonny hopes he can get steadier work soon so his wife can have a baby. Then they want to make sure the child is brought up in the church. Meanwhile, they attend services every Sunday. He says it isn't something he believes in; it's just a basic part of who he is.

Religious faith has been a part of all three of these lives. And yet these cases show how tenuous the connection may be between faith and economic behavior. It is unclear exactly what role, if any, faith has played in guiding Miriam, Bill, or Sonny in their work. Indeed, their career patterns seem to have been influenced more by circumstances and economic considerations than by anything else. Did religious commitments play a role in their selection of jobs? Does spirituality make them work harder? Or better? Are they happier than other people? More ethical? Do they feel themselves "called" to their work? And if so, what does this mean? We need to know more about each person to answer these questions. But we already have reason to expect—from what we considered in the last chapter—that the answers to these questions are not simple.

This chapter examines the complex relationships between religious commitment and work in our society. We all know that work itself is quite varied. Different people mean different things when they talk about work; they, of course, work at different kinds of jobs, value different things about their work, and derive varying levels of satisfaction from it. People also differ in the extent to which they bring religious ideas to bear on their work. Thus we need to consider the specific aspects of work that may be influenced by religious commitment: job selection, work values, job satisfaction, the concept of the calling, and manifestations of faith within the workplace. I argue that religious commitment plays a more important role in guiding work than has generally been acknowledged in the scholarly literature on this subject, especially the literature that instructs us to think about work strictly from a market or organizational orientation. But I also suggest that prevailing cultural assumptions have weakened the influence of religious commitment in the workplace. We have come to think of religion—at least implicitly—as a way of making ourselves feel better and have largely abandoned the idea that religion can guide our behavior, except to discourage activities considered blatantly immoral. We believe economists and advertisers when they tell us that careers and work habits are matters merely of personal preference. We look to religion, therefore, to make us happy about our preferences, not to channel them in specific directions.

In giving up its ability to shape our behavior in the workplace, contemporary religion has lost a great deal of its power. We might not want the clergy telling us which career to pursue, but if their advice makes no difference to us at all (and if what we understand from reading scripture or attending religious services makes no difference either), then we must acknowledge that something is lacking in the way we think about religion. Yet there is a positive side as well. Even if faith has only small effects on how we think about work, these effects can nevertheless be significant. And they need to be understood, especially by people who believe their faith should have greater consequences than it does for the way they live. Work plays such a central role in our lives that it surely must remain of interest to religious leaders and practitioners. Indeed, as a recent study conducted among church and synagogue members in Chicago concludes, "many Christians and Jews hunger for more support from their religious communities in relating their faith to their work lives."[1]

For the majority of us, time spent on the job is one of our most serious commitments. Indeed, except for sleeping, the average person spends more time working than on any other activity. Consider the following:

- In the U.S. labor force, the typical person spends nearly two thousand hours a year at his or her job, not counting work that may be taken home on weekends or evenings. Between the late 1960s and the late 1980s this figure actually increased by 163 hours, meaning that the average American was working about one month longer on the job each year than a generation earlier.[2]
- Two-thirds of the American labor force claim they are in fact working harder than five years ago; half say they wish they could work fewer hours than they do.[3]
- Among full-time male workers in professional and managerial occupations, one in three works more than fifty hours a week.[4]
- Compared with a generation ago, when fewer than one married woman in four was employed outside the home, two-thirds of married women are now gainfully employed.[5]
- By the time he or she is four years old, the average child has begun to think about the question "What am I going to be when I grow up?" Usually this question is taken to mean, "What line of work will I choose?"[6]
- Although young people have always been faced with career decisions, these decisions now continue throughout life: three-quarters of the U.S. labor force have been in more than one occupation during their adult lives (one person in six has been in five or more); 35 percent wonder if they are in the right line of work; and 28 percent say they feel seriously burned out with their jobs.[7]
- Reversing previous trends, a growing number of employers are now extending the mandatory retirement age and encouraging many employees to work until they are age 70. Economic projections, moreover, suggest that an increasing share of the population will have to work at least part-time during retirement itself to make ends meet.

- Despite their complaints about it, work remains a meaningful and valued activity for most people: 82 percent of those currently working say their work is "very meaningful," 80 percent say it is "absolutely essential" or "very important" to their basic sense of worth as a person, and 71 percent say they are "very interested" in doing well in their job.[8]

Clearly, then, work is an economic activity to which most of us are deeply committed. We work long hours as a matter of economic necessity and feel the burdens of that work and of shouldering responsibilities that often seem to be more than we can bear. But we also regard our jobs as a source of personal meaning and fulfillment. Many of us experience tensions and pressures in our work that also cause us to want guidance and support. Some of us at least seek this guidance and support in religion.

What Is Work?

What counts as "work" in the first place depends on the situation and on the cultural norms and assumptions governing those situations.[9] "Are you working?" means something different when a representative of the Census Bureau asks it than when a parent is encouraging a child to finish a page of arithmetic. Most generally, work means any expenditure of energy. Thus it makes sense to ask if a person's heart has been working too hard or to talk about homework, spiritual work, or works of art.[10] Traditionally, the link between faith and *works* has been conceived to include virtually all the ways in which piety may affect behavior. In narrower terms, work has come increasingly to mean gainful employment.[11] If a person has a job, then we say this person is in the workforce.

But even a seemingly straightforward equation of work with gainful employment becomes complicated when we think about all the possible ways of making a living in contemporary society. It does so partly because of the possibility of being self-employed or of working on commission without actually being considered an employee. There are more serious ambiguities as well. Someone who has a job but is not working at it because of a temporary leave or illness is still considered employed. A person who is unemployed but is actively looking for a job is considered part of the labor force but not part of the active labor force. In other cases, working for pay is the critical dimension. A person who does volunteer work, therefore, is unlikely to be considered working, while someone who makes furniture in the basement and sells it is likely to be.

I mention these definitional issues only to point out that as soon as we ask about the influence of religion on work, we are already acknowledging that its influence is limited in one significant respect. Although religious traditions may have defined work at one point (for example, in the story of Adam and Eve), we are now likely to be talking about the ways in which work is understood by our employer or the Internal Revenue Service. Religion's power to define the basic categories in which we think about work has thus eroded.

Defining work as gainful employment has become dramatically more prominent in the two centuries since the Industrial Revolution. One reason is that an increasing number of people depend on monetary remuneration. In traditional societies, people may work to support themselves and yet not participate in markets in which goods and services are exchanged for money. With most economic activities now involving monetary remuneration, a sharper line can be drawn between work as gainful employment and activities done purely for personal pleasure or gratification. That this distinction is still somewhat arbitrary is, of course, all too apparent. People who mow their own lawns may be considered engaged in a leisure activity. And yet if they did not do this work themselves, they would have to hire someone else to do it (and perhaps work harder themselves to pay for this service). The other reason why work is officially regarded as gainful employment is that official designations themselves have become more important. One of the most effective mechanisms devised by governments to collect revenue has been to levy taxes on the income derived from work. Governments, therefore, have a monetary stake in maintaining neat definitions of work and to find ways of classifying activities (baby-sitting, for example) as work that in previous times might have been considered something else.

The most contested category of work in recent years has been housework. Married women still do far more housework than their husbands, despite the fact that nearly as many women as men are also gainfully employed members of the labor force.[12] Norms of etiquette have become ambiguous as a result of this dual nature of work. Asking someone if she "works" made little sense at a time when very few women were gainfully employed. Under those circumstances, the answer would have been "of course" (cooking, cleaning, etc.). But with women involved in the labor force and doing household duties as well, the same question must now be amended to include something like "outside the home." In addition to such norms, the question of household work has also been hotly contested because of the power and gender inequality implied. Beyond housework, much evidence also suggests that paid employment tends to be perceived differently, depending on whether it has traditionally been regarded as "women's work" or "men's work."[13]

Religion thus figures into the definition of work in at least one important way. Religious teachings have often been interpreted in such a way that women were encouraged either not to participate in the labor force at all, or if they did participate, to subordinate such activities to household duties not expected of their husbands. While many of these traditional teachings have been challenged, there is still some evidence that the more religiously committed a woman is, especially when commitment is to conservative religious organizations, the less likely she is to participate in the labor force, or to do so full-time.[14] And some evidence also suggests that religiously committed women are more likely to do housework themselves than to share it with their husbands, while religiously committed men are more likely to let their wives do the housework than to share it.

The idea that staying out of the paid workforce is simply a traditional role that women who are being exploited by their husbands have adopted is increasingly being rethought, however. What religious commitment may provide for some women is an alternative sense of who they are and of what the role of paid work in their lives should be. Miriam Zellers, for example, explains that it was difficult for her to give up her career to become a mother. More than anything else, it was her faith that helped her define motherhood as a career and to understand its importance. "It was not something I felt I should take lightly," she says. "I felt I'd been given three gifts [my children], and what I did with these gifts was as important as any job fulfillment I would have."

The other way in which religion is relevant to the definition of work is that theologians and religious leaders have been in the forefront of attempts to challenge the views of work promulgated by the marketplace or the state. Recognizing that work has historically been regarded in a wide variety of ways, they have tried to suggest new ways of thinking about it. For example, some theologians have taken responsibility for images of work in their own traditions that regarded it as a curse, or as a necessary evil, and have tried to present a more positive image. Others have tried to challenge the notion that only gainful work is important, thereby encouraging people to engage more actively in voluntary deeds of kindness.[15] The Fuller Seminary theologian Miroslav Volf, for instance, argues that conventional definitions of work are alienating and focus too much on earning money; in contrast, he suggests, we should think of work as any purposeful activity performed by free and responsible individuals and that preserves both the dignity of the individual and the integrity of nature.[16]

For present purposes, I rely primarily on official definitions of work, focusing our attention on attributes of jobs and considering work as a form of gainful employment. As we shall see, there is much to be learned about this important dimension of contemporary economic behavior. To the extent that some religious views raise questions about the very definition of work, they generally do so, it might be added, with reference to these official definitions.

Choosing a Job

One of the most important decisions young people make nowadays is choosing a job, a career, or a line of work. In the past, fewer choices were available, but religion often decisively influenced those choices. For example, a younger son of a devout Catholic family might have been designated from childhood to become a priest. Or a member of a persecuted religious minority may have found it impossible to gain admission to college or to become an employee of the government. Today, most discussions of how people choose jobs focus either on the resources needed to acquire particular jobs or on the attributes of jobs that may attract certain kinds of people to them. The resources needed to obtain a job include having the right kind of training and experience, and these may in turn depend on other resources, such as the social status of one's parents. To take an obvious example, children whose parents have college educations and work in white-collar occupations are themselves much more likely to enter professional and managerial jobs than are children from blue-collar backgrounds. Other important resources include individual talents, personality traits, knowing the right people, or simply being in the right place at the right time. Discussions that focus on the attributes of jobs emphasize many of the same factors but do so from the standpoint of recruitment. Thus, some occupations require specialized training, so they recruit people with certain kinds of education. Or, at a given time, new opportunities open up, say, in television or computing, so people select these jobs simply because they are available. Bill Williams's work as a biostatistician, for instance, can be understood largely in terms of the training he received and the opportunities that became available to him.

These theories, then, pay little attention to the role of religion. They do not rule out religion as a consideration but assume its effects will be minimal, compared with other social influences. Placed in historical context, these theories also suggest a diminishing role for religion in postindustrial societies like the United States. The reason is that job markets have become more complex than in the past. At one time, inherited attributes, including the religious affiliation of one's parents, might have determined where one could get a job. But now such factors as scoring highly on a standardized college placement test and then majoring in a certain subject are important. There are, however, at least three perspectives from which to see that religion may still have a significant influence in the selection of jobs.

First, religious values may encourage people to select occupations in which these values can be realized. Most religions, for example, attach value to understanding their particular creeds and to helping other people gain greater religious understanding. People who hold these values may be more inclined to consider entering the clergy or may hold the clergy in higher esteem than people who do not share the same values. In a wider sense, religious commitment is often associated with wanting to help the needy or to be of service to others. These values might encourage persons of faith to enter professional occupations, especially the so-called helping professions such as nursing or teaching. We might not be surprised, for example, to learn that Bill Williams's religious training was one of the reasons why he went into cancer research. In contrast, religious traditions that try to discourage greed might deter people from being attracted to an occupation that has come to be associated in the public's mind with greed. For example, in recent years stock brokers have been criticized because of several widely publicized incidents in which they appeared to be motivated primarily by greed.

Second, religious beliefs and activities may become an interest that substitutes for, or precludes receiving, the rewards that might come from other occupations. In this view, religious commitments function mainly as alternatives to the workplace. People who have been unable to obtain the kind of job they desired may shift their interests increasingly toward religious activities. Through these activities, they find friends and perhaps even beliefs that diminish the importance of careers. For example, doing church work, such as teaching Sunday school classes or helping clean the building each week, comes to be regarded as more pleasing to God than holding a job that requires a high level of commitment and responsibility. Over time, it may also be that these alternative interests make it harder for people to move into more prestigious jobs because they lack the requisite experience, do not associate with the right people, or are not motivated to seek such jobs. In this view, someone like Miriam Zellers may do volunteer work at her church because she has been frustrated in pursuing her career.

Third, religious commitments put people in a certain context that, quite apart from any specific features of the religious beliefs themselves, expose them to some occupations more than others. This perspective takes into account that religious commitment is associated with different regions of the country and with different social classes largely because of historical factors. A higher percentage of the population attends religious services regularly, for example, in the Bible Belt, located in the Midwest and South, than in other parts of the country. It may be, therefore, that active churchgoers are more likely to work in certain blue-collar occupations and on farms than other people simply because these occupations are more common in the Midwest and the South. In this perspective, then, religious commitment has an indirect influence on job selection, influencing where people live or whom they know, but not directly shaping their beliefs in a way that would lead to certain kinds of careers. This view would alert us to the possibility that Sonny Nicos's father operated a restaurant because of certain ethnic ties that were reinforced by his religion. In Sonny's own case, these ties may be weaker, allowing him to choose a career on the basis of other considerations.

The current debate over the relationship between religion and the so-called new class illustrates how all three of these arguments might apply in our own setting. The new class is said to be a characteristic of postindustrial societies like the United States. It has developed because these societies have emphasized higher education and technology, and have moved away from heavy industry and manufacturing toward services and the professions. It is composed broadly of college-educated people, or can be defined more narrowly in terms of employment in the professions.[17] A number of scholars have argued that religiously committed people tend to be underrepresented in the new class.[18] This underrepresentation is perhaps due to a conflict between religious values emphasizing dogma or divine revelation and scientific values emphasizing reason and empirical evidence. Or it may stem from the inability of religious people to acquire the cultural capital (education, knowledge, social graces) needed to participate in the new class. And there may be reason to think that the new class has simply put down roots in large cities and on college campuses where religious influences have been weaker from the start.

While all three of these perspectives suggest possible religious influences on career selection, there are several reasons to think that these influences may be less important now than in the past. Most people attend secular high schools and colleges, and it is in these contexts, more so than in religious organizations, that careers are discussed. Moreover, in a religiously pluralistic society like the United States, it is common for people to have contact with members of a wide variety of religious organizations. It may also be that people choose occupations more on the basis of how much they will get paid, or whether the work suits their talents, rather than thinking about its connections with their religious beliefs. Given all these possibilities, clergy are also likely to say it doesn't matter what career a person chooses. Religious organizations thus abrogate their authority and leave the job selection process entirely to the marketplace.

What do we learn from the survey? It is worth noting that some of the evidence indicates that *attitudes* toward various lines of work may still be influenced by religious commitment. For example, people who attend religious services every week and say their religion is very important to them are more likely than people with less interest in religion to say they admire teachers, nurses, and therapists. They are also more likely to admire housewives. And, not surprisingly, they are more likely to admire clergy.[19] Some of these differences suggest that religious commitment elevates the importance of caring and thus makes people think more highly of those who enter the caring professions. Miriam, Bill, and Sonny all expressed admiration for such professions, even though their own careers were quite varied.

But these evaluations seem not to influence very much the actual careers people enter. Part of the reason is that other considerations become more important. People may admire nurses, for example, but be uninterested in becoming one themselves because they feel their talents lie elsewhere or they are interested in a less stressful job. Another reason is that values in our society are quite malleable. We tend to think of our values as a matter of personal taste, preference, or whim, rather than something expressing fundamental truths. We also learn to be tolerant of others' whims or personality traits. Thus, when people who valued compassion and who themselves were actively involved in volunteer work were asked what they thought of stockbrokers, for example, most said this would not be their own preference, but they admired stockbrokers who were honest and hardworking, figuring that they probably could be decent, compassionate people as well.[20] We are, in short, very reluctant to judge the moral worth of various occupations in absolute terms (possibly basing these judgments on religious values), even though we clearly accord some occupations higher status than others. We also recognize the limitations of our own occupations. Thus, many people who say they are satisfied with their jobs still say they would not recommend those jobs to their friends. This means that other factors, such as job availability, can have a more decisive influence. Our culture has, in other words, taught us to be flexible enough to fit into whatever niche the job market may provide.

When people are asked why they chose their line of work, they respond in ways that point to reasons other than religious commitments. Approximately half, for example, say that money was one of the major reasons why they pursued their present occupation, almost half (44 percent) say the opportunity to use their talents was a major reason, and nearly this many (41 percent) say circumstances just led them into it, or mention (40 percent) the challenge it presented them (see Table 3.1). A reason such as wanting to use one's talents or desiring a challenge could, of course, be part of a person's understanding of God or of other religious teachings. Yet, the values of using one's talents and of seeking challenges are so widespread in our culture that people hardly have to be religious to hold them. The high proportion who choose their career on the basis of monetary concerns is also significant. This finding is consistent with the concern often expressed about the level of materialism in our society. One layman put it in these words: "The measure of success today is too materially driven. You don't see people espousing careers that will do anything but benefit them materially. There's very little sense of feeling called to your work."

When working Americans are asked directly about the role of religion in their job choices, most say their decision was not influenced by religion. Specifically, 75 percent say no, it was not, 12 percent say maybe religious values influenced their decision, and only 10 percent

TABLE 3.1

Reasons for Choosing Line of Work

Question: "Following are some reasons people give for getting into their present line of work. Which ones were most important for you? Which one was the most important reason of all?"

	A Most Important Reason	The Most Important of All
The money	53	29
The opportunity to use my talents	44	15
Circumstances just led me to it	41	15
The challenge it presented me	40	12
Freedom to make my own decisions	30	5
Flexible hours	29	6
Knowing people in this line of work	29	4
The chance to become successful	25	6
Wanting to grow as a person	23	3
Parent or relative in this line of work	13	3

say religious values definitely influenced their decision. Even among persons who attend religious services every week, fewer than a quarter (22 percent) say religious values definitely influenced them in deciding what kind of work to pursue. This is a striking finding. People were not asked if religious values were the determining factor, only if their faith had any influence at all on their choice of careers. And the vast majority—of active churchgoers and of the unchurched alike—denied that faith had made any difference. Miriam Zellers, Bill Williams, and Sonny Nicos are typical in this respect. When asked if religious values influenced their decision about a career, all three denied that religious upbringing had entered into their thinking at all.

In the case of Sonny Nicos, for example, religious upbringing gave him a basic respect for other people and for himself, and an understanding of how people should be treated, but these values could be applied in any job situation. His actual choice of career, therefore, was not in any direct way influenced by religion. In fact, high school was a time when he got away from religion, rebelling against it because it represented something his mother had made him do rather than something he himself wanted. In high school he discovered an interest in sports and this, more than anything else, was what attracted him to the idea of operating a camera at sporting events. It's fun. And he is sure God is happy about it as long as he is happy. "I'm pretty lucky," he says. "I do something I really enjoy. I've always felt that is the most important thing."

Further doubt about the role of religion arises when the actual occupations of various people are examined. A comparison of broad occupational categories in the U.S. labor force as a whole and among the third of the labor force who attend religious services most often, for example, reveals very few differences. The religiously involved, for instance, are somewhat more likely to be represented in the professions and somewhat less likely to be employed in managerial positions, but these differences are quite small and mostly disappear when other factors are taken into consideration (see Table 3.2).[21] In other ways, the employment characteristics of the two groups differ little as well. The religiously involved are only slightly less likely to be employed full time than in the labor force as a whole, and this difference is probably attributable to gender differences. Self-employed people, employees of nonprofit firms, and employees of government organizations are somewhat more likely among the religiously active than in the labor force at large, but again these differences are relatively small.[22]

Findings such as these, of course, raise specific doubts about the alleged relationship between religion and the so-called new class. It may be that considering the professions in general is too broad to be a valid indicator of new class employment. A more likely explanation for the lack of a relationship, however, is that religious communities themselves have been undergoing change. Research conducted during the 1950s and early 1960s showed that *denomination* was significantly associated with levels of education and types of occupation. Presbyterians, for example, tended to be in higher-status occupations, while Baptists tended to be in lower-status occupations.[23] In some studies, Catholics also tended to be in lower-status occupations than Protestants. Studies conducted in the late 1970s and 1980s generally showed these differences to be diminishing or in some cases no longer important at all.[24] But *religious orientation* was becoming a more important feature of American religion in general, conservatives often differing substantially

TABLE 3.2

Employment Profile

Percent of respondents whose work has the following characteristics among the total labor force and among weekly churchgoers:

	Total Labor Force	Weekly Churchgoers
Employed full-time	79	75
Employed part-time	21	25
Professional worker	24	27
Manager/executive	7	5
Business owner	3	3
Sales worker	6	8
Clerical worker	12	12
Service worker	13	12
Skilled worker	16	16
Semiskilled worker	10	9
Laborer	3	2
Work 0–39 hours/week	34	37
Work 40–49 hours/week	48	45
Work 50+ hours/week	18	17
Self-employed	15	19
For-profit organization	69	64
Nonprofit organization	9	13
Government organization	17	18

from liberals on many lifestyle characteristics.[25] But even this factor was shown to be a function of the times, rather than an endemic characteristic of religion itself. While much research during the 1970s showed that religious conservatives tended to be underrepresented among the college-educated, for example, other research showed that conservative Protestant sects were rising rapidly in levels of educational attainment. By the end of the 1980s, some of the differences in education that had been noted in earlier studies were clearly beginning to disappear.[26] Still, the overall occupational structure tends to reflect the past more than it does the present. Thus, religious conservatives continue to be somewhat underrepresented in the professions.[27] With rising levels of education, religious conservatives may, however, be entering professional and semiprofessional occupations in larger numbers. If so, there may still be value conflicts that require what has been called "cognitive bargaining." And, for this reason, better educated religious conservatives may continue to feel more comfortable in managerial positions than in the professions. But job selection itself may for the most part be a function of factors other than religious commitment.

More nuanced characteristics of jobs also suggest that religiously involved people do not differ much from the rest of the population. The third of the labor force most actively involved in religious services, for example, is no different from the rest of the labor force in saying their job involves a lot of pressure, is highly competitive, is physically exhausting, or is emotionally draining.[28]

This evidence tells us that people with deep religious commitments can be found in virtually all segments of the labor force. Certainly, there may be exceptions where this rule does not apply. For example, deeply religious people probably do not hold jobs as mob leaders, prostitutes, or drug dealers (although there have been some notable cases to the contrary). Some evidence indicates that religious commitment tends *not* to go hand in hand with careers in certain branches of higher education, such as teaching in the humanities or social sciences.[29] At the local level, there may also be businesses that for various reasons tend to hire only fellow fundamentalists, Jehovah's Witnesses, or Polish Catholics. But the pattern in the labor force as a whole does not seem to be greatly influenced by these exceptions. For better or worse, religiously active people are distributed widely throughout the labor force, experiencing the same kinds of job demands and pressures as everyone else.

Religious leaders have largely accommodated to this situation, regarding it as natural and healthy. Advice books written by religious leaders for young people thinking about career options, for example, often encourage prayer and reading the Bible. But the leading of God is said to come about primarily through circumstances. Doors will open for one career and close on another. The reason is likely to be something about one's talents, interests, or training. That religiously committed people can enter virtually any career, moreover, is regarded in this literature as a good thing because it means God's people will be filling important roles throughout the society.

A parish priest in Chicago who counsels young people on a regular basis about career decisions illustrates another reason why religious teachings may not be expected to guide people into particular lines of work. "I ask them what they're looking for," he explains, "and if the job is going to be able to provide for them the types of things that they're looking for. I emphasize much more the sense of accomplishment than the money aspect, although you can't deny the money aspect. Is this going to make you happy and are you going to feel that you've accomplished something with your life after 40 years of whatever it is?" In his view, God doesn't expect people to choose one job or another, just to think about the question seriously and do something satisfying.

If religious teachings are largely indifferent with respect to particular careers, then churches can appeal to all segments of society. They run no danger of offending anyone—for example, race car drivers, casino operators, or movie stars—because all occupations are considered equal in the eyes of God. This is good for the churches in many ways. It means more potential members and contributors and it means that the churches can be a witness to the value of acceptance, rather than exclusion. As one religious leader writes, the best way to dampen people's enthusiasm for their vocations is to "invent a hierarchy of vocations and deny [that] vocations [are] all of equal importance."[30] But if religion counsels people only to pursue careers by thinking about the same criteria they would if they were not religious, there may be little reason for those who are worried about career decisions to look to the churches. Thus, religion must be relevant to the workplace in some other way, if it is to be relevant at all. It either influences *how* people behave within their various lines of work or remains separate from the ways in which people conduct themselves at work.

The main point, then, is that people with deep religious commitments can be found in all segments of the workforce; they are neither particularly disadvantaged nor privileged; nor are they free of the problems and anxieties that other people experience in connection with their work. Religion has, we might say, adapted to postindustrial society. Faith commitments are sufficiently malleable that most people can participate fully in whatever sector of the workforce for which they feel suited without experiencing restraint or being excluded on the basis of their creedal orientations. This also means that work is a realm that is likely to intersect in some way with individuals' religious commitments. That is, most individuals who work also have some kind of religious commitment, and most individuals with deep religious commitments also work. How the two realms influence each other is therefore an important issue to consider in the remainder of the chapter.

Work-Faith Connections

If religious leaders have often been content to counsel people to enter whatever line of work that may be of interest to them, they have been more divided in their views of how much people should actually try to connect their faith to their thinking about work. On the one hand, religious teachings can be found suggesting that people should bring biblical principles to bear on their work, lead godly lives in the workplace, and demonstrate God's love through the quality of their work. On the other hand, religious leaders have sometimes been reluctant to draw close connections, fearing that they did not themselves understand what people did during the work week or feeling that work was a kind of neutral zone, a place where people did what they were told in order to make a living. One group of clergy with whom I discussed these issues, for example, admitted they knew little about the day-to-day activities of their parishioners in the workplace. Another pastor remarked that secular work had become so technical that he felt incapable of offering anything but general advice.

Compared with the emphasis devoted to prayer, Bible reading, and family matters, applications of faith to the workplace have sometimes been minimal, judging from anecdotal comments from laity about their experiences in Sunday school classes and Bible studies. One parishioner who participated in a congregationwide effort to address this gap, for example, acknowledged that he had "never really talked at church before in depth about how I spend my time the rest of the week." In recent years, some religious leaders have, therefore, begun to call for greater attention to be paid to the relationship between faith and work. In Illinois, Catholic newspapers have initiated a column that profiles the work experiences of laity and invites them to reflect on how their faith affects their work. Men's and women's Bible study groups are also using new study guides and popular books that aim to connect spirituality with work. Miriam Zellers, for instance, belongs to a Bible study group that talks a lot about child rearing and relationships between spouses but also is concerned in principle at least, as its leader says, "with viewing our work and all our decisions in the light of eternity."

The American labor force is itself quite divided in terms of its efforts to connect thoughts about faith with thoughts about work. When asked how much they had thought during the past year about "how to link your faith more directly with your work," 33 percent of working Americans said they had thought about this a great deal or a fair amount. Among persons who said they were members of a church or synagogue, this proportion was 46 percent. And among persons who attended religious services every week, it was 60 percent. Although this figure is probably not as high as many church leaders would wish, it does, therefore, indicate that many people are at least interested in making their faith relevant to their work. It also indicates that many people have learned to compartmentalize the two.

Bill Williams would be typical of the majority of church members who largely keep work and faith in separate compartments. Asked about the connection, he says,

> I don't allow my value system to be dictated by the church. I have to take responsibility for my own decisions. But I guess overall my values don't differ that much from what I was taught. I still believe that I treat people the way I want to be treated. I try and function that way, even as a manager. The people who work under me, I treat them the way I want to be treated, so therefore I can very rarely go wrong, because I'm not a sadist who will mistreat myself. So generally it works. And I still try to be a good person and treat people well.

In short, there is not that much to think about. It simply makes good sense to treat others fairly and honestly.

The role of religious organizations in encouraging thinking about faith and work is perhaps not as minimal as some critics have suggested, however. For example, one book on the subject says an informal poll of church members revealed that 90 percent claimed to have never heard any sermons or lessons on relating their faith to their work.[31] But the more systematic evidence provided by the Economic Values Study suggests a considerably higher figure. For instance, 40 percent of all church or synagogue members said they had heard a sermon within the past year that had inspired them to work harder (among weekly attenders, this figure was 52 percent). Parishioners, for the most part, also seem to feel that clergy understand the problems they may be experiencing in the workplace. For example, only 24 percent of church members in the labor force agree with the statement, "Members of the clergy have very little understanding of what it is like in the real workaday world." Still, evidence also suggests that most parishioners do not feel strongly enough about linking their faith and their work to engage in actual conversations with the clergy about this topic. Only 20 percent of church members, for example, say they have talked about their work with a member of the clergy during the past year.

We shall want to see in subsequent sections whether those who think about this connection actually differ in their work values and attitudes from those who do not think about it. For the moment, though, it is worth noting that the culture as a whole is not all that is divided about the relevance of faith to questions about work—individuals themselves are divided. They pick up the mixed signals that the culture emits. They learn from secular sources that a job is a job, period, and that one need not bring religion into the picture. They learn from some religious leaders and teachings that faith should inform all of life and, recognizing that work is a large chunk of their life, they realize that there should be some connections. But they also hear religious people saying they keep the two in separate compartments. Perhaps this is why so many of us think about the connection between faith and work. We don't know what the relationship should be. So it troubles us—from time to time. We may remain confused or feel ambivalent, giving lip service to the possibility that faith matters but not being able to say how it should matter.

Work Values

Does religion heighten the value of work or diminish it, or do the two have anything to do with each other? Historical studies suggest that the Judeo-Christian tradition was associated with a positive rise in the value of work. The ancient Greeks regarded work as a necessary evil. In many other societies, common practice was to work as little as possible, especially if one were a member of the aristocracy and could force others to do the work.[32] In contrast, the biblical tradition encouraged hard work and an investment of one's talents in useful pursuits. The Puritans were perhaps the epitome of this orientation toward work.

An opposing view can also be found in contemporary religion, however. This perspective suggests that work is a form of idolatry, perhaps an addiction, that gets in the way of believers' spiritual lives. It argues against careerism, pointing out the devastating effects it can have on one's family and personal life. Religious leaders have sometimes adopted this perspective because they wanted members of their churches or synagogues to spend time doing religious rather than secular work. Arguing against viewing hard work as a moral virtue may also be an adaptation of contemporary religion to postindustrial society. If hard work is no longer as important as it once was for sheer economic survival, a religious faith that encourages people to relax and enjoy life may be more attractive than one that embraces a rigid work ethic. In short, changing economic circumstances reinforce mixed signals about the value of work.

A third alternative can be identified by thinking about the ways in which contemporary society has become secularized since the Industrial Revolution. This perspective suggests that faith neither encourages nor discourages hard work because work has simply become institutionalized as part of the way in which most people live their lives. People have to work hard to make a living, or at least to attain the standard of living they desire. A system of rewards has been institutionalized in most work settings that encourages hard work as a way of receiving promotions, bonuses, and salary increases. Because they have to work hard, this argument suggests, most people then turn this necessity into a virtue by claiming it is of *value* to do so. They believe in the value of working whether or not they are people of faith. Religious beliefs may have had something to do with the rise of a work ethic to begin with. But at present, religion is unlikely to be associated one way or the other with how much people value their work.

A general sense of how widely work is valued in the American labor force can be obtained by looking at Table 3.3. According to these figures, 81 percent of employed Americans regard their work as either absolutely essential or very important to their basic sense of worth as a person. On the surface at least, this figure suggests a very high level of commitment to jobs and careers. It is, for example, a considerably higher proportion than that who say the same thing about their hobbies, leisure activities, or community. It is also higher in the labor force as a whole than the proportion who say their relation to God is this important.

Table 3.3 also shows how people who attend religious services every week compare with the total labor force. In terms of the sheer proportion who value their work, there is no difference at all (81 percent of the weekly attenders also say their work is very important to

TABLE 3.3

Personal Values

Question: "How important is each of the following to your basic sense of worth as a person?" (Percent "absolutely essential" or "very important")

	Total Labor Force	Weekly Churchgoers
Your family	95	97
Your moral standards	93	97
Taking care of yourself	87	87
Helping people in need	82	90
YOUR WORK	81	81
Being able to do what you want to	77	69
Paying attention to your feelings	75	75
Living a comfortable life	74	68
Being successful	73	68
Your relation to God	69	94
Your community	58	67
Your hobbies or leisure activities	51	45
Making a lot of money	47	39

them). The main difference, though, is that the religiously involved are much more likely than the labor force as a whole to say their relation to God is very important (94 percent as opposed to 69 percent).

What does this mean? A better sense of it can be obtained by considering the evidence in a little more detail. If most people who are religiously involved value *both* their work and their relation to God, which do they value more? Most, it appears, do value their relation to God more. For example, 67 percent say this relation is absolutely essential to their sense of worth as a person, whereas only 32 percent say the same thing about their work. So one way of looking at it is to say that work is a high value, but relating to God is an even higher value. Consequently, people may love their work but ultimately know it is something they can also get along without. Miriam Zellers illustrates this attitude when she says, "I am fulfilled, confident, I like my life, and I have all the choices I need, so going to work doesn't prove anything; it just adds another dimension."

But does this mean work is then diminished in importance? No. At least not in absolute terms. In fact, among weekly attenders the proportion who say work is absolutely essential is slightly *higher* than in the labor force as a whole. And among those who think a lot about the relationship between their faith and their work, it is even higher. Thus, it appears that valuing one's relationship to God places work in a secondary position relative to that value but on the whole enhances the importance of work in absolute terms.[33] Putting it differently, we might say that faith encourages people to recognize that work is important or meaningful by placing it in a context that also includes service to God; work, therefore, is certainly not to be pursued zealously at the expense of everything else, but one should be responsible and do one's work to the best of one's ability.

There are, of course, other ways in which work can be valued besides being considered an important part of one's personal worth. For example, doing well in one's job can be a value that some people believe in more strongly than others do. Or there is also a small literature on whether work is considered an intrinsic value (important in its own right) or an extrinsic value (important only as a means of making money). Does religious commitment also increase the likelihood that work will be valued in these ways?

The answer depends on what specific orientation toward work is being considered. If it is doing well at one's job, then it appears that religious commitment is positively associated with this orientation, although not very strongly so.[34] We might suppose that religiously committed individuals would spend longer hours at their jobs each week because they feel a stronger need to do well at work. However, there appear to be no correlations worthy of note between hours worked and religious factors.[35] An intrinsic commitment to the value of work is widely held in American society generally, and this orientation does not seem to be significantly more common among religious than among nonreligious people. For example, about four out of five people in the labor force agree with the statement, "Even if I had enough money, I would still work," and this proportion is about the same among those who attend religious services regularly and those who do not (and among people who say religious commitment is very, or not very, important to them). On this basis, we might say that there is merit to the arguments about secularization: American culture has institutionalized the value of doing well in one's job and the number of hours that one should work to such an extent that religious convictions make little difference on these matters.

If work is compared with family, though, a different pattern emerges. One way of saying that work is an extrinsic rather than an intrinsic value, for example, is to regard work as a means of serving one's family. The religiously committed are more likely to hold this view than people who are not religiously involved. They are also more likely to say their work takes second place compared with their family.[36] Furthermore, when asked about various factors that might motivate them to work harder at their jobs—money, competition, promotions, praise, among others—the religiously committed are significantly more likely than other workers to say they would be especially motivated by trying to benefit their families.[37] More broadly, the churches have, of course, emphasized the family. Work, then, is less likely to be regarded as an end in itself but as a way of contributing to one's family. In this way, faith influences the meaning of work—how people understand it. Nonetheless, it is worth repeating that the number of hours people actually work is not affected. Thus, despite the fact that they value their families more than other people do, the religiously devout spend no less time working.

What then does valuing one's family mean? In Miriam Zellers's case, of course, it gave her a reason to stay out of the labor force for a number of years and, when she started working again, she did so because she needed money to help send her children to school. Judging from the survey, religious commitment influences reasoning such as this more than it does the decision to work or not to work. Religious commitment may also be a source of messages that run counter to those one receives in the labor force itself. For example, Miriam Zellers says she tells her daughters they are "getting too independent" and she encourages them to "get rid of the things that separate you because when your father and I are gone you are going to need each other." Her daughters have not quit their jobs as a result of their mother's advice, but they may feel more ambivalent about working long hours or moving away from one another.

None of these orientations gets at the idea of a religiously sanctioned work ethic, however, quite as well as the simple notion that work is pleasing to God, while laziness is not. On this score, the Puritan work ethic is still very much alive in American culture. In the labor force as a whole, a majority (53 percent) agree that "People who work hard are more pleasing to God than people who are lazy." Among church members, 62 percent agree, and among those who attend religious services every week, 68 percent agree. In a later chapter, we shall see that this attitude influences how people think about the poor. For now, it also reinforces the conclusions I inferred from some of the other results. If work is pleasing to God, then the meaning of work is somewhat different for those who believe than for those who do not. Working hard makes God happy, whether it brings economic rewards or not. In practice, however, this belief seems to affect how people think about their work more than it does how—or how much—they actually work.

Job Satisfaction

Few aspects of work have been studied as much as workers' satisfaction or dissatisfaction with it. Although the reasons for this research are varied, they stem mainly from the fact that employers are interested in knowing the conditions under which employee satisfaction will be high and the conditions under which morale may become problematic. The assumption in much of this literature is that productivity will also be higher if satisfaction is at a high level. From the viewpoint of the employee, it is, of course, equally important to gain knowledge of what work situations may be the most conducive to personal happiness.[38]

Most research on job satisfaction has focused on the ways in which it may be affected by characteristics of the job itself. Thus, it has been common to examine the effects of different supervisory styles, levels of compensation, hours of work, chances for promotion, composition of the work group, and content of the work being performed. It has made sense to examine factors such as these because they represented conditions that might be possible to manipulate if managers and workers better understood their effects. Some of the literature has also recognized other factors but has generally attributed them to personality differences among workers.[39] In other words, researchers generally assume that religious orientations make no difference or—if they do—are irrelevant to the things managers want to know about.

For present purposes, we must reverse the standard approach and ask what conditions *outside* the workplace may affect job satisfaction, particularly whether or not adherence to religious belief systems and involvement in religious organizations may make a difference. Although the standard literature would subsume these under "personality variables," we must recognize that they do not so much reside in some deep-seated personality trait as they do in the roles and beliefs that constitute individuals' involvement in the wider social world.

There are several reasons to think that people with strong religious commitment may have higher levels of job satisfaction. One is that religious belief may devalue the importance of work to the extent that it simply makes less difference to the individual whether or not the job is objectively pleasant or not. Miriam Zellers, for example, says she doesn't really care what people think of her when she is working because she knows God loves her; in contrast, she speaks disparagingly of a son-in-law who claims to be a Christian but is still worried about appearing successful. Another possibility is that religious belief may elevate the importance of work to the point that even trivial tasks become more meaningful and therefore provide greater satisfaction. Still another is that religious belief may offer tangible sources of advice or support that help tide the individual through trying times.

Previous research lends some support to the expectation that individuals with higher levels of religious commitment will also have higher levels of job satisfaction.[40] Some research on stressful life events, such as experiencing a divorce or being fired from one's job, suggests that the impact of such events is diminished when individuals have several different roles from which they derive their sense of worth. Thus, being an active church member might make it easier to be happy at work simply because all of one's eggs, so to speak, were not in the same basket. Other research has demonstrated that religious beliefs and activities may be helpful for alleviating stress and may be associated with a more positive attitude toward life in general.[41]

One caveat from previous work is that relationships between religious commitment and job satisfaction are fairly meaningless unless the religiously committed actually experience stress or other unpleasant job conditions in the same degree as other people do. It could be, for example, that religiously committed people tend to be from different social strata, or perhaps even from different family backgrounds, that somehow made it possible for them to escape some of the trials of

TABLE 3.4

Problems in the Workplace

Question: "In the past year, which of these have you experienced in your work?" (Percent who have experienced each of the following among total labor force and among weekly churchgoers)

	Total Labor Force	Weekly Churchgoers
Wondering if you were in the right line of work	35	31
Feeling seriously burned out	28	26
Having to do things that were against your better judgment	24	19
Having an argument with your boss	20	14
Taking a cut in pay	13	10
Seeing something you thought was illegal	12	10
Being reprimanded	12	8
Feeling your work was compromising your values	12	10
Being laid off	10	8
Felt that you were being discriminated against	10	8
Having to do something you thought was unethical	9	7
Felt that you were being sexually harassed	4	4

the typical working environment. What we have already seen about the distribution of jobs among the religiously committed, of course, casts some doubt on such conjectures.

As shown in Table 3.4, churchgoers are scarcely any more immune to the psychological, emotional, interpersonal, and ethical problems that arise in the workplace than anybody else. On virtually all of the items shown, there are some slight differences. But these are mostly attributable to the fact that regular churchgoers are somewhat more likely to be from middle-class occupations than is true in the labor force as a whole.[42]

Nor are persons who are religiously oriented any less subject to experiencing stress in the workplace than other people are. In the labor force as a whole, one person in seven claims to be bothered by stress in the job almost every day. Another one in seven is bothered by job-related stress several days a week. In all, 55 percent are bothered at least once a week. These proportions are just about the same among persons who attend religious services every week. One person in eight experiences stress almost every day and one person in two experiences stress at least once a week.

On more specific kinds of stress, the data also indicate clearly that work creates conflict and frustration for the religious just as much as for the nonreligious. About a quarter of people in the labor force who attend religious services every week, for example, complain about stress from having to meet deadlines and from needing more time for themselves and for their families. These are about the same proportions as in the labor force as a whole. In both groups, about one person in five complains of stress from having to work too many hours, from bureaucracy and red tape, and from having to do too many different things. One person in six experiences stress from conflict with co-workers, and nearly this many have trouble with their supervisors (see Table 3.5).

The important point, then, as far as religious organizations are concerned is to understand how frequently their members are experiencing problems in the workplace. Believers may be admonished to get along with their bosses or to work hard so that there will be no reason for them to be reprimanded. But the data indicate that reality does not live up to these ideals. With burnout facing a quarter of their members, doubts about their careers being expressed by nearly a third, and anywhere from 5 to 10 percent being faced with sexual harassment, discrimination, or requests to engage in unethical behavior, religious organizations must become actively involved in supporting and guiding their members in these difficult situations.

What is also evident, though, is that religious involvement seems to go hand in hand with higher levels of overall job satisfaction, despite

TABLE 3.5

Sources of Stress

Question: "Which of these, if any, is currently a source of stress in your work?" (Percent answering yes to each of the following among the total labor force and among weekly churchgoers)

	Total Labor Force	Weekly Churchgoers
Not being paid well enough	34	29
Wanting other things in life	30	24
Having to meet deadlines	30	30
Needing more time for myself	27	26
Not enough time for my family	26	25
Working too many hours	24	20
Feeling burned out	23	19
Bureaucracy and red tape	23	22
Doing too many different things	23	22
Conflict with co-workers	18	17
An unsupportive boss	15	10
Having to make decisions	13	12
Feeling my work doesn't count	13	9
An unpleasant work environment	11	7

these various sources of stress. When members of the labor force were asked to rate their satisfaction with their work on a scale from zero (low) to ten (high), for example, 58 percent of those who attend religious services weekly rated their work an "8" or higher, compared with 50 percent of those who attend services several times a month to as little as several times a year, and only 45 percent of those who attend seldom or never. Other measures of religious commitment, such as how much they had thought about the relationship between faith and work or how many friends they had in their congregations, yielded similar results. These relationships, moreover, did not disappear when other factors, such as the kind of occupation in which one was employed, gender, or age, were taken into consideration.[43]

Why then are religious people somewhat more satisfied with their work than nonreligious people? One possibility, as mentioned previously, is that they are simply prone to be Panglossian about everything. Religious people are, for example, more likely to say they are, on the whole, happy with their lives. They are also more likely to look back on their childhoods and say they were happy then. There is some empirical evidence, too, that religious involvement seems to be associated with a rosier attitude toward life in general, and this attitude then influences how people respond when asked about their work.[44] But the fact that religious people are just as likely as nonreligious people to admit that stress, pressure, and emotional exhaustion are part of their jobs suggests that a Panglossian attitude is not the only explanation.

A more likely explanation comes from considering what people faced with unpleasant situations at work may do about them. The possibilities are enormous, ranging from doing nothing at all, to going jogging to blow off steam, to seeking outside help or support. In recent years, much attention has been devoted to helping employees find effective ways of dealing with stress. Some options, it appears, work better than others to revitalize people and make them feel better about their jobs. In the survey, for example, people who talked about job-related stress with their spouse and engaged in physical exercise generally had higher levels of job satisfaction than those who did not; in contrast, coming home and watching television and keeping it to oneself were associated with lower levels of job satisfaction.

Religious commitment is probably conducive to higher levels of job satisfaction because religiously oriented people are more likely than nonreligious people to engage in two kinds of activities to alleviate job-related stress. One is religious-specific activity, such as praying, meditating, or seeking help from a member of the clergy. The other is religion-related activity, that is, behavior, such as talking with friends and family or even seeing a therapist, not necessarily restricted to religious settings but encouraged by the fact that religious involvement helps tie people into broader communities and supportive networks. These activities are more common among persons who regularly participate in religious services than among those who do not.[45] They are also associated with being in religious fellowship and support groups more generally. And they are all positively associated with higher levels of job satisfaction.[46]

The value of such coping mechanisms is perhaps even more evident with respect to serious job-related problems, such as burnout, than for maintaining overall job satisfaction on a day-to-day basis. People who attend religious services regularly, who associate with friends in their congregations, who pray, and who think a lot about their relationship to God are significantly less likely than their counterparts to say they have experienced serious burnout in their jobs during the past year. These effects hold when other characteristics of employment and religious affiliation are taken into account.[47]

Apart from alleviating stress, religious commitment also appears to contribute to job satisfaction just by helping people establish a center in their lives. God becomes a kind of sounding board, a partner in the internal conversations people have about their jobs while at work or before starting their day. In fact, a majority of the labor force as a whole (51 percent) says that "Praying in the morning helps me have a better day at work." Among church members in the labor force, this proportion rises to seven in ten, and among weekly attenders at religious services, to eight in ten.

An example of how prayer may help people feel better about their jobs is provided by Miriam Zellers. She remembers feeling very uncertain about what to do when she first started her job as dietician for the school lunch program.

> I remember asking God if the whole purpose of this job was to better feed the children and to increase their nutrition, then would he help me find the right suppliers, the right kind of people who would not try to cheat me because they knew I was brand-new, and that they would make me aware of any bargains that were coming up or any ways I could be planning long-range to perhaps save money and still keep the welfare of the children up front.

Praying this way gave her the confidence to make day-to-day decisions and helped her remember the main goal she was trying to achieve.

New Meanings of "The Calling"

No discussion of the relationship between religion and work would be complete without special attention to the doctrine of the calling.[48] The Protestant reformers' belief that each individual was called by God to whatever occupation he or she was pursuing made work in the present life more important than it had ever been before. The faithful were thus challenged to live dutiful, responsible lives before God by working diligently in their occupations, rather than regarding such work as a necessary evil, and to consider it as important as time spent in prayer, serving the church, or preparing for life in heaven. The calling in this sense provided motivation that might otherwise have been lacking for the multitude of shopkeepers, artisans, and merchants that contributed to the rise of industrial empires and that spread capitalism to virtually every corner of the globe between the seventeenth and nineteenth centuries.

The doctrine of the calling has also been interpreted in different ways. Martin Luther stressed responsible work activity as part of the divine law of good works that were supposed to follow from a life of faith. But for Luther, good works were always secondary to having faith in God's grace. Vocational commitment was partly encouraged by this view, but not as much as it might be. Calvin's emphasis on the calling as a privilege of serving God seemed to provide greater motivation. In part, though, this was because of the broader framework in which Calvin's understanding of the calling was situated. That framework emphasized predestination—the divine foreordaining of individuals to be part of the chosen few or part of the damned—and this belief, together with a view of the inscrutable nature of divine will, left the believer in utter uncertainty. Thus, the calling was not simply a privilege of serving God; it was a way that the believer could gain some *sign* of divine favor as well. In addition, the Calvinistic system was more thoroughly rationalized and stressed discipline both in worship and in individual piety to a greater extent than Lutheranism.

My reason for reviewing these traditional understandings of the calling is to point out that contemporary interpretations probably vary as well.[49] The idea of being *useful* to other people and to society at large by working diligently in one's chosen field of endeavor, for example, was already evident in Catholic theology, came to be emphasized in Puritan writings, and eventually formed the basis of eighteenth-century utilitarian individualism. It is thus not so much a matter any longer of comparing Protestants and Catholics, or Lutherans and Presbyterians, to see how they understand the calling, but of envisioning how the calling itself may have been altered since the sixteenth century by the various forces of secularization.

Two such possibilities illustrate the kinds of change that may be worth considering. We will then be in a better position to consider some contemporary evidence. One is that the calling, rather than unsettling people and challenging them to work harder or be more aggressive economically, may actually have the opposite effect. Some of Calvin's own writings, for example, suggest that believers were encouraged to consider their calling in order to be more *content* with their station in life and to avoid envying those in higher positions or feeling superior to those in lower positions. Whereas the standard interpretation would suggest a connection between feeling oneself called by God and being more committed to hard work, this interpretation would perhaps argue for a stronger connection between the calling and measures of job satisfaction. The other possibility is that understandings of the calling may have shifted toward the pietistic interpretation found among Quakers, Methodists, and various Brethren sects. In this view, the calling has less to do with worldly activity in the workplace itself than with an introspective attitude about one's relationship to God. The pietistic tradition in American culture has always been strong, and now, coupled with the privatization of religion that some have envisioned as well as a growing interest in inner feelings, it may be that the calling has shifted in this direction.

Before considering what the calling means in contemporary society, we must pause to ask whether it has any meaning at all for most people. We have already seen that a relatively small percentage of the American labor force believes religious values had any influence on their actual choice of a career. This finding would lead us to doubt that many people experience a calling while they are young that literally tells them to go into vocation X because God wants them to do so. Qualitative interviews also reveal that not many people, even ones with strong religious convictions, think very much or very clearly about the doctrine of the calling, at least in the abstract.

A sizable minority of the American labor force, however, has some sense of having been called to their line of work. Thirty percent, for example, agree with the statement, "I feel God has called me to the particular line of work I am in." Among church members in the labor force, 40 percent do so, and among persons who attend religious services every week, this figure is 46 percent. Thus, we might say that among the most actively religious segment of the population, the idea of a calling is meaningful to about one person in every two. The fact that Protestants and Catholics do not differ much is indicated by relatively small differences in overall proportions among the two who agree with the statement (35 percent and 31 percent, respectively). As might be expected, religious conservatives (45 percent) are more likely to believe in a calling than moderates (32 percent) or liberals (19 percent).[50]

Neither Bill Williams nor Sonny Nicos feels called to his particular line of work. Miriam Zellers, however, provides an example of someone who has a sense of being called. Not having spent her life in a single career, she associates the calling less with a particular occupation than with the unique set of talents she feels God has given her and the opportunities she has to use these talents.

> All of us were given life by God. We're like snowflakes. No two are alike. Whatever our gifts are, they were given to us. We had no choice about it. But we do have a choice how to use them. If I ignored God, and didn't use my gifts, I would not be showing the love he's shown to me. If I didn't understand his love, then I'd be a person who couldn't do horizontally what I know he vertically does for me.

But does believing one is called make any difference to the ways in which people approach their work? If the standard argument is correct, we would expect people with a calling to be more intrinsically oriented toward their work. Work itself would have meaning because it was given divine legitimacy by the concept of the calling, whereas otherwise it might be regarded simply as a way of earning money or providing for one's family.

One indication that a sense of calling does give people a more intrinsic attachment to their work comes from reconsidering the reasons for choosing one's line of work examined in Table 3.1. People who believe they are called to their line of work are more likely than others to list reasons like "the opportunity to use my talents" and "wanting to grow as a person." They were less likely to select reasons like "the money" or "circumstances just led me to it."[51]

Another sense of how the calling may influence orientations toward work can be obtained by considering what people say their motivation is for working hard and doing their job well. The motivational factors that distinguish most clearly between those who have experienced a calling and those who have not are trying to fulfill one's own potential and trying to help other people. Money, competition, and fear of losing one's job, in contrast, run in the opposite direction (see Table 3.6).[52]

TABLE 3.6

Sources of Motivation

Question: "How much does each of the following motivate you to work hard and do your work really well?" (Percent who said each one motivates them "a great deal")

	Among Respondents Who:	
	Felt They Had a Calling	Did Not Feel They Had a Calling
Trying to fulfill your own potential	75	64
Knowing you've helped someone	75	62
Doing it to benefit your family	62	58
A supportive working environment	63	54
Being paid more money	42	52
Praise from your boss	47	40
Hope of a promotion or award	33	35
Competition	26	30
Fear of losing your job	12	18

In other words, it appears that some of the utilitarian meaning, in the classic sense of contributing to the good of others, is still associated with the calling. But so may be the inward focus on self that has sometimes been associated with contemporary pietism.

When people themselves choose among various definitions of the calling, these meanings also appear. The most common understanding of the calling is, as Miriam Zellers's comments illustrated, that God wants people to do something useful with their lives. The closely related idea of making the best use of one's individual talents is next likely to be chosen. Both of these responses are more likely among persons who themselves have experienced a calling than among other people. In addition, a substantial minority (like Sonny Nicos) feel God simply wants them to be happy. And another sizable minority believe

God doesn't care, or they have no opinion on the subject (see Table 3.7).

This tells us that the utilitarian understanding is still associated with the concept of a calling. If this is the dominant view, the introspective or emotional meaning of the term is nevertheless quite prominent in contemporary culture as well. One indication of just how prominent is that two-thirds of the labor force agrees that "God wants me to have the kind of job that will make me happy," and among church members three out of four agree. Among those who feel they have experienced a calling this proportion rises to 90 percent.

Also suggestive of the introspective meanings that have become associated with the calling is the fact that two thirds of those who have experienced a calling say they "need a lot of time to be quiet and reflect on things," 61 percent say "getting in touch with your feelings is more important than doing well in your job," half say "exploring my inner self is one of my main priorities," and an equal number say "working on my emotional life takes priority over other things." All of these statements, moreover, elicit greater agreement among those who have experienced a calling than among those who have not.[53]

If the calling has come to have introspective connotations, one of the reasons why may be that religion in general is used in our society for therapeutic purposes: it emphasizes counseling, personal adjustment, self-esteem, and simply feeling good about oneself. Given the demands of the contemporary workplace, it may be especially therapeutic for people to have some sense that their religious faith helps them in this context. A clear indication that the calling connotes such an orientation is that one of the strongest differences between those who say they have been called and those who have not is that the former say praying in the morning helps them have a better day. This statement is much more highly related to the calling, in fact, than the statement about hard work being pleasing to God.[54]

Miriam Zellers's view of the calling helps us understand this therapeutic orientation. Her example of snowflakes is instructive because the calling—and the gifts associated with it—are important to her not because they lead her to pursue a particular line of work but because they reinforce her sense that she is special. "If God hadn't given me these gifts," she asks rhetorically, "who would I be?" Knowing she is unique, she says, gives her confidence. Indeed, her sense of calling counteracts the workplace more than anything else. In the workplace,

TABLE 3.7

Understanding of the Calling

Question: "Which of the following statements comes closest to your view?"

	Among Respondents Who:	
	Felt They Had a Calling	*Did Not Feel They Had a Calling*
God wants us to work at whatever makes us happiest	18	19
God wants us to find work that best suits our individual talents	29	18
God wants us to do something with our lives that will be useful to the world	43	34
God doesn't really care what kind of work we do	4	16
Other	2	4
Don't know	5	10

everyone is a cog, a replaceable part, but as a snowflake, she can never be duplicated.

On balance, then, what difference does it actually make in people's work lives whether they feel they have been called to their work? Standard arguments about the calling's relation to the work ethic notwithstanding, the two groups do not differ in terms of how many hours a week they work.[55] Nor are the two any different in their likelihood of saying they are working harder now than five years ago. The one is also no less likely than the other to say they would like to work fewer hours than they do. The biggest differences are that those who feel called to their work score higher on job satisfaction, are more likely to say their work is meaningful, and are more likely to say it is important to them to do well in their jobs.[56] Apart from their work, they also feel closer to God.

Witnesses in the Workplace

A final dimension of the faith-work connection that bears brief consideration is the extent to which people try to bring their religious commitments into the workplace in a *public* way. It is one thing to say a silent prayer while sitting at one's desk, but quite another to talk about one's faith with co-workers or to be part of a religious group that meets in the workplace.

In recent years there has been much debate over the norms of bringing religion into various aspects of public life. Most of this debate has focused on the question of how (or whether) religion should be brought into the political arena. But the workplace has also attracted increasing attention. Recognizing that most religiously committed people spend far more of their time in the workplace than they do in churches or synagogues, or even in their neighborhoods, some religious leaders have called for a more aggressive effort to share religious beliefs with co-workers. Others argue that this would be inappropriate, that the workplace should not be a mission field, but that religious people should be witnesses simply by working hard, doing well at their jobs, and leading ethical lives.

The workforce itself is divided in terms of these styles. On the whole, approximately a third claims to have discussed their faith with someone at work during the past year. Among members of churches or synagogues, this proportion rises to nearly half (47 percent), and among those who attend religious services every week it is even higher (58 percent). Protestants are somewhat more inclined to have done so (42 percent) than Catholics (33 percent). And religious conservatives are considerably more likely to have done so (50 percent) than religious moderates (38 percent) or liberals (31 percent). The data also suggest that discussions of faith in the workplace are probably stimulated by people consciously thinking about the connections between their own work and their faith. An equally important factor, though, is that some people are simply very interested in their faith and their relationship to God in general, and thus bring this interest with them to the workplace.[57]

Discussions of this kind are probably informal in most cases and depend to some extent on informal norms operating in the work environment. Women, for example, are more likely than men to engage in such discussions, and people living in the South are nearly twice as likely to do so than those living in the Northeast. Actual participation in religious groups that meet in the workplace is much less common. Only 4 percent of the labor force as a whole is involved in such a group, while among church members the figure is 6 percent, and among weekly attenders, 10 percent. Whereas 6 percent of Protestants claim to be in such groups, only 3 percent of Catholics do. And 8 percent of religious conservatives are, compared with 4 percent of moderates and only 2 percent of liberals.[58] Another way to assess the relative importance of these groups is by comparing them with fellowship groups of other kinds. In the labor force as a whole, about one person in five is involved in some kind of religious fellowship group. From other research, we know that most of these groups meet in churches or in homes, study the Bible and pray together, and provide emotional support to their members. Fewer than one in seven of these groups, it appears, meets in the workplace.

An example of someone who tries hard to witness in the workplace is a man (whom I introduce at greater length in a later chapter) who works as a computer service and repairman.[59] He has a "heavy heart" about his working environment: "I'm the only Christian in the office and I'm the only one that I know of who has any interest whatsoever in spiritual things or the Lord." He is offended by his co-workers' language and by what he considers immoral behavior. "We have so many people who are divorced, remarried, and living with people. They have three girlfriends. I guess they are very typical of the people in the world today who don't know the Lord." He says he feels as if he is living in Sodom or Gomorrah. But he stays because he feels obligated to witness to his co-workers. A few years ago, he worked with another man who shared his beliefs, and they talked a lot to each other about their faith, but then that man retired. Now, it is more difficult to say anything. Not long ago, his sister died in an automobile accident and that gave him a chance to talk with his co-workers about death and the possibility of divine judgment. Otherwise, he just tries to be a witness through his actions and by mentioning some of the things he does at church.

Faith as Therapy

Since the inception of systematic research on the correlates of work in the 1930s, interest has focused primarily on conditions in the workplace itself. Much of this interest was inspired by the theories of

Frederick Taylor at the turn of the century.[60] Taylor's view that work could be more productive if it were managed "scientifically" made it imperative to examine features of the workplace that could be manipulated. The theories being advanced at the same time by Max Weber, as well as by Émile Durkheim, Georg Simmel, and other founders of modern sociology, however, were at heart fundamentally opposed to the economistic views of scholars like Taylor. Cultural phenomena that could not so easily be manipulated were examined and shown to have a decisive impact on the meaning of work. Religion was one such phenomenon.

Religious commitment continues to have an important influence on how work is understood. It challenges economistic definitions of work that deny the value of activities such as caring for children, performing household duties, or serving in churches or other voluntary organizations. It teaches that work is more pleasing to God than laziness and that God wants individuals to find work that utilizes their talents, makes them happy, and serves others. It also encourages people to find satisfaction in their jobs and motivates them to engage in activities, such as prayer, meditation, or talking about their problems with others, that may be conducive to alleviating job-related stress.

In other ways, however, the relationships between faith and work bear serious evidence of secularization. The vast majority of people do not take religious values into consideration at all in choosing their careers, and overall employment patterns suggest few influences that might be attributable directly to religious commitment. The religiously involved are not much different from anyone else in the degree to which they value their work or the amount of time they devote to it. Relatively few think a lot about the connections between their faith and their work or avail themselves of the counsel of clergy on such matters. Only a minority of the labor force feel called to their work, and many have little understanding of what it means to be called. In addition, the influences that are evident between religion and work seem to depend mainly on differences in sheer level of religious interest and not very much on variations among faith traditions. Spirituality, it appears, has some generic effects on thinking about work, but its effects do not show much evidence of the power of specific doctrines, teachings, or subcultures. Indeed, many people seem to think of spirituality in generic terms—as Bill Williams says, "spirituality comes from within"—rather than something associated with particular practices.

All this would suggest, perhaps correctly, that the workplace has become an autonomous sphere subject to few influences by religious institutions. Yet it is also clear that many religious leaders continue to be interested in the workplace, and that individuals themselves exercise enough discretion over their choices in the workplace that religious commitment could have more of an impact than it does. One reason why it does not, then, must be traced to the nature of religious discourse about work itself.

Religious teachings concerning work have, it appears, come to focus almost entirely on subjective or psychological issues. People are counseled to recognize that their work matters to God. They are told that if they pray about their work they will experience peace of mind. When choosing a career, they will feel more confident if they have asked themselves what God would like them to do. They believe that God is interested, above all,in their own personal happiness. As long as they pursue their happiness, therefore, they are following God's desires.

A tentative conclusion that can be drawn from considering the relationship between faith and work, therefore, is that religious commitment has come to play a kind of therapeutic role in relation to economic behavior in postindustrial society. It may not encourage people to work harder, or to work less hard, but it makes them feel better about how much they do work. Rather than providing guidance, religious conviction contributes meaning—that is, work becomes more interesting, if one stops to think about it, because it has cosmic significance. And rather than defining the meaning of work in specific ways, religious beliefs simply make work more satisfying. In this view, work is, as Miriam Zellers explains, "mainly about attitude," and thus, as she also believes, "it can always be, to me at least, pleasurable." It is, of course, desirable that work be meaningful. So, in this respect, the role of religion is important. In a secular society, however, this may be one of the few roles it still can play.

Chapter Four

Ethics in the Workplace

M anny Rodriguez started working in the sixth grade, delivering newspapers before school. In high school he worked at a grocery store near his home on the North Side of Chicago. After graduation his sister got him a job in the mail room at an insurance company. A year later he moved to the bookkeeping department, where he worked for three years as a technical assistant. Eventually he became an insurance broker handling marine accounts. Manny's mother made sure he went to catechism class as a child and sent him to church every Sunday. It was the one good influence in his life, she thought. The rest of the time he seemed to hang out with a gang. He was the only one of the bunch who finished high school. By the time he was eleven, he started lying to his mother about church, telling her he'd gone when he hadn't. When he got married at nineteen, the priest refused to perform the service because Manny hadn't been to confession for a long time. Manny has been alienated from the church ever since, though he does still believe in all the basic beliefs of Christianity. He also feels the church taught him to be a basically good, ethical person.

Harold Bentley went to college for two years, quit, was drafted, spent four years in the army, including a year in Vietnam, eventually finished college, and became a school teacher. A year later he decided to switch careers and took a job at a finance company. After several years of working nights in the repossession department, he got a job at a bank. For the past ten years he's held various positions at the bank, most recently a middle-level position in the commercial lending department. He describes his religious background as "very conservative, almost fundamentalist." He attended a Scandinavian church in rural Minnesota. All the members believed it was wrong to work on Sundays, even to mow the lawn. Harold says he is still quite conservative in his religious views and attends church regularly but isn't nearly as strict as his parents. Asked to state his most basic values, he says, "hard work—and a real sense of ethics."

Teri Silver works in southern California at the headquarters of one of the nation's largest investment firms. She's part of a growing division that handles technical problems involving the company's computerized records system. She starts a typical day by checking the accounts that were posted overnight to make sure everything is okay. Then she runs interference between the professional staff who understand investments and the programmers who understand the computers. This is the sort of work she's been doing ever since high school. Now at twenty-nine, she is taking evening classes at a local junior college, hoping eventually to earn a degree. She's interested in religion, believes in God, but describes the rest of her religious beliefs in one word: "confused." As a child, she complained so much about going to catechism class that her mother let her quit. She remembers singing "Michael, row your boat ashore" at the suburban parish her parents attended and learning the Ten Commandments. But she says she doesn't really know any Bible stories. She feels especially confused now because the boyfriend she lives with is Jewish. She's attracted to his faith but not sure she really believes it. She also figures her parents' church would reject her for "living in sin." She insists, though, that she is a thoroughly ethical person. "I'm honest, don't lie, don't cheat," she says. "I'll call in sick once in a while when I'm not, but I don't do that very often."

The question of ethics in the workplace has become a matter of supreme public concern in recent years. The Watergate break-in and cover-up that led to Richard Nixon's resignation from the presidency initiated a major round of discussion about the importance of professional ethics in the 1970s.[1] In the 1980s, additional interest in the topic was fueled by insider trading scams on Wall Street, by the savings and loan crisis, by a number of fraud cases in the medical and scientific research communities, and by acts of censure against several members of Congress.[2] Some studies have suggested that willingness to engage in unethical and even illegal activities may be quite widespread in certain settings. One survey, for example, revealed that 80 percent of business executives had driven while drunk.[3] Another study estimated that white-collar crime in the United States amounts to about $40 billion a year.[4] Still another study found that between 10 and 25 percent of all job seekers falsify their credentials.[5] It is not surprising, therefore, that public opinion polls reveal deep misgivings about the ethical standards of business leaders and other public figures. In a series of polls conducted by the Gallup Organization, for example, only about one person in six rated business executives highly on ethical standards and honesty.[6] In another survey, 86 percent of the public said "corruption in business" is a serious or extremely serious problem in American society.[7]

Manny Rodriguez, Harold Bentley, and Teri Silver have all faced ethical dilemmas in their work. Each has, on occasion, been asked to bend the rules or to keep his or her mouth shut about activities that were probably questionable on ethical grounds. The head of Teri Silver's company was actually sent to prison on charges of conspiracy to engage in criminal conduct. Each of these people insists that he or she behaves scrupulously. Indeed, it is interesting that all three, without prompting, volunteer that behaving ethically is one of the values they have cherished since childhood. Yet it is not exactly clear what they mean by ethics, or how firmly their behavior is guided by ethical convictions. Certainly, it is unclear what gives legitimacy to their sense of ethics. And it is unclear what the connection may be between their sense of ethics and their religious views.

An Ethical Life Is an Honest Life

Given the public concern that has arisen about unethical conduct, many scholars have turned to an examination of such misbehavior itself, asking why business leaders, for example, can do things that land them in jail. If the statements of such people themselves are examined, the interesting thing is that guilt is seldom admitted. People accused of unethical conduct generally argue that they were actually behaving ethically but were somehow trapped by circumstances, ambiguities in the law, or changing expectations about what was proper behavior. It is easy to dismiss these avowals and regard them as attempts by the guilty to keep their self-respect or to bargain for leniency. It is, however, worthwhile to begin by taking these statements at face value. Certainly a person's sincere belief that he or she is behaving ethically should be considered part of our understanding of what ethics means in contemporary society.

Accused villains are not the only ones who protest their innocence. In the labor force at large, 88 percent of employed Americans claim they "always behave ethically in my work." Manny Rodriguez, Harold Bentley, and Teri Silver are among this 88 percent. Each denies ever having done anything that he or she thought might have been unethical. The people we met in Chapter 3—Miriam Zellers, Bill Williams, and Sonny Nicos—say the same thing. These responses are curious, though, because the labor force survey also found that one person in three claims to have observed others at work doing unethical things. If a third of the work force actually is engaged in such behavior, then it is puzzling that only one in ten has any sense of doing so.

The puzzle becomes even more interesting when people are asked about engaging in specific activities that might, by some criteria, be considered questionable, unethical, or indeed, illegal. In the labor force as a whole, four people in ten admit to having arrived at work later than they are supposed to within the past month, nearly this many say they have covered for someone who had made a mistake, almost a third say they have bent the rules in dealing with someone, more than a quarter have bent the truth a bit in what they told people, one-fourth have used office equipment for personal uses, a fifth have not asked questions about something they suspected was wrong, one in seven has taken time off from work that they should not have taken, and 3 percent have charged for illegitimate expenses (see Table 4.1).

Some of these activities, it might be noted, are even more common in certain segments of the work force. For example, managers and business executives are significantly more likely than people in other occupations to say they have bent the rules; professionals are significantly more likely than other people to have used office equipment for personal purposes; clerical and salespeople are the most likely to have bent the truth; and blue-collar or service workers are the most likely to have taken time off or not asked questions about possible wrongdoing. On the whole, *three quarters* of the labor force has done at least one of these things within the past month (half have done at least two). And yet, scarcely anyone feels he or she has ever done anything unethical.

We could perhaps dismiss this discrepancy as a result of some research error (perhaps people misunderstood the question). But other research also points to the relatively widespread practice of certain kinds of ethically questionable behavior. A study of business managers, for example, found that more than half believed it necessary to bend the rules to get ahead.[8] A study of secretaries found that more than half would comply with a supervisor's instructions to alter board minutes or change the date on a postal meter, even though they knew it

TABLE 4.1

Incidence of Questionable Behavior

Question: "In your work, have you done each of the following any time during the past month?" (Percent responding yes)

	Labor Force
Arrived later than you're supposed to	40
Covered for someone who had made a mistake	36
Saw other people doing things that might be unethical	32
Bent the rules in dealing with someone	29
Bent the truth a bit in what you told people	27
Used office equipment for personal uses	26
Not asked questions about something you suspected was wrong	21
Taken time off from work that you shouldn't	14
Charged for expenses that might not be legitimate	3

was improper.[9] Another study found that 78 percent of business executives had used the company phone for personal long-distance calls. In the same study three out of four had taken supplies for their personal use. And 35 percent had overstated deductions on tax forms.[10]

The discrepancy between people's perceptions of themselves as ethical beings and what actually seems to be going on in the workplace provides a useful starting point for understanding what ethics means in our society. The reason why most people can believe themselves to be perfectly ethical, despite working among unethical people and in situations widely regarded as ethically dubious, is that many people, when pushed to say what ethics means to them, say it basically means nothing more than being honest. Without being pushed, many people also inadvertently speak of ethics and honesty as if they were the same thing. Teri Silver, for example, says the most vivid experience she can remember that has always encouraged her to be ethical happened in second grade. Asked by her teacher to write a poem, she wrote down one she knew by heart from hearing her grandmother tell it over and over. Teri's teacher

was so impressed by the poem that she submitted it to a schoolwide poetry contest, which Teri won. Unfortunately for Teri, her mother found
out what she had done and marched her to the principal's office to confess. Teri claims she has tried hard ever since to be *honest*.

Asked if he had ever had to do anything unethical, Manny Rodriguez also focuses on an issue of honesty. "One time I was asked to
withhold some information to make something look better," he says. "I
was real uncomfortable with that, because I've always been pretty honest. I feel I'm honest, and that really bothered me. I ended up telling
everyone what I was instructed not to." Asked if he could think of any
other ways in which ethical questions came up in his work, he said no.

In the labor force as a whole, about one person in three chooses "always trying to be honest" as the best definition of ethics when presented with a list of five alternatives. Among those who attend religious services every week, this proportion is even higher, rising to
about four people in ten (see Table 4.2).

When ethicists try to define their subject matter, they, of course, include standards about telling the truth. But ethics in general, religious
ethics, and even ethics in the workplace are typically conceived to include a much wider array of topics.[11] Discussions of business ethics,
for example, often stress relationships between business and government or the enforcement of professional codes about dealing with
clients, while discussions of workplace ethics from a religious perspective may include topics such as fair labor practices, economic justice, the environment, and establishing sound priorities for the use of
one's time and money.[12] To equate ethics with personal honesty, therefore, is to restrict greatly the domain to which ethics applies.

Why? It does so in part because honesty serves as a kind of minimum standard. One's behavior may contribute to the burning of rain
forests and the perpetuation of world hunger, and yet, as long as one
tells the truth, ethics is not a problem.[13] But honesty also means less
even than it could. Some books on the subject, for example, suggest
that an honest employee is one who works hard, never engages in
"time theft" by taking undue breaks, and avoids "energy theft" of the
kind that might result from being emotionally or mentally distracted.
Most of the people we interviewed in depth did not see it that way.
Honesty meant little more than not telling a bald-faced lie. A lawyer
who cheated on his expense reports, for example, had worked out a
system in his own thinking whereby free dinners were simply a way of
paying himself back for working overtime. As long as he was honest to

TABLE 4.2

The Meaning of Ethics

Question: "Which one of the following statements do you think is the best definition of ethics?" (Percent choosing each statement)

	Total Labor Force	Weekly Churchgoers
Always trying to be honest	30	39
Being able to decide what's right or wrong	30	29
Behaving in a responsible way	19	16
Doing your best	10	6
Feeling good about what you do	6	5
Other	2	2
Don't know	3	3
Question: Does ethics, in your view, mean . . .		
Something that applies in the same way to everybody, no matter what the situation	48	56
Something that varies depending on the circumstances you are in	48	41

his own system, he didn't care whether the records themselves were exactly honest. Many people, we discovered, felt it was honest to bend the truth as long as they had a good reason for doing so.

The other reason that people are able so easily to be ethical in an unethical world is that ethics has become so highly variable, so dependent on personal definitions and circumstances, that its meaning can be readily modified. This malleability is evident in the fact that about half the labor force regards ethics as something that depends on circumstances rather than as a universal that applies to everyone no matter what the circumstances.[14] It is also evident in the fact that about a third of the labor force define ethics as an individual's ability to decide what is right and wrong. A statement such as this can be taken in different ways. But judging from other comments, it often seems to emphasize individual

feelings or intuitions, which make ethics subjective, rather than regarding ethics as an objective standard or set of principles about
which people might be able to agree collectively.[15]

Definitions of ethics that emphasize being responsible or doing
one's best also tend to subjectivize the concept and turn it into such a
general principle that it is incapable of guiding specific behavior.
Harold Bentley, for example, says being ethical in his work and in the
rest of his life, which he considers extremely important, basically
means (as it does for others) being honest. But his definition of honesty, then, turns out to focus mainly on being reliable and responsible.

> When you say you're going to do something, you do it. You do it the best
> way you know how to. It may not be always correct, it may not be exactly
> what the other person expects, but your intent is there to do what you
> say you're going to do. And to me that's extremely important. If you have
> any ethics, you don't play games with other people's thoughts and feel-
> ings. It's responsibility. When you say you're going to be some place at a
> particular time, you're there. People can depend on you. Being very de-
> pendable. And trying to do the best you can with what you have.

There are, of course, good reasons why people find it in their interest
to think of themselves as ethical beings in an otherwise ethically suspect
world. To be ethical is to be a good person, to have self-esteem, especially in an era when feelings and ethics are so closely associated. But a
perception that does not conform to reality is also problematic, particularly if it results in an overly high appraisal of oneself, an overly cynical
view of one's co-workers or of business and government leaders, or a
lack of confidence in social institutions. As Robert Nisbet observes, many
Americans combine an "enveloping fear" of institutions with an "unwillingness to admit the usefulness of ethical codes."[16]

The Role of Religion

Religion has always been regarded as a source of ethical behavior.
People may be encouraged by their participation in religious communities to do what is right for a wide variety of reasons. In some religious communities, ethical behavior may depend to a great extent on
beliefs about the importance of good works and correct behavior for
securing rewards in an afterlife. Good behavior may be encouraged in
other settings as a way of pleasing God. It may also be reinforced by
the example set by priests or lay leaders. The informal norms of the

religious community itself may be very important as well. For example, many Protestant denominations during the past century encouraged their members to avoid such vices as card playing, dancing, cigarettes, and alcohol. The coercive element of such tutelage should not be ignored either. Conformity to the ethical standards enjoined in religious teachings has been enforced by the strict punishment of children, by the threat of being ostracized from the religious community, and by the prospect of divine intervention itself.

Some research suggests that religious commitment is in fact an important deterrent of many kinds of behavior considered to be unethical, illegal, or deviant, at least in terms of middle-class conceptions of morality. Active membership and participation in religious services, for example, has been shown to be negatively associated with such activities as engaging in premarital, extramarital, or homosexual relationships, drinking alcohol, and cheating on exams.[17] At the same time, research has also found areas of behavior over which the influence of religion is weaker than had been supposed. For example, child abuse and other forms of family violence may be fairly widespread among active church members.[18]

With concern about workplace ethics becoming more widely discussed in the society at large, religious leaders have turned their attention increasingly to this subject as well. Numerous books and articles offer advice about workplace ethics from a variety of religious perspectives. The topics addressed have been wide-ranging, from matters that might be considered little more than etiquette, such as getting along with abrasive co-workers, to questions of honesty and responsibility, to wider issues having to do with social justice and the environment. Although the perspectives of various religious authors vary widely, there is considerable agreement on the importance of workers thinking more seriously about questions of right and wrong in the workplace.[19]

That religious commitment does have some influence on workplace behavior that may be considered questionable from an ethical standpoint is evident from the data in Table 4.3. Workers who say religion is very important in their lives are less likely to have engaged in each of the activities shown within the past month than are those who say religion is fairly important, and both are less likely to have done each of the items listed than are people who say religion is not very important to them. From these data, it would appear that religious people are somewhat more likely to avoid such activities as bending the rules, arriving late, taking time off that they shouldn't, or using office equipment for themselves than are nonreligious people.

What is also obvious from Table 4.3, however, is that the differences between religious and nonreligious people on these items are not great.[20] Only a minority of workers in either category have actually done each of these activities within the past month. And yet, among the most religious, this minority is often almost as large as it is among the least religious. In absolute terms, at least a third of the most religious have engaged in several of these activities and a quarter have engaged in some of the others.

Evidently, religion is only one of the influences that shape how people think about workplace ethics. This should not surprise us, of course. Most religious people do not work in a religious environment, and their religious leaders may not speak very often about the workplace. It is, therefore, quite easy for religious just as for nonreligious people to be guided by secular understandings of ethics. In the workplace, these understandings are especially likely to be governed by assumptions implicit in the culture of the workplace itself.

The Culture of the Workplace

If religion often has only a small impact on how people think about ethics and how they conduct themselves at work, an important reason is that the workplace itself has come to provide its own understandings of ethics, and even more than that, its own well-established procedures that sometimes obviate the need for ethics at all. Both of these developments are characteristics of postindustrial society. Complex economic conditions make many kinds of workplace behavior difficult to police but provide regulations that prevent some of the worst excesses from occurring. For example, an institutionalized system of auditing accounts and of co-signing vouchers makes it so unlikely for stealing from the organization to go unnoticed that employees may seldom need to give the ethics of stealing any thought at all.[21] Evidently enough areas of discretion are left over, however, to justify concern about the general issue of ethics. The fact of the matter is that people do think about ethics in the workplace, and they develop understandings of what constitutes ethical behavior and why such behavior is more or less common.[22] These understandings uphold the importance of ethics, encourage people to believe they are acting ethically all the time, and yet provide very little that may ever stand in the

TABLE 4.3

Religion and Ethics

Percent who had done each of the following within the past month among those who said religion was:

	Very Important	Fairly Important	Not Very Important
Arrived later than you're supposed to	36	41	45
Covered for someone who had made a mistake	31	38	41
Bent the rules in dealing with someone	21	30	37
Bent the truth a bit in what you told people	22	28	33
Used office equipment for personal uses	21	27	33
Taken time off from work that you shouldn't	11	13	19
Charged for expenses that might not be legitimate	2	3	5

way of the business of the organization. To the contrary, they probably function mainly to ensure that the organization's business gets done.

As one example, we can return to Harold Bentley's earlier comments about ethics. For him, honesty does not mean thinking about truth, or telling it under all circumstances; it means the kind of dependability that comes from straight talking: follow through on what you say; if you don't intend to do something, don't say it in the first place. Everything is left up to individual discretion. The only constraint is to make what you do consistent with what you say. It is still possible to withhold both. But more important, dependability means performing your job to the best of your abilities. The assumption clearly is that ethics will not conflict with carrying out your job. Defined this way, ethics is good for business, just as it is for interpersonal relations. Mean what you say, keep your promises, show up when you are supposed to—these are the dicta that make ethics and good business compatible.

We might refer to this kind of perspective as a "self-regulating" view of ethics in the workplace. It is in everyday discourse quite similar to a long tradition of argumentation in the published literature about the morally uplifting aspects of business and trade. Simply to subject oneself to the discipline of being a reliable trading partner or of making the calculations necessary to be a good merchant, this literature suggests, transforms a person into a responsible individual who abides by the norms of the community.[23] In this perspective, ethics becomes a kind of autonomous system that can be understood entirely within the framework of the workplace, rather than needing any external validation or grounding in an ultimate or transcendent sense of reality. When ethics becomes honesty and when honesty means behaving responsibly, then ethics is unlikely to conflict with working hard and performing one's tasks well. The self-regulating view of workplace ethics also includes some other assumptions.

One is that violations of ethics—basically, *dis*honesty—become economically disadvantageous. Implicitly, this assumption places morality and money on the same plane. Honesty, it is assumed, will pay off monetarily. Dishonesty therefore is wrong primarily because it will cost you. Moreover, the market itself encourages honesty because the clever player in the market will sift out dishonesty and turn it to economic advantage.

Asked to give an example of what it meant to be honest, Harold Bentley related the following story. As a small child he remembered his parents going to a car dealer to purchase a new automobile. When his father finally made an offer, the salesman excused himself to go ask such and such a person to approve it. But while the salesman was away, his father went to a pay phone and called the dealership, requesting to speak to the same person, and was told no such person worked there. Confronting the salesman with this fact, his father got an even better price on the car than before.

Once ethics has been justified in terms of economic logic itself, it then becomes easy to draw other economic implications. Through a simple reversal of the causal connection between honesty and monetary gain, for example, it becomes possible to argue that some people are excusably dishonest because they simply cannot afford to be honest. Others are honest through no virtue of their own but because they have more economic resources. In talking about his bank, for instance, Harold Bentley says, "We represent very wealthy clients. And they're able to afford to be honest. It's more, I think, the very small business-man who often has to bend the rules a little bit." By implication, ethics becomes a function of economic circumstances.

In the survey, 58 percent of the labor force agreed that "being ethi-cal will pay off economically," while only 35 percent disagreed. This view was most likely to be taken by managers and business executives and least likely to be held by professionals. Active church members were somewhat more likely to agree with it than the religiously unin-volved. The notion that ethical behavior makes good economic sense was also documented by another study in which two-thirds of the cor-porate executives queried agreed that high ethical standards would improve their company's competitive position.[24]

A closely related assumption is the view simply that "honesty is the best policy"—a dictum that many of our respondents used in talking about ethics. Teri Silver, for example, used these words in summariz-ing what she had learned from the poetry incident. In this view, being ethical may not pay off in cold cash, but it certainly is in your best in-terest to be honest. If your mother catches you, you get punished. If the boss does, you may get fired. Whether ethical behavior is ab-solutely right or not, therefore, doesn't matter very much. It is easier to justify ethics on utilitarian grounds.

In the contemporary workplace, it is often difficult to know what is the honest thing to do, even if one believes that honesty pays. Consequently, two other assumptions about ethics become part of contemporary corporate culture, if not part of the wider culture as well. One is that there are many gray areas where it is impossible to know for sure what is right and wrong. In the workplace, these gray areas are concerned to a considerable degree with how much or how little employees should be expected to abide by their employers' rules. On a statement such as "it is okay to bend the rules sometimes at work," for example, the labor force is about evenly divided between those who agree and those who disagree. The other assumption is that being honest, there-fore, means being honest with oneself, that is, with how one feels at the moment. Nearly three-quarters of the labor force agrees with the statement, "You just have to do what feels right and hope for the best."

Although not a workplace issue, Teri Silver's feelings about living with her boyfriend provide an example of how being honest with oneself becomes a definition of ethics. Her parents don't approve of her living arrangement. By focusing on how she herself feels, she is able to resist her parents' definition of ethical behavior. When she is truly honest with herself, though, she realizes that she would also prefer to be married. The problem with paying attention to her feelings, therefore, is that her feelings speak to her with mixed voices. They do not stand apart from her situation but depend very much on the various roles she is playing, whom she is interacting with, and what her mood happens to be on a given day. When she applies the same logic to the workplace, it is very hard not to let her feelings be influenced by the demands of her job.

A corollary of the assumption that ethics mostly is a matter of feelings is the idea that legitimate differences of opinion may be present among any group of co-workers. It is thus quite possible for individuals to excuse themselves from taking responsibility for the behavior of their co-workers. This may, for example, be a reason why a third of the people surveyed said they had seen co-workers do things they *thought* might be unethical, and yet only one in ten had tried to blow the whistle on perceived wrongdoing. It is also consistent with the fact that 45 percent *disagreed* with the statement, "I feel responsible to make sure others I work with behave ethically." Why not? If ethics is just differences of opinion, then any serious dispute must be resolved as would be a business decision. Higher management would need to be concerned, but the average employee would not.

The hierarchical structure of the workplace also provides an additional way of coping with ethical issues. Manny Rodriguez says he's glad he doesn't have more authority in his company. He's seen employees being manipulated into bad situations just so management could fire them. He figures he'd feel bad about the ethics of doing that. But he feels OK about his own work. In comparison with the dilemmas upper management faces, he feels that his own compromises are relatively minor.

Another corollary of the view that ethics is a matter of feelings is that it becomes easier over time to do things that may be questionable. The reason is that an informal norm develops: the norm says, in effect, this is the way things are done here; no conscious decision is required—no thinking, no feelings. A salesman, for example, said it was "accepted practice" in his company to promise a customer delivery in a week, even though it might not be realistic to expect delivery within three weeks. In his own opinion, this was probably unethical. But, he noted, "I've never been told to do that; it's just something that is unsaid." Consequently, he said he had never actually had to take an ethical stand on the matter. Another man who worked for a real estate company said he and his colleagues normally price properties before they have all the necessary information and then just "fix it" so the numbers come out right. He says this practice doesn't bother him in the least. "Nobody asks any questions; it doesn't matter."

How people view their workplace, therefore, is a key to understanding whether they feel it is possible to be ethical or not. From the qualitative interviews we conducted with people in many different working environments, it appears that the organization is typically seen as a mixed environment of opportunities and temptations (or more simply, of things you like and things you don't). But it is *not* seen as a totally controlling environment. Most individuals feel they have a good deal of control over such matters as determining their daily schedule or setting long-range work goals for themselves. This sense of being able to exercise discretion is what allows them to feel they can be ethical in an unethical world as well. They have room to maneuver, to beat the system, to maintain their integrity against external pressures. Discretion is what makes honesty possible—not exactly to say yes or no to a request to be dishonest but discretion to exit the system, or at least to avoid conflict by deciding whom to talk with, where to go, what to say, and what not to say. For example, when Teri Silver's boss asked her one time to keep something secret from the auditors, she didn't confront him with the ethics of what they were doing, nor did she use her discretion to speak out; instead, she used it to schedule herself in a different part of the building that day where she knew she wouldn't see the auditors.[25]

One final assumption about the workplace is also important. Most people have stories to tell about unethical or questionable behavior they have witnessed or heard about at their place of employment. In the survey, 91 percent of the labor force agreed with the statement, "As far as ethics is concerned, no organization is perfect." This is probably a true statement, but the interest people demonstrate in telling stories to prove it is true suggests that more is at stake than simply an accurate rendition of the facts. What, then?

We might suppose realizing the ethical compromises inherent in the workplace would put people on their guard, encouraging them to be all the more scrupulous themselves, especially since they all believe they are behaving ethically. But something different seems to be the consequence. The point of painting the environment in negative terms seems to be to make oneself look better by comparison. If one's organization is not perfect, then it is possible to justify a little questionable behavior on one's own part because at least it wasn't as bad as what else was going on.

The thrust of these observations is that our workplaces give us a great deal of discretion in deciding how to behave and we are, accordingly, able to behave in a way that we believe to be highly ethical. Yet, we are also quite capable of deceiving ourselves, making so many compromises that even our co-workers think we are behaving unethically, but failing to see the problem ourselves. Ethical decisions are, of course, complex; often there are no simple guidelines; and we have to temper our behavior according to how we evaluate the situation. The problems come when we are guided entirely by the implicit norms of the workplace itself. Thus, we may tell ourselves we are ethical because we haven't told blatant falsehoods, whereas the reason we have avoided doing this is that we have run to the far corner of the building rather than speaking up. The few rules we bend and the few corners we cut may not amount to anything serious in themselves, but they may also reflect an attitude conducive to the more serious scandals that have afflicted our society in recent years. We need to consider more carefully what this attitude is and how it may be related to our religious convictions.

Underlying Value Orientations

Implicit in the foregoing discussion is an assumption that ethics in the workplace is actually rooted in underlying value orientations.[26] Even though much of what people may say about ethics is limited to discussions of dishonesty and is conditioned by their understanding of the compromises required in the workplace, ethics always requires some sort of legitimating view of the world.[27] Faced with a tough decision, an individual may feel intuitively that one course of action is preferable to another. If a conversation were to take place about the decision, some sense of the criteria or arguments justifying it would probably surface.[28] These might reflect a broader outlook on the world, albeit one not very carefully thought out or explicitly articulated. But they would at least indicate some half-formed views about what is right or wrong, what is appropriate or inappropriate under certain conditions, or what ends the individual should be oriented toward in making decisions. What are these views and what difference do they make?

From the remarks we have considered thus far and from others like them, I have identified six underlying value orientations that influence how people actually think and behave with respect to particular ethical decisions: individualistic utilitarianism, corporate utilitarianism, emotivism, altruism, moral absolutism, and theistic moralism.[29] All these orientations come together in the contemporary workplace; few individuals are guided by only one of them. Together, they help us to understand the ambivalence many of us feel about ethical decisions in our work and why the situation, rather than principles, determines what we do. Let me describe each orientation briefly, and then we can consider evidence on what difference they make.

Individualistic utilitarianism stresses that an important consideration in making any decision must be its practical consequences for the individual making that decision: a decision that advances the interests of the individual is therefore better than a decision that fails to advance those interests. In this way of thinking, self-interest tends to be given precedence over other considerations, such as what may be absolutely right or wrong, or what might be in the best interest of others. What may compose the self's "interests" can include material possessions, power, pleasure, or the avoidance of pain, hunger, insecurity, or violence. These interests are generally assumed to be innate, or at least fundamental, dispositions or appetites that must be respected, but individualistic utilitarianism also emphasizes the individual's freedom to select from a long list of personal desires or wants.[30] Self-interest may also be regarded as the basis on which to build larger economic systems or social programs that contribute to the wider good of society. Although formal ethical and philosophical systems have been constructed around assumptions about individualistic utilitarianism, in everyday life it is more typically expressed in simple maxims such as "looking out for Number One," "covering one's behind," or "just trying to get ahead."[31]

There are many examples of individualistic utilitarianism. A typical one is provided by a young legal assistant in Boston who describes how the attorney she works for shuffles funds back and forth among different accounts. This seems questionable to her. Yet she admits she's kept quiet. She says she's afraid of losing her job. She doesn't consider herself particularly self-interested and certainly not unethical. Rather, she believes you have to make decisions in terms of what you know or are able to calculate and what you don't. She knows for sure that she needs her job. She is less sure what would happen if she spoke up. She also figures the attorney knows more than she does. "When you've just had one year of training," she says, "you don't know if it's right or not." Just recently, the attorney has been sued, so she has more doubts than before. But she still isn't sure she should jeopardize her own position by speaking up. Manny Rodriguez, Harold Bentley, and Teri Silver also show signs of this orientation in some of the things they say about ethics. They are not ruthless in pursuing their self-interest, but they are guided by such concerns as keeping their jobs and getting ahead.

Corporate utilitarianism gives priority to the expected outcome of a particular decision for one's employer or the organization for which one works. This way of thinking emphasizes loyalty, following the rules, and doing what those in authority have decided. It is in some ways similar to what studies of moral reasoning discover when they observe children justifying their behavior in terms of family loyalty or the rules that have been established for them by their parents. In the workplace, however, what is in the company's best interests may be subject to much greater calculation and may be much more difficult to determine. It is, in this respect, similar to individualistic utilitarianism; both interests and wants must be considered, but individuals now act more as agents of the organization than on behalf of themselves.[32] They adopt what William Whyte some years ago termed an "organization ethic" that "rationalizes the organization's demands for fealty and gives those who offer it wholeheartedly a sense of dedication in doing so."[33] As we have seen, corporate cultures may justify ethical behavior up to a point by asserting that such behavior will ultimately pay off economically. Beyond this, however, corporate utilitarianism may legitimate compromises of absolute ethical principles in the interest of getting a job done. It may, of course, be quite consistent with advancing the self-interest of the individual employee as well. Maxims associated with corporate utilitarianism, therefore, may range from "the boss said to do it" to "nobody was getting hurt" to "business is business."

. The logic of corporate utilitarianism can be illustrated by the manager of a travel agency in Los Angeles. He admits he often has to do things that may be considered slightly unethical. The main consideration, he says, is "how am I going to do it and not get caught." Chuckling to himself at how clichéd this sounds, he elaborates:

> I know I've got to do it for the company. And there's some way to do it. It's just how do you do it. The parameters that have been set up have to be broken. We do this all the time. It's just, how do you do it? And I guess if you looked at strict ethics, you're not supposed to do it, but that's just business. Everybody does it. Some just do it a little better than others.

Emotivism emphasizes feelings as a standard for determining what is ethical and what is not; in the extreme, it holds that moral judgments are nothing but expressions of preference, attitude, or feeling.[34] In some discussions the rationale for emphasizing feelings is that ethical decisions are too complex or variable to make on the basis of rational arguments, thus leaving intuition as the only means of summarizing these unexpressed (and inexpressible) arguments. In other discussions, feelings are regarded as a valid guide for making decisions because of some physiological link.[35] Thus, it may be argued that a person simply "knows" what is the right thing to do because doing something else will make that person feel anxious or guilty, or as one discussion suggests, "if you do something that goes against your own innate sense of what's right, you can't help but feel bad."[36] In practical matters, emotivism also tends to emphasize that different individuals may feel differently about a given situation, depending on their physiological makeup, desires, and experiences. Its adaptability to particular situations has been one of the objections levied against emotivism at least since Kant raised them more than two centuries ago, but contemporary moral philosophers also point out that such adaptability may be quite desirable in a complex society like our own.[37] Some versions of emotivism also encourage the realization or expression of feelings as a desirable end in itself.[38]

Feelings have been emphasized in a wide variety of moral frameworks. In the Judeo-Christian tradition, for example, the idea of following one's heart or conscience often gave some credence to the voice of feelings. In the past, however, conscience was thought to be an inner voice, more than an actual feeling, and this voice was thought to be in need of sustained counsel and training. In recent years, emotivism has come to focus more on the attainment of pleasurable feelings.[39] Behaving ethically may, for example, make one feel good about oneself, contribute to one's self-esteem, or enhance one's pride. Because these feelings are widely valued in American culture, discussions that ultimately root ethics in other considerations sometimes appeal to emotivist arguments as well. A statement like "probably the greatest benefit of cultivating integrity is the sense of confidence and self-respect you'll feel," for example, is not atypical in popular religious literature on ethics.[40]

An assumption made by most advocates of emotivist ethics is that some form of principled introspection will be a part of the decision-making process. Feelings will be a valuable indicator of what to do because there will be some sort of unease, perhaps something that cannot be put into words, if the anticipated behavior is inconsistent with what the person knows to be right and good.[41] From the ways in which people describe their own decisions in the workplace, however, it is clear that feelings can be the basis of a very different sort of decision-making process. A man who sells hearing aids, for example, says he sometimes charges customers when they come in to have the tubing replaced and other times provides this service for free. He apparently recognizes that this practice has ethical connotations because he brings it up in the context of discussing ethics. But he says his decision depends entirely on how he feels at the moment. If a customer has been friendly and he feels good, he doesn't charge; if he's in a bad mood for some reason, he charges. The main point, he says, is that he doesn't feel bad about it, no matter what he decides. The remarks I described earlier about Teri Silver's attitude toward living with her boyfriend also illustrate the emotivist orientation.

Altruism emphasizes the well-being of other people as an important consideration in deciding what is right and wrong; at minimum it requires, to quote the philosopher Thomas Nagel, "a recognition of the reality of other persons [and] the equivalent capacity to regard oneself as merely one individual among many."[42] This emphasis does not necessarily require the individual to sacrifice self-interest in deciding what is right or wrong, but it does require the individual to take into account the needs of others, perhaps even giving them priority.[43] In theory and in practice, it has often been associated with arguments against the desirability of following strict, unalterable rules of conduct. Rather than saying stealing is always to be avoided because it is wrong, for example, the altruistic view might point out that stealing would sometimes be justified because serving the needs of one's family or overthrowing an oppressive political system would require it.[44]

Altruism is probably seen by most people as a high ground on which to engage in ethical behavior. But it may well conflict with an ethics of always being honest or loyal to one's company or scrupulous in the observance of rules. It can also provide a rationalization for not doing what one had been taught was right. In the workplace, people often talk about bending the rules precisely as a way to get beyond organizational red tape in order to help people. The employee of a real estate company who was quoted earlier, for example, regards the legal rules governing loan ratings as silly obstacles that get in the way of getting things done. Thus, he tries to help his clients by fudging these rules. He means that as long as someone benefits, and as long as nobody gets hurt, it doesn't matter. Bill Williams, as we saw in Chapter 3, is another example of someone who is guided by altruism. When he talks about ethics, he says he mainly tries to be fair and help other people.

Moral absolutism assumes that certain activities or standards for deciding on the appropriateness of activities are always right or always wrong. Prohibitions against stealing, lying, or killing fall into this category. This mode of reasoning tends to be what the sociologist Steven Tipton has referred to as "regular" or "rule governed" in that it stresses the importance of asking what the relevant rules or principles are for deciding what to do.[45] In practical applications of this view, it may be recognized that ambiguity will exist, say, about what exactly constitutes stealing, lying, or killing. Consequently, this orientation should not be regarded as one of rigid or blind obedience to a set of arbitrary and simplistic ethical rules. Moral absolutism nevertheless emphasizes the underlying principles or standards as important in themselves. These standards, moreover, are assumed to be knowable, either through reason or from being imprinted in some way on the individual's conscience.[46] Behavior that might otherwise be regarded as trivial, or even as damaging to one's self-interest, might be encouraged as a way of upholding, dramatizing, or clarifying an absolute moral standard. The ordinary maxims that indicate moral absolutism typically assert that something is right or wrong not because it has certain consequences or because it can be defended on some other basis but simply because it *is* right or wrong. Although moral absolutism may be incorporated into other styles of moral reasoning, therefore, it also represents a mode of thinking that includes its own metaphysical or naturalistic assumptions about ethical rules.

Part of what reinforces moral absolutism in an otherwise relativistic culture is that some ethical issues are also matters of legality. For example, a man who had worked several years for a company that made medical instruments says his predecessor had cultivated relationships with employees in competitor companies, sometimes exchanging information about products and prices. "That," he explained, "posed a moral dilemma for me, but it posed a legal dilemma too, because you get into your anti-trust laws and regulations. I didn't like it at all." He tried to handle the situation by staying on the high ground and not talking with competitors at all. "I personally will not do things that go against my moral code." And when that was not good enough for his boss, he quit.

Theistic moralism emphasizes obedience to God, or attempting to do what would please God, as the ultimate standard for determining what is ethically appropriate or inappropriate. This view often complements moral absolutism by justifying arguments about what is right or wrong in terms of divinely revealed wisdom (the Ten Commandments, for example). But more important, it tends to relativize other considerations by asserting the importance of serving God as the overall end to be achieved by particular activities. An action is thus right not simply because it leads to good consequences, or even because it is reasonable, but because it has been commanded by God or is deemed to be pleasing to God or consistent with the spiritual dimension of life.[47] Insofar as God is considered a monotheistic being who governs all of reality, theistic moralism typically emphasizes the universalistic qualities of ethical principles. It may, however, acknowledge the validity of variations in the interpretation and application of these principles, especially when complex ethical issues are being faced in a society as diverse as ours.[48] Maxims indicating theistic moralism would include sayings like "God wouldn't approve," "what is the biblical view?" or "what would Jesus want me to do?"

The story is told about a psychiatrist, David Allen, who was one of the first African Americans on the Harvard Medical School faculty and who was asked to mediate some of the racial tensions that erupted in Roxbury in the early seventies. As he was walking down the street, watching apartments burning and seeing stores being looted, he said under his breath, "I wish Jesus Christ were here today because he could resolve it." And a small voice said to him, "But I am. Only now I live in you. And through you." The doctor who told this story said he tries to take this approach in his work. "I ask myself what Christ would do if he were here, and the answer is often different from what I would naturally do."

As another example of theistic moralism, consider the following statement:

> Our company was started about 35 years ago by one man. He was a Christian. He started the company as a ministry to the Lord. He didn't ever start a meeting without a prayer, asking God to bless the meeting. He had ten principles of management hanging on the wall. The first one was this company is dedicated to Christ. That was where we started. That was number one. When he was at the helm, I never saw or heard anything from management, other than you do what Christ would do.[49]

Miriam Zellers is also an example of someone who tries hard to "think what Jesus would do," as she puts it, when she is faced with difficult ethical choices.

The data presented in Table 4.4 give some sense of how widely these various value orientations may be held in the American labor force. These, of course, are not mutually exclusive orientations. In a pluralistic culture such as ours it is common for people to draw legitimation for

TABLE 4.4

The Importance of Value Orientations

Question: "Suppose you had a tough decision to make at work. Would each of these be a major consideration for you, a minor consideration, or not a consideration in making your decision?" "Now, which one would you give the most weight to of all?"

	Total Labor Force	Weekly Churchgoers
Individualistic utilitarianism:		
What would benefit you the most		
Major consideration	41	3
Give the most weight	9	4
Corporate utilitarianism:		
What would benefit your company or employer		
Major consideration	63	65
Give the most weight	12	7
Emotivism:		
Whether you would feel good about it		
Major consideration	72	76
Give the most weight	15	12
Altruism:		
What would benefit other people most		
Major consideration	64	71
Give the most weight	11	9
Moral absolutism:		
What you thought was morally right		
Major consideration	79	86
Give the most weight	30	29
Theistic moralism:		
Trying to obey God		
Major consideration	52	79
Give the most weight	14	32

their behavior from a variety of these orientations. Individualistic util-itarianism is a fairly common orientation, given that 41 percent of the labor force say the response "what would benefit you the most" would be a major consideration if they had to make a tough decision at work. This orientation, however, is not as widespread as some of the others, nor as widespread as some critics of American society have suggested, although it is possible that people are more self-oriented than they are willing to admit in a survey. Corporate utilitarianism is actually more widespread: nearly two-thirds of the labor force say "what would ben-efit your company or employer" would be a major consideration.

Emotivism and altruism are both quite popular orientations, it ap-pears. "Whether you would feel good about it" would be a major con-sideration for nearly three-quarters of the labor force. "What would benefit other people most" would be a major consideration for nearly two-thirds.

Moral absolutism is actually the most prevalent orientation, at least judging from the fact that 79 percent of the labor force say "what you thought was morally right" would be a major consideration. It is true that this statement allows for considerable subjectivity ("what you thought") in deciding on moral issues. In comparison, theistic moral-ism seems to be considerably less prevalent, indeed, ranking lower than any of the other five except individualistic utilitarianism. Only half of the labor force say "trying to obey God" would be a major con-sideration. Again, the evidence suggests that religious convictions may not be guiding people's behavior in the workplace as much as re-ligious leaders would hope.

When people are forced to say which value orientation they would give the most weight to of all in making a tough decision at work, the most frequently chosen response is "what you thought was morally right." This fact may be reassuring to those who believe it is indeed important to bring moral and ethical considerations into the work-place. Yet in absolute terms only three people in ten actually chose this response. The other 70 percent are divided about equally among the other five categories. At least a tenth of the work force say they would do whatever benefited themselves the most, about the same say their company's interests would be uppermost in their minds, emo-tivism comes in slightly ahead of the others in prevalence, altruism is given preference by about one person in ten, as is trying to obey God.

Table 4.4 also indicates how these various value orientations may be in-fluenced by religious commitment. When persons who attend religious services every week are compared with the total labor force, several interesting differences appear. One, of course, is that churchgoers are substantially more likely to say trying to obey God would be a major consideration and to give this the most weight of all. It is perhaps interesting, however, that only one weekly church attender in three would actually choose pleasing God above all the other considerations. Another interesting result is that churchgoers are significantly less likely to choose the individualistic utilitarian response. In other ways, though, what is perhaps most interesting is that churchgoers resemble the total labor force so closely. They are, for instance, no less likely than others to give major consideration to what would benefit their employer. They are slightly more likely to give major consideration to their feelings and to what would benefit others. And about the same proportions in both columns say they would give the most weight of all to what is morally right and to what would benefit others. It is worth emphasizing that these questions are not asking people to make simplistic decisions about what they would actually do when faced with difficult ethical choices—only whether they would try to do what was right and whether they would try to please God. Even religious leaders who have tried to encourage parishioners to think in complex ways about ethical issues could surely agree that religious conviction should have these kinds of consequences. Yet the evidence suggests that churchgoers are not being stimulated to think very differently from anyone else. The question also remains open as to whether these various considerations make much difference to the ways in which people actually behave in the workplace.

To answer this question, we need to compare people with different value orientations. Because survey respondents were asked to say which one of the various statements shown in Table 4.4 they would give the *most* weight to, we can use these responses as an indicator for making such comparisons. In doing so, however, we must keep in mind that most people said they would actually attach major importance to at least several considerations. This means that their responses to the question at issue are somewhat forced. A person who selected the "moral absolutism" response may have also been inclined to emphasize feelings in deciding on what was morally right. A different person, giving the same response, may be oriented more toward trying to obey God. We should, therefore, not expect strong differences to appear in the data simply on the basis of classifying people according to these particular statements.[50]

The likelihood of people in the various categories having engaged in some of the questionable or unethical activities we considered earlier is shown in Table 4.5. Overall, individualistic utilitarians are the most likely to have engaged in these activities. On average, for example, about a third of the respondents in this category say they have done each activity. Corporate utilitarians, emotivists, and altruists fall in the middle. On average, about 28 percent of the people in each of these three categories say they have done each activity. The moral absolutists and theistic moralists fall at the low end of the continuum. On average, only one person in five in each of these two categories has engaged in each activity.

Although the percentage differences are sometimes small enough to be attributable to sampling error, it is also interesting to note how people in each category responded to some of the particular items shown in the table. For example, individualistic utilitarians are much more likely than any of the others to take time off from work when they shouldn't. In contrast, corporate utilitarians seem to be guided at least to some extent by loyalty to their employer. For instance, they are less likely to cover for someone else or to bend the rules than are individualistic utilitarians. The emotivists seem to be guided by their feelings in ways that enhance their personal freedom. For example, they tend to arrive late, bend the rules, and use office equipment for their own purposes. But compared with either category of utilitarians, they are less likely to cover for someone else. Altruists, in contrast, are relatively more likely to cover for someone and bend the rules. But they are relatively unlikely to bend the truth. Finally, the moral absolutists and theistic moralists resemble each other very closely. They do not differ from others much in their tendency to arrive late. They are most different from the others in terms of not covering for others, not bending the rules, not bending the truth, and not using office equipment. The theists are most different from the absolutists in being less likely to bend the rules or the truth.

Again, readers should be reminded that some of these differences are small enough to be statistically insignificant. Yet, depending on how the data are interpreted, there are some notable differences as well. For example, individualistic utilitarians are twice as likely as moral absolutists or theistic moralists to bend the truth. Moral absolutists are only a third as likely as individualistic utilitarians to take time off from work when they shouldn't. Both kinds of utilitarians, as well as the emotivists, are four times as likely as the moral absolutists

TABLE 4.5

Value Orientations and Ethics

Percent who had done each of the following within the past month among those whose value orientation was:

	I	C	E	A	M	T
Arrived late	41	41	44	39	36	39
Covered for someone	49	42	36	42	29	29
Bent the rules	35	29	34	39	25	20
Bent the truth	40	32	30	31	21	16
Used office equipment	26	29	29	31	23	22
Took time off	26	15	17	10	9	11
Charged for expenses	4	4	4	3	1	2

Key: I = Individualistic utilitarianism; C = Corporate utilitarianism; E = Emotivism;
A = Altruism; M = Moral absolutism; T = Theistic moralism

to say they have charged for expenses that might not be legitimate.[51] Moreover, multivariate analysis of the data shows that the various orientations are quite strongly associated with how likely or unlikely it is for someone to take a relativistic stance toward bending the rules.[52] These findings suggest that religious teachings *could* make a difference to the ways in which people behave in the workplace if these teachings could be brought to bear more effectively on the underlying value orientations that guide people in their ethical decisions.

In the labor force as a whole, the two most common value orientations are emotivism and moral absolutism, at least judging from the numbers who give these responses the most weight and who say each would be a major consideration. These two orientations, as just seen, also tend to be associated with different likelihoods of engaging in questionable behavior: emotivists score significantly higher on most items than do moral absolutists. And yet, both orientations are so widespread in American culture that most people probably combine them in subtle ways as they face complex ethical questions. For example, when asked in another question what they would do if they were facing an important ethical dilemma at work, 74 percent of the moral absolutists said they would be very likely or fairly likely to "make the decision mainly by paying attention to your feelings." For this reason, it may be helpful to consider another concrete example—one that shows how a strong sense of moral absolutes and an emphasis on personal feelings come together in making difficult ethical decisions.

Estelle Cavenah, 29, works as a staff trainer for a health education service in southern California. If she were to be classified as having one underlying value orientation, it would be moral absolutism. She believes firmly in being honest and in following the rules. For example, listen to what she says about reporting mileage expenses:

> If I drive from home to a clinic site which is close to my home, and it's only seven miles, and my normal commute from my home up to where I work is twenty miles, well I wouldn't report that seven miles because it's on my way to work. I would normally drive by there anyway. But, what happens is that it makes my reporting inconsistent, because I report some things and I [don't] report others. So my manager told me that I needed to report it. But I feel unethical claiming money from the company that I don't think I deserve.

She also walks down the street to do personal xeroxing, rather than using the company machine. Her co-workers say it doesn't matter if she uses the company machine. But she claims it does, even though it is a little thing.

As a health worker, she also confronts much more serious ethical dilemmas. For example, she counsels women about pregnancy, birth control, adoption, and abortion. The issue of abortion is especially difficult for her.

> I have had to struggle with that a lot, because I really don't think abortion is okay. I really do think that you're murdering, or killing, a potential life. So what I did is, I went and saw some procedures, some abortions, and I talked to people about them, and I came to the conclusion that yes, I still feel that it's not a good thing. Abortion is just really not the ideal. But I don't have the right to impose my views on other people. So I do teach the procedure and I always pray before the class that the truth of the procedure will really sink into the participants' hearts and that they will be able to see for themselves what goes on in an abortion and that they will not go out and encourage it when they're in the clinics. So that's how I've dealt with that.

On both the mileage and abortion issues, she is convinced she knows what is morally right. Both issues, in her view, raise questions about fundamental standards of right and wrong: stealing and killing. She feels so strongly about both that she has discussed them with her supervisor. In the first case, she has enough discretion in her work, and the issue is sufficiently small, that she is able to go against her supervisor's advice. In the second, she also uses discretion to her advantage but has less room to maneuver. It is important, however, to understand that emotivism also plays a significant role in her thinking. Intellectually, she knows the mileage issue is small, but it looms larger because it affects the way she feels about herself. A dogmatic moral absolutist might resolve the abortion issue by saying it should not be taught or encouraged in any way. Emotivism helps her compromise. She tells herself she feels good about the way she handles it. More important, it gives her a way to legitimate the opinions of others. In saying she doesn't have the right to impose her views on others, she turns a moral absolute into a "view," and recognizes that how others feel about it is a legitimate consideration as well. We might disagree with how she handles these issues. But the important point is that her combination of moral absolutism and emotivism helps her to think hard about ethics in the workplace and to do what she believes is right without taking an utterly rigid stance on what she does. At the same time, it is clear that an emphasis on personal feelings can make it easier to rationalize what we do.

Participation in Religious Communities

This example also illustrates some additional ways in which religion influences ethical behavior and some of the limits of this influence. The reason Estelle Cavenah feels as strongly as she does about ethical issues is that she has a strong religious faith and is an active member of a religious community. It is significant that she chooses not to explain her stand on particular ethical issues, even abortion, in terms of her religious beliefs. Whereas a theistic moralist would make these connections explicit, she leaves them implicit. She recognizes that she works in a secular context. Her college education and exposure to the mass media also make her reluctant to use religious arguments. It makes more sense to her simply to state a moral position but then legitimate it as a personal view, a conviction, something she feels strongly about. The fact that she acknowledges the right of others to hold different views is consistent with her religious beliefs as well. She is a pluralist who regards religion largely as a matter of personal conviction.

These are all, as I have suggested, traits of American religion at the end of the twentieth century.

Religion does influence her ethical views more significantly than it does those of many other people, however, primarily by providing an alternative source of identity. She is trying to witness to her faith by her life in the workplace. Her religious involvement gives her a source of strength as she tries to be a public witness. She draws a very strong boundary between who she is as a person and the rules of the workplace. She regards these rules as rather petty and bureaucratic, as opposed to her own standards, which are more fundamental and important to her. And in the case of mileage reporting, because she isn't being asked to do anything very serious, she takes the occasion to turn this into a kind of ritual, an occasion to dramatize her belief in honesty. Her moralism works for her because it is reinforced by an alternative community outside the workplace.

We already saw some evidence of the role of participation in religious communities when we considered the tendency of active churchgoers to emphasize obedience to God as a moral consideration. A better sense can be obtained by considering the relationships between ethics and membership in religious fellowship groups. As noted in Chapter 3, such groups are quite widespread in American society. At least 20 percent of the labor force claim to be an active member. Other research shows that such groups are quite diverse, cutting across denominational, confessional, and ideological lines, and including men and women from all occupations. But these groups, usually consisting of no more than about twenty people, also develop strong primary attachments, provide deep emotional support, and contribute to spirituality in numerous ways.[53]

The members of religious fellowship groups are substantially more likely than nonmembers to believe that moral absolutes exist and to say these moral standards are vital to their own sense of personal worth (see Table 4.6). They are also better positioned to receive advice about ethical issues from sources outside the workplace itself, especially from clergy. For example, nearly half say they would be very likely or fairly likely to consult a member of the clergy for advice if they were facing an important ethical dilemma at work, compared with only a quarter of nonmembers. Members are also less likely to agree that bending the rules at work is acceptable. And they are less likely to say they have actually bent the rules within the past month.

TABLE 4.6

Ethics and Fellowship Groups

Percent of those in the labor force who were in a religious fellowship group, or who were not in a group, who gave each of the following responses:

	In Fellowship Group:	
	Yes	*No*
Say moral standards are absolutely essential to basic sense of worth as a person	74	51
Agree strongly that certain values must be regarded as absolutes	71	47
In facing an important ethical dilemma at work, would seek advice from a member of the clergy	46	24
Agree it is OK to bend the rules sometimes at work	32	52
Have bent the rules in the past month in dealing with someone	20	31

In all these ways religious participation seems to have an important influence on ethical considerations, at least when it draws people into small, primary groups.

Such groups can serve as a kind of counterculture, helping to combat the more relativistic or utilitarian norms that may prevail in the workplace. Their members, for example, are decidedly more likely than average to say they would try to obey God when making an important ethical decision, and less likely to say they would do what most benefited themselves. But even these groups are unable to insulate their members entirely from the broader culture. Emotivism is pervasive even among the members of such groups. For example, two-thirds agree that "you just have to do what feels right and hope for the best," and 70 percent say they would be very likely or fairly likely to "make the decision mainly by paying attention to your own feelings" if they faced an important ethical dilemma at work. These percentages, moreover, are about the same as they are among nonmembers.

There is also a fairly pervasive tendency in American culture to believe that people should mind their own business when it comes to ethical questions. Thus, a person may feel strongly about abiding by strict moral standards and yet feel it would be inappropriate to police the behavior of co-workers or clients. Estelle Cavenah's feeling about not imposing her views of abortion on anyone else is one example. Another example is the way in which people respond when asked what they would do if they saw something at work they thought was ethically wrong. Nearly half (49 percent) say they would actually "tell them you thought what they were doing was wrong" (about the same percentage that agrees they feel responsible to make sure their co-workers behave ethically). But this leaves at least as many who have good reasons for keeping their mouths shut. For example, about a quarter say it would depend on how they were feeling at the moment. Twelve percent say people probably have their reasons for doing what they do. Seven percent say it just isn't appropriate to say anything. And eight percent aren't sure what they'd do.

Participation in religious communities does not seem to protect people very much from adopting the norm of minding their own business on ethical matters. Among members of fellowship groups, for example, the proportion who said they would definitely confront someone rose only to 54 percent. Otherwise, about the same proportions said it would depend on how they felt or that it probably wouldn't be appropriate to speak up. Other kinds of religious involvement, such as church membership or regular participation in religious services, showed similar results.

Training in Ethics

When workplace ethics became a matter of public concern in the 1970s, the public sought to deal with the problem primarily by calling for more explicit training in the subject. Within a few years, business, law, medical, and other professional schools were offering (and sometimes requiring) courses in ethics. Professional associations developed codes of ethical conduct that new recruits were expected to know, and corporations often encouraged employees to attend seminars on the subject. Prior to that time, ethics had often been taught in separate courses at the undergraduate level, and training was certainly provided in many elementary and secondary schools, in homes, and in churches and synagogues. Business managers and professionals had been expected to behave ethically simply as a matter of personal pride and common decency. But this was the first time that widespread interest was expressed in training programs specifically concerned with the problem of workplace ethics.

In the face of continuing public concern about moral and ethical corruption, there is still a widespread conviction that better training is the answer. In one national survey, for example, 69 percent of the public said "teaching ethics and values in business schools" would help a lot to make America a better society, and another 25 percent said it would help a little.[54]

More than two decades have passed since that initial wave of interest in teaching courses about ethics in the workplace. How successful has the effort been? What proportion of the labor force has actually received such training? Does it appear to make a difference in the way they behave? Does religion still have a place in providing such training?

Asked if they had ever received some kind of training in ethics, such as taking a course in it, either as part of their work or outside their work, 14 percent of the labor force said they had as part of their work, 9 percent said they had outside their work, and 5 percent said they had done both. But nearly three-quarters of the labor force has received no ethical training of either kind. Because the interest in such training has been relatively recent, it might be expected that younger people would be more likely to have taken courses than older people. When persons younger than thirty-five were compared with older persons, and when additional comparisons were made with people over age fifty, though, no significant differences were found. It is the case, however, that such training is significantly more likely among college graduates and people working in the professions than in other occupations. For example, a quarter of college graduates have received training in ethics as part of their work, 17 percent have received such training outside their work, and 10 percent have experienced both. Among men and women employed full-time in the professions, these percentages are about the same. There is, then, at least modified evidence that some success has been achieved in actually providing training in ethics. Clearly, however, most of the labor force has not yet been reached by such courses.

That such training may also make a difference in how people think about ethics is indicated by the significant differences evident in the value orientations of those who have had training and those who have not. People who have received training in ethics as part of their work tend to be more likely to emphasize corporate utilitarianism, altruism, and moral absolutism, and less likely to emphasize individualistic utilitarianism. Those who have received training in ethics outside the workplace are not as oriented toward corporate utilitarianism but are more likely to adopt the altruistic and moral absolutist orientations. People with no training in ethics are most likely to say they would do what would benefit themselves the most. They are also likely to say they would be guided by how their family would react.

A specific example of the value of training is given by an appraiser. When asked if he ever confronted ethical questions in his work, he responded:

> I am posed with that problem at least every other day. I have had people attempt to bribe me. I have had people threaten me. I have had a sheriff in my office. I have worked for the IRS. I have been examined and cross-examined about those exact issues and I have to constantly be aware. I'm bombarded with ethical dilemmas constantly because of the work I do. Just constantly.

What has helped him the most is periodic training.

> I just spent three days in a class, and the title of the class was Standards of Professional Practice and Conduct. About half the class was dealing with ethical problems, ethical requirements. Reporting and just how to avoid advocating, and bias and prejudice and incompetency. I get training in it, that's how I cope with it.

A course of this kind makes the norms that otherwise remain implicit more explicit. It may not resolve all the gray areas people confront in their work, but it does help prevent custom from taking over completely. It provides external standards and even language, from seminars or from case studies, that serve as a counterdiscourse to the unspoken expectations affirmed by routine behavior.

The role of religion is evident partly in the fact that persons who have received training in ethics outside their work are more likely than others to be oriented toward theistic moralism. The reason for this is probably that such training was actually associated with their religious upbringing or with their current religious involvement. Active attenders at religious services, members of religious fellowship groups, and participants in Sunday school classes were all more likely than others to say they had received some kind of training in ethics outside their work.

Questions remain, however, about the overall effectiveness of courses in ethics as the solution to wide-ranging ethical dilemmas in the workplace. Often such courses focus more on technological, legal, and governmental issues than on matters of day-to-day personal behavior in the workplace. Full-time workers who had taken courses, for example, were no less likely to have engaged in the various kinds of questionable activities considered earlier in the chapter than workers who had not taken courses. Nor were they any less likely to agree that it is OK to bend the rules at work. The one attitude they were significantly more likely to hold was that being ethical would pay off economically. Yet utilitarian thinking of this kind may be insufficient in guiding either everyday behavior or thinking on major ethical dilemmas.[55]

A Limited Impact

I have tried to suggest in this chapter that sacred tradition remains relevant, but in limited ways, to the issue of workplace ethics. Few questions are as thorny, or as important, as questions of ethics in the workplace. Most employees enjoy high levels of discretion in deciding how to perform their work. Discretion of this kind is a cherished feature of postindustrial society. But the possibility for misconduct is also quite high, as some well-publicized scandals in business and politics have shown. Ethical questions have also become more complex as a result of new technology and a host of legal constraints and governmental guidelines. Most people, nevertheless, simplify the realm of ethics greatly by equating it largely with personal honesty. As long as they do not blatantly tell a lie, they feel they are behaving properly.

Although the family, neighborhood, ethnic group, schools, and religious communities have always been sources of thinking about ethics, it appears that the workplace itself has increasingly become a subculture in which particular understandings of ethics are encouraged. These understandings include a number of assumptions that maintain a modicum of moral order but seldom interfere with the daily business of the workplace. Among these are the belief that ethical conduct pays off economically, that misconduct does not pay, that each individual worker is probably ethically superior to any of his or her co-workers, that no organization can be expected to be perfect, that there are many reasons why the rules need to be bent, and that people should mind their own business in matters of ethics, letting upper management worry should anything serious occur. These implicit norms appear to function fairly well in most situations, seldom standing in the way of business itself, but they also suggest why scandals and white-collar crime have become so common in our society. If people feel they are honest but have only a shallow notion of what honesty is, and if they feel they can cut corners as long as they feel good about it—leaving it to others to blow the whistle, but refusing to do so themselves—then it is not surprising that ethics in the workplace has become a slippery slope.

Workplace ethics is also influenced by value orientations that may be widely diffused in the culture at large. Individualistic utilitarianism, a view that emphasizes self-interest, is widespread, as is corporate utilitarianism, one that emphasizes the interest of the organization for which one works. Emotivism, stressing the importance of individual feelings in making ethical decisions, is prevalent as well. A number of people hold an altruistic orientation that encourages them to try to benefit others. Moral absolutism of some kind, urging people to follow certain standards deemed valuable in their own right, is still widespread. Theistic moralism adds some sacred sanction to these standards by encouraging people to obey God. Utilitarian and emotivist orientations appear to accommodate a wider range of questionable conduct in actual life than do moral absolutism and theistic moralism.

Religious commitment is associated with opting for a theistic or absolutist orientation toward ethics. When religious commitment includes active participation in a small primary group, such as a fellowship, it can make a considerable difference to the ways in which people think about moral standards and to their willingness to engage in questionable workplace behavior. The religiously committed, however, have also been deeply influenced by emotivism and by the norm of minding their own business in matters of ethics. Explicit training in ethics still occurs in religious settings but increasingly appears to be associated with secular programs ranging from college courses to instruction provided by professional organizations.

On balance, ethical behavior is still an important aspect of the workplace over which religious beliefs can exercise some influence. A substantial minority of the American labor force claims that trying to obey God is a significant consideration in making ethical decisions. A sizable minority say they would contact a member of the clergy if faced with a truly difficult ethical dilemma. And those who say religion is important in their lives and who participate more actively in religious communities are significantly less likely than others to engage in some kinds of ethically questionable behavior. When ethical decisions have become as complex as they have, small fellowship groups and other religious communities can perhaps be an especially valuable place in which to discuss these decisions and to introduce values that might not be present in the workplace itself. One of the respondents we interviewed explained this idea as he described how his Sunday school class helps him think harder about decisions at work.

> How do people know we're any different from anybody else? We say we are Christians, but how would anybody know? So we discuss the Bible and we discuss our lives, and we say, how will this idea affect what we do at work?

Yet the forces of secularization are also very much in evidence. Religious understandings of ethics are often highly subjective, oriented largely toward personal honesty and influenced by the economistic thinking that governs the workplace. For those who may think religion has become completely irrelevant to the workplace, plenty of evidence suggests that religious considerations still matter. Certainly religious leaders themselves would argue that they should. But those who believe religious commitments should make more of a difference than they do also need to understand that organizational and cultural forces have become much more important than religious convictions in shaping how people think about ethics and how they make ethical decisions at work. As one man observed, "There's just things in life that you have to do, even though the church says you shouldn't."

Chapter Five

Orientations Toward Money

Lovella Medina grew up in South Philadelphia except during the summers, which she spent at the Jersey shore, and the winters, at the family home in Miami Beach. She remembers there was an exclusive dress shop near her house. She'd go there anytime she felt like it and buy anything she wanted. "My father always used to say, `you and your credit cards, you're going to get me in jail.' Then he'd just laugh. No, money was never a problem." But her father did play the numbers, and somewhere, deep down, Lovella knew he *could* land in jail. So money was never really a source of security. That came from family. And from the church. Going to Catholic school exposed her to all the teachings about Jesus and the Virgin and the saints. She's always celebrated Christmas and Easter. She can still recite stories from the Bible about money. But she's not quite sure she understands them. God, to her, is a mystery. "Like, maybe God decides to strike somebody with polio because they love their money too much. I don't know. I don't think for God. God thinks for God."

After high school Murial Johnson got a temporary job with the board of education as a camp counselor. Since then she's worked as a crossing guard, sold Avon products, Tupperware, and insurance, driven a truck, and worked at the post office. Right now she has three part-time jobs and is training to be a police officer. Pregnant with her fifth child, she has to earn as much money as she can to support her family. Being black in Chicago has never been easy. But Murial works hard, lives frugally, and is faring better than many of her neighbors.

She hasn't gotten married because she doesn't want some "irresponsible man" telling her what to do with her money. In high school she took her lunch money (thirty-two cents) to the store and bought cookies, sold them to her classmates at a profit, then used the money the next day to buy more. She's always been clever that way. Murial is a Baptist. As a child she went to church every Sunday and to choir rehearsal on Wednesdays. Lately, she hasn't gone much. The biggest sinners are in church, she says. "You can't go to church without it being a fashion show." In her view, God doesn't want people to be materialistic. "God just wants people to learn to strive together."

Doug and Linda Hill used to be Baptists. Living in Tennessee, it was hard to be anything else. A few years ago, though, they switched to an independent Bible church. They used to fight a lot about money. Doug would come home tired from servicing computers all day. Linda would be worn out from her job at a local day care center. They'd fight about whether to go out to eat, and if not, who was going to fix dinner. Usually Doug was the tightwad, Linda, the spendthrift. At their new church, they've been hearing a lot about money. They've studied some Sunday school lessons about family finances and heard some sermons on stewardship. They still disagree with each other about how much money to spend. But Doug and Linda both say they have a greater appreciation of each other's views. Now, when they go over their budget together, they try hard to figure out what God would want them to do.

All religious traditions have had much to say about money. In India the Rig-Veda says the giver of money receives a life of light and glory. Mesoamerican religions taught that money had a soul and should be exchanged only after prayer and fasting. When money consisted of precious metals, the mining of these metals was often surrounded by religious rites. In Sumatra, for example, other metals could not be carried into the gold mines lest the spirit of gold flee. The Dyaks of Borneo believed the soul of the gold sought revenge on those who mined it. The Egyptians buried coins with the dead in case currency might be needed in another life. The Hebrew prophets taught that all riches were ultimately gifts from God. Christian and Muslim apocalyptic writings liken heaven to a city filled with gold, silver, and precious stones. The early Christians taught that Jesus had been betrayed for thirty pieces of silver. Andean missionaries explained salvation to indigenous peoples by likening it to the expiation of a financial debt. Biblical writings are also replete with admonitions about saving,

greed, generosity, and the wise investment of money. Virtually all religions have taught their followers to give money or its equivalents in
acts of worship. Religions often prohibit the sale of sacred objects, too,
the implication being that their sanctity is lost if they are bought and
sold.[1]

In our own society, most of us have been taught to think of money
in purely secular terms. Reading *Money* magazine, paging through the
Wall Street Journal, or taking a course in economics, we gain the impression that money is simply a medium of exchange. We are taught
that money is best understood by economists, not by priests, that we
should be rational about it, not superstitious, and that how we spend it
should be determined by our desires and preferences. In scholarly
settings, money is regarded as a specialized commodity that circulates
according to its own laws of supply and demand, rather than being
connected in any way with the beliefs and values of religion or other
cultural traditions.[2]

If we think about our own views of money, though, we know that it
is much more than economists lead us to believe. It has *meaning*. And
it is thus connected with our beliefs and values—whether we admit it
or not. Historical studies show that money has meant different things
to women than it has to men. A term such as "pin money" suggests at
least one way in which money has been given a gendered identity.
Psychological studies show that money is interpreted quite differently
by children in different families. From our own experience, we know
that a twenty-dollar bill means something very different to us if we
have received it as a birthday present from our grandmother or if it is
the first money we have ever earned, than if it is simply the change we
receive at the supermarket.[3] To an economist, a dollar may be nothing
more than a dollar when one puts it into a bill-changing machine. But
to a human being, a dollar can mean the reward for hard work, an expression of love by a parent to a child, a chance to do something fun,
or all that stands in the way of starvation ("my last dollar").

These considerations suggest that religious convictions may still be
important if we are to understand our attitudes and beliefs about
money. Indeed, examples are not hard to find. To see that money is not
simply a universal medium of exchange but one that has different
meanings in different settings, all we have to do is think about the
thousands of religious congregations that take up an "offering" each
weekend. This money is ritually set apart from ordinary money. It is

collected in special receptacles during a religious service. Usually it is consecrated in some way, often by a prayer recited by an officially designated person. Some explanation of why people give may be offered and the deity's blessings may be invoked in exchange for these gifts.

Other examples abound. Religious customs often dictate how money is handled at weddings. In some traditions, a special envelope is circulated during a reception following the wedding ceremony in which guests discretely place cash or checks for the bride and groom. In other traditions, the giving of money itself is considered bad taste, but gifts may be registered or purchased at well-known department stores so that exchanges for more desired commodities can be made. Funeral and burial customs supply similar examples. Religious holidays evoke norms about how money should be given. More broadly, some traditions may teach that money is a powerful source of temptation, while others may regard it as a divine resource to be invested wisely.

To say that money is treated differently in some contexts than in others does not quite get at the important issues, however. Certainly money could be given special meanings during religious ceremonies and yet be treated pretty much with indifference to religious teachings 99 percent of the time. A student of biblical texts could recite numerous teachings about money, and yet we would not know whether those teachings actually influence the way people think about money.

The important questions are whether religious teachings influence how people think about the place of money in their own lives and whether such thinking in turn affects their behavior. Especially in our own time, when we seem to be consumed by the earning and spending of money, we need to know whether religious convictions help people to keep money in perspective, whether they may in some way encourage our desire for money, or whether these convictions have become irrelevant. As one of the women we interviewed put it: "We've been living as if prosperity would last forever, but we're in for a lot of terrible surprises; there's got to be some way to see that money isn't the true source of happiness."

My argument is that religious teachings do remain relevant to the ways in which we think about money, but that they also give us mixed signals. We are taught to be diligent with our money but also not to worry about it; most of us, moreover, interpret religious teachings about money in our own way, without much input from clergy or from fellow believers, and we are greatly influenced by the messages we learn from the secular culture about money. It is not surprising that many of us, like Lovella Medina, are simply confused.

Yet the problem cannot be overcome by blaming ourselves. It is a symptom of the complex times in which we live. A brief glimpse at the past again demonstrates how much things have changed. In a society such as Puritan Boston we might expect religious teachings to have a powerful effect on attitudes toward money. Puritans were encouraged to live their entire lives in subjection to religious principles. A merchant like Robert Keayne, moreover, would have a hard time keeping his finances secret from his neighbors or the clergy. In an industrial society such as the nineteenth-century United States, we might also have expected a close connection between religious teachings and views of money. Wealthy industrialists could take pride in their money, believing it was God's blessing, while the laboring classes could dismiss the importance of money relative to the far glory of an afterlife. In our own postindustrial epoch, these historic teachings are still a part of our cultural heritage. But personal finances are much easier to shield from public scrutiny than ever before. Individuals and families can make huge sums of money and purchase lavish consumer goods without members of the clergy—or even their friends—ever knowing it. The average middle-class American, living in relative comfort compared with the rest of the world, may also find more subtle ways in which to think about the Bible and its admonitions against greed.

Making the Connection

A relatively high proportion of the American labor force believes there is a connection between religious faith and money. Indeed, given what we saw in Chapter 3 about faith and work, it is interesting that people seem, on the whole, more inclined to recognize a connection between faith and their money than between faith and their work. Presented with a statement that denies any connection, for example, only about a fifth of the labor force (22 percent) say they agree that "God doesn't care how I use my money," and this proportion drops to a seventh among weekly churchgoers. (In comparison, it will be recalled, a majority of weekly churchgoers denied that God had called them to their line of work.)

Other ways of posing the issue also suggest that Americans are fairly willing to see a connection between faith and money. For example, about one person in two agrees that the Bible contains valuable teachings about the use of money. Among weekly attenders at religious services, this proportion rises to about three in four (see Table 5.1). For some Americans, the possibility of learning about money from the Bible is no more than an abstract idea. But a substantial number actually claim they have thought about such teachings in the recent past. In the labor force as a whole, this is true of nearly a third, while among weekly churchgoers more than half say they have thought a great deal or a fair amount about what the Bible teaches about money in the past year. Approximately the same proportions also say they have thought this much about the connections between religious values and their personal finances.

It is important not to exaggerate these connections. The proportion who say they think at least a fair amount about faith and money is actually about the same as that (as we saw in Chapter 3) who said they think this much about faith and work. Yet, when we considered more closely what it meant to think about faith and work, we discovered that it often made little difference to the way people lived their lives. We shall want to keep that possibility in mind here too. It is also the case that posing a more stringent definition of "making the connection" quickly reduces the proportion who do this. For example, if devoting a "great deal" of thought to the connection between religious values and personal finances is the criterion, then only one person in eight in the labor force does so, and among weekly church attenders the proportion is only one in four.

Why are some people more interested in thinking about faith and money than others? To some extent the differences seem to be rooted in factors that may have little to do with religion itself. Better-educated people, for example, think more about it than less-educated people. People who earn higher incomes express more interest in it than people with lower incomes. And women do more so than men. But taking these and other such factors into account, we note that overall levels of religious involvement do make a considerable difference to the likelihood of drawing a connection between faith and money. Frequency of attendance at religious services makes a significant difference. How important religion is in a person's life generally makes a significant difference. Taking these factors into account, we observe that religious conservatives are more likely to make the connection than religious moderates or liberals, probably because the former are more often taught to think about ways in which they should subject their entire lives to biblical teachings, whereas the latter are encouraged to interpret biblical teachings in more diverse ways. And taking everything else into account, we see that Catholics are more likely than Protestants to draw the link.[4]

TABLE 5.1

The Bible and Money

	Total Labor Force	Weekly Churchgoers
The Bible contains valuable teachings about the use of money (Percent who "mostly agree")	51	77
In the past year, how much have you thought about what the Bible teaches about money? (Percent responding "a great deal" or "a fair amount")	29	57
In the past year, how much have you thought about the connection between religious values and your personal finances? (Percent responding "a great deal" or "a fair amount")	31	61

We would, of course, expect at least most of these factors to make a difference. It is reassuring that they are not just artifacts of other differences between the more religiously involved and the less involved. And yet it is important to press a little more deeply to see what it is about religious involvement that makes the difference.

For instance, we might suppose that seeing a connection between the Bible and teachings about money would depend mostly on what people believe about the Bible more generally. This is true to some extent, but only in a particular way. About three-quarters of the American labor force believe the Bible is the inspired word of God, while a quarter doesn't (or isn't sure). We might guess that the former would be much more likely than the latter to believe the Bible contains valuable teachings about money and to have spent time thinking about these teachings. Not so. Apparently belief in biblical inspiration is too general or vague to make much of a difference. What does make a difference is believing that the Bible should be taken literally. About a quarter of the labor force hold this view. And they are significantly more likely than others to make connections between the Bible and money. This, incidentally, is the case even when other factors, such as frequency of church attendance and a conservative religious orientation, are taken into consideration.[5]

It might be disturbing to some at least to think that encouraging biblical literalism was the only way to encourage people to think more about the relationship between their faith and money. Other things, however, also make a difference. One is the kind of experiential piety that composes a believer's relationship to God. People who say they think a lot about their relationship with God, for example, are significantly more likely to believe the Bible has valuable teachings about money and to think about these teachings than are other people, even when we take into account many other religious factors.[6] One man who illustrates this type of connection, for instance, said simply that he wants his faith to influence his money because his faith is the "very foundation of his life." He thinks a lot about God and so it is only natural to say, "I wonder what God would want me to do."

Another factor that actually makes some difference is whether people have heard sermons on the topic. In the labor force as a whole, 26 percent say they have heard a sermon on stewardship in the past year, and 21 percent have heard one about personal finances. If people who are not members of churches or synagogues are excluded, these proportions rise to 40 and 32 percent, respectively. And among those who say they attend religious services every week, the proportions are 57 and 43 percent, respectively. It is perhaps noteworthy, given the fact that clergy generally *have* to discuss finances at least once in awhile just to keep their congregations solvent, that more regular attenders claim to have heard a sermon that inspired them to work harder (52 percent) than one that dealt with personal finances. Yet, these are on the whole substantial proportions. And having heard such sermons does improve the chances that people will believe the Bible contains valuable teachings about money as well as the likelihood of thinking about religious values' implications for their finances, again if we take into account other factors.[7]

Some perspective on these findings can be added by also noting two kinds of religious involvement that do *not* increase the chances of making faith-finance connections. One is childhood religious training. It, at least, does not seem to retain a direct link with thinking about faith and money as an adult. It does increase the likelihood that adults will do other things, such as attend religious services and listen to sermons on finances, that encourage such thinking. But in the absence of these adult activities, the residual effect of simply having been religiously involved as a child is nil.[8] The other factor that makes no difference, when other things are taken into account, is having friends in one's congregation. There is a line of sociological argumentation that suggests such informal ties are probably more important than beliefs and teachings.[9] Thus, one might suppose that having religious coequals with whom one could discuss personal finances would be important. But apparently not. And, in fact, there is a reason why it is not important that we shall come to in a few pages. Lest sociological argumentation be dismissed entirely, it *is* the case that people involved in small fellowship or support groups are somewhat more likely to make the connection between faith and money than people who are not involved.[10]

The four people introduced at the beginning of the chapter illustrate some of what we have just been considering. Neither Lovella Medina nor Murial Johnson think very much about the relationship between religion and money. They figure there is one but don't worry much about it, other than to take a cynical attitude once in awhile when they do. Doug and Linda Hill, in contrast, are exposed to sermons on a regular basis and attend a fellowship group that draws explicit connections between the Bible and money. They are also quite conservative in their religious views, including holding the belief that the Bible should be taken literally.

On one issue, however, all four agree: greed. Murial Johnson probably put it best: "[Religion] has kept me from being totally greedy." She explains, "I could've made a lot more money, or stuck with a job just for the pay, and said, `Forget everybody and everything else.' Maybe I'd be a millionaire, but not know my kids." She says God has helped her keep things in perspective.

Greed and the Quest for Money

Religious thinkers have always counted greed among the major human vices, categorizing it with such evils as lust, anger, envy, pride, gluttony, and sloth. Readers of the Hebrew and Christian scriptures can find countless examples of greed resulting in divine punishment. In most of these instances, money, gold, land, and other material possessions were at issue, not simply an aggressive attitude or a compulsive lifestyle. While greed has a variety of connotations in contemporary society, it is not uncommon to define it, therefore, in monetary terms, or as Solomon Schimmel does in a recent study of the topic, as "the inordinate love of money and of material possessions, and the dedication of oneself to their pursuit."[11]

In the United States, most people (71 percent of the labor force) still agree that "being greedy is a sin against God"; this figure rises to

83 percent among church members and to 89 percent among those who say they have thought a lot about biblical teachings on money. This view is widely shared in contemporary religious books and in articles about money, and it has been reinforced greatly in recent years by scandals in the business community that have evoked editorials and public debate about the dangers of greed.[12]

It appears, however, that regarding greed as a sin is quite easy for most Americans to reconcile with the desire for a lot of money. Thus, while 86 percent of weekly churchgoers say greed is a sin, only 16 percent of them say they were ever taught that wanting a lot of money is wrong, and in fact 79 percent of them say they wish they had more money than they do.[13] Most churchgoers can thus deplore the greed they see in others but remain insensitive to its impulses in themselves.

Miriam Zellers might be one of the 16 percent who have been taught that wanting a lot of money is wrong: she attends church at least once a week, gave up a career to do volunteer work at her church, and thinks a lot about the implications of her faith for the ways in which she handles her money. Yet she is among the vast majority of regular churchgoers who have escaped the implications of Jesus's warnings about the quest for money. All she was taught in church as a child was that you should not "trample other people" to get money. As an adult, she says, her Christian friends have made it clear to her that "making a lot of money is not a sin." An even louder message came from her parents. Although they were faithful churchgoers, they wanted a better life for her and encouraged her to be a success. "I always knew," she acknowledges, "that success had a dollar sign on it." In raising her own girls, she has applied the same logic: "As strong a Christian as I am, I also knew that I wanted them to go away to good colleges where they would come out prepared to make a good living—and if they married right, so much the better." Only in recent years has Miriam begun to question some of these assumptions.

The lack of teaching in the churches about the dangers of wanting a lot of money is perhaps one reason why so many people in an affluent country like the United States can also retain strong interests in religion. Indeed, the admonition against greed appears to be rooted more in broad cultural understandings than in exposure to specific religious teachings or experiences. Taking other pesonal characteristics into account, people who have heard a sermon about personal finances or one on stewardship within the past year, for example, are no more likely to say greed is a sin than anyone else, nor are they any more likely to say they have been taught that wanting a lot of money is wrong. Even regular church attendance and participation in fellowship groups fail to have any discernible impact on responses to these statements, compared with the effects of a broad interest in cultural religiosity.[14]

Specific religious activities may fail to have more of an impact on thinking about greed because warnings against greed are simply institutionalized as part of American culture in general. Certainly it is possible that such admonitions are common in families and in schools, and that they emerge informally in interactions among friends. Any school child can learn about the evils of greed, not from reading the Bible but by hearing the story of Midas, or perhaps later, reading Chaucer's tale of the greedy brothers. That so many people regard greed as a "sin against God" suggests, however, that there is still a strong religious connotation. Thus, another possible reason why this belief can be so easily reconciled with wanting and having a lot of money is that greed itself is vaguely defined. In the comments of people we interviewed, for example, it sometimes meant being totally obsessed with money, rather than simply wanting it badly; being stingy, rather than having a lot of money and being willing to share it; doing illegal or unethical things to get one's money; simply forgetting to thank God when one prospered; or displaying some psychological insecurity that might have nothing to do with money at all.

An even more important reason why religious admonitions against greed have no more effect than they do is that other, predominantly secular understandings of money have penetrated the thinking even of those who are religiously active. One is what might be called the "psychologization" of money. According to this view, money itself is neither good nor bad; all that matters is a person's attitude toward it. Like the emotivist ethics we considered in the last chapter, this orientation can make it very difficult to know whether a person (even oneself) is greedy or not. Some contemporary religious writers, for example, try to discourage greed by telling their readers it will make them unhappy. "Am I unhappy?" asks the reader. "No? Well, then, I must not be greedy either."

The Bible itself encourages this orientation, of course, in stating that the *love* of money is the root of all evil, not money itself, or even the pursuit of money. The concern expressed in the Bible about money is often interpreted not as an admonition against having money but against thinking about it too much or attaching too much value to it. At a time when love implied behavior, this distinction was less problematic—to think properly about money also meant that one behaved accordingly. But now that love has in so many settings become little more than a good feeling, it becomes more difficult to pin down greed to anything concrete. That people may be willing to seize on this distinction to keep teachings about greed from interfering with their actually having money is suggested by one of the statements in Table 5.2. This statement, asserting simply that "money is the root of all evil," elicits agreement from far fewer people than the one about greed being a sin.

A related understanding that, as it were, protects money from moral accusations is captured in the statement included in our survey, "money is one thing, morals and values are completely separate." About two-thirds of the labor force as a whole, and about the same proportion of those in the labor force who attend religious services every week, agree with this statement. Thus, although many people say they think about the connection between their faith and their finances, there is also an implicit tendency to think of money as being in a category all its own.

What belies the belief that money really is separate from morals and values is that most people turn right around and *connect* it to their values. About two-thirds connect having money with freedom, while three-fourths admit that having money makes them feel good (see Table 5.2). Freedom and feeling good are two of the most widely held values in American culture in general. The fact that money is linked to both these values means that having it and wanting more of it makes a lot of sense to most people, whether or not they also believe that it is wrong to be greedy. Indeed, the signals telling us to do things that make us feel good are much stronger than the ones telling us not to want a lot of money.

If religious commitment exercises relatively little restraint on wanting a lot of money, it nevertheless does make some difference. We saw in Table 3.3 that regular churchgoers are somewhat less likely than the workforce as a whole to say they value making a lot of money. The differences are small. Yet a more detailed analysis of these responses shows that they are in fact influenced by religious participation, even when other factors are taken into consideration. An active churchgoer illustrated why this may be so in remarking that he had always learned at church that "Christ should be the center of your life" and he knew that "money has an insidious way of drawing you into its control." In addition to church attendance itself, all of the following are associated with *not* regarding making a lot of money as an essential value: thinking a lot about one's relationship to God, having heard a sermon in the past year on stewardship, having friends in one's congregation, and being a member of a fellowship group.[15] If the churches are failing to inhibit Ameri-

TABLE 5.2

Attitudes Toward Money

Percent who "mostly agree" with each statement:

	Total Labor Force	Weekly Churchgoers
Being greedy is a sin against God	71	87
Money is the root of all evil	46	51
Money is one thing, morals and values are completely separate	68	67
Having money means having more freedom	71	65
Having money gives me a good feeling about myself	76	72

cans' desire for a lot of money, the churches are, then, at least discouraging this desire from getting totally out of hand.

The other way that religious commitment deters the pursuit of money is by discouraging people from doing some of the things it might actually take to realize this ambition. It is one thing to admit a desire for more money (as most people do), but quite another to make the sacrifices necessary to pursue this desire seriously. What religious commitment does, perhaps more than anything else, is provide people with alternative identities and loyalties so that they are less willing to make these sacrifices. Thus, when asked what they would be willing to do to have a lot more money than they have now, weekly churchgoers were significantly less likely than those who attended less regularly to say they would work longer hours each week, take a less interesting job that paid more, move to a different part of the country, or play the lottery.[16]

If clergy want to curb Americans' appetite for money, it may be, therefore, that the most effective way of doing this is by pointing out the sacrifices one would have to make to become rich, rather than directly challenging the desire for wealth. There is a danger in this approach. Criticizing the *means* of obtaining wealth, but not challenging the *goal* itself, may result in people feeling that the churches are giving hypocritical—and frustrating—messages about money.

Attitudes Toward the Rich

The same religious teachings that warn of greed and wanting money too much often make their point by showing how the rich may have a hard time entering the kingdom of heaven. After his encounter with Jesus, for example, the rich young ruler is described as going away "sorrowful" because he is unable to part with his wealth to follow Jesus. Other biblical stories tell of rich men building bigger barns instead of thinking about their own souls or of rich men making a display of their wealth and failing to consider the needs of the poor.

Living in one of the richest countries in the world, most Americans seem to have difficulty believing that such stories should be taken very seriously. Only 30 percent of the labor force, for example, agree that "riches get in the way of our truly knowing God." Among church members, this proportion rises only to 37 percent, and among those who attend religious services every week, only to 42 percent. Apparently the majority of regular churchgoers have trouble believing Jesus really meant it when he talked about the difficulties the rich face in realizing the kingdom of God.[17]

Lovella Medina knows the passage in the Bible about it being harder for a rich person to enter the kingdom of heaven than a camel to pass through the eye of a needle. She figures that means there is a human tendency to be corrupted by power (note that power is the issue, not money itself). She doesn't figure this passage applies to her father. Despite his wealth, she says, people still respected him and he respected them. As for the Bible, she says its teachings about money are just contradictory. One person "gets bitched at because he didn't invest his money" and somebody else, because he "didn't give it away." This is why God seems so mysterious to her.

Murial Johnson, in contrast, is one of the 30 percent who does feel money conflicts with religious values. Never having had very much of it, perhaps she is more willing to envision the tension. She says, "Most people are turned around by money. They forget about the Bible and their values. They just say, `I worked hard for it, so you can't touch it' and they forget to be human anymore."

Doug and Linda Hill fall into the 30 percent too. They both think riches can conflict with spirituality. And yet, their arguments typify what many of the people we interviewed said, essentially softening the biblical teaching and finding other ways in which to give the rich more credit. Linda says the trouble is mainly that the rich have so many responsibilities that they may not have the time to devote to their spiritual lives. Doug sees the problem more as being lured by a false sense of security. But both admire the rich because they also believe the rich have simply been "blessed abundantly" and that it is "the Lord's choice" to do so. Neither believes the rich may have done anything immoral to obtain their wealth. Thus, as long as the rich behave responsibly, they are actually carrying out a special mission for God.

The data shown in Table 5.3 provide another way of understanding what is going on when religiously oriented people in the United States consider the rich. Each statement describes a certain kind of person

TABLE 5.3

Attitudes Toward the Rich

Percent who say they admire each kind of people a lot (8–10 on a 10-point scale)

	Total Labor Force	Weekly Churchgoers
People who make a lot of money by working hard	80	77
People who take a lower-paying job in order to help others	69	72
People who have a lot of money and still work hard	66	66
People who work hard but never make much money	60	64
People who give a lot of money to charitable causes	59	69
People who spend a lot of money traveling	17	17
People who inherit large sums of money	14	16
People who do not work hard because they have a lot of money	8	9

who represents different combinations of wealth, the lack of wealth, hard work, and other activities. Respondents were asked to indicate how much or how little they admired each kind of person, using a scale that ran from zero (low) to ten (high). By comparing the responses of regular churchgoers with the entire labor force, we can see how much of a difference religious involvement may make. More important, by comparing the responses (vertically) to the various statements, we can gain a better sense of what people may admire most or least about wealth.

The first point to be made is that the horizontal comparisons between the total labor force and those in it who attend religious services every week show very few differences. More detailed statistical analysis shows that some of these are statistically significant, and that the same is true of the relationships with some other religious variables, but these differences yield no consistent patterns, other than the fact that religious commitment is consistently associated with higher regard for wealthy people who give their money to charitable causes.[18]

The more important point pertains to the considerable differences evident in the table as one makes vertical comparisons among the responses to the various statements. What is clearly in evidence here is the American work ethic: among the most widely admired are people who make a lot of money by working hard and people who have a lot of money but who still work hard.[19] Even people who work hard but do not make much money are highly admired by a majority of respondents. Conversely, admiration is withdrawn from people who appear to be lazy. What is also apparent, though, is that somewhat greater value is attached to work that leads to monetary success than to work that does not. The data also indicate a lingering belief in the value of altruism, whether it be in the form of rich people giving away their money or ordinary people not pursuing riches in order to help others. Nevertheless, it is striking that we, on the whole, admire those who work hard and make a lot of money more so than we do those who take a lower-paying job to help others.

Several tentative conclusions can be drawn from these results. Religious people do not seem to think about the wealthy with any special frameworks that other people do not share. Riches are generally regarded favorably because of the assumption that people have worked for them. Some added benefit comes from simply being monetarily successful. Apart from hard work, generosity legitimates wealth. And then there is some residual admiration, either because of the glamour associated with being rich or because of good-heartedness that encourages people to think well of others in general. From this evidence, there is no reason to think that religious teachings have, as some critics suggest, *encouraged* us to admire the rich and to seek riches ourselves. These orientations are already pervasive in American culture, among both the religious and the nonreligious. However, it also appears to be the case that religious teachings do little to prevent us from adulating the rich. The churches may be, as they often claim, the special friend of the poor (more on this in Chapter 7), but they are certainly no enemy of the rich.

Lilies of the Field

Another way in which religious teachings bear on the topic of money is by counseling people not to worry about it. Jesus encouraged his followers to consider the lilies of the field: through no effort of their own they were beautiful, simply because God made them that way. The Apostle Paul wrote that he was indifferent to being "abased" or being able to "abound" as long as he was following God. Modern writers have been more critical of such teachings, arguing that they prevent people from throwing off oppression. Karl Marx, for example, characterized religion as the "illusory happiness of the people" that needed to be replaced by a more just economic system that would bring true happiness.[20] In contemporary social science, deprivation theory has drawn on this argument, suggesting that religious commitment may actually be more pervasive among the economically disadvantaged or among those with special economic concerns because it helps reduce their anxiety.[21] The therapeutic motif evident in contemporary religion points to a similar argument. As we saw in Chapter 4, religious convictions seem to operate at the level of moods and feelings, more so than at the level of morals and behavior. In our work, it helps us to be cheerful and to cope with stress, rather than altering the actual work we choose to do. We might expect the same pattern with respect to money. Perhaps religion does less to alter behavior or values than to make people feel better about themselves, including fretting less about their bills. To move beyond broad generalizations, however, we must understand three widely held assumptions in American culture.

First, there is a strong tendency to deny that money and happiness have anything to do with each other. In part, this assumption reflects the thinking we considered earlier that places money in a separate conceptual category, arguing that it is just "hard currency" having no intrinsic connection with thoughts, values, beliefs, or feelings. In part, it grows out of the egalitarian ethos on which American democracy itself is founded. Believing that all persons are equal, we psychologize this ideology by assuming that everyone has an equal right to pursue (and achieve) happiness, whether rich or poor. Thinking that money and happiness are unrelated also reflects the argument that Linda Hill made about the burdens of wealth. The truth is, most people can think of stories about wealthy people who are unhappy, and they gladly tell these stories as evidence that there is no intrinsic connection between wealth and happiness.[22] When surveyed, only one person in nine believes the wealthy are happier than other people, while twice that many claim they are less happy, and the remainder see no relationship at all.[23]

Second, there is an equally strong tendency in American culture to recognize that money and happiness often *are* related.[24] As already seen, about three-quarters of the American labor force agrees that "having money gives me a good feeling about myself." There was also a strong relationship in the survey between saying one was bothered by "not feeling good about yourself" and being worried about bills or feeling anxious or guilty about money.[25] Furthermore, not feeling good about oneself was more common among persons in lower income brackets, while (as in many other studies) overall happiness was greater in higher income brackets.[26] Valuing money and material possessions as much as we do, and believing that even our personal freedom depends on having money, we find it hard to deny that money does affect our feelings. We are thus torn by conflicting messages. One part of our culture—perhaps the messages our parents were willing to put into words—tells us that money doesn't *necessarily* result in happiness. But another part—perhaps the one we secretly cherish and that is reinforced by the glamorous images we see on television and in movies—convinces us that it would be nice to find out if wealth and happiness go together.

Third, American culture also requires a high degree of responsibility from each of us in matters of money, thereby contributing to the likelihood of experiencing anxiety about such matters. Were the issue simply one of having money or not having it, people could perhaps decide at some point that they were going to be content with what they had. Financial responsibility, however, requires that serious attention be given to *how* one spends money: making wise purchases, not spending it too conspicuously, having the right attitude toward it, and even not worrying about it. Some of these ideas are rooted in religious teachings and (as we shall see) are still influenced by religious commitment. But they are also conditioned by the mass media, parents, teachers, and even advertisers who counsel spending, but spending wisely.

Despite the fact that American standards of living are generally quite high, there is plenty of worry and anxiety about money, then, and these concerns do influence how people feel about themselves.[27] Most Americans wish they had more money than they do, most feel anxious about their purchases and monetary decisions, most worry about their bills, and many feel guilty about their expenditures (see Table 5.4). Other evidence points to the same conclusions. For example, 53 percent of the labor force says the statement "I worry about meeting my financial oblig-

TABLE 5.4

Money Worries

Question: "In the past year has each of the following bothered you a lot, bothered you a little, or not bothered you?"

	Total Labor Force
Wishing you had more money than you do	
Bothered a lot	53
Bothered a little	35
	88
Worrying about how you were going to pay your bills	
Bothered a lot	28
Bothered a little	44
	72
Feeling anxious about purchases or other decisions about money	
Bothered a lot	27
Bothered a little	46
	73
Feeling guilty about the things you were spending money on	
Bothered a lot	16
Bothered a little	39
	55

ations" describes themselves at least fairly well. Sixty-three percent say they "think a lot about money and finances," and more than half (55 percent) say they have "a lot of financial obligations."

Because Marxist and deprivation theories have often focused on religion as a kind of palliative for the poor, it is also important to note that financial worries are by no means restricted to the poor, even though they are indeed more common among the poor. In the poorest third of the labor force, for example, 61 percent say they worry about their financial obligations. But 53 percent also do in the middle third, and 39 percent do in the upper third. And the main reason for this, of course, is that financial obligations expand as people's wants and standards of living expand. In the upper third, for instance, 65 percent say they are trying to save money for retirement, 40 percent are saving for their children's college expenses, 39 percent are paying off credit card debts, and a quarter are meeting high mortgage payments. For these reasons, there is also plenty of worry to go around.[28]

Does religion make a difference? Does it encourage people to cut back on their financial obligations? Does it help them to worry less about the obligations they do have? Does it alleviate guilt? Does it provide techniques, such as prayer, for attaining peace of mind about financial concerns?

Although many religious leaders—from historic figures such as Francis of Assisi to contemporaries such as Mother Teresa or the Protestant writer Richard Foster—have championed a life of simplicity, there is little evidence that religious commitment actually encourages the majority of people to cut back on their financial obligations. It may have this effect on certain kinds of consumer wants (see Chapter 6), but on the whole, it appears that religiously committed people are just about as likely to incur major financial obligations as the less religiously committed. Certainly, this is how they themselves see it. For example, those who attend religious services every week and say religion is very important to them are just about as likely to say they have a lot of financial obligations as those who seldom attend religious services and say religion is not very important. When more detailed categories of expenditures are examined, the same conclusion emerges. The religiously committed are somewhat less likely to incur certain expenditures (e.g. high mortgage payments) but are *more* likely to incur others (e.g., saving for their children's education).

Religious commitment does, however, have a modest effect in reducing the chances of people worrying about their financial obligations.

The most consistent effect is from actually spending a lot of time thinking about one's relationship with God. Even when differences in other kinds of religious commitment, such as denomination or church attendance, are taken into account, those who spend more time thinking about their relationship with God are less likely to be worried about their bills, less likely to feel anxious about money decisions, and less likely to feel guilty about their purchases. Although they are weaker, some other forms of religious commitment also have this effect. For example, those who have heard sermons on personal finances or on stewardship recently are less likely to feel anxious or guilty about money. So are those involved in fellowship groups.[29]

A woman in her fifties whose husband earns a six-digit income illustrates how not worrying about money can easily be reconciled with feeling good about the ample material possessions that one has. "I love pretty things, a beautiful home, beautiful clothes, and expensive travel," she explains. She is also a woman of faith, so she adds, "I know that God has given me all these things. So I'm just not going to fret about getting more and more and more."

It is also important that some forms of religious commitment actually *increase* the likelihood of worrying about money. Specifically, regular church attendance is associated with a greater likelihood of worrying about one's financial obligations and with a greater likelihood of feeling guilty about one's purchases (controlling for other background characteristics). There are at least two reasons why this may be the case. But we shall want to consider each in a later section.

The fact that thinking about one's relationship to God has the most consistent effect in reducing the chances of worrying about money also raises the possibility that prayer is a significant way of dealing with such worries. We will consider what people actually pray about in greater detail in the next chapter. Suffice it to say, however, that indeed a lot of people resort to prayer in dealing with money. In the labor force as a whole, 31 percent say they have prayed about money matters within the past year. Among church members, 42 percent have done so. And among those who attend religious services every week, the figure is 55 percent. Protestants, it may be worth noting, are significantly more likely to pray about money matters than Catholics, but when regular attenders are compared, the differences disappear.

Apparently these prayers are answered. At least a large number of people say they have also thanked God for a financial blessing. In fact, the number who have done so within the past year is actually higher than the proportion who have prayed about money matters. In the entire labor force, 49 percent have thanked God for a financial blessing within the past year. Among church members, 64 percent have, and this proportion rises to 76 percent among weekly attenders.

Doug and Linda Hill illustrate how prayer—and faith more generally—help to reduce anxieties about money. Linda says she reminds herself as often as she can that "we are children of a sovereign God who owns everything and knows how much we need." Prayer is her way of doing this: "I have to verbally give it to the Lord and leave it there." She adds,

> Sometimes we get into financial difficulties because of our own foolishness or our own extravagance, but more often than not we are there just because of the general pressures of, you know, doctor bills that come up that we're really not expecting or clothing needs that we have not budgeted or school expenses.

Prayer makes her feel better because "the Lord knows about that and usually takes care of it." Doug feels the same way. In his view, good Christians should be joyful and content. When things go wrong, he tries to remember this. Sometimes he thinks about the biblical story of Job. It makes him feel better to realize that somebody else had it a lot worse than he and Linda do.

Many of the people we talked to did not pray about their finances at all. But among those that did, there was a striking tendency to emphasize peace of mind. "The Lord will make our cup full to overflowing," was the way Doug Hill put it, "and we're full to running over when we have the peace of God in our hearts." He believes the Bible also teaches that "contentment is great gain" and that being discontented is a sin. This, then, is another indication of how faith has become therapy in our culture. An orthodox believer like Doug Hill insists—as religious teachings have in the past—that the purpose of life is to "bring honor to God." In concrete terms, however, the way to glorify God is not to live according to certain moral standards, not to spread the gospel, not to minister to the sick, and not to accomplish some other mission in life, but simply to be happy.

The Taboo on Discussing Money

Observers who have lived in other societies note that Americans are much more reluctant to talk about money than people elsewhere. It is considered impolite here to ask other people what their income is, for example. There are also cultural norms against revealing one's good or bad monetary fortunes. Many families feel it is important to shield their own children from knowing too much about the family budget— perhaps to keep them from worrying, but perhaps more often to keep them from asking for so much.[30] These norms, of course, do not apply universally. Close friends may find it helpful to compare notes about what they paid for items of clothing. Or a support group may provide a place in which people with worries about money can give voice to their anxieties. But such exceptions stand out mainly because of the more general norm in our society against discussing money.

It is difficult to identify the sources of a longstanding norm such as this. Some of the people we talked to indicated that they learned it inadvertently from their parents. Mom and dad just never talked about important financial decisions in front of their children, so the children grew up thinking that was the way they should behave as well. In other cases, people remembered being told specifically as a child that it was inappropriate to discuss money matters. When they could hear their parents arguing about money in the next room, they figured they knew why it was inappropriate.[31] A number of people also reported that it was the policy in their place of employment not to disclose salaries. That way, employees were less likely to compare notes and make demands.

Religion is probably one of the sources of this taboo as well. Admonitions against pride, bragging, and showing off can be interpreted to mean that someone who has experienced good financial fortune should not talk about it. Doing so would only make one's friends feel bad. Misfortune, in contrast, might result in tight-lipped behavior as well, especially if religious norms encourage people to be self-sufficient, rather than saying anything that might be construed as a plea for help.[32] How widespread this taboo actually is can be seen in the survey results. When asked how often in the past year they had discussed various aspects of their personal finances with people outside their immediate family, 82 percent said they had never or hardly ever discussed their income, 89 percent said they had not discussed their family budget, 76 percent said this about their major purchases, 75 percent said they had not discussed worries they might have had about money, and 92 percent said the same about their giving to charities.[33]

The role of religion can also be seen in the survey. Among those who seldom or never attend religious services, about a quarter claim that all or most of their friends have told them how much money they make, but among persons who attend religious services weekly, this proportion drops to about one person in eight. On specific financial issues, church members differ most from nonmembers in being reluctant to talk about their incomes and what their major purchases cost. Regular church attenders differ most from infrequent attenders in their reticence on discussions about income and money worries.[34]

One would think that religiously involved people might be less isolated from their friends and neighbors and for this reason actually more inclined to discuss money with them. Especially within the same church or synagogue, where there are presumably shared beliefs and values, money might well be an appropriate topic of discussion. When those who attended religious services every week were asked how often they had discussed their personal finances with various *kinds* of people, however, a surprising pattern emerged. The *least* likely group with whom conversations about personal finances had taken place were fellow church or synagogue members: 95 percent said they had never or hardly ever discussed personal finances with them. Nearly as unlikely were members of the clergy, with whom 93 percent had not had conversations. In comparison, such conversations were somewhat more common among fellow workers (88 percent had not had them), and among friends (82 percent had not had them).

Perhaps norms have simply emerged in religious communities over the years against discussing money. Certainly the proverbial "church gossip" who spreads tales about everybody else in the congregation may be seen as a reason to clamp a tight taboo on such discussions. But whatever the reasons, we are now in a better position to understand some of the other findings we have noted in passing. We saw, for example, that having friends in one's congregation did not increase the chances of drawing connections between one's religious values and one's personal finances. The reason is probably that these friends never discuss personal finances. We also saw that church attendance did not alleviate people's worries about money (in fact, it aggravated them). The reason for this may be that formal teachings encourage people not to value money and not to worry about it, and yet people do value it and do worry about it. In the absence of any frank discussions of the topic, they then simply feel guilty and anxious. The fact that fellowship groups reduce such worries indicates that the norm of silence can be circumvented when there is sufficient trust to do so.

If religious leaders want to help people apply their faith to their finances, therefore, it seems clear from this evidence that breaking through the barrier against talking about money must be a first step. At present, the norm is to suffer—or rejoice—in silence. People hear so many contradictory messages about money from their churches and from the secular culture that they become confused. Their confusion raises their anxiety but does not prevent them from following the path of least resistance. They still want money, spend it, and shoulder heavy financial burdens. Were they to discuss their feelings about it more openly, they would at least be able to confront some of their own ambivalence. Once articulated in public, moreover, feelings may also find ways of influencing behavior itself.

Understandings of Stewardship

Although religious organizations convey norms about greed or hints about how to have monetary peace of mind, their most systematic teachings on the subject of money generally fall under the heading of stewardship. In the Judeo-Christian tradition, believers are taught to regard themselves as stewards, or caretakers, of what ultimately belongs to God. In the parable of the good steward, for example, Jesus likens the master of the house to God and the stewards to employees of the master who are regarded more highly or less highly depending on how they have invested the master's money while he journeyed in a far land. In the twentieth century, stewardship has increasingly come to be associated with fund raising and pledge drives in local congregations, and we will want to consider this aspect of stewardship in some detail (see Chapter 8). But stewardship also has broader connotations. Here we ask whether people understand it at all, and if so, what their understandings are.

Although stewardship sermons are routinely preached in nearly all churches, only a quarter of the American workforce claims to have heard such a sermon within the past year. Among church members, only 40 percent have. And even among those who attend religious services every week, a bare majority (57 percent) have heard such a sermon. Perhaps stewardship Sunday is a good day to stay home and read the newspaper. Or perhaps clergy find it so awkward to talk about stewardship that parishioners don't realize it when the topic is being discussed. In any case, it comes as no surprise that many Americans have little understanding of stewardship at all.

Of the people we interviewed, many responded simply that the word *stewardship* was not part of their vocabulary. Others struggled to give it a definition but came up with little more than notions of being responsible or using one's talents wisely. Lovella Medina was one of the few who referred the question back to Jesus' parable of the talents. She was able to recount the story with fair precision. Yet the conclusion she drew was that the master was pretty arbitrary ("you never know how to take these things"). In the survey, close to 40 percent of the labor force said they didn't know what stewardship meant or that it wasn't very meaningful to them. Of the remainder, only 22 percent said the idea was very meaningful. Even among those who attended religious services every week, fewer than half (42 percent) said it was very meaningful to them. Moreover, it seems doubtful that hearing sermons on the topic does much to enhance this figure, given that the same proportion said it was very meaningful among those who had heard a sermon on it as did regular attenders in general.[35]

Religious leaders themselves are quite divided about what exactly stewardship means. Sermons on the topic are quite often preached during a congregation's annual pledge drive. These sermons may encourage members to give a certain proportion of their earnings to the church. But it is not hard to find sermons, tracts, and books that define stewardship more broadly, for instance, as responsible living or the wise use of one's talents. Another meaning, sometimes conveyed in children's Bible stories, is that stewardship means recognizing that God created the world—the implication being that one should therefore be thankful or reassured of things working OK. Stewardship has also come to be associated with environmentalism.

Given these diverse meanings, it is little wonder that the public defines stewardship in a variety of ways (see Table 5.5). Judging from the survey, we see that the most common definition is the idea of using one's talents wisely. The next most common is the view that stewardship means remembering God as creator. This is followed by the environmentalist view. And the least common understanding pertains to giving money to the church

We can also see from the table that people who have actually heard a stewardship sermon in the past year differ to some extent in their understandings from people who haven't. Yet these differences tend to be outweighed by the similarities. Using one's talents responsibly is still the most common understanding. This is still followed by the idea

TABLE 5.5

Understandings of Stewardship

Question: "Which of the following statements would be the best definition of stewardship?"

	Heard Stewardship Sermon		Total Labor Force
	Yes	No	
Giving a certain percentage of your money to the church	19	7	10
Using your individual talents in a responsible way	46	38	40
Taking good care of our planet	6	14	12
Remembering that God made everything	21	14	16
Other	3	1	2
Don't know	4	25	20

that God made everything. But then the environmentalist view is less common among persons exposed to stewardship sermons, while the idea of giving to the church is more common. More detailed statistical analysis of these responses shows that hearing stewardship sermons does substantially increase the likelihood of thinking in terms of church giving, even when denomination and level of attendance are taken into account—a finding that should encourage clergy to keep preaching these sermons, even if they do not affect attitudes and values deeply. Attendance itself also has a significant impact on selecting the view that stewardship means giving to the church. The notion of using one's talents responsibly seems to be rooted more in a kind of general interest in religion, including church membership and belief in the Bible. The environmentalist definition, in contrast, is selected more by nonmembers than by members. The view that stewardship means thinking of God as creator is associated most strongly with thinking a lot about one's own relationship to God, but is also influenced to some extent by childhood exposure to the Bible.[36]

Thus, there are ways in which specific religious experiences and activities influence our understandings of stewardship. The more important conclusion, however, is that stewardship is not meaningful to most Americans—or even to many active churchgoers. And stewardship, when it is discussed, is presented in so many different guises that people can interpret it pretty much as they like. When they do so, moreover, they prefer vague understandings that make little difference to how they should behave from day to day. In a society as diverse as ours, it is not surprising that religious leaders have tried to make the idea of stewardship relevant by linking it with all sorts of different ideas. The negative result of this nod to diversity, however, has been to leave people confused about—and often uninterested in—the topic entirely.

Confusion and disinterest were evident in the remarks of most of the people we interviewed in depth. Lovella Medina, as I mentioned, thought stewardship involved using one's talents, but she doubted that God would reward those who did so more than those who did not. She also regarded stewardship as a teaching that pointed—rather obliquely—to the possibility that God was present in all of creation. "Everything is God," she explained. Thus, if you do "what you can" for people, that is creating, too, and you are an extension of God. Asked how this belief influenced her life, she told the following story.

> One time I was out walking with my daughter. It was a spring day and everything was beautiful. So I said to her, "You know, ever since time began, people would make a circle as a symbol of eternity and then they would stand in the middle and look at the sun and worship it."

She said this, she explained, not to bring glory to God—which she regards as a strange idea—but just to appreciate nature.

Of the people we talked to, Doug Hill had the most to say about stewardship. He is interested in the topic and thinks it is important. But even his comments show how many ideas come together around this concept and how hard it is to know what to do with these ideas. He says the main idea is to "be responsible with what God has entrusted to you." For him, this means being responsible with his time and his money. But he says he is seldom able to make decisions on the basis of what he regards as responsibility because he is constantly juggling the opinions of his family, his friends, his boss, and others he knows. So, he admits, "it's frustrating." About all he can do is "be careful and wise." He also gives money regularly to his church. Even that causes him trouble because he can never decide exactly how much he should be giving. But it does make him feel better to give. In a "helter-skelter" world, as he puts it, being able to "honor the Lord" in a small way reassures him that he is at least doing something right.

Financial Responsibility

The idea that one can be a faithful steward by using one's talents wisely may be so bland that it means very little. But religious leaders have also tried to concretize this teaching by applying it to the ways in which people handle their money. There is a long tradition of religious thought about the importance of budgeting money and making careful decisions about expenditures.

Most Americans claim they have a budget of some kind: in the survey, three out of every four persons did. But whether these budgets serve much of a purpose is another matter. Most people, it appears, do not have budgets that actually tell them very precisely how to spend their money. In the survey, 48 percent said they had a budget that "provides general guidelines," and 19 percent said they had a budget but "don't follow it very closely," while only 9 percent said they "follow a strict, itemized budget." Harold Bentley, the banker we met in the last chapter, is fairly typical in this respect. He says he and his wife have never really sat down and made out an actual budget. But things have been tight enough over the years that they have just gotten in the habit of not buying "frivolous" things. That, to him, is what a budget means.

Given these overall patterns, it does not appear that religious teachings about the importance of budgeting have had a very significant impact on the American public. Nevertheless, there is evidence that they have made some difference. Among persons who say they have thought a great deal about what the Bible teaches about money, for example, the proportion who follow a strict itemized budget rises to 15 percent, whereas among those who have not thought about these teachings, it sinks to only 7 percent. But if religious commitment has little impact on budgets themselves, it may influence family finances indirectly.

Doug and Linda Hill illustrate how thinking about biblical teachings concerning money can influence the family budgeting process.

Doug explains that the budget itself doesn't actually amount to much because most of their expenditures are fixed. The purpose of the budget, he says, is "really just to meet the bills we have." To do this, he and Linda try to be frugal. For example, in setting their air conditioner in the summer, they find the temperature at which it gets so hot they just can't stand it and then "back it off one degree." They don't have enough money to make investments. But Doug does have "a saving thing at work" that takes some money out of his paycheck each month. Biblical teachings come in mainly in helping them keep their sanity while they struggle to pay their bills. Rather than fighting about them, they've tried to use the bill-paying process as a time of drawing closer together as a couple. Doug, for example, says Linda is much more artistic than he is, and he's come to appreciate her spontaneity and creativity more as a result of working with her on family finances. Their faith, then, has done less to tell them specifically *how* to budget their money than to undergird their marriage so they can work together better in making financial decisions. Again, we see faith functioning as a kind of therapy.

Whether or not the application of religious teachings actually helps people to use their money wisely is a more difficult question to answer. The reason is that people differ in what they think constitutes a wise use of money. To some, prudence requires extreme caution in making purchases. For others, a wise use of money may entail a greater sense of spontaneity. Sermons and inspirational books can probably be found arguing for both these approaches. On balance, though, religious teachings have probably argued more for discipline and rational thinking in the spending of money than anything else. The good steward buys things that are practical, thinks about their use value, and makes sure to get good quality for the money.

Table 5.6 shows the responses to a variety of questions of persons who said the idea of stewardship was very meaningful, fairly meaningful, or not very meaningful. If religious teachings about stewardship encourage people to be more financially responsible, we would expect to see differences on most of these items. Indeed, this is the case. Gift giving provides one interesting indication, because the labor force as a whole is relatively divided in terms of giving practical gifts rather than ones that may be just for fun: 34 percent say a preference for practical gifts describes their own behavior very well, 38 percent say it describes them fairly well, and 26 percent say it does not describe them

TABLE 5.6

Financial Responsibility

	Responses of Persons Who Said Stewardship Was		
	Very Meaningful	*Fairly Meaningful*	*Not Very Meaningful*
I prefer to give gifts that are practical, rather than just for fun	41	35	27
I'd rather give something I made than something I bought	26	21	18
I prefer not to loan money to relatives or friends	33	30	26
To have a lot more money . . . willing to get more education	42	36	31
In buying a new car . . . would think a lot about will it get good mileage	81	77	73
Think a lot about how having a car fits my basic values	49	44	34

very well. Among those who say stewardship is a very meaningful concept, the proportion who give practical gifts rises to 41 percent, whereas among those for whom stewardship is not a meaningful idea, it falls to 27 percent. The former are also somewhat more likely than the latter to prefer giving homemade gifts rather than something they've bought, although the differences are not great.

Doug Hill illustrates how someone who tries to be a good steward applies the concept of stewardship to gift giving. "I never know what to get people," he says. "I don't want to spend too much, and yet I want to get them something that is meaningful." He says he generally tries to find something that will be useful. Until recently, he thought flowers were a waste of money because they just wilted and died. But now he wonders if flowers can also be considered useful because they "can hold good memories." His interest in stewardship does not connect directly to these reflections. Instead, he thinks of himself as a practical person and is reinforced in this belief by his understanding of stewardship, but then he receives so many different signals from the culture about what it means to be practical that he is unsure how to behave.

With such a maxim as "neither a borrower nor a lender be" in the popular religious culture, it is interesting to observe that those who are more oriented toward the idea of stewardship are also more likely to say they prefer not to loan money to relatives or friends. The fact that they are more willing to contemplate getting more education as a way of earning more money suggests that stewardship may still be associated with the idea of trying to invest one's talents in a profitable way.

If they were considering buying a new automobile, people who say stewardship is very meaningful would also differ from other people to some extent in the considerations they deem important. While most Americans say good mileage would be an important consideration, the likelihood of doing so is even higher when stewardship is very meaningful. So is thinking how having an automobile fits with one's basic values, and even whether having one at all is consistent with the environment (not shown in the table).[37]

Applying the idea of stewardship to one's life may also increase people's confidence that they are spending their money wisely. The data show, for example, that a quarter of those who say stewardship is very meaningful give themselves an A for the way they handle their money (another 44 percent, a B), whereas only one in seven do so among those for whom stewardship is not very meaningful. Though the percentages are small, it may also be worth noting that stewardship can set up a standard that some people find impossible to attain: 3 percent give themselves an F (compared with 1 percent of those who say stewardship is not meaningful).

These results may help us to understand why faith so often seems to play a therapeutic role, helping us to feel better, rather than greatly influencing how we actually behave. Stewardship is no longer a very meaningful idea, but to the extent that it does have meaning it encourages us to be more cautious and practical in how we think about money. Echoes of the Puritans and Benjamin Franklin are still present. In today's world, however, we often do not know for sure what it means to be cautious and practical. We receive mixed messages, for example, about the kinds of gifts we should give and whether or not we should loan money to our friends. We are left feeling anxious—especially when other norms tell us never to discuss our finances with anyone else. So feeling that God cares about us, praying, and believing we are somehow guided by our spiritual concerns helps us to feel better.

Compartmentalization

Money has come to be the domain of financial advisers, bankers, investment brokers, and economists. But religious teachings have always regarded money as a matter of the heart. Avoiding greed, not worrying about money, and yet being good stewards in the use of one's money have always been central tenets of religious tradition.

The evidence we have considered in this chapter suggests that these teachings have become problematic in contemporary society. On the one hand, many people give lip service to the notion that greed is a sin or that stewardship is a somewhat meaningful concept. On the other hand, many people seem not to understand these ideas very well, turning them into bland statements about personal responsibility, rather than religious teachings that actually make a difference in how they lead their lives. Those who are actively involved in religious communities generally understand these ideas better than the rest of the population, but even among this group, many seem to be little exposed to, and little influenced by, teachings that draw strong applications for the handling of money.

Noting the prevalence of greed in American society, some observers suggest that religious convictions are either ineffective or downright hypocritical. Barbara Ehrenreich, for example, writes that "our traditional values have always been bigotry, greed, and belligerence, buttressed by wanton appeals to a God of love."[38] Her opinion is overly cynical. Yet a sober-minded assessment would also ask whether religious faith has done more—at least by default—to encourage the pursuit of wealth than to deter it. Certainly it is valuable to keep the idea alive that greed is wrong. But if this idea does little to influence behavior, then religious leaders who articulate it may be doing little more than giving tacit assent to the status quo.

Religious commitment in contemporary society appears to have little effect on the levels of financial responsibility that people shoulder.

The simple life advocated by St. Francis, Thomas Merton, Richard Foster, Mother Teresa, and others is beyond consideration, even for the most religiously oriented. Indeed, religious commitments themselves encourage people to take on financial responsibilities, such as providing good educations for their children or investing money for old age. Nor do the religiously committed regard money, or those who have a lot of it, very differently from other people. Attendance at religious services produces little effect. Protestants and Catholics basically hold the same views on these matters. Even the differences between religious conservatives and religious liberals are relatively small.

There does, however, appear to be some lingering effect of the ascetic religious orientation that reinforced a more rational spirit in the handling of money during the industrial epoch. Although the doctrine of stewardship holds little meaning for many people, those who consider it particularly significant in their lives tend to be more practical and careful in their financial dealings than most other people. They are somewhat more budget-conscious, practical in the gifts they buy, cautious about lending money, and pragmatic in their purchases.

The therapeutic orientation we observed in discussing work is also evident in orientations toward money. If religious commitment does not deter people from wanting money, at least it helps them worry less about whether they have it or not. Part of the reason is that money is relativized: even if it is important, it may not be as important as meditating or thinking about God, and religious attachments help anchor a lifestyle that deters people from making the adjustments that would actually be required to pursue wealth. Many people also pray about financial concerns, testifying that prayer gives them peace of mind. Most of this therapeutic activity occurs in private, in what has been called the devotional aspect of personal religious commitment, because formal participation in religious congregations still encourages a taboo against actually discussing monetary matters. Only participation in small, intimate fellowship groups seems to break through this taboo.

If a single word had to be used to describe the relationship between religion and money, however, it would be compartmentalization. Even though financial responsibility and a therapeutic orientation are both part of contemporary religion, most people seem not to differ very much from their counterparts, whether or not they are religiously oriented. There is a kind of mental or emotional gloss to contemporary religious teachings about money that prevents them from having much impact on how people actually lead their lives. Prayer, for example, seldom leads people to buy one brand of automobile rather than another. It just makes them feel better about their purchase after the fact. Stewardship encourages people to think of themselves as responsible persons in the handling of their money, but it also says little about what responsibility actually means. Although many people claim to think about the connections between their faith and their money, something seems to encourage them to draw a fairly sharp distinction between these two realms. In the next chapter we will try to probe more deeply into the nature of this distinction.

The practical implications of what we have learned depend greatly on the perspectives and needs of different individuals. For many of us, compartmentalization is probably the most comfortable way of dealing with the relationship between our faith and our finances. Keeping the two apart is expedient. We can fall back on familiar habits—which may be ethically sound—rather than having to think about every decision anew. But for those who want their spirituality to inform their lives more deeply, it is evident they must work hard to unite their faith with the monetary dimension of their lives. Otherwise, it is easier to be a fan of spirituality than a follower.

A tennis player we talked to provided a vivid description of the difference between fans and followers:

> I used to think I was a follower of Bjorn Borg because I thought he was the greatest, but I realized I was just a fan because I didn't really work at my game and didn't try to develop a two-handed backhand or anything.

Most people, this man believes, find it easier to be fans of their faith as well. For instance, he finds himself saying "Go Christ go, yea for Christianity." "But when it comes to paying the price," he says, "forget it. It's too hard to go the extra mile."

It is unlikely, given the complexity of our lives, that simple formulas can be found for the ways in which we should spend our money or think about what it means to be stewards. But the absence of simple answers does not mean there are no answers at all. We must spend more time thinking about the issues. And we must do so not in the extreme privacy of our hearts but with the help of others—our friends and families, the people in our congregations, and our clergy. Taking charge of our own lives requires us to do this. As we look to the future of our nation, we cannot let ourselves be guided only by the near-sighted wisdom of Madison Avenue. We must also be instructed by the ancient wisdom contained in our religious traditions.

Chapter Six

The Meaning of Materialism

Warren Means attended Catholic elementary and secondary schools, graduated from college in economics, and served four years in the air force. By age twenty-eight, he had worked his way up to controller of a small aeronautics firm but then decided it was time to move on. After two years earning an M.B.A. at Harvard, he took a position at one of the nation's largest banks, eventually enlarging his responsibilities until he had oversight of approximately $1.2 billion in loans. Then, realizing he had risen as far as he could, he quit and with a few other investors bought a small air transport business that specializes in international freight. Ten years later, following some internal financial structuring that left him a wealthy man, Means has built the firm into an operation that handles about $40 million in sales annually. It's been a long time since he's been to church, although he still considers himself a Catholic. He's been busy. But he's also a bit miffed at the church. It taught him that money was the root of all evil and to think badly of the money changers in the temple. He was never quite able to reconcile those views with being a banker. "I guess I must have been a very bad person!" he says facetiously. He dislikes materialism as much as the next person, but he figures the best way to reconcile religion and the material world is by keeping them apart. "Money," he says, "is a technical matter. If you tried to follow the Bible, you'd never get anywhere!"

Growing up in a Beverly Hills mansion, Karen Kelsey learned early that it's nice to be wealthy. She rode horses, bought expensive clothes, and traveled. She was also given a fine education, graduating from one of the most elite universities in the country. After college she landed a policy job in Washington, D.C. Her plan was to attend Harvard Law School and then take a job on Wall Street. Along the way, though, the road to power began to lead away from her values. For as long as she could remember, the Jewish faith had taught her the importance of being ethical, honest, compassionate, loyal to her family, and responsive to the needs of others. She didn't see much of this on Capitol Hill. Indeed, the congressman she worked for was doing things she knew were plainly illegal. When she threatened to blow the whistle, he blackballed her. During college, she had also read a lot about Christianity and Buddhism. She felt that *how* you lived your life was more important than *how much* you accumulated. Becoming increasingly disillusioned with politics, Karen Kelsey toyed seriously with the idea of becoming a clinical social worker. She had a decision to make.

Gene Atwood has been practicing law for five years. He grew up in a middle-class neighborhood in southern California, went to public school, and graduated from one of the state universities. His law degree and M.B.A. are from UCLA. Specializing in corporate law, he now earns more in a year than his father did in five. Gene's parents were faithful Episcopalians who took him to church regularly as a child. Looking back, he feels they were sincere but restricted their faith pretty much to Sundays. He wants his own faith to do more than that. He feels he has to work at it to keep his priorities straight. Now a member of a Presbyterian church, he attends the adult Sunday school and participates in a men's fellowship group. The issue he's struggling with the most is materialism. His firm seems to give top priority to making a profit. Most of its clients are corporations that have the same goal. Gene isn't sure if he can be comfortable in this environment much longer. More generally, he worries that materialism is corrupting our society. "Nordstrom [department store] isn't real life," he observes. He's glad some of the excesses of the 1980s seem to be over. But he also feels children are exposed to too much materialism at too early an age. People need to think about deeper values in life, he says. "What do we really put our faith in," he asks, "materialism or God?"

Materialism has in fact become a topic of growing concern in recent years. Analysts of American culture suggest that we are increasingly preoccupied with how much or how little we earn, with shopping, with having the newest electronic gadgets at our fingertips, with buying designer sneakers, with wearing the latest fashions, with buying luxury automobiles, and with creating an ambience of material ease in our homes. Religious leaders charge, as Gene Atwood does, that many Americans put their faith in materialism rather than God. Pollsters accuse teenagers and college students of being particularly materialistic. Retailers hope they are. Other people, Karen Kelsey being one, worry that materialism may be corrupting our deepest values. Judging from opinion polls, we note that virtually everyone perceives materialism to be a social problem. And the vast majority believe our society would be better off if there was less emphasis on money and material things.

But there is clearly an irony here—perhaps a number of ironies. The American public voices concern about the reign of materialism in our society while wandering the corridors of the mall. Somehow we have been able to convince ourselves that materialism is bad for our collective health, but we proceed in our individual lives as if nothing mattered more than a fat wallet, especially one made of expensive leather. The religious leaders who fret about materialism eclipsing the faith would seem to have ample backing. At least church attendance and belief in God would suggest that religious allegiances run high. But somehow this level of religious intensity, replete with teachings about the trade-off between God and Mammon, has been unable to curb the national obsession with material goods. Indeed a number of prominent religious leaders have themselves become subject to charges of materialism and greed.

When people raise concerns about materialism, therefore, we need to suck in our breath, forgo the temptation to join the deploring, and ask ourselves what can possibly be happening. How can a culture as thoroughly materialistic as ours generate such sweeping condemnations of this very materialism? Given the prevalence of such concerns, why don't they influence our behavior any more than they do? And if religion is a source of these sentiments, how is it possible for us to be as religious as we are and still pursue the forbidden fruits of the marketplace with such abandon? In short, we need to concentrate on the *meaning* of materialism.

One perspective on materialism is provided by Karl Marx. He and his disciples declared that materialism is simply an inescapable feature of capitalistic societies. Turning Hegelian idealism on its head, Marxist theory asserts that ideas, including religious beliefs, are at root reflections of the relations of human beings to the means of production and of the asymmetric relations that exist between those who own the means of production and those who do not. Dialectical materialism thus provides a way of understanding the power struggles, ideologies, and evolution of modern societies. A sympathetic reading of Marx suggests that materialism has a more decisive influence on our beliefs and values than we are even able to realize. In this view, American society could indeed be thoroughly materialistic and yet generate an antimaterialistic ideology as a form of false consciousness that prevents us from seeing ourselves as we truly are.[1]

But it is clear that Warren Means does not have Marx in mind when he denies being materialistic while arguing that it is OK to be devoted to the pursuit of money and material goods, nor does Gene Atwood as he worries about the conflict between materialism and God. In American culture, materialism generally means much less than it does in Marxist theory, if only because there is seldom a full-blown theory of society or of human nature that goes with it. At the same time, materialism also means much more in American culture than it does in Marxist theory. Why it does is what we consider in this chapter.

My argument is that materialism is a category that carries deep meaning in American culture and that this meaning depends in large measure on the distinctions we draw between the material realm of life more generally and other parts of our lives. These distinctions set materialism apart in our thinking and shape our attitudes toward it.[2] To understand how we can hold such seemingly contradictory—if not outright hypocritical—attitudes toward materialism, therefore, we need to consider its deeper symbolic meanings.[3]

The main question I want to consider is what do we set the material realm—and thus our understandings of materialism—apart from? In referring to Marx and Hegel, for example, I have already noted how materialism may contrast with idealism. In this sense, materialism connotes something solid, physical, and tangible, while idealism suggests something more ephemeral, invisible, and intangible. Materialism in popular usage can also imply a crass, grasping, or greedy orientation, which contrasts with perhaps a more thoughtful, sophisticated, temperate, or balanced outlook on life. These and other meanings are all associated with materialism in our culture. And yet, for present purposes, the one that is of greatest interest is suggested by Gene Atwood: the contrast between materialism and God, or between materialism and spirituality, faith, or religion.

In considering the relationships between money and faith, we have already touched on the present topic. But here, I want to go beyond a consideration of money, asking more broadly what materialism means in American culture and how this meaning is shaped by our understandings of religion. The presence of widely held religious commitments and of deeply engaging material commitments in our society suggests the importance of this question. Addressing it will give us an opportunity to consider more fully how the prevalence of religion in contemporary American culture may influence our understandings of materialism. But as with any pair of concepts, there is a reciprocal effect as well: considering the meanings of materialism will also give us a way to understand the role of religion in postindustrial America. Indeed, it will provide a somewhat different perspective from conventional understandings that draw contrasts between the sacred and the profane or between religious commitment and secularity.[4]

There is another reason, too, for being interested in the relationship between the material and the spiritual. American culture—perhaps any culture—is built on a foundation of paradox. The paradox of intense individualism being present in the same settings as a deeply altruistic spirit, for example, is one.[5] The simultaneous presence of spirituality and materialism in our society is clearly another. If, as most observers agree, America is pervaded from end to end with an interest in spirituality and yet is also pervaded with materialism, how is this possible? How can a single culture hold together these basic commitments, which many people even today regard as inherently incompatible?

We are able to hold together such incompatible commitments, some readers will undoubtedly argue, because Americans are fundamentally hypocritical. Look at your favorite villain from the world of religious television: isn't that person just pretending to be spiritual in order to rake in millions of dollars and live in a mansion? Or to go back to Murial Johnson's comment in Chapter 5, aren't most church services just pretenses for a fashion show? Indeed, hasn't American religion championed a "gospel of wealth" that promotes the pursuit of riches, despite its frequent protestations of being concerned about the poor and the downtrodden?

I want to be clear at the outset that the question being raised is not one of sincerity. To reduce the question of spirituality and materialism to one of sincerity is to put it on grounds that lead nowhere. It may be interesting to judge people around us (especially those claiming to be devout) as hypocrites, but what does that accomplish?[6] Our purpose is rather to gain a better understanding of how American culture is put together. The point is not whether it is "OK" for the society to be vastly interested in spirituality and deeply committed to materialism at the same time but that this is the way things actually are. Taking that fact as a starting point allows us to learn how these two relate to each other, and, thus, how the meaning of each is shaped by the other.

The Spiritual and the Material

The place to begin is to recognize that the distinction between the spiritual and the material is a fundamental characteristic of Western civilization. This is a broader distinction than the one we might have in mind when we say that someone is materialistic and someone else is devoted to spirituality. But it is the broader distinction on which these narrower assertions ultimately depend. Hebrew writings draw the distinction between two realms sharply in the oppositions portrayed between God, or service to God, and characteristics of the temporal world. In the story of the fall of Adam and Eve, for example, Eden represents a kind of spiritual state in which direct communion with God is possible, work is unnecessary, and death absent, whereas the world outside of Eden is characterized by distance from God and the necessity of work. Other Hebrew writings, such as the story of the golden calf or of the angel's visit to Sodom, draw the contrast with even greater clarity. In classical Greek thought a similar distinction is present, especially in the view that the spiritual realm embodies purity, truth, beauty, and symmetry, and that the material realm is at best an imperfect approximation of the spiritual. Christianity also carried forward the basic distinction between spirituality and the material, especially in Jesus' teachings about serving God and Mammon or rendering unto Caesar what was his and unto God what was God's.[7]

Our society has been the beneficiary of this legacy. Throughout most of its history, American culture has also incorporated the basic distinction between spirituality and the material realm. Countless homilies and sermons have warned believers of placing their trust in material possessions rather than God. Theologies recognizing God as creator of the material world, still recognized by a majority of the American population, explicitly distinguish the two realms.[8] A separate clergy, set apart perhaps by dress, celibacy, and a vow of poverty to do God's work, has itself provided a tangible contrast between the spiritual and the material realms. And despite widespread discussion of changing clergy roles, a substantial minority of the population still believes the clergy are doing God's work more than anyone else (a belief that is considerably higher among Catholics, incidentally, than among Protestants).[9]

The contrast between spirituality and the material realm was perhaps easiest to sustain when society itself was organized largely into separate domains. Jesus' recipe rendering different offerings to God and to Caesar implies such a separation of domains. Medieval dualism separating the supernatural from the natural was to some extent reinforced by the church's organization as an entity separate from (if not unrelated to) the temporal powers of princes and merchant elites. The same dualism was often evident in mercantilist societies as well. Here, materialism could still be defined largely in terms of money itself and the possession of money or being involved in monetary transactions. Charges of usury, or of exacting excessive profits from one's trade (as in the case of Robert Keayne), were the clearest examples of a distinction being reinforced between fundamentally incommensurable realms.

The advent of industrial society raised new questions about the material realm but also provided a means of maintaining the distinction between it and spirituality. In addition to monetary transactions, machinery now became the primary symbol of materialism. When concerns were expressed about materialism, they were thus fears about the rape of the natural environment by mills, slag heaps, and railways, and about the demoralizing effects of workers being drawn away from the land and into the factories. If materialism was more difficult to exclude from everyday life, it nevertheless was kept in place by the logic of strict scheduling that went hand in hand with industrialization. The rational budgeting of time that would prove so effective in factories of the nineteenth century was already at work among eighteenth-century figures such as Benjamin Franklin, helping them to compartmentalize the time they spent producing material wealth from the time they spent reading, thinking about God, and otherwise cultivating their spiritual life. Indeed, industrialization itself was based on the premise that everything could be organized rationally, thereby minimizing its socially disruptive consequences. Military units, prison cells, academic disciplines, and above all the organization of work itself were all symptomatic of this premise. The location of mills at one end of town made room for a domestic culture to develop at the other. Smoke-stacks signaled that the real activity of the factories was in the furnaces situated at their base. Church steeples signaled that the real activity was in the heavens to which parishioners and clergy lifted their voices on Sunday mornings.

In the past half-century the transition from industrial to postindustrial society has again impinged dramatically on the distinction between the material and the spiritual. Most important is the shift from production to consumption. In industrial society the average worker came against the leading edge of material expansion primarily in the workplace itself—as a producer. The rawest effects of the material realm could thus be cordoned off by protecting the home, by keeping women and children out of the labor market, by limiting the work week, by creating parks, and by encouraging people to have family devotions in the evening or to attend church and Sunday school on weekends. In postindustrial society the meaning of materialism has moved decidedly from production to consumption. When people complain about materialism, they are registering concern primarily about the lure of advertising, the fact that television commercials bring consumer wants into their living rooms, and the fear that the innocence of childhood may be exploited by the advertisers of consumer goods. Consumption cannot be bracketed so easily by the simple arrangement of places or schedules, especially when mass media penetrate private life and public life alike.

For the distinction between spirituality and the material realm to be maintained in postindustrial society, it has thus become necessary for the individual to draw more subtle symbolic boundaries. Rather than materialism being external to private life, it is now more likely to be distinguished from some intangible aspect of personal life. The inner self, for example, may be set off and protected from the distractions created by goods, clothing, and entertainment. We are surrounded, for example, by the clothes we buy, the records we listen to, and the television advertisements we watch, but we draw a distinction between these material goods and our attitudes about who we are and what is really important in life. It may be very difficult for us to draw this distinction in our behavior—for instance, by finding some time, place, or activity that is "really me" and uncontaminated by material goods—so we draw the distinction in our minds.

Materialism also retains its sense of artificiality, connoting goods resulting from the manufacturing process, whereas spirituality may be associated with aspects of life that are more pure, real, or natural. We draw this line in our everyday speech. We say, for example, that the jewelry we wear or the makeup we put on is cosmetic; we complain of products that are cheap or that break easily; we say we want quality and value in our products, implicitly admitting that they generally lack quality and value; and we view advertising cynically and register doubt that its claims are accurate. These orientations suggest that the material world is not truly the real world. We illustrate the same beliefs when we say we want more out of life than just a lot of pretty things. We also talk about the search for depth within ourselves, for breakthroughs in our relationships with others, and for a way of living that is not caught up in the pursuit of material goods. As postindustrial society comes increasingly to provide services as well as goods, and as it depends more heavily on the symbolic manipulation of images, these distinctions, however, become more difficult to sustain. Spirituality may thus be associated with the inner life, with nature, or with an underlying core of reality, but so may be the messages used to sell automobiles, hiking boots, and soft drinks.

Scholarly thought has also contributed to the process of change by advancing a sustained attack on the dualism of spirituality versus the material. The collapse of a two- (or three-) tiered cosmology has been one of the most significant developments.[10] This collapse has blurred the boundaries between the spiritual and the material in the same way that the barrier between nature and culture has been blurred by economic developments in postindustrial society, and it reflects the growing importance of symbol manipulation, image creation, and constructed knowledge in contemporary society. This thinking has clearly had an impact on popular culture as well. A person like Karen Kelsey, who has studied Buddhism, practiced meditation, taken philosophy courses, and received training in psychotherapy, finds herself uncomfortable distinguishing sharply between a spiritual and a material realm. Yet even her thinking continues to be influenced by the fact that such a distinction has been common in American culture. And for other people, as we shall see, the distinction continues to make a great deal of sense.

The barrier separating spirituality from the material world is thus a product of changing social conditions. It exists as part of our cultural heritage, but its meaning varies from one century to another. At present, its meaning is again being reshaped by the growth of postindustrial society. Ours is nevertheless a pluralistic society. People are exposed to different conditions, depending on their work or income. Some may be more at home with material goods because they have wealth or because they work in banking and finance. It is inevitable that such diversity be reinforced by the complex economic circumstances in which we live. Even more so, different family traditions and ethnic subcultures, as well as educational experiences and avocational interests, situate individuals differently with respect to the heritage in which spiritual/material distinctions have been drawn. Some people have been raised to think that the material and the spiritual are quite different, while others have drawn this distinction only implicitly. It is, for this reason, possible for individuals to draw the distinction in different ways and yet participate fully in the paradox of harboring anti-materialistic sentiments in a highly materialistic society.

Careful analysis of both the Economic Values Survey and the qualitative interviews suggests that Americans symbolically differentiate between the spiritual and the material in several distinct ways. Each is rooted in a distinctive style of religious thinking and behavior. The first derives from paying concerted attention to questions of religion and spirituality; the second, more from neglecting such questions; and the third, from emphasizing intuition or feelings in dealing with them. A brief description and an example of each is in order.

The first way of distinguishing the spiritual from the material is most clearly evident in the survey in responses to a question asking people how much they think about the two. When asked how much they had thought about "the differences between spiritual growth and material possessions" in the past year, 39 percent said they had thought about it a fair amount or a great deal. Some perspective on this figure can be obtained by recalling (from Chapter 5) that 31 percent say they think this much about the connection between their religious values and their personal finances, while 29 percent say this about what the Bible teaches about money. Thus a substantial minority of the public draws a conscious distinction between the spiritual and the material. The critical issue is whether or not those who think about the differences are also the ones who think about the connections.

The data show clearly that the two are largely the same people.[11] More generally, thinking about the differences is related to similar (in fact, more) religious experiences and attitudes as is thinking about the connections. Drawing this sort of distinction is strongly associated with attendance at religious services (taking into account other personal characteristics), and once attendance is taken into account, with participation in Sunday school classes and fellowship groups, with thinking about one's relationship with God, with believing the Bible is literally true, and with understanding the concept of stewardship.[12] In other words, the more religiously active a person is (by almost any criterion), the more likely that person is to think about the differences between spirituality and material possessions.

Gene Atwood illustrates this reflective way of drawing the distinction. He has thought a lot about what the Bible teaches, not only on his own but at church and in the men's fellowship group he attends. He tries to read the Bible each week and keeps a journal of his thoughts about his spiritual life. The distinction between spirituality and every other aspect of reality is sharpened by the fact that he experienced a turning point in his life, a time of spiritual awakening that involved a conscious decision to put his faith in Christ and try to be more obedient to Christ's teachings. At the same time, he talks about having a materialistic streak. In contrasting his values with those of his parents, for example, he says he is more religiously oriented, on the one hand, but also more materialistic ("more willing to pay the personal costs to achieve material success"). He isn't sure where this second trait comes from but suggests a different source than his religiosity (perhaps "society" or "some psychological need"). He also senses that the two realms imply different priorities. For instance, his materialistic side wants a new house in the foothills; his spiritual side wants to spend more time helping the needy. The language of priorities is, in fact, one of the ways in which his thinking reinforces the distinction. In talking about money, for example, he says he asks "what would God want me to do?" and assumes the answer would probably be different from what he wants to do.

The second way of distinguishing the spiritual and the material occurs through tacit assent, rather than from sustained reflection. It can be understood best in the survey from the responses to the question about money being different from morals and values. As we saw in Chapter 5, 68 percent of the labor force agrees that "money is one thing, morals and values are completely separate." Thus it is fairly common, one would think, for people to have heard this sentiment expressed, say, by their parents, friends, or in the media. That this sentiment does not depend on thinking about religious issues or participation in religious communities is evident in that it is negatively associated with thinking about one's relationship to God, attendance at religious services, participation in Sunday school classes, and understanding the idea of stewardship, and is unrelated to thinking a lot about the differences between spiritual growth and material possessions. (It is, however, positively associated with believing that the Bible should be taken literally.[13])

Warren Means illustrates this kind of thinking. Recall that he no longer attends religious services but still believes in the basic religious tenets he was taught as a child. He also regards materialism, especially money, as a separate realm, describing it as a technical matter. He chafes at religious teachings that seem to criticize making money, working in finance, or having material possessions. Thus, he compartmentalizes the two realms, arguing that the church should mind its own business and let those who really understand business get on with theirs. To make his point, he refers to the Bible story about Jesus throwing the money changers out of the temple. "The money changer," Means argues, "was nobody other than the foreign exchange trader at the airports today." There was nothing inherently wrong with being a money changer (indeed, they provided a service), unless the exchange rate they charged was unfair. "It's just a commercial transaction, that's all it was." Markets, he asserts, operate according to their own principles; sometimes they are subject to adjustments; but that's all it is; nobody is to blame. And money is just money, something that facilitates trade. "There is no inherent goodness or badness about it." In the process, he affirms the long-standing dualism in Western culture between the spiritual and the material.

The third way of drawing this distinction may be rooted in a more recent phenomenon in American culture, although precedents can be found in nineteenth-century transcendentalism or, centuries earlier, in Gnostic and Manichean writings. This perspective implicitly dissociates the spiritual from the material by contrasting the inner life with the outer world. It does so by conceiving of spirituality as an inner quest, or perhaps as an awakening of some inward potential, generally through introspection and involving an emphasis on emotions and feelings. In the process, materialism comes to be regarded as an externality, or as a more superficial aspect of reality, perhaps even a distraction from the quest for spirituality.

The survey offers ample evidence of this introspective orientation. As we observed in Chapter 4, it manifests itself in the way many people think about ethical issues, especially in the current emphasis on feelings as a guide to what is morally appropriate. It emerges in the responses to a variety of other questions as well. Sixty percent of the labor force agree with the statement, "I need a lot of time to be quiet and reflect on things." Almost as many (58 percent) agree that "getting in touch with your inner feelings is more important than doing well in your job." Nearly half (45 percent) agree that "exploring my inner self is one of my main priorities." Four in ten (43 percent) agree that "working on my emotional life takes priority over other things." Three in four say that paying attention to their feelings is at least "very important" to their basic sense of worth as a person. And one in four say this is "absolutely essential." Thus, on average, about half of the public seems to be very strongly oriented toward the value of their inner emotional life. What is most important for present purposes, however, is that introspective orientations seem to be associated with drawing distinctions in the survey between the spiritual and the material. Indeed, these statements about feelings, emotions, and the inner self are positively associated *both* with thinking about the differences between spiritual growth and material possessions *and* with agreeing that money and values are completely separate.[14]

Karen Kelsey illustrates this introspective way of thinking. She is, as we have seen, quite thoughtful about her life, her values, and her religious beliefs. But she also illustrates the way in which many Americans distinguish between their own spirituality and materialism in the wider society, and how they themselves lead their lives. She believes everyone in the United States is materialistic insofar as they have more than other people, and she says this criticism applies especially to the rich. She denies, however, that she herself is materialistic, asserting that she shares this trait only to the extent that "society allows people to have unequal amounts of material." She hastens to explain that she doesn't go out shopping just to find happiness in the stores.

What is she trying to say? Where one derives happiness is somehow the issue for her. In response to another question, she provides some clarification. This time she asserts plainly that she doesn't think materialism is bad. The reason, she says, is that everything depends on a person's basic sense of selfhood. If that sense comes from having material possessions, then there is a problem. If it doesn't, a person can have all sorts of possessions.

Spirituality to her is not something metaphysical or set fundamentally apart from the material realm. Rather, it is a part of her self, not even an essence but something that "flows into" everything she does. She also talks about it as something in her that she is supposed to share with others. She describes it as the reason people have what they have, or as the beneficial purpose to which they apply their skills. In her own life, she is trying to "grow" spiritually, by which she means coaxing the spiritual part of her out into the open and realizing its potential as fully as possible before she dies. Since it is so wrapped up with her self, she worries about compartmentalizing it. She feels that a split between it and any other part of herself is potentially harmful.

There is, nevertheless, a dualism in her thinking because she regards materialism as a commitment of scarce energy. She explains:

> Becoming a deeper, more ethical, more balanced whole person takes an incredible amount of time commitment and energy. And if your time commitment and energy is going into making money, or maintaining a boat or a house, that's time taken away from other things. And it gets difficult to have spent all your time pursuing money and then somehow expect to have reached some level of whatever people call the pre-death God state.

Different as they are, all three of these perspectives result in a distinction being drawn between the spiritual and the material. Part of the answer to the question of how Americans can be spiritual and materialistic at the same time is thus that we accomplish this feat by engaging in cultural work. We in fact draw a distinction between spirituality and the material realm, placing the two in separate cognitive categories. Virtually everyone with whom we spoke did this. The differences in how people accomplish this task, however, are also of some significance. The nature of the distinction influences how the spiritual and the material can be connected. Having drawn the distinction, we do not simply keep the two categories totally separate. Instead, we let them come together. Our understanding of the one inevitably influences our understanding of the other. How people pray, and the kinds of answers they receive, are in particular a way in which the importance of these differences become evident.

Prayer and Miracles

We saw in Chapter 5 that a substantial number of Americans pray about material things and an even larger number give thanks to God for their material blessings. Prayer is thus an important way of bridging or transcending the gap that most people perceive between the spiritual realm and the material realm. In fact, it can be thought of as a kind of exchange in which an individual sends forth a signal of some kind to God and in return perceives an answer from God, perhaps in the form of peace of mind or perhaps in some material gift itself. But as with all social exchanges, the transaction depends greatly on the kind of relationship thought to exist between the two parties. In the present case, the character of this relationship is heavily contingent on the way in which spirituality is separated from the material realm in the first place.

I want to emphasize that prayer and miracles are not only leftovers from some sacred feast of the past but are very much a part of our daily lives in contemporary society. The reason they continue to be important is not simply because our religious institutions remain powerful in disseminating ideas about prayer and miracles. These ideas are, of course, important. In other societies the decline of religious institutions has progressed to such a point that it may seldom occur to people to pray or to interpret events as miracles. But in our society we do both of these things, and doing so actually makes sense to us because of the way in which we understand the material world. Comparing how different people view prayer and miracles is thus a way of seeing what these connections are.

Let us consider Warren Means. Separating the spiritual from the material as sharply as he does, he finds it difficult to pray at all, especially about finances. His world view makes God into a metaphysical being who exists in an entirely different reality from the present world. That leaves the material world completely to human decisions. A person has to be wise, responsible, ethical, and aware of where to find expert advice. But this extreme separation of the two realms, ironically, also allows for anything out of the ordinary to take on truly miraculous proportions. To illustrate, Means mentions a recent business transaction in which he was about to lose $300,000. Suddenly, something happened, and he wound up breaking even. He describes this as a miracle and suggests that "somebody up there" must have been watching out for him.

Remarks such as this were fairly typical in the interviews with people who drew a sharp but implicit contrast between the spiritual and the material. They believed the material realm was hermetically sealed 99 percent of the time, functioning according to its own laws, and responding in a more or less rational way to the decisions people made in everyday life. But still believing in a distant God of some kind, they also found it useful to resort to this deity to account for the unexplainable. God functioned as the proverbial deus ex machina, intervening on rare occasions in ways that they could describe only as miracles. The rest of the time, God made no demands on the material realm. People were not supposed to cheat and steal or become too greedy, but that was just common sense, part of the natural order of things, not something that required any knowledge of God to understand.

If we compare Gene Atwood with Warren Means, we see a quite different view of prayer, miracles, and God. Consistent with the more thoughtful separation he draws between spirituality and the material realm, Atwood tries to pray regularly about his work and his finances. This effort is required by his sense that the material realm should be subjected to the spiritual realm, but it also gives him a recurrent way in which to emphasize the distinction itself. He, too, has witnessed what he might describe as a miracle, a breakthrough by the spiritual into the material world, but he has a different understanding of miracles than Warren Means does. He recounts the following story:

> When I was in law school, one of the guys' wife was very ill and they had little money. And they had gone from doctor to doctor. As a group we decided we would fast a given day for her and pray at lunch. I recognized in fasting and praying how selfish I was, because that process forced me to give up something as simple as a meal. I realized how reluctant I was to do that for someone else. Unbeknownst to us, when we met at lunch time to talk about and pray for this woman, God had healed her through a faith healer at a church the night before. I attribute her healing to God's hand; it seemed miraculous. But I also look at it as having taught me how selfish I was and what God really desires all of us to be: to grow beyond ourselves and to begin to care for others. I also see that as a miracle.

We will want to come back to part of Gene Atwood's statement later. But certainly this statement is remarkable in the way it portrays miracles. Being healed of a serious illness is miraculous, but in the story itself it is scarcely worth paying much attention to. Judging from other remarks, both from Atwood and from people who talked in similar ways, we can venture two possible explanations for this down-playing of the miraculous healing. One is that people like Atwood have such a rational understanding of the world that they are actually some-what skeptical about the possibilities of genuine ruptures in reality. The other, though somewhat at odds with the first, is that God is also so close at hand (much closer than Warren Means's God) that it is sim-ply less remarkable when some intervention of this kind occurs.

Atwood is also typical in that he appears to struggle a lot more with how to reconcile the spiritual and the material in his own life. When he and his buddies prayed, he did not come away with a vague feeling that everything would be all right. He came away with a kick in the pants. God was trying to send him a message that he needed to behave in a different way. Others described similar experiences. They prayed, but they also struggled with wondering whether they were praying correctly and with what God was trying to teach them.

An emphasis on introspection and feelings presents a third alterna-tive. For Karen Kelsey, miracles do not bring two fundamentally dif-ferent realms together; they merely depend on how a person sees things.

I have trouble with the word miracle because something is only a mir-acle if it wasn't within the realm of possibility and shouldn't have hap-pened. And a miracle is just something that happened that we can't un-derstand or explain or take responsibility for.

Thus, she describes miracles as "a further growth in one's understand-ing of what's possible and a greater perception than one had before."
She gives a simple but telling example:

I was on a Buddhist meditation retreat—it was my first one ever. I had been meditating for about 72 hours, you know, with sleep in the mid-dle, maybe five hours of sleep, but non-stop, no talking. And all of a sudden an image of a man I knew appeared to me and I saw his right pinky glowing red on the knuckle. And I thought, oh, no, there's can-cer on his pinky. And when I got back home, I phoned him and I said, what were you doing at 9 o'clock on Saturday night (which is when this happened). And he said, oh, my father was burning a cancerous mole off my right pinky. He was in Washington, D.C., and I was in western Massachusetts. I just can't even imagine how come that came into my head. I don't think about it as a miracle, but I think of it as potential that's unused and at this point, misunderstood or not understood.

For people like Karen Kelsey, prayer is not so much an act of communication with a separate entity known as God but a message to oneself. It becomes a way of altering one's perspective. Thus, prayer seldom involves "asking for" something material; it is more likely to emphasize a changed attitude toward something material. As she explains, "I don't believe God actually gives us anything material, unless of course you count the planet we live on." A miracle, then, is not so much an intervention of the spiritual into the material realm but a sudden breakthrough in how one perceives reality.[15]

I am suggesting that the distinction between the material and the spiritual is fundamental to the nature of prayer and miracles in our society. This connection becomes evident when we see that people who draw the distinction in certain ways also tend to pray and understand miracles in ways that are consistent with it. It has thus been necessary to emphasize the differences. But there are common features as well, and these features are even more important than the differences. In each of the cases we have considered, prayer and the possibility of miracles helped, in turn, to dramatize the distinction between spirituality and the material world. We might even venture that one of the reasons prayer and miracles remain prominent in our society is that we need ways of dramatizing this distinction. But if so, what might that be? And how might the character of prayer help us to decide?

The most striking feature about all the stories of prayer that we elicited from people in our study was that they emphasized good feelings, thankfulness, and a positive attitude more than anything else. They were never prayers imploring God to heap vengeance on an enemy. Seldom were they petitions requesting God to spare an individual from some terrible event or even petitions seeking better understanding of misfortune or suffering. They nearly always involved some unanticipated stroke of good fortune: an unexpected job opportunity, a check in the mail, a beautiful spring day, peace of mind, and so on. They were the kind of prayers and miracles one would expect in a relatively affluent society such as ours.

Postindustrial society in fact provides unprecedented levels of material comfort for most of its members. A threshold of physical security can at least be counted on most of the time. But postindustrial society also creates uncertainty—indeed, it depends on uncertainty. Efforts to plan, predict, and control make no sense if everything is already utterly certain. They make sense only if the unexpected can still happen. Pharmaceuticals and therapists, for example, provide ways to control emotions. But there would be no need for either if emotions were already completely predictable. Thus an exceptional feeling of serenity remains mysterious, and for many people it may be an occasion for thoughts about miracles. Postindustrial society also generates unexpected outcomes by virtue of the sheer complexity of its institutions. A billion-dollar deal may be the result of hundreds of people having put long hours into preparing reports, but when it takes place it may still seem miraculous to any of the individual participants.

Whether a person distinguishes the material world from a spiritual realm with conscious effort, tacitly, or intuitively, therefore, the distinction becomes a way of leaving our horizons open. Prayer and miracles do this as well. They allow us to say there is more to life than this, the material world does not subsume us. In postindustrial society unanticipated goodness is perhaps the most visible evidence that this is the case. We know that material abundance may be an important reason for these moments of goodness. But we do not want to believe they are the only reason. Having a new Toyota, for example, may help us drive out into the desert to view the sunset. But even if our goal is to sell Toyotas, we must hold to the assumption that the sunset itself was not produced by an automobile company. It may be that some of our antimaterialism itself is rooted in this assumption.

Materialism as a Social Problem

We have already considered some anecdotal evidence suggesting that materialism is viewed negatively in American society. The sense that Americans are too materialistic for their own good could, of course, be nothing more than the perspective of a few social critics. Before proceeding further, it is important, therefore, to establish just how widely materialism is seen as a problem.

When asked straight out what they think, three-quarters of the American labor force says "materialism" is a serious or extremely serious social problem. Just about the same proportion says the same thing about "too much emphasis on money." A better sense of what this figure means can be obtained by considering other social issues that may be so regarded (see Table 6.1). For instance, more of the public registers concern about the condition of the poor or the shape of the nation's schools than they do about materialism. This is probably not surprising, given the amount of media attention such issues have received. But materialism is as widely regarded a social problem as something like the breakdown of families, an issue that has also received widespread coverage. It is somewhat *more* widely perceived as a social concern than "people turning away from God," although the fact that two people out of three regard the latter as a serious social problem is again testimony to the prevalence of certain kinds of religious orientations in the United States.

It is also worth emphasizing that materialism is said to be a serious social problem by *considerably more* people than several other issues that have attracted widespread attention in the scholarly, self-help, and therapeutic literatures. Individualism has been attacked repeatedly in these literatures, and yet, the fact that fewer than one person in two regards it as a serious problem suggests that many Americans continue to regard individualism as a virtue rather than a vice. Best-selling books about self-expression, personal growth, and problems of "co-dependency" and other dysfunctions have counseled people to pay more attention to their feelings, rather than closing down on their emotional life. But the data suggest that a majority of working people either believe they are already paying enough attention to their feelings or that not doing so ranks low in the scale of social woes. Despite evidence that many Americans are working harder than ever before, there also does not seem to be widespread concern that overwork is itself a serious problem. In all these comparisons, materialism looms as an issue of importance.

Qualitative information gives a clearer sense of why people believe materialism is a problem. We saw earlier that Gene Atwood believes materialism diverts time and energy from higher values. Karen Kelsey associates materialism with an unfulfilled (and unfulfillable) longing for security, recalling from her own childhood that "we had all this nice silver and jewelry, just endless amounts of material things; but I grew up in terror that the next day we would be out on the street." Murial Johnson, whom we met in Chapter 5, living amid poverty all her life, associates materialism with middle- and upper-class indifference: "If people weren't so worried about having a yacht, so many cars, or this brand of a car, then maybe they would worry more about

TABLE 6.1

Perceptions of Social Problems

Question: "How serious a problem do you think each of the following is in our society—extremely serious, serious, a small problem, or not a problem?" (Percent responding "extremely serious" or "serious")

	Total Labor Force
The condition of the poor	92
Problems in our schools	92
The breakdown of families	91
Political corruption	88
Corruption in business	84
Selfishness	81
The breakdown of community	76
Too much emphasis on money	75
Materialism	74
People turning away from God	68
Individualism	45
People not being in touch with their feelings	45
People working too hard	35

other people having something." Bible-church members Doug and Linda Hill are especially concerned about the effects of materialism on children. They feel television advertising is stripping children of their respect for parents and encouraging them to want things before they are ready for them.

Some of these opinions are shared widely. Asked simply whether they agreed or disagreed with the statement "our society is much too materialistic," 89 percent in the Economic Values Survey said they agreed. Ninety percent agreed that "children today want too many material things." Seventy-five percent agreed that "advertising is corrupting our basic values." On a different question asking "if there was less emphasis on money," 23 percent said the society would be "a lot better off," another 47 percent said it would be "somewhat better off," while 20 percent said it would be "no better off and no worse off," and only 4 percent said it would be "worse off."

Dualism and Materialism

Earlier in the chapter we were considering the differences between the spiritual and the material realms. In the last section I shifted specifically to the question of material*ism*. There is a connection between the two, as I have suggested, but the one does not necessarily imply the other. "Material" can refer to the physical world or to nature, while materialism conjures up images of yachts, new cars, and television commercials. So what is the connection?

The connection is perhaps so straightforward as to seem uninteresting, but it is nevertheless worth emphasizing because it shows both the overall importance of religion in American culture and the significance of variations in religious understandings. In simplest terms, spiritual/material dualism is the cultural precondition from which negative evaluations of materialism arise. Without this prior dualism, we would have no way of arguing that anything might be fundamentally wrong with an emphasis on money and material possessions. Seeing a yacht would simply make us admire the craftsmanship that went into constructing it or the wealth its possession symbolized. Only by having a sense that there is some other reality, an order of being that transcends the material world, is it possible to adopt an alternative perspective. Certainly it would still be possible, say, to criticize the yacht in terms of another yacht (that went faster) or a material alternative (a Ferrari). But deeper, far-reaching criticisms would be out of the question. It would be impossible to say, as Gene Atwood does, that "Nordstrom is not reality" without having some notion that a different reality existed. It would be equally improbable for someone to charge advertising with corrupting our values unless he or she had a sense that values came from somewhere else in the first place.

We have already seen that the distinction between the spiritual and the material can be constructed in a variety of ways. Were we to adopt a broader horizon, we would need to consider surrogate meanings of the term *spiritual* as well. Hegel's idealism would need to be pitted against Marx's conception of the material world. Marx's own dialectic vision of society, in fact, poses a kind of spiritual alternative (the classless, stateless society of the future) to the present vale of woe (although Marx certainly would not have called it a "spiritual" alternative). In American society, both of these alternatives might be present in some sectors of the population: an idealistic disdain for the material world among intellectuals, or a political critique of capitalist society rooted in alternative conceptions of economic justice. But American culture is especially indebted to its *religious* heritage for the capacity to distinguish the spiritual from the material. Whether it is a fairly orthodox rendition of the tradition (such as Gene Atwood's), a decidedly secularized version (Warren Means's), or a more introspective alternative (Karen Kelsey's), religious tradition supplies a valued conception of the spiritual that can serve as a conceptual alternative to a more negatively evaluated image of materialism.

A rough approximation of this claim can be seen in the evidence presented in Table 6.2. If religious tradition is in fact a source of negative sentiments toward materialism, we would expect those who value religion more highly to more often regard materialism as a serious

TABLE 6.2

Materialism as a Social Problem

Percent identifying each as "extremely serious" or "serious":

	Among Persons Who Said Religion Was Personally:		
	Very Important	*Fairly Important*	*Not Very Important*
Materialism			
Extremely serious	35	24	22
Serious	48	48	41
Either	83	72	63
Too much emphasis on money			
Extremely serious	36	26	19
Serious	48	47	43
Either	84	73	62

social problem. Judging from the table, we see that they do. They are also more likely to say "too much emphasis on money" is a serious social problem. It may, of course, be that these relationships are spurious, resulting from differences in gender, level of education, or social class between the more and the less religious. A detailed statistical analysis of the data, however, reveals that these results hold up when other factors are taken into account and when different measures of religious commitment and concern about materialism are examined. Thus, taking account of gender, age, education, working full- or part-time, and family income, we note that frequency of attendance at religious services is also positively associated with regarding materialism and too much emphasis on money as serious social problems, with saying that less emphasis on money would make the society a lot better, with agreeing that the society is too materialistic, and with agreeing that advertising is corrupting basic values and that children want too many material things.[16]

Yet critics would point out that none of this bears directly on the issue. Does the dualistic separation of the spiritual from the material itself encourage a negative orientation toward materialism? Contrary to the arguments that have been presented for why it should, a reasonable case could be made for precisely the opposite. If people put the material realm in a different category from spirituality (or other values), then surely they could believe that nothing was inherently wrong with materialism. Warren Means's view that money is just a technical matter would be a case in point. It is thus an empirical question as to whether distinguishing the spiritual from the material actually undergirds negative sentiments toward materialism.

The best evidence we can extract from the survey data indicates clearly that drawing this distinction *is* associated with regarding materialism negatively. Having found that religious attendance made a difference, we included this factor, along with all the other background characteristics, just to make sure what was happening wasn't a result of a more generic form of religious commitment. We then added the question about how much people had thought about the differences between spiritual growth and material possessions. In every case (seven questions), there was a significant relationship between having thought more about this difference and expressing negative sentiments about materialism. Having seen how a religiously committed person like Gene Atwood (or even a thoughtful person like Karen Kelsey) viewed materialism, we found that these findings seemed to make sense. But we were also interested in the other kind of separation evident in people like Warren Means. Following the same procedures, we thus used the question about money being one thing and morals and values being completely separate. This question had the added advantage of not being associated with measures of religious commitment at all: those who were not religiously oriented were just as likely to agree with it as those who were. This statement also predicted negative sentiments toward materialism (even more strongly than the other statement).[17] It is, of course, not an inevitable logical deduction that distinguishing the spiritual and the material should lead to a negative view of materialism. But this is why research evidence is needed. Such evidence indicates that people who draw this distinction are indeed more inclined to view materialism negatively.

What Is It About Materialism?

In some of the comments quoted earlier, we saw that materialism could be disliked for a variety of reasons. We can understand its relation to the distinction between spirituality and the material realm a little better if we consider its meanings more closely. Materialism, after all, is a very broad concept, and this is probably why it is so widely regarded as a social problem. Some people think of their childhood insecurities; others see rich people cold-heartedly sailing their yachts; others see children being corrupted by television commercials.

Putting it differently, we can say that materialism is a symbol. It stands for something else, just as a valentine card or a bouquet of red roses stands for something else. To be precise: materialism is a generalized symbol that stands for evil in our culture. In a society that has largely ceased to personify evil in some tangible being (Satan), materialism has become the devil. Sensing that something is wrong with society, people easily point their finger at materialism.[18] And there is a connection with how they pray and think about miracles as well. The positive good fortune that characterizes prayer in our society has the clear disadvantage of paying too little attention to evil. Yet evil is absent from no society, not even ours. Having banished it from our prayers, we have, so to speak, had to reinvent it. Materialism has become our way of talking about evil.

The value of having a generalized symbol of evil is that it can be blamed for virtually any problem that happens to be of interest. "The devil made me do it" is the same logic that can be applied to, say, blaming the national debt on materialism, or the drug problem, or lax performance among high school graduates on their SATs (none of which is to say that materialism may not *in fact* be part of the problem). Thus, in the survey, people who registered more concern about families, political corruption, schools, and just about all the problems shown in Table 6.1 were also more likely to say the society was too materialistic and would be better off with less emphasis on money.[19]

But if materialism serves as a catchall for speaking about social ills, what does this have to do with religion or spirituality? Does materialism have any special meaning that might put it directly in conflict with spirituality? One way of answering these questions is to look more closely at the relationships between perceptions of materialism as a social problem and perceptions of other kinds of problems. We might suppose that perceiving the condition of the poor as a social problem would be associated quite strongly with perceiving materialism as a problem because both have to do with money and its distribution. Given what we now know about the importance of separating the spiritual from the material, we might also suppose that "people turning away from God" would be a problem closely associated in the survey with negative perceptions of materialism. In contrast, something like "the breakdown of community" might be of concern to a rather different sort of person than would care about materialism. In short, examining the statistical relations among various kinds of perceived social problems provides a way of understanding the meanings associated with it.

Doing this yields a strikingly clear result, although one that is probably easier to understand after the fact than to have anticipated. When all the social problems listed in Table 6.1 were examined jointly to determine which ones best predicted responses to the statements about materialism and about too much emphasis on money, quite a few of those statements turned out not to be associated with materialism very strongly (or at all). Being concerned about the condition of the poor was not a factor. Nor was concern about corruption in business or politics. Even concern about people turning away from God, moral corruption, and the breakdown of families were not associated with concern about materialism, if we take everything else into account. What did make a difference was a cluster of issues defined by a concern about individualism, a concern about selfishness, and a concern about the breakdown of community.[20]

This result takes us back to something we considered earlier in Gene Atwood's story about the miraculous healing. What he emphasized most pointedly was not the healing itself but that God used the occasion to teach him about *selfishness*. Fasting (the sacrifice of a material comfort) was pitted in the story against praying for a spiritual solution to the woman's medical problem. And the lesson learned was about being so selfish that such a sacrifice was difficult.

Other people we talked to made similar arguments. Without any prompting to do so, Doug Hill drew the following connection: "Materialism basically is self-centeredness, if you want to put those two in categories, they are the same category." Murial Johnson saw a basic trade-off between being materialistic and having a sense of community responsibility because, in her words, "as long as you're worried about the bottom line and how much you possess, you worry less about anyone else." Karen Kelsey said it was how people *understood* the trade-off that mattered: "You may be very materialistic and you may also be helping the world, so it isn't a problem. But [to do that], you have to get your *sense of self* less wrapped up in material things."

If we were to think of spirituality and materialism as two islands, then, we would see individualism (that is, selfishness) as the bridge connecting the two. And it would be on this bridge that the fundamental conflict would have to be fought out. Materialism, to many Americans, is a problem because it connotes selfishness, an individualistic emphasis on self-interest that devalues the community and the need to care about others. Selfishness is a problem, in turn, because religious tradition champions love, compassion, reaching out to the community, caring for others. It is this, more than anything else about religion in contemporary society, that butts up against the pervasive materialism to which we are exposed.[21]

Personal Materialism

Yet this is not all of the story. If materialism is so widely considered a serious social problem, why does this perception not haunt individual Americans any more than it does? Especially if materialism is considered a problem not because of abstract social conditions (economic laws, business, profit seeking) but because it suggests an absorption with one's self, then how is it possible for most Americans to cherish money and material possessions as much as they do?

The extent to which people value material possessions has already been implied in figures cited in Chapter 5 about money making people feel good, being associated with freedom, and factoring into their basic sense of personal worth. A more direct indication of how much material possessions are valued is given by responses to questions about specific possessions or activities (Table 6.3). Four people out of five say it is at least fairly important to them to have a high-paying job. Nearly as many say this about having a beautiful home, a new car, and other nice things. Three out of four give the same responses to wearing nice clothes, as do almost as many about traveling for pleasure. And half say this about eating at nice restaurants.

It is true that some people value material possessions considerably more than others do. If three people out of four, on the average, consider such possessions at least fairly important, only one in four says they are *very* important. How much such possessions are valued also depends to some extent on the wherewithal people have at their disposal. People with higher incomes are more likely than those with lower incomes to value big-ticket items, such as expensive homes and vacations. But these differences are not large, and there are actually no differences among income groups on items such as valuing nice clothes or eating out at nice restaurants.

To find that Americans are interested in material possessions is, I confess, about as surprising as discovering that grass is green. The reason for pointing out the obvious is that it provides the context in which to ask how people reconcile this interest with their concerns about materialism. Three additional points need to be made about this relationship. First, people who are more concerned about materialism in the society at large *are* less likely to value material possessions themselves. The differences are relatively small (about ten percentage points on average), but they are significant.[22] Second, religious commitment is also negatively associated with valuing material possessions (also not strongly, but the relationships are significant).[23] And third, that still leaves quite a lot of overlap, that is, people who are religiously committed, who worry about materialism as a social ill, and yet who value material possessions themselves. In short, there is enough overlap that most people have to do some negotiating with themselves to explain why their lifestyle isn't really in conflict with their values.

How people do this can be grasped only by listening to what they say about themselves. Let us begin with Karen Kelsey because she is

TABLE 6.3

Personal Materialism

Percent who say each of the following is absolutely essential, very important, or fairly important:

	Total Labor Force
Having a high-paying job	80
Having a beautiful home, a new car, and other nice things	78
Wearing nice clothes	75
Being able to travel for pleasure and see interesting things	72
Eating out at nice restaurants	50

particularly articulate on the subject. She begins with a simple syllogism (that puts her in a bad spot): all Americans are materialistic, I am an American, so I am materialistic. But she also believes she is somehow not materialistic. So she embarks on several (partially successful) attempts to explain why. Her first attempt could be summarized as an it's-pretty-hard-to-know argument. She says her parents recently offered to buy her a new car and, wealthy as they are, put no limit on what she could spend. She recalls, "I couldn't decide on what was indulgent, what was reasonable, what was safety, what was gas efficiency, what was style. I just had no way of understanding what was wasteful and what was not. It was a very difficult decision for me." She didn't mean she lacked information or intelligence. What she meant was that materialism is quite subjective: who can say, what may be indulgent for you may not be for me; it's all in how you look at it. She wound up getting a modest sedan that was far cheaper than her parents could have afforded, but she was still unsure if she had been guided more by her practical needs or by the materialism inherent in the culture.

Her second argument is that she is not materialistic because she actually denies herself things she would like. At least she can point to specific examples. She says she never buys clothes, just wears things her mother throws away. And she never buys shoes. "My shoes will have a million holes in them and I'll just keep wearing them, when I shouldn't do that. I should buy new ones. I won't go on trips. I won't spend money on a lot of things." The point here is that the initial syllogism can be turned to an advantage. If all Americans are materialistic, then at least I'm not as materialistic as some. And I know I am not because I make token sacrifices—like wearing worn-out shoes.

Finally, she bridges into a third argument that complements the second by showing how she gives money and time away. With the money she saves on shoes, she's building up a fund that she intends to devote (sometime in the future) to the needy. She thinks maybe helping poor kids get therapy would be a worthwhile cause. This reminds her that she is also donating some of her own time as a therapist to people who cannot pay the full amount. And given that she could have been a Wall Street lawyer, earning a lot more money than she does now, she feels even more justified in saying that she's not really that materialistic.

These three arguments came up so often in other interviews that it would be a mistake to credit Karen Kelsey with having invented them for her own interests. Indeed, it makes more sense to regard them as scripts, readily available in the cultural tool kits of most Americans, to be used whenever some fine-tuning on one's self-understandings may be required. The it's-all-subjective argument allows people to say, in effect, you have to take my word for it because you cannot know my thinking on the matter. The I-don't-spend-that-much argument provides a sliding scale of values that can always be confirmed with ritualized references to some material temptation forgone. And the I-give-my-money-away argument demonstrates, symbolically probably more than literally, that one is not too attached to material possessions to be aware of human needs.

Whether religion itself has much to do with making these scripts available is a different matter. Insofar as religion regards *love* of money as the evil, and insofar as greed is considered an attitude rather than an action, religion may encourage the it's-all-subjective argument. Not spending as much as one could probably has more to do with the marketplace than with houses of worship. In our interviews, few people at least gave examples of anything that had to do with religion. The third script, though, is particularly important because it demonstrates an absence of selfishness. If this is primarily how religion challenges materialism, then it makes sense that people have ways to show they are not selfish. (It also makes sense that religious organizations provide such opportunities for giving, as we shall see in Chapter 8.)

Materialism and Religious Organizations

If people are able to excuse themselves from being materialistic, they are nevertheless less willing to excuse religious organizations for seeming to be so. The reason can again be understood in terms of the basic framework we have considered throughout the chapter. The spiritual and the material are separate, and fundamentally different, realms. The material realm becomes problematic when it creeps out of its borders, infringing on alien territory, as it were, by causing people to be so devoted to their material pursuits that they violate sacred standards limiting selfish behavior. The spiritual realm can, incidentally, become problematic in the same way: creeping out of its borders to tell someone like Warren Means that he may be a sinner just because he handles a lot of money in the banking business. But the spiritual realm becomes even more problematic if it seems to absorb too much from the material world, that is, if spirituality itself seems in danger of being subverted by materialism.

As representatives of the spiritual realm, religious organizations and religious professionals are especially subject to public fears about the symbolic intrusion of materialism. Clergy, as noted before, are widely regarded as God's emissaries, doing spiritual work in a special way. If pushed, most people would probably admit that clergy need material possessions as do everyone else, and indeed may be entitled to the same lifestyles their congregants enjoy, rather than needing to demonstrate their piety by living in abject poverty. But there is also considerable misgiving about clergy becoming too materialistic. When a television preacher is shown living in a lavish mansion or is accused of engaging in illicit sexual behavior, the one evokes almost as much public dismay as the other. Both are perceived as a special kind of corruption, perhaps excusable among ordinary mortals but not acceptable in a realm deemed to be holy and pure. For those who are already alienated from religious organizations or uninvolved, such scandals provide useful rationales for staying uninvolved. These scandals merely symbolize what is regarded as a more widespread subversion of the spiritual by the material. In the Economic Values Survey, 43 percent claimed it was true that "churches are too eager to get your time and money," a figure that declined to 25 percent among weekly attenders but rose to 59 percent among persons attending only once a year or never.

An important implication of this interest in keeping the spiritual unsullied by materialism is that people are also uneasy with appeals from religious organizations to give of their time and money.[24] Such appeals are easily categorized as examples of religious organizations becoming too materialistic. There is an irony here, however, because people also want religious organizations to encourage them (or people "out there") to be less materialistic. One of the ways in which this might be done, of course, is by encouraging charitable giving through religious organizations. But that sort of appeal is unpopular because it makes these organizations seem materialistic.

The relative weight of these orientations can be seen in responses to two questions in the Economic Values Survey. Asked whether churches and synagogues should encourage people to be less materialistic, a substantial minority said this should be emphasized a lot more, and virtually everyone said it should be emphasized at least somewhat more. In comparison, only about one person in eight said religious organizations should pay a lot more attention to encouraging people to give more time and money to religious programs; indeed, only about half thought this should be emphasized even somewhat more. Regular churchgoers were more likely than infrequent attenders to want more emphasis given to both. But the relative emphasis was still heavily on less materialism rather than more giving (Table 6.4).

A Basis for Transcendence

To summarize, this chapter has been principally concerned with the *symbolism* associated with materialism in American culture and how that symbolism is related to our understandings of spirituality. The symbolic dimension of material goods has been widely acknowledged in scholarly discussions. Advertisers exploit this dimension when they try to sell new cars by associating them with beautiful scenery or

TABLE 6.4

Materialsim and Religious Organizations

Percent who said churches and synagogues should do each of the following among persons in the labor force who attended religious services:

	Weekly	Monthly	Yearly
Encourage people to be less materialistic			
A lot more	39	25	24
Somewhat more	44	53	38
Somewhat less	9	13	13
A lot less	2	2	5
Encourage people to give more time and money to religious programs			
A lot more	19	12	7
Somewhat more	46	44	23
Somewhat less	23	30	31
A lot less	4	5	17

when beer commercials associate drinking with sexual prowess. But it has generally been assumed in discussions of such symbolism that everything worked to the advantage of the seller: sunsets and semi-nude bodies made people want to buy more. None of this literature has tried to make sense of an equally prevalent sentiment in American culture: that there is something wrong, corrupting, askew about our society's emphasis on materialism.

There is indeed widespread concern about materialism in contemporary social life. It can be found in many scholarly books and articles arguing that business has too much power, that television is subverting the values of young people, and that high-brow tastes in music and literature are giving way to low-brow interests in material objects such as video games and barbecue grills. It can also be found in statements by ordinary people. They worry about their children's obsession with material possessions, about the influence of advertising on the nation's values, and about their own desires for more and finer things than they can ever afford. Survey data reveal that a very large percentage of the population believes materialism is a serious social problem and thinks the society would be better off if there were less emphasis on money.

It is easy to dismiss this concern about materialism in view of the fact that most Americans actually seem willing to run up huge credit card debts and to purchase a vast assortment of consumer products. To an economist (or marketing agent) it might make little difference that people also worry about materialism. But it should, even for economists, because those who worry about materialism actually are somewhat less inclined to value material amenities themselves. If we are interested in understanding the relationships between religion and economic behavior, however, it is absolutely crucial to take this concern into account.

We are able to regard materialism as a problem because of the long-standing division in Western culture between the spiritual and material realms. This division makes it possible, as we saw, to compartmentalize thinking about money from religious teachings. But it also supplies a basis for recognizing that there are values that transcend those advanced by economists and advertisers. Thus, people who think a lot about the differences between spiritual growth and material possessions are more likely to be troubled about materialism than those who think less about these differences. The same is true of people who emphasize an introspective orientation toward spirituality, distinguishing its inward, emotional nature from the outward, physical nature of the material world. Even those who radically separate money from morals and values are inclined to recognize that materialism in itself may be problematic.

A negative view of materialism is most likely to be reinforced by religious commitment, it appears, when materialism is understood to involve selfishness or individualism. Were materialism understood strictly in economic terms, it might lead to proposals to curb it through social policy initiatives. Or if it were truly understood to be a pervasive social problem rooted in basic cultural assumptions and related to a wide variety of other problems, we might address it through our schools and universities or through other forums for public debate. But when it is regarded as selfishness it becomes a matter of conscience. And conscience is private, hidden from view, and easily separated from the ways in which we actually behave. Conscience, however, has traditionally been regarded as a subject worthy of moral consideration and thus of religious tutelage. Were religious organizations to do more to discourage materialism (as most people want them to), they would probably be most successful, therefore, by emphasizing the connection between materialism and selfishness.

But we have also seen that it is much more difficult for most people to acknowledge that they themselves may be too materialistic than it is for them to criticize materialism in the abstract. It may be only human nature to excuse ourselves from the blame we attribute to others. But assertions about human nature provide no understanding of how this process of excusing ourselves actually works. Listening to people talk reveals that personal materialism is easy to deny because of arguments that make it entirely subjective, that show how it is not so bad because it could have been worse, and that demonstrate one's lack of actual selfishness through acts of kindness. Religious organizations provide settings in which these charitable acts can be performed. But giving money to these organizations may also be deterred by fears that these bastions of spirituality are themselves becoming corrupted by materialism.

Having considered some of the implications of drawing symbolic distinctions between the spiritual and the material, we can conclude by offering a somewhat broader interpretation of the relationship between religion and economic behavior than we could in considering work and money by themselves. On the basis of statistics alone, we would be hard-pressed to say that religious teachings have a powerful influence on thinking about materialism. Religious commitment is associated with considering materialism a social problem and with devaluing personal possessions, but the relationships are not strong. The role of religion nevertheless extends beyond merely making individuals more content, more thoughtful, or more financially responsible.

Religious understandings are part of the deep structure of any society's cultural orientations. In the present case, the distinction between spirituality and the material is a fundamental ordering principle. It establishes basic categories that influence how other assumptions and ideas hang together. The fact that these categories are so widely taken for granted makes it difficult to demonstrate how they function. We have been able to show, however, that they are reinforced by several different orientations toward religion (not only a particularly thoughtful or pious orientation), and that they do shape understandings of materialism that, in turn, raise certain problems for the ways in which individuals understand their own material possessions, as well as their giving behavior and their views of religious organizations. It is certainly conceivable that contemporary culture would be very different were it not for this distinction between the spiritual and the material.

Yet it is only partially correct to conclude that American religion stands in significant opposition to economic forces because of the antimaterialistic sentiments it reinforces. At a deeper level, these very sentiments help to sustain postindustrial society. The capacity to produce goods and services has now far outstripped the ability of most consumers to buy them. Affluence notwithstanding, the gap between the conceivable and the attainable has never been wider. Bombarded by constant appeals to want more, buy more, and spend more, we thus need a way to rationalize what we realistically cannot have. It helps to point to some gadget and tell ourselves that wanting it would be materialistic. Our antimaterialistic sentiments are also a way of telling ourselves that we are better than we might seem, not under the control of advertisers but free to choose, and capable of determining our own values. And these are messages that postindustrial society itself requires. It is precisely this freedom, these values, these deeper definitions of who we are that provide the challenges for the next wave of consumer goods and services.

There is thus enormous synergy between religion and economic life in our society. We have kept the spiritual realm distinct, even separate, despite the forces of secularization. But we have domesticated it, stripping the sacred of moral authority and allowing it to break through only occasionally and for good purposes, such as helping us out of a jam or salving our conscience when we succumb to the appeals of Madison Avenue. This kind of spirituality feeds on the uncertainties of contemporary life but also reinforces our sense of concern with materialism. It points to something higher, open, and perhaps absolute. At the same time, the spiritual infuses the material realm, giving it values to aspire to, slogans, and inspiration, but also detaching us from it, providing a way of explaining why we don't have more things, why we shouldn't want them, and yet why it is good for us to have what we do. This view of spirituality has adapted us well to contemporary social conditions. A religion that focused mainly on death, illness, hunger, and other physical needs would not serve us very well. Instead, our sense of spirituality is psychologically uplifting and therapeutic, a buttress of individuality, freedom, and diversity, a spirituality concerned with our true self, interested in how we think, depicted in images, oriented toward planning and introspection. If our spirituality turns too blatantly against money, we can question, rethink, and discard it. Our religious impulses, therefore, caution us against becoming too materialistic, but their prompting is limited because we are thoroughly embedded in a world of material goods.

Chapter Seven

The Poor and Economic Justice

Pam Jones was born in Indiana but spent most of her childhood in Puerto Rico, where her father had gone to do service work after giving up a lucrative medical practice. Helping the needy was deeply valued by the Mennonite church in which Pam was raised. At the Mennonite college she attended, students were encouraged to put this value into practice. She spent one summer doing hospital work in Puerto Rico, a semester in Colombia learning about Latin American politics, and another semester at a language institute learning French. After college she did volunteer work for a year with elderly people in France, helping feed them and giving them medications. Her sense of what she was "really good at," though, had always drawn her more toward technical subjects. She spent the next year getting a master's degree in computer science and is now employed as a software engineer for a large corporation specializing in communications. Pam has always felt a deep personal sense of responsibility for the poor. Her parents emphasized simple living to free themselves to be of service to others. In deciding on engineering as a career, Pam realized she would not be directly involved in helping the poor through her work. Someday, she says, maybe the company will give her a chance to work in an underdeveloped country. In the meantime, though, she tries to live her life in a way that furthers the cause of social justice. She and her husband are fixing up their basement to house refugees that their church is sponsoring. They have been giving financial assistance to a single mother in their community. They have also been refusing to pay the share of their taxes that goes for military expenditures. Pam feels that charitable efforts help, but she also believes the problems in our society are deeply rooted in greed. "The only thing that's really going to help the poor," she says, "is for rich people to start living at a lower level."

Ricardo Alvarado grew up in East Los Angeles, worked in a factory after high school, and eventually earned a bachelor's degree in sociology. His main interest during college was the free clinic where he did volunteer work. After graduation he continued working there for awhile, switched to another community clinic program, counseled teenagers for several years, and is now an administrator at a nonprofit agency that oversees community health programs sponsored by the state of California. Ricardo's parents required him to attend Mass every Sunday during childhood and adolescence. He never believed as unquestioningly in the church's authority as his parents did. But he attributes much of his interest in helping others to the church's teachings. His parents wanted him to get a steady job that would bring in a good income, and his teachers encouraged him to put his Mexicano identity aside. So doing volunteer work in the barrio depended a lot on his own convictions. Faith, he says, doesn't involve institutions as much as it does the life of the spirit. "It comes around to personal satisfaction with your life, what you've accomplished during that time, what you've done with the resources you have." For him, that means serving the poor. "I could have moved into a more capitalistic, materialistic position," he says. "But to really serve our country, you need to serve others instead of yourself. If people would just get involved, we'd have a much better society."

John and Mary Phelps live in a comfortable suburban home in Minnesota. Married two years ago, they are trying to save money to start a family. John has an M.B.A. and has worked in banking and marketing. Mary is a graphic designer. Both were raised in devout Catholic homes, and both are now actively involved in what John describes as "a progressive Catholic community that has a very rich liturgical tradition that is at the core of the community." Revolving around that core, he says, "are social justice causes galore." At one time, for example, the church basement was the epicenter of an international movement to boycott products of a company that was thought to be exploiting Third World people through an aggressive advertising campaign for packaged infant formula. At other times, the church was heavily involved in the nuclear disarmament movement and in protesting apartheid in South Africa. It has made a big difference in the Phelps's lives as well. Last year, John abandoned the marketing firm he was with to take a lower-paying job in the human services/social justice realm as an economic development person. His job is to promote small businesses in the inner city by helping people obtain loans and guiding them through the government's maze of ordinances and regulations. Asked what role his religious faith played in his decision to enter this line of work, he explained that it had changed what he identifies with the most. "I guess I get more and more fulfillment out of working for a cause, working for groups that are ostracized, disenfranchised, oppressed, or just plain left behind by our society."

No discussion of religion and economic behavior would be complete without considering the responsibility that people like Pam Jones, Ricardo Alvarado, and the Phelpses feel toward the poor. Religious teachings have always included admonitions about the dangers of economic injustice. Working to help the needy and to promote greater economic equality has long been regarded as a way of fulfilling the biblical mandate of loving one's neighbor as oneself.

Yet there remain many unanswered questions about the relationship between religious teachings and efforts to promote economic justice. With middle-class Americans being as devoted to their jobs, making money, and pursuing a comfortable lifestyle as they seem to be, is it realistic to expect them to be interested in the plight of those less fortunate than they are? Even if they were, are the problems so grave that individual efforts and small-scale programs make little difference? Has the so-called capitalist or market system on which American society is based become so deeply entrenched, and does it enjoy such widespread legitimacy, that few changes of any significance could even be contemplated? And with religious organizations focusing on individual spirituality, meaningful worship experiences, music, youth programs, and small groups, is it likely that religious commitment is going to challenge people to be concerned about economic justice as well?

One might take an optimistic stance toward all these questions, arguing that certainly religious organizations have concerned themselves with addressing the needs of the poor, and that certainly

these efforts have made some difference. Yet there is another trou-
bling issue. In his study of grassroots Christian thinking about
economic justice, Stephen Hart writes, "Christians are far from
united with regard to the implications of faith for economic life,
and are struggling with one another (and inside themselves) to define the social role Christianity will play."[1] Evangelical Protestants,
he observes, often take a radically different view of matters economic than do members of liberal Protestant churches or of
Catholic parishes. Moreover, as Craig Gay has recently demonstrated, evangelical Protestants are themselves deeply divided on
economic issues, and as Gene Burns (among others) has shown, so
are Catholics.[2] It may well be, therefore, that religious leaders have
sparked debate about economic justice, but that the debate itself
has become self-defeating, inspiring so many contradictory ideas
that none of them wind up mattering very much. And if this
debate, as Hart suggests, occurs within individuals' own thinking,
as well as between groups, the voice of conscience may be a faint
and wavering cry indeed.

Clearly it is not possible in the present context to consider the
wide range of proposals put forth by religious leaders to promote
economic justice in recent years, let alone to trace their historical
evolution. Other studies can readily be found for such information.
What we do want to consider is how the American workforce re-
sponds to several key dimensions of this debate: do they think about
their responsibility to the poor at all? what is their understanding of
the needs of the poor? how do they feel about the economic system
more generally and the possibilities of reforming it? and what do
they want religious organizations to be doing on behalf of economic
justice?

Some evidence on these questions already exists from various
surveys and public opinion polls. Here we want to add information
about how these issues relate to the economic values and beliefs
that make up such a large part of our outlooks toward our own lives.
How does working hard and trying to make a lot of money influence
our attitudes toward the poor? What difference does it make to be
exposed to teachings about stewardship or materialism? And, if
Hart and others are right, do people with different religious orientations also differ in their views of the poor and other economic
issues?

Responsibility Toward the Poor

If pressed to define economic justice, most religious leaders (or policy experts, for that matter) would probably point out that the concept carries many connotations that go beyond a discussion of the poor. Rich people exploiting the middle class would qualify for consideration, as would certain claims about fair prices, equitable wages, and safe working conditions at all levels of the social hierarchy. But thinking about the poor is clearly an appropriate place to begin. Religious leaders have sometimes been hesitant to make pronouncements about aspects of economic justice they considered beyond their level of technical expertise (such as monetary policy or tariffs), but they have generally found plenty within the sacred texts of their traditions to warrant assertions about the poor.

Perhaps the most fundamental issue is simply whether religious teachings require believers to feel responsibility toward the poor. From the Mosaic law, to the jeremiads of the diaspora prophets, to the teachings of Jesus, there is ample reason to assert that people with the means to help, or people in positions of authority, bear a divinely sanctioned responsibility to alleviate the suffering of the disadvantaged. Yet, as Lovella Medina pointed out, religious teachings may also seem to convey contradictory advice. Jesus' saying about the poor "always being with you" is an example of a teaching that has often been used to deny responsibility toward the poor.

We asked a number of the people we interviewed to address this teaching—and this interpretation of it—specifically. Did they think it excused people of means from helping the poor? Scarcely anyone was willing to go that far. Ricardo Alvarado said it was just a way of "passing your responsibility." John and Mary Phelps both laughed it off as being too simplistic to take seriously. "You're also supposed to be with the poor and try to help them," John observed, "not just lock your doors and have a party." Pam Jones pointed out that it may be impossible to *eliminate* poverty, but one should still try to alleviate it: "Maybe you can't make ten people comfortable, but you can make two of them comfortable; so that's what you should do."

We did find in the survey, however, that people vary considerably in how much they have actually thought about their responsibility to the poor. While everyone might agree at some level about the reality of such responsibility (as we saw in Chapter 6, 92 percent thought the "condition of the poor" was a serious social problem), only about half of the labor force say they have thought about their responsibility to the poor at least a fair amount in the past year (see Table 7.1). Indeed, only 20 percent say they have thought about it a great deal, while 45 percent have thought about it only a little or hardly any

Blacks and whites are about equally likely to have thought about it, as are persons from upper-, middle-, and lower-income groups. Older people and the better educated have thought about it more, as have women, while people on the East Coast claim to have given it less attention than people in other parts of the country. The largest differences, however, are between people with an active religious involvement and those who are religiously uninvolved. Thus, church members are significantly more likely to have thought about it than nonmembers, and those who attend religious services every week are about twice as likely to have considered it as people who attend once a year or less.[3]

Contrary to popular impressions that associate such thinking with religious liberalism, religious conservatives are substantially more likely to have thought about it than either moderates or liberals. Much of this difference, though, can be attributed to the fact that conservatives are on the whole more active in their churches than liberals.[4] Protestants run slightly ahead of Catholics on such thinking, but the same caveat applies to interpreting these differences.

If we were to ask what *specifically* about religious involvement encourages thinking about responsibility to the poor, we would have to rely on more detailed statistical analysis of the survey data to answer this question. Such information suggests two important factors. One is involvement that encourages people to be thoughtful about their relationship to God in general. In other words, an understanding of spirituality that says, in effect, knowing God requires intellectual effort also spills over to an individual's thinking about his or her responsibility to the poor.[5] The other is involvement that includes specific instruction, not so much about the poor but about believers' responsibility in the use of their money. Sermons on stewardship, coming to regard it as a more meaningful concept, and thinking about biblical teachings concerning personal finances all make a notable difference, even when level of religious involvement is taken into account.[6]

Such information also suggests two characteristics of religious involvement that do *not* encourage thinking about responsibilities to the

TABLE 7.1

Responsibility to the Poor

Question: "In the past year, how much have you thought about . . . your responsibility to the poor?" (percent responding "great deal" or "fair amount")

Total U.S. labor force	53
Church attendance	
Weekly	76
Monthly	47
Yearly or less	37
Church member	
Yes	63
No	40
Religious preference	
Protestant	58
Catholic	51
Other	52
None	35
Religious orientation	
Conservative	67
Moderate	54
Liberal	48
Stewardship sermon	
Yes	77
No	44
Race	
White	53
Black	53
Income	
Low	54
Medium	55
High	50

poor. The first is developing a kind of subculture of friends within one's religious community. It might be supposed that such a subculture would reinforce thinking about economic justice. But apparently it is too easy for such subcultures simply to reinforce a comfortable lifestyle. In any event, when level of attendance at religious services is taken into account, those with more friends in their congregations actually think *less* about their responsibility to the poor.[7] The second is a moralistic attitude. The view that it is morally wrong to have nice things when others are starving, it appears, often accompanies thinking about responsibilities to the poor. But when other kinds of religious involvement are taken into account, this view becomes relatively insignificant.[8]

It is worth pausing to emphasize, therefore, that religious commitment, at least certain kinds of it, does encourage people to think more about their responsibility to the poor. If two-thirds of all church members—and three fourths of all the people who attend religious services every week—think a fair amount about their responsibility to the poor, this is a lot of people. Furthermore, the fact that at least half of regular churchgoers have heard a sermon on stewardship in the past year and that nearly this many are involved in a fellowship group or Sunday school class becomes all the more significant because such involvement does appear to stimulate thinking about the poor.

Responsibility to the poor can, of course, mean many different things within popular religious understandings. It is clear, however, that it is associated with other expressions of concern for the poor. We already saw that upwards of 90 percent of the public think the condition of the poor is a serious problem, so it would be hard for those who think a lot of their responsibilities to be much more sympathetic. But they are. On average, about one person in two thinks the condition of the poor is an *extremely serious* problem, but among those who have thought a great deal about their responsibility to the poor, this proportion rises to three in four (see Table 7.2). There is also some indication that thinking about one's responsibility to the poor is associated with a favorable attitude, at least toward certain kinds of poor people. Those who work hard but make little money are admired substantially more often by people who have thought a great deal about their responsibility to the poor than by other people.[9] Both of these attitudes, it is worth noting, are also more common among the actively religious than among the nonreligious. They are reinforced especially by frequent

TABLE 7.2

Attitudes Toward the Poor

	Among Those Who Had Thought About Their Responsibility to the Poor		
	Great Deal	*Fair Amount*	*Little/ None*
Percent who said the condition of the poor is:			
Extremely serious	75	60	49
Serious	22	36	41
A small problem	2	4	7
Not a problem	0	0	0
Percent who admire people who work hard but never make much money (a lot)	43	32	26
Percent who agree that the poor are closer to God than rich people are	29	23	16

attendance at religious services and by having a better understanding of stewardship.[10]

Part of what responsibility to the poor is understood to mean, therefore, surely must reflect the teachings of religious leaders themselves. One of the oldest of such teachings is the idea that the poor are actually of special interest to God, and thus of particular importance to those who wish to demonstrate their love for God. The Catholic social teaching that has been called an "option for the poor" has especially been concerned with this argument in recent years. "The Scriptures indicate that those who are poor and defenceless have nobody to turn to but God," explains one author. "[God] has a special care for the victims of injustice and those who are poor; and they in turn can more easily accept his care and protection."[11]

Some of the people we talked to had their own, somewhat romanticized views of why the poor might be especially close to God as well—views that often paralleled the arguments we considered in Chapter 5 about the rich being distant from God. For instance, Lovella Medina believes the poor probably hold a special place in God's heart because they care more for each other and are more frugal. "Poor people help each other more because it's more convenient for them," she suggests, "and they swap babysitters and things like that." Speaking from his evangelical perspective, Doug Hill offers another reason why the poor might be closer to God: "Oftentimes the Lord works in our lives because of finances, because of the lack of money. It might drive us to the Lord a lot more because we don't have money."

But judging from the survey, we note that not many Americans are willing to credit the poor with having an inside track on God's favor. Compared with the 30 percent who say riches get in the way of knowing God, only 20 percent agree that "the poor are closer to God than rich people are." Not surprisingly, poor people themselves are more inclined to accept this view than wealthier people. But this tendency appears to be more a function of lack of education than of low income itself.[12] Consistent with theological teachings, Catholics are also somewhat more likely to hold this view than Protestants.[13]

Those who attend religious services regularly are more inclined to believe this statement than people who attend less often. There is thus a tendency for this view to go along with thinking more about responsibility to the poor as well. If level of attendance is taken into account, however, this relationship becomes much weaker. The religious factors most associated with this view are biblical literalism and praying about one's finances. On balance, this view seems to be grounded less in broad understandings of stewardship than in a kind of thinking that perceives God as a source of material blessings. If God is especially concerned about the poor, it may make some sense to think that God will also be there if particular material needs arise. Extending this logic very far, however, would clearly raise questions about why God allows the poor to be poor at all, unless the reason is their lack of faith.

Taking stock momentarily, we observe that it seems obvious that a large number of people spend time thinking about their responsibilities toward the poor, that this thinking is associated with at least a recognition of the seriousness of the condition of the poor, and that it is especially pronounced among the religiously involved, probably being reinforced by religious thought in general and by teachings about stewardship in particular. If this is the case, then an outsider to American society might well be surprised by the realities of everyday life. Knowing that religious leaders have often pressed for social action on behalf of the poor, this outsider might be surprised to find that there was virtually none. She would be surprised to learn that people like Ricardo Alvarado or John Phelps, who actually make career choices aimed at helping the poor, are quite rare, as are people like Pam Jones and her husband who engage in quiet forms of civil disobedience against government policies. Knowing that religious people have mobilized in huge numbers to protest in front of abortion clinics, and that large religious movements have emerged to fight pornography and to turn back court rulings against school prayer, she would undoubtedly be surprised to learn that religious movements oriented toward passing legislation to help the poor have foundered for want of public support. Having heard about Americans' fears that materialism, advertising, and corruption in business are perverting the nation's values, she might wonder why religious people were seldom interested in reforming their economic system. And knowing how often religious movements have been involved in political efforts to install new regimes or to initiate new economic policies in other countries, she might ask if such were not the case in America as well.

If we are to understand the peculiar linkages between religious commitment and economic justice in American society, therefore, we must go beyond saying that religious involvement encourages people to be concerned about the poor. We must also recognize that there are countervailing cultural pressures at work as well. These pressures work at cross-purposes with taking responsibility for the poor. And yet some of them are reinforced by the same kinds of religious commitments. Together, they channel the ways in which responsibilities toward the poor are expressed. They do not render religious people mute or ineffective, but they do direct their energies. And they do so not so much by directing them onto battlefields of acrimonious public debate, as some observers have suggested, but by focusing them overwhelmingly on one particular kind of social response.

Images of the Poor

To understand why the American public registers concern about the poor but does relatively little to turn this concern into a broad range of social and economic action, it is necessary to start by probing more deeply into the ways in which poverty is perceived. Religious thinking clearly influences some of these perceptions, but they are rooted in broader cultural traditions within American society as well.

Let us return briefly to the idea that the poor may be closer to God than other people. If this idea were widely believed, it would presumably encourage greater efforts on behalf of the poor. But what kind of efforts? Someone like Lovella Medina can romanticize the poor, saying that their simplistic lifestyle is godlike, but be inspired to do little more than point out that some of her best friends are poor and that she tries to help them if they are really in a jam. Even a more thoughtful interpretation is likely to encourage efforts to ameliorate the suffering of the poor but not to alter fundamentally their position, for to do so would presumably make them of less interest to God.

The more important point to be made about this idea is that it simply is not widely accepted in the first place. Even among those who have thought the most about their responsibility to the poor, three-fourths reject it. Why? In part, because it flies in the face of popular religious understandings themselves. In American culture, God is an equal-opportunity employer. The poor are, therefore, no worse off and no better off in the sight of God than anyone else. The proper approach is neither to condescend to them nor to romanticize them, but to "have solidarity with them," as John Phelps puts it, "so that *together* we can accomplish something."

Calvinist notions about an "elect" minority being saved, while the majority are destined for perdition, have admittedly died hard, especially among fundamentalists and evangelicals who regard a "born again" experience as being essential to salvation. But even this notion credits the individual with complete "freedom to choose," making it quite unlike its Calvinist predecessor. Certainly it is difficult for people to believe God would discriminate on the basis of how much or how little wealth a person had accumulated. "It's not that you're a worse person if you're rich or a better person if you're poor," says Lovella Medina, "it's a question of your heart."

The same logic people invoke to explain why a rich person can still gain entry to the kingdom of heaven applies to the possibility that the poor might have an easier time gaining admission. The rich person will be denied entry only if some egregious moral failing has become evident, or if material pursuits have become an obsession. Wealth alone, or its absence, is not the issue. In similar manner, the poor may have certain advantages, but these can readily be balanced by certain disadvantages. If the poor do not have the burden of being responsible for managing huge fortunes, they may become obsessed with material pursuits simply because they have no other choice. And if the rich can be faulted for moral impurity, so too can the poor. Indeed, the poor may be more sorely tempted to lie, cheat, steal, cut corners, abandon their families, and destroy themselves because economic conditions make their lives difficult.

Ricardo Alvarado provides a glimpse into this way of thinking about the poor. Because he works with people who are at least 100 percent below the poverty line every day, he understands that poverty is not simply the fault of individuals; it is a feature of the organization of society. "It's because of capitalism," he says, "you're taught to make as much as you can and keep it; it doesn't allow for being non-competitive; some people just get squeezed out." But he also believes economic conditions make people poor chiefly by destroying the moral foundations of their lives. Citing the poorest person he can think of as an example—an individual whose life "revolved around drugs, and who was obsessed by acquiring drugs, and had only friends who were associated with it"—he says this man was not only monetarily bankrupt but "spiritually" impoverished as well. "He had no guidance, no goals, no sense of life's worth."

If God leaves it largely up to the individual to be moral or not, there is, nevertheless, some lingering belief that God may in fact ordain some people to be poorer than others. In American culture it is difficult to find this view expressed in bold, predestinarian terms, especially not with the implication that God singles out particular individuals by name and says, Tom, sorry, but you have to be poor. There is more willingness to believe that God may give particular individuals a talent for making money than for not making it. But, perhaps ironically, religious thinking does combine with social science views of poverty to suggest that being poor is simply a feature of all societies and, in this sense, can be understood as part of God's plan for humankind.

The basis for assuming that "the poor will always be with you," therefore, is clearly present. Yet the question of why some particular people are poor, rather than others, appears to devolve the issue immediately to the level of individual behavior. In other words, rather than a systemic interpretation of the problem leading to a systemic view of its solution, the systemic diagnosis provides a framework that says, in effect, this is the way it will always be, and then individual attributes are credited with causing people to stay in poverty or to move out of it.[14] The range of relevant attributes is itself considerable. But images of what it has taken the middle class to escape being poor surface most readily, and of these, popular understandings of work, laziness, and financial responsibility are especially apparent.

Religious commitment adds authority to these understandings when it translates them from middle-class values into divine absolutes. For those who take the Bible literally, the message can be very clear. As Doug Hill explains,

> Scripture indicates that if a man is not willing to work, he shouldn't eat. I think that's a very basic principle, and I think it's a principle we forget when we come to handing out government money to people. It means making a judgment call sometimes. But I think the basic principle still stands. If a man is not willing to work, he shouldn't eat, period.

From considering understandings of the poor, we arrive at an argument that can be instrumental in turning a cold shoulder toward them, namely, because they are assumed to be lazy and irresponsible.[15] Given the widespread humanitarian concern that is also part of American culture, however, this argument can also lead to a more ameliorative orientation. In fact, two possibilities can be logically sustained: one, that social reforms must be made that do more to enable those who are willing to do so to work hard and take responsibility for themselves, and two, that charitable efforts must be devoted to helping particular individuals who are otherwise deserving recover from misfortune. Both of these have support. To understand why the second is often favored more than the first, though, it is necessary to turn our attention to understandings of the economic system itself.

The Economic System

Let us acknowledge at the outset that most people claim not to understand the American economic system very well. Those we interviewed sometimes prefaced their remarks on economic issues with dismissals such as "I'm no expert" or "if I knew, I'd be president." And it is little wonder that they did, given that economics claims to be a science and that the media so often describe even economists as being puzzled about such issues. In the Economic Values Survey, only 11 percent said they understand "very well" how our economic system works, and even among those who said they had thought a great deal about their responsibility to the poor, only 18 percent did. One reason why many people seem indifferent to public debates about economic injustice, therefore, may be simply that they feel these discussions are better left to the experts. As critics suggest, one of the dangers of the increasing reliance on technical expertise in modern societies is that the mass public becomes "inattentive," speaking a language of personal life but having no way of bridging into the public discourse of large-scale institutions.

Despite not understanding it very well, most people nevertheless believe the economic system is capable of being reformed. In the labor force as a whole, 32 percent say it is possible to make many significant changes, and 44 percent say a few significant changes are possible, while only 18 percent believe economic forces are pretty much beyond control. Significantly, those who have thought more about their responsibility to the poor tend to be more optimistic about change than those who have thought less (see Table 7.3).[16]

TABLE 7.3

Views of the Economic System

	Among Those Who Had Thought About Their Responsibility to the Poor		
	Great Deal	*Fair Amount*	*Little/ None*
Percent who said:			
It is quite possible to make many significant changes in our economic system	40	34	28
It is possible to make a few significant changes in our economic system	36	47	44
Economic forces are pretty much beyond our control	20	15	20
Our economic system is:			
The best system we could possibly have	6	6	6
Basically okay, but in need of some tinkering	27	31	30
In need of some fundamental changes	50	54	51
Needing to be replaced by a different system	14	7	7

One might wonder, then, if the system can be so readily reformed, why more effort does not go into reforming it. The question is even more puzzling in view of the fact that most people think basic changes are needed. Only 6 percent of the labor force say the economic system is the best we could possibly have. Another 30 percent say the economic system is basically sound but could stand some minor changes. Thus, 51 percent say the system needs some fundamental changes, and another 9 percent say it needs to be replaced by a different system entirely. The last response is also more common among people who have thought a lot about their responsibility to the poor than among people who haven't, although the other responses show few differences (see Table 7.3).[17]

One person who thinks the economic system needs a radical overhaul is Karen Kelsey, the therapist. Not only her formal education but her reading in Buddhism has helped her to think in systemic terms.

> In terms of systems, we've made some choices about how we want the world to be. By definition, some people get helped and some people don't get helped. Because of the way we've decided to petrify society, some people pay a price. Society wasn't made for them, to accommodate them and to give them what they need. I think society, which is such a big word (I hate to use it), is increasingly accommodating the needs of fewer people, and so there are flaws in the system which need to be changed so that more people aren't ending up poor.

But her view is clearly the exception rather than the rule. Most people want change, not a different system. It is thus the nature of change that deserves closer scrutiny.

To understand why the system, according to most Americans, could use change rather than basic restructuring, we must go back briefly to what we discovered about materialism in Chapter 6. Materialism is, we suggested, a symbol of evil. As such, it provides a language for talking about social ills without attributing them to the economic system itself. To be sure, there are systemic connections, as in the case of people who argue that advertising promotes materialism or that capitalism is at fault. John and Mary Phelps illustrate this point of view very clearly when they argue that commercial pressures are "omnipresent." As John observes,

> It's hard to imagine a place where you could go in America and be free from the commercial pressures that are omnipresent in your life,

whether you're driving down the street looking at the side of a bus, to your little boy looking at the TV every five minutes saturated with ads. It's hard to get away from it anywhere.

But, it will also be recalled, what seems to trouble people the most about materialism is the selfishness it implies. And that, while perhaps encouraged by capitalism or by advertising, is understood in American culture as a human tendency, a kind of moral failure, rather than an economic or political failure. Moreover, religious teachings that warn believers against such temptations as greed and envy provide a strong rationale for believing that it is these moral failings, more than anything else, to which poverty and economic injustice must be attributed. Here is Pam Jones responding to a question asking her about the causes of poverty:

> Greed. It's like why is there war? Because you're greedy and you want more. Why are there so many poor? I'm aware of people really living high off the hog, and they have more than they can even really enjoy. So when we talk about quality of living, I think we live at such a high standard that it's not worth it. To have real fancy wallpaper in your room, to me that doesn't really improve my quality of living very much. But to know my neighbors and have a good relationship with them, to have a refrigerator so that food doesn't spoil, those are some basic things.

Greed, then, is a moral failing. Being concerned about it leads people like Pam Jones to live simply and to worry about the corrosive effects of advertising. It is, however, not so different a view from those of people miles apart from her in political ideology. For instance, Doug Hill says men should be the bread winners and women should stay at home. He believes there is a "fundamental imbalance in society today" because "men are not doing what they're supposed to do." Materialism has encouraged them to send their wives into the workplace, and this has messed up the family, causing its basic values to erode.[18] Pam Jones would disagree violently with this analysis. Yet the common assumption underlying both arguments is that materialism is more than anything else a moral problem.

Most needed, given an analysis of this kind, is moral tutelage that encourages people to be less greedy (or to reassert traditional gender roles), not radical reform of the economic system itself. A different system would do no good unless something else was done to curb greed. Churches and synagogues would have a special role to play in this scenario, but even if they succeeded in curbing greed, it is not clear in this logic whether the poor would be served. "Trickle-down" economics would suggest that the poor may be better off because of American materialism than despite it, the reason being that materialism creates jobs and generates tax revenue. The best argument for why less materialism would be beneficial to the poor is that wealthier people would then give away some of their money to the poor instead of spending it on consumer goods. This logic, however, fits most readily with yet another important assumption about poverty.

That assumption attributes poverty not so much to moral shortcomings as to unfortunate events. Poverty exists not because of the way economic relations are organized but because of a lay off here, a plant closing there, a nasty divorce, the early death of a parent, a dysfunctional upbringing, or a thousand other separate circumstances. As John and Mary Phelps both argue, "everyone has their own sad story." Some are ex-offenders, some have lost their job, it just depends.

Recognizing that poverty consists of special cases is not incompatible with arguing that a systemic response is needed to deal with their aggregate effects. Some of the people we talked to argued that the economic system is still at fault because, like a spoiled child, it does not pick up after itself. Plant closings are inevitable in a competitive economy but leave human misery in their wake. The solution might be government programs for job training, low-cost housing, and short-term loans. Still, the view that each person is a distinct "sad story" is far more conducive to saying that adjustments are needed rather than a fundamental overhaul. And it also influences the kind of adjustments that make the most sense.

How to Help the Needy

To hear newscasters tell it, political debate on matters of poverty and economic justice revolves around differences of opinion on specific proposals: enterprise zones, aid to dependent children, low-income housing, job-training programs, and the like. It is revealing, however, that when the public is polled on welfare issues, one of the most striking results seems to have less to do with any of these specific proposals and more to do with a minor variation in question wording. The results of one poll will illustrate: when asked, "are we spending too much, too little, or about the right amount on welfare," 44 percent of the public said too much, while only 23 percent said too little. But when asked the same question about "assistance to the poor," only 13 percent said too much, while 64 percent said too little.[19] Clearly, the public is more interested in helping the poor than in providing them welfare.

The larger lesson here is that the various attitudes we have been considering apparently channel the widespread responsibility most people say they feel toward the poor in a way that drastically weakens support for federal social welfare programs. But if this is the case, what do people favor as strategies for helping the needy? The figures in Table 7.4 indicate what is most and least favored. Before considering the numbers themselves, we find two points worth emphasizing. One is that

TABLE 7.4

Strategies for Helping the Needy

Question: "To help the needy in our society, do you think each of the following would help a lot, help a little, or not help?" (percent responding "a lot")

	Thought About Responsibility to the Poor		
	Great Deal	*Little/ None*	*Total Labor Force*
If more people gave a few hours a week to doing volunteer work	70	39	50
Spending more money on government welfare services	30	21	24
If everyone just worked harder at their own jobs	34	28	29
Getting businesses to take a more responsible role in their communities	70	54	59
If more people took an active role in their churches	65	24	37
Policies to promote faster economic growth	54	42	46

"the needy" is a far less culturally loaded term than "the poor." As we have already seen, many people think there are substantial numbers of the poor who are not really needy, if only because they are assumed to be capable of working but simply unwilling. The other is that most newscasters and pollsters do not focus on the list of options shown here when discussing the needy. But these options are clearly the wider array that frame people's thinking about the needy.

The results show clearly how little confidence the American public has in government-sponsored social welfare programs. Only one person in four thinks such programs would help a lot (a third say it wouldn't help at all). In comparison, there is much greater confidence that volunteer efforts would help a lot. Moreover, those who have thought more about their responsibility to the poor are much more likely to express confidence in volunteer efforts than in government programs.[20]

Further indication of some of the assumptions we have already considered can also be seen in these results. The assumption that the economy is basically sound, despite perhaps needing some changes, is probably behind the fact that so many people believe economic growth, hard work, and better business are all effective ways of helping the needy. There may well be an implicit message to the so-called welfare chiseler who is "just lazy" in the fact that more people believe hard work will help the needy than believe this about welfare programs. And where the favored volunteer efforts should be located is suggested by the fact that so many people—especially among those who have thought more about their responsibility to the poor—believe active church involvement would be a good way to help the needy. What people actually like or dislike about social programs and other efforts to help the needy can be understood best by considering how they talk about these efforts.[21]

Efforts on behalf of the needy regarded as the most likely to help are ones tailored to individual circumstances. This is why local programs, nonprofit agencies, and religious organizations are so often championed as opposed to federal welfare programs. There may be as much waste in the former than in the latter, but the former are thought to be more flexible, more suited to each "sad story" than anything mandated on a national scale. John Phelps, for instance, insists that it makes more sense to support agencies concerned with economic justice than ones just "doling out charity." The way to do this is to compare particular programs and see which ones are doing the most good. But he means the ones that draw people in and empower them. He sees no way of doing this through a single, universal policy. Instead, programs are needed that make people feel as if their specific circumstances are taken into account.

Interestingly enough, the same underlying logic is expressed by people who, unlike John Phelps, want social programs to play a much smaller role in helping the poor than they do now. Doug and Linda Hill are quite upset about the waste they perceive in the federal welfare system. They cite case after case of people using food stamps to buy better meals than do people who work for a living. But what galls them the most is that welfare programs seem intent on treating everyone the same, rather than respecting individual differences. If supporters of social programs want individual circumstances to be recognized, so do Doug and Linda; they simply want talent and hard work to be recognized along with sloth and misfortune. Indeed, they believe there is a religious principle involved that is as important as the idea of God wanting people to be equal. Doug explains:

> I think everybody is equal before the Lord. I don't think there's anybody who has an inside track to the Lord at all. But when it comes to living here on this earth, there are hardly two people who are equal. And I think we do ourselves a disservice in government and society when we think that everybody has to be equal.

It is worth following this thread a little further, because it illuminates why popular understandings of the poor are more commonly associated with charitable efforts than with favoring social welfare programs. People have different talents and abilities. It follows that there will be different levels of compensation, a reason incidentally that many people believe the present economic system is basically fair. The notion of equality flies in the face of rewarding such differentials. It is as ludicrous, Doug Hill says, as "the king having to walk when the servant rides on the horse." This rhetorical flourish masks the possibility, of course, that equality can also mean something quite different; for example, equal opportunity, respect, dignity, or even access to decent housing and health care. The train of thought, however, moves away from equality to the reality of economic inequality. Social justice should be concerned with maintaining a system in which ability and hard work are rewarded, and thus it becomes relevant more for protecting the middle class than the poor.[22] What is most needed for the poor is charity. A fair system is, after all, a harsh system because some well-intentioned people will always suffer misfortune. Thus, the biblical mandate of "helping the fatherless and widow" comes into play. Mercy enters the picture where justice leaves off. It is concerned more with helping the downtrodden back on their feet, rather than preventing them from falling in the first place. It requires individual attention, kindness, and compassion.

Social programs that help the most are also ones that help people help themselves by getting their families together, by training themselves and their children, and by learning to resist temptation and to occupy a productive role in society. Ricardo Alvarado explains,

> The key to poverty is education. The better the education, the more educated the individual, the better that they can help themselves. It depends on where they are and where they have to go. If it's the grammar school kid who doesn't have enough to eat, is hungry at school, then you hit it there. If it's a high school kid who's being tempted by drugs and outside influences, then you apply it there. If it's the high school grad who can't afford to go to college, then that's where it goes. But it all feeds into education. Because that's the only way out of poverty.

The underlying logic is that poor people who are not lazy but willing to work hard and interested in being self-sufficient should be given a chance. Whether the best way to do this is through a government program or individual giving, the assumption that the poor must be deserving places strict limits on how far compassion should be extended. Doug Hill makes the point very clearly.

> I think poor people fall into two categories: people who are poor because they are lazy and prefer to live on welfare rather than do something honorable to earn a living; and people who, because of the lack of education, cannot get a good job in order to sustain a wife and a home and four children and run a car and keep groceries on the table. Those are the ones that I would prefer to help. But people who are poor because they are lazy, I really have very little compassion for.

What separates those who favor large-scale efforts and those who oppose them is mainly how widespread they think these traits are among the poor. Banker Harold Bentley (whom we met in Chapter 4) implicitly believes most poor people, for whatever reasons, are not in-terested in being self-sufficient.

> There's always going to be some people that are poor. A lot of it can be self-inflicted. They've caused their own problems. And no matter what you do, you can give everybody money, have them on like a social se-curity type check. Some are going to blow it and they're always going to be poor. Sometimes they don't have a good sense of values. Don't have a good work ethic.

In contrast, someone like Pam Jones says she has known (and dated!) a few lazy people, so she knows they exist (and even respects them), but she assumes most poor people want to work hard and be-come self sufficient. So she is in favor of programs "to give them a chance."

Yet, even those who believe that most poor people are willing to work hard may be missing an essential point. "Just get a job," Mary Phelps explains, fails to consider that the poor may not have the re-sources to do that.

> Sure, there's a job bank they can go to and they can maybe line up an interview. But how do they get there? They don't have any clothes to wear. They have all these obstacles that come up that people in the middle class and upper middle class can't even relate to. They just don't understand it and until there's an understanding, the haves prob-ably will not be able to fully help the poor.

She, too, would be in favor of "work fare" programs as the "best" solu-tion were it not for two additional assumptions that deeply influence her thinking.

The first is that greed and materialism do not operate simply at an individual level, preventing the rich from giving to the poor instead of buying toys. These problems, she believes, have social policy implica-tions as well. Middle-class Americans want their toys so they vote for politicians who favor holding taxes down. But taxes would clearly have to increase to provide better health care, housing, and a host of other services for the poor. Fundamentally, the problem may be one of the heart, but it has ramifications in the public square.

The second is that justice itself is an important concept. Whereas many people think about the income differentials between the rich and the poor and say these are simply the way our system works, John and Mary Phelps look at them as a matter of injustice. He remembers reading a Dr. Seuss book as a child in which one group received all sorts of special privileges because they had a star on their chest and another group didn't because they lacked a star. Having a comfortable middle-class existence seems to him like having a star on your chest. However you may have gotten it, it doesn't entitle you to certain things, like self-esteem, respect, decent housing, or good medical care, anymore than not having one should disenfranchise you from these amenities. Only if people are outraged by this sense of injustice, as he was as a child, he believes, will true change come about.

The Role of Religious Organizations

The belief that more people taking an active role in their churches would help the needy a lot is perhaps the most important notion to understand if we are to come to grips with religion's relationship to thinking about the poor. From the in-depth conversations we had with people who expressed many different views of the poor, it became evident that church involvement was considered relevant for a variety of reasons. For people like Doug and Linda Hill, it was relevant for at least three reasons: it would help the "have's" to behave more compassionately, it would help the "have not's" to take greater responsibility for their own lives, and both groups would find the divine salvation that would cure their poverty of spirit. For people like Pam Jones, Ricardo Alvarado, and John and Mary Phelps religious involvement was favored mainly as a way of encouraging deeper thinking about the needs of the poor and as a vehicle for mobilizing volunteer efforts. In the Phelpses' case, the church was also an important means of promoting activity on behalf of economic justice.

Although religious organizations have often been criticized (sometimes by their own leaders) for not doing enough on behalf of the poor, the majority of the American labor force believes they are actually doing a good job in this area (see Table 7.5). Among the most actively involved, this proportion rises to about two-thirds. Significantly, a larger proportion of people with low incomes than with higher incomes feel churches are doing a good job helping those in financial need.

An important reason why people are convinced their churches are doing an effective job helping the poor is that they can cite firsthand examples. They may not know how government programs work, or they may not know what happens when they send a check to United

TABLE 7.5

Churches' Role in Helping

Question: "Churches do a good job of helping people who are in
financial need" (percent who say statement is mostly true)

Total U.S. labor force	53
Church attendance	
Weekly	66
Monthly	58
Yearly or less	37
Church member	
Yes	62
No	42
Religious preference	
Protestant	57
Catholic	55
Other	54
None	29
Religious orientation	
Conservative	66
Moderate	60
Liberal	46
Stewardship sermon	
Yes	66
No	49
Race	
White	53
Black	51
Income	
Low	58
Medium	52
High	45

Way, but their congregation is small enough that they can feel directly
involved and see the fruits of their labors. One modest but fairly typical example comes from Pam Jones. About the poorest person she has
ever known personally was an unwed mother who didn't have a job.

"She was actually part of our small group and that was one of the places where we set up the fund through the church and so she didn't know who was giving her money," Pam recalls. "We kind of had to canvass people so that we knew about how much she'd be getting a month, and we made a commitment to give her so much a month for a while, for the child care when she went back to work." This project worked out partly because the woman got back on her feet. She also showed appreciation, which gave the donors a good feeling about what they had done. Perhaps most important, her behavior demonstrated, as it were, that she was a worthy recipient. She became like the donors themselves, working hard at her job, taking a small apartment that she could afford, and showing how frugal she was by buying secondhand furniture.

Just by bringing middle-class people into personal contact with the poor, church programs also help reinforce the idea that disadvantaged people should be helped. The reason is often that seeing a need firsthand brings out some compassionate or altruistic sentiment. A person with an acute need is someone who must be helped. This sort of thinking is relatively straightforward. What is perhaps more interesting is how such firsthand contact transforms the way in which the *character* of the poor is understood. All too often, their character is diminished implicitly in efforts to account for their situation in the first place. They symbolize the opposite of character traits thought to be the basis of middle-class success and security. The poor are thus credited, as we have suggested, with limited intelligence, an inability to plan, having made bad choices, falling in with bad friends or marrying irresponsible partners, being weak-willed with respect to drugs and alcohol, or simply being lazy. Firsthand contact through church programs reverses those perceptions, making the poor more like "us."

It may be a little thing, like having a good sense of humor, that becomes a redeeming quality. Mary Phelps provided the following example. Admitting that, despite her concern for the poor, she has seldom really known anyone who was actually poor, Mary was drawn to the example of a poor woman with whom she had interacted in her parish to illustrate why she holds the poor in high esteem. The woman's poverty is easy to understand because she has been an alcoholic and married a man who abused her. But her ebullient spirit makes up for these moral failings: "The one thing that I just adore about her is she always laughs. There is some inner life in her, even though on the outside she is just this awfully miserable person who has nothing. She always seems to be able to smile."

John Phelps reinforces the impact of this story by noting that he has a lot more contact with poor people because of his work than his wife does. What he too emphasizes, though, is the role of personal contact in overcoming negative impressions. Many of the people he sees have notable deficiencies that John knows are scorned by the middle class: poor speech, dirty clothes, body odor. But he says he likes these people. Why? Because they are "pretty straight-shooting, very warm individuals, just kind of call-it-the-way-they-see-it types, friendly."

Feeling a common bond of humanness is one of the most powerful sources of altruistic behavior. If this bond is absent, or if, as Mary Phelps observes, "the middle class refuses to accept the poor as human beings, or even `see' them," little possibility exists of economic justice. What then is there to criticize about people like John and Mary Phelps who find reasons to feel "at one" with the poor? It is possible to admire this orientation and yet to point out that it makes the poor embody middle-class values, and perhaps even makes accepting them contingent on their conformity to these values. Being warm, good-natured people, the poor can be trusted. What if they were cold, diffident or crafty? They may be admired because of a down-to-earth attitude that makes them seem particularly "real" or genuine. They may be especially admired if they continue to work hard, despite suffering misfortune.

An interest in economic justice may start with empathic identification with the poor. It may be inspired by the sense that these people are "just like us," and so their rights should be enforced just as ours are. But if those rights become contingent on poor people having the same moral virtues as the "respectable" middle class, then departures from these traits provide a way of avoiding responsibility. True empathy requires more than remaking other people to conform to our own image. It requires rethinking our own identity as well. The poor may be a mirror for the middle class. But that mirror should register the faults of the middle class as well as its virtues.

In the Judeo-Christian tradition empathy that truly draws people together is defined as compassion, to suffer with, or to feel the same way as another person. The Good Samaritan is emblematic of this kind of empathy. Despite the ethnic differences that separate him from the man wounded on the Jericho road, he perceives suffering as a common human element. The injured man is required to pass no test of worthiness to receive his help.

Having studied Buddhism, Karen Kelsey has come to a very similar understanding of compassion:

In the Buddhist sense of compassion, if you're becoming less detached and living in the present moment, you're going to feel the need of others. So you walk by a homeless person and you feel their suffering and then you say, well geez, do I really need to have X amount in the bank? Shouldn't I relieve this person's suffering?

And yet she recognizes that empathic identification with those in need puts her in tension with the material comforts she has grown used to as a middle-class American.

It's a constant battle that I can't resolve. Should I have property? Should I have a house? I mean, everything about the way I live my life is in conflict with my ability to feel what it's like to be another human being with less.

Even though she's found no easy answer, she continues to think about the question, reading about it, talking about it. "I can't live with not having made a decision," she says, "so I guess I'll keep trying."

The other caveat to emphasize is that religious involvement encourages people to favor church efforts to assist the needy, but only up to a point. While close to 80 percent of the labor force say they would like churches to emphasize "job training, housing, and other services for the poor" more than they do now, only about a third want to see "a lot" more emphasis devoted to such efforts. Among those who attend religious services every week, moreover, this proportion is actually *lower* than among those who attend less often (see Table 7.6).[23]

From one perspective it is understandable that active churchgoers do not want their churches to be turned into welfare organizations. They recognize that the primary role of the church must include worship, prayer, religious instruction, and the nurturing of personal spirituality. Yet, from another perspective, it is also clear that this view of the churches further orients American thinking about where welfare efforts should be focused. It means that voluntary efforts other than those sponsored by the churches themselves must shoulder most of the responsibility for helping the needy.

Not Doing More

We began this chapter with the question, Why do so many people worry about the condition of the poor, take their responsibilities

TABLE 7.6

View of Churches Doing More to Help

Question: "Would you like to see churches and synagogues emphasize providing job training, housing, and other services for the poor
a lot more, somewhat more, somewhat less, or a lot less?"

	A Lot More	Somewhat More	Somewhat Less	A Lot Less
Total U.S. labor force	36	42	8	3
Church attendance				
Weekly	31	47	10	4
Monthly	38	46	7	3
Yearly or less	37	34	8	4
Church member				
Yes	33	47	9	4
No	39	36	7	3
Religious preference				
Protestant	35	43	10	4
Catholic	38	48	7	2
Other	35	47	6	5
None	32	25	5	7
Religious orientation				
Conservative	33	45	11	4
Moderate	35	46	10	3
Liberal	42	38	6	4
Race				
White	34	43	9	4
Black	42	36	7	3
Income				
Low	38	41	7	2
Medium	37	41	11	2
High	31	47	7	6

toward the poor quite seriously, and yet mount few organized efforts to promote economic reform? It is possible to quibble with the basic premise of this question: perhaps people don't care about the poor, or perhaps they really do take action to help them. With respect to the former, we presented quantitative and qualitative evidence showing that concern for the poor is widespread and that religious involvement increases it. With respect to the second, we will consider more in the next chapter how religious involvement encourages charitable giving, including deeds of kindness for the needy. But what we are trying to understand here is why concern for the poor leads to volunteer efforts rather than to greater support for basic economic reform.

If religious commitment encourages people to think about their responsibilities toward the poor, then, we have suggested, there must be cross-pressures that channel this thinking, perhaps muting what most Americans are willing to support. One of these cross-pressures has to do with public images of the poor. While thinking about responsibilities toward the poor is accompanied by a more sympathetic attitude toward them, this orientation is muted by all of the following: denying that the poor are any closer to God than the rich on grounds that God treats all people equally, recognizing that the poor may be especially subject to temptations and other moral failings that help explain why they are poor, and believing that God created a system of differential talents and rewards that ensures some degree of poverty at all times and places.

A second set of cross-pressures arises when Americans reflect on the nature of the economic system. In part, it is difficult to consider very seriously proposals for basic economic reform because large numbers of people claim not to understand the economic system well at all. Yet, there is considerable faith that economic changes are possible and even widespread agreement that some fundamental changes (but not an entirely different system) are needed. The cross-pressures arise because American culture encourages us to view economic problems essentially in moral terms. Whether a person attributes these problems to greed or to men shirking their God-given male roles, the logic is still that morality is at fault, rather than something endemic in the economic system itself. Those who regard the suffering of the poor as serious can nevertheless attribute it to happenstance rather than failings that can be corrected through economic reform.

All this leads to the belief that poor people can still be helped by a variety of volunteer efforts and social programs. But these programs in turn are shaped by understandings of what is fair and likely to work. Indeed, "likely to work" has an important dual meaning, for the program must be effective, but its recipients should also be willing to work. Volunteer efforts and localized social programs are preferred over national programs because they take into account the individual circumstances and moral worth of recipients. Being deserving is especially important, and this often means showing gratitude, and being friendly, matter-of-fact, and conscientious—all traits that middle-class Americans admire in themselves. Thus, they favor efforts by their churches and synagogues, up to a point, to help the poor. But they have misgivings about taking these programs too far, especially if notions of economic justice run counter to ideals of hard work, respecting individual differences, and rewarding individual abilities.

Religious thinking is not at all of one mind on these issues. Some believers favor systemic reforms, while others insist that volunteering is best. Yet the differences between supporters of social welfare programs and those who favor individual caring often pale in contrast to the broader assumptions that undergird the thinking of both. Much of the difference revolves around arguments about how many or how few of the poor are willing to work hard or turns on different understandings of equality. Broad agreement is present on assumptions about the moral roots of poverty, the role of individual differences, and the desirability of certain middle-class values. Deep support for economic justice, or deep involvement in the suffering of the poor, is difficult to mobilize because of these cross-pressures.

None of this is to deny what is actually being done on behalf of the poor or in the interest of economic justice. As we shall see in the next chapter, Americans engage in massive charitable behavior, and religious organizations greatly encourage this activity. If it falls short of what its proponents would wish, one of the reasons is the cultural logic that is at odds with doing more. This logic in fact channels thought and energy toward voluntary social programs such as those sponsored by religious organizations. It also limits the effectiveness of those programs.

Chapter Eight

Charitable Behavior

"He was a real task master, my father, physically and verbally abusive, always made me work hard. I hope I'm a bit kinder and gentler." It was hard work that helped Steve Young rise from boyhood on a small truck farm in Idaho to become owner and president of a $250 million business. It was his desire to be kinder and gentler that pushed him to sell it and, at age forty-three, turn his attention to philanthropy and volunteer work. A typical day starts at 5:30 A.M. with an hour of exercise. After cooking breakfast for the children and taking them to school, Steve spends an hour reading history, philosophy, or some other subject that interests him. His financial affairs may take until early afternoon. Then he spends most evenings visiting the sick, helping a family with some particular need, and doing church work. He's in charge of what is known as a "stake" in the Mormon church, an organization of ten "wards" (congregations), each of which is likely to have around two hundred families. In Steve's stake there are 4,700 people. To help him with his responsibilities, he has two lay counselors, an ecclesiastical board consisting of twelve men, a youth director, and about seventy staff members who oversee various programs and services. Each year the stake's budget for welfare services alone is approximately $200,000. Helping migrant workers, for example, has been a big item in recent years. Steve is convinced this type of activity can make America a better place to live. "I don't like the harshness of the capitalist system," he says. "I don't like the aggressiveness and the competition. It's brutal and its raw. I detest it. There has to be a way to balance that."

223

Rachel Eisen operates a small interior design business from her home in suburban Philadelphia. It takes most of her time but allows her to be there when the children need her. Besides, she enjoys the contact with customers and the chance to express herself creatively. Rachel has also devoted much of her time to her community. It all started, she explains, when her son went to kindergarten and became the target of some blatant anti-Semitism. She realized more clearly than ever before the importance of her Jewish identity. But there was virtually nothing available on an organized scale to help her rediscover her identity. So with the help of a few neighbors, she planned a campaign to start a temple, bought some land, and raised money for a building. "We were building it for our children and for future generations," she recalls. Serving first as chair of the building committee, then of the membership committee, and finally as president of the congregation, she found her volunteer efforts taking all her time. Since then, she's remained involved in one capacity or another, serving on various boards and contributing financially. Being part of the community has deepened her faith. She doesn't consider herself particularly religious, but she does believe in God, in the basic tenets of Judaism, and in just living well. The main rule of charity, she says, is that "it begins at home."

For the past fourteen years, Mike Kominski has driven a cement truck for a living. A union member, he earns a good wage. In fact, he recalls, his income doubled the year he joined the union. A typical day starts at 4:30 A.M. He gets to the plant about six, warms up the truck, and picks up his first load and delivers it at a construction site. He follows this routine the rest of the day. Some days he's finished by midafternoon, many days not till 6 P.M. He's lived in the same blue-collar town all his life. And over the years, he has become increasingly involved in the community. Several years ago, for example, when the town council threatened to drill a water well on his block, he organized his neighbors and persuaded the council to build it elsewhere. Since then, he's served on the planning board and the town council himself. Mixing with blue-collar people all day, he feels, gives him a real advantage in knowing how they think. He always tries to look at proposals in terms of how they may affect the poor and the elderly. Mike was raised in the Catholic Church and, until recently, attended Mass every Sunday, went to confession, and did parish work. "I went the whole nine yards," he says. Eventually the routine became so familiar that he decided he needed a change. Now he and his wife are attending a Pentecostal church. It's different, more lively, more oriented toward warmth and support. The most decisive event in Mike's life, though, was almost being killed a few years ago in a motorcycle accident. Feeling that God must have spared him for a reason, he's decided to devote his life to helping others. This is why he's become active in town politics. It's also why he spends his entire paycheck each year before Christmas to buy food for the homeless. "They always ask which organization I'm from," he says, "and I just say, `No organization, I'm just doing it myself.'"

Steve Young, Rachel Eisen, and Mike Kominski are but three examples of the millions of Americans who give money each year to religious organizations, who volunteer their time to these organizations, and who are inspired by their religious commitments to be of service to other people. Such efforts are well worth understanding. They are habits deeply ingrained in American culture. When Alexis de Tocqueville visited the United States in the 1830s, he was especially impressed with the voluntary associations that, in his view, served as vital underpinnings of democratic processes.[1] Helping one's neighbors had been part of American religious traditions long before Tocqueville.[2] And since then, charitable behavior has grown enormously, providing a wide variety of services to the needy and supplying the time and financial support on which religious organizations themselves depend.[3]

Charitable behavior is thus a vital link between sacred tradition and economic life in two important ways. It is itself a form of economic activity insofar as it represents time and money that could have been devoted to other purposes. If faith motivates people to give their time and money to charitable causes, rather than spending longer hours at work or buying more consumer goods for themselves, then this is an important way in which religion influences economic behavior. Charitable activities also provide the means for religious organizations to influence economic behavior in other ways. Stewardship sermons do not just happen; they have to be written, usually by someone with specialized training, and delivered, usually in person, to an audience that meets in a physical structure. All this requires economic resources. For religious organizations, most of these resources depend on charitable giving.

In this chapter we consider what is known about giving money to religious organizations and volunteering time to them, adding information from the Economic Values Survey and in-depth interviews. I am interested not only in how much money and time people give but in how attitudes toward religious organizations influence these activities. What people say would motivate them to give more is especially important to consider because of widespread concern about declining levels of giving relative to rising operating costs. I also consider evidence on religion's role in motivating compassionate behavior beyond what takes place in religious organizations themselves. Finally, I discuss some of the recipients of religious organizations' efforts and how some of these efforts actually help the needy. This chapter, then, extends the discussion presented in Chapter 7. Having examined a number of reasons why Americans prefer to channel their assistance to the needy through voluntary organizations, we now want to ask what role religion plays in actually mobilizing such efforts.

Giving to Religious Organizations

The history of giving to religious organizations reveals that levies were assessed on ordinary people for religious purposes from the time that specialized religious functionaries, such as priests and shamans, came into existence. But there have also been remarkable variations in how such assessments were made. Until the early modern period, many societies collected money for the support of religious organizations through a regular system of taxation. Some of the money went to the state, some to the church. At present, this system is still practiced in countries that have a state-sponsored church.[4] In the United States, religious giving has always been relatively free of the coercive powers of the state. Yet the state plays a role even today, for example, by exempting such giving from federal income taxes. Coercion of a different sort has often been present as well. Having to pay rent for one's pew or to pay a membership fee has a coercive aspect to it, at least for those who wish to be members in good standing of particular religious congregations. The same is true of appeals for money that suggest a fixed percentage of one's income be given to the church as a condition of staying in good favor with God.

Coercive means of raising support for religious organizations have given way in the United States to measures that rely largely on a combination of marketing appeals and individual conviction. The appeals range widely, from ones that encourage believers to give as an expression of their thankfulness to God, to ones that promise miraculous healings, special prayers that only clergy can offer, or material benefits themselves (in a favorable cost-benefit ratio). Appeals common in the industrial milieu of the nineteenth century are still widely in evidence. Believers are encouraged to give as a way of disciplining themselves, of giving thanks to God for blessing their labor, and of helping to provide for the moral instruction of children and the disadvantaged. Increasingly, however, new appeals appear to be more consistent with what we have noted in previous chapters about the characteristics of religion in postindustrial society. Giving and volunteering are encouraged because these activities make the donors feel good. Being generous is said to be a way of relieving stress, gaining diversion from the routine of ordinary life, and enhancing one's self-esteem. It may be a way of retaining some of the warmth and intimacy of private life despite the impersonal forces of large-scale institutions. And it may be a token or symbol, not of one's labor but of one's ability to withstand the corrupting influences of advertising and materialism.

One of the most common ways of making such appeals is through the stewardship sermon. As we have seen, some 40 percent of all church members say they have been exposed to such a sermon in the past year, as have 60 percent of those who attend services every week. Individual conviction enters the picture because appeals must always be made with reference to some values or beliefs on the part of the individual. Those who do not believe faith is important, or that it has anything to do with their finances, are likely to be unmoved even by the most ardent appeals.

The amount of money raised in the United States each year by religious organizations is in many respects staggering. Total giving to charitable organizations of all kinds, both in absolute figures and as a proportion of income, is higher in the United States than in virtually any other advanced industrial society.[5] By the early 1990s, this giving had risen to more than $100 billion annually, and of this figure, more than 50 percent went to religious organizations.[6] When giving only from private households is considered, the proportion of all charitable giving that goes to religious organizations rises to 64 percent. More than half of all households, according to a 1990 study, give money to religious organizations, on average donating about $715 per year (or $375 if averaged over all U.S. households).[7]

Still, this giving amounts to far less than the traditional "tithe," or 10 percent, that has often been suggested in religious literature, or even the 5 percent proposed more recently by some charitable organizations. Moreover, there are also huge variations in levels of giving within the population, some families making donations in the thousands of dollars, while most who contribute at all give less than a few hundred, and many give nothing at all.

The role that appeals and conviction play in explaining these variations in religious giving can be understood to some degree by considering the evidence presented in Table 8.1. People who attend religious services regularly are far more likely to give in substantial amounts than people who attend less frequently. This is not surprising, but it is important to consider the magnitude of these differences. Certainly they are far greater than those separating people simply on the basis of available income. Other things matter as well. Protestants on the average are more likely to give than Catholics, and religious conservatives are so inclined more than moderates or liberals. Participation in Sunday school classes or fellowship groups and actually having heard a sermon on stewardship in the past year are also associated with greater probabilities of giving. Indeed, nearly 20 percent of these people give more than $1,500 annually, whereas among those who have not participated or have not heard a stewardship sermon, only 5 percent give this much. These factors, incidentally, make a difference even when level of attendance at religious services is taken into account.[8] These results also parallel those of other studies, including national surveys and special surveys focusing on populations such as blacks and Jews.[9]

The same factors, it is worth noting, also appear to be associated with giving to other, nonreligious charitable organizations, indicating that religious giving may "begin at home," as Rachel Eisen says, but extend to other needs as well. In the Economic Values Survey, moreover, those who were religiously involved were more likely than the uninvolved to say they gave *regularly*. While only 44 percent of the entire labor force said they "give on a regular, planned basis" (with 46 percent saying they "give when you happen to feel there is a need"), the proportion who gave regularly rose to 50 percent among church members and to 61 percent among those who attended services weekly.

Other religious factors significantly associated with religious giving include thinking a lot about what the Bible teaches about money, thinking a lot about the relationship between one's faith and one's work, thinking a lot about one's responsibility to the poor, believing that one has received a divine calling, and regarding stewardship as a meaningful concept.[10] All of these matter independently of how often a person attends religious services or what that person's religious orientation is. Certainly it is important for religious organizations to draw out the specific connections be-

TABLE 8.1

Giving to Religious Organizations

Percent who gave at least $500 last year to religious organizations of all kinds:

Among persons in the labor force:	
All church or synagogue members	25
High income	41
Medium income	28
Low income	19
Attend services weekly	36
Attend services monthly	15
Attend less often	3
Protestants	27
Catholics	17
Conservatives	35
Moderates	20
Liberals	23
Fellowship group members	39
Nonmembers	18
Sunday school class members	39
Nonmembers	18
Heard stewardship sermon	39
Did not hear sermon	14

tween faith and personal finances if they want people to give generously. A broader perspective requires us to recognize, though, that religious giving occurs not only within a specifically religious framework but in the context of a much wider range of personal values.

The Culture of Religious Giving

In seeking the broader context in which religious giving occurs, we are sometimes strongly tempted to treat it purely as an economic matter. Indeed, data on such giving have now accumulated to the point that social scientists have begun creating econometric models to determine whether one additional stewardship sermon will bring in X dollars or whether three new fellowship groups per congregation might be an equally effective strategy.[11] But giving is always more than economics, especially when it occurs in religious settings.

It is also a symbol. How much one gives, religious tradition itself teaches, is less important than the spirit in which one gives. To give grudgingly, for self-aggrandizement, or for public display is a less worthy form of charitable behavior than giving in a spirit of thankfulness or from a sense of genuine compassion for the needy. This is why religious giving is carefully surrounded with ritual: prayers remind those in attendance why they are giving, the gifts are set apart and consecrated, and connections are drawn between monetary gifts and teachings about service and devotion to God. All these are formalized and made explicit. But *implicit* cultural frameworks are also deeply embedded in the wider society.

A framework that governs a great deal of thought about religious giving is one that prevails in the wider economy as well: an emphasis on economic responsibility. People want their money to be used wisely and effectively. This point may seem obvious. But there is a surface reason and a deeper reason for this emphasis on responsibility. The surface reason is that money should not be wasted, especially if it is given, as virtually all charitable giving is, with some goal or purpose in mind. "If your resources belong to God," Steve Young explains, "then you have a responsibility to use them wisely." The deeper reason is that charitable giving has become a symbolic extension of oneself. A rich person may make it so by giving $100 million to a college on condition that it be named after himself. In quieter ways, religious giving permits donors to tell themselves they are truly sincere in their faith, genuinely compassionate, and, among other things, responsibly investing in a worthy cause. Rachel Eisen says,

> I've always been very proud of the fact that I've donated something, some money to an organization that I've worked in. If I can see what it's done, or see that it's bought something special, that makes me feel good.

The driving forces behind this emphasis on responsibility are also twofold: they come from the culture at large, especially the world of work and consumption in which "quality merchandise at a fair price" is deemed a virtue, and from religious teachings about stewardship, stressing not only giving itself but the responsible investment of one's talents. Miriam Zellers is an example of someone driven to give responsibly by both of these forces. She tries hard to be frugal and carries this idea with her as she thinks about giving to religious causes. For instance, she is increasingly concerned about investing in religious programs that will have "long-term" consequences, especially as she grows older herself. With some amusement at her own seriousness, she admits that "God will still be here, of course, long after I'm gone," but she asserts "I want to make one less problem for God to be concerned about by doing a better job of planning." Her emphasis on rational giving is thus a reflection of who she is.

But another factor in our society makes us give as an extension of ourselves. Many of us have trouble knowing who we are. Our very identity is confused because of the mixed signals we receive from advertising, schools, churches, and our various subcultures. We are also torn by playing different roles in different settings—having to act one way to please our boss, another way behind the boss's back, and still another way in the presence of our children. As a result, we devote a great deal of energy to figuring out who we are. And the way we handle money is an important part of the process. As we saw in previous chapters, we feel good when we have money and disparage ourselves when we can't pay our bills. Yet we struggle in private with these feelings about ourselves and about money. Giving money is one of the few things we can do in public to show we are really good, decent, responsible people. Our giving—and our desire to give responsibly—thus have important symbolic implications for how we think about ourselves.

Even Miriam Zellers, for example, recognizes that a part of her derives happiness from having enough money to buy the things she wants. She asserts, "I'm not some wonderful saint." But she also realizes that being able to give away some of her money makes her feel even better about herself than having it or spending it on the things she wants. In a way that she considers curious, she says that giving "freely" makes her feel more secure. By giving some of her money away, she convinces herself she is not really dependent on having money and material goods. She is just herself—and could be happy even if she lost all her money.

Most people believe religious organizations actually do a good job of putting the money they receive to wise and responsible uses (see

232 _God and Mammon in America_

Table 8.2). There is, however, an undercurrent of doubt rooted in concerns about charitable organizations in general, some of which have been heightened by exposés revealing that officials had used donations for their own purposes.[12] It is particularly relevant to religious giving, not because exposés have found greater evidence of corruption than elsewhere but because public expectations are, ironically, both higher and lower. They are higher in that religious organizations are expected to be pure, sacred, especially careful with how they use their money; lower, because they are also expected to be a bit removed from the real world of tough economic decisions (much as are college professors and scientists whom we call "eggheads"). Thus, a substantial minority of the public (40 percent of the labor force), and even among the most active churchgoers (a quarter), fear religious organizations are not using their resources wisely, and this minority is substantially less likely to give than are those who have greater confidence.[13] Some of this concern, the data also suggest, might be allayed if people simply had a better idea of what religious organizations do with their money. Nearly half of all church members, for instance, say this added information would probably encourage them to give more (see Table 8.3).

The relevance of economic responsibility to religious giving suggests a second important cultural framework, namely, the separation of spirituality and materialism that we considered in Chapter 6. We saw there that cultural categories tend to differentiate these two realms, making it particularly dangerous or problematic when the caretakers of one seem to be influenced too much by values of the other. A distinction of this kind runs in several directions, depending on what sort of encroachment on symbolic boundaries is at issue. Let a television preacher be discovered living in a multi-million-dollar mansion and some hackles are raised. Let it be shown that the same preacher has actually bilked donors (and worse, engaged in perverse sexual behavior as well) and the public outcry becomes far greater. At that point, wealth or comfortable living has indeed been redefined by the public as greed, entailing a sense of selfishness and moral corruption as well. Mike Kominski, for instance, says he never, ever gives money to television preachers because they're raising money for material purposes—such as personal pleasure or political causes—rather than spiritual purposes—such as missions or feeding the hungry.

TABLE 8.2

Attitudes Toward Church Finances

	Total Labor Force	Weekly Churchgoers
Percent who agree:		
Churches use the money they get wisely and responsibly	60	77
Giving money to churches is more important that giving it to other organizations	32	57
I'd rather give money to a needy family than to a church	58	37
I'm more likely to give money to a church if someone I know personally asks me	44	42
It annoys me when churches ask me to give money	36	24

But let another preacher, say, one who lives in a modest dwelling, pay too much for repairs to the parsonage roof, and the public is actually somewhat relieved (one wouldn't expect a spiritual person to be any good with money). Thus, it restores public confidence in the orderliness of its cultural distinctions to believe, for example, that Mother Teresa of Calcutta is unconcerned about money or to know that generations of preachers, from Cotton Mather to John Wesley to Billy Sunday, died with virtually no money to their name.

If it is important to keep the spiritual and the material separate, it is therefore dangerous for religious organizations to concern themselves too much with appealing for donations. As shown in Table 8.2, about a quarter of active church members say it annoys them when churches ask for their money. Moreover, relatively few (about one church member in fourteen) say they would be inclined to give more if their church simply put more emphasis on giving, while a substantial number (nearly a third) say they would be inclined to give *less* (see Table 8.3). This fact, of course, flies directly in the face of fund-raising wizardry that says, in effect, all you have to do to get more money is ask.[14]

The distinction between the material realm and spirituality is so deeply embedded in our culture that many of us seldom think about it. By assuming that religious institutions should be exclusively concerned with spirituality, however, we excuse ourselves from taking responsibility for the material support of these institutions. We tell ourselves we are just interested in what is truly spiritual—perhaps groveling in our own quest to discover the sacred deep within our souls. We refuse to give money to churches and synagogues because they are spending money needlessly or showing too much interest in lavish artifacts. Or we give but in token amounts. Ironically, our insistence that spirituality remain unsullied helps keeps our money safe in our own pockets.

A third set of assumptions that helps define religious giving—one that is better understood by fund raisers—emphasizes what is often called the personal touch. They include the rather familiar notions that giving is more likely if the donor is approached by someone personally and that giving may be more generous if the recipient is actually a needy individual, rather than some organization or cause. But these notions also reflect deeper understandings in American culture. Despite the growth of large-scale organizations in the twentieth century (corporations, government bureaucracies, even mega-churches), or perhaps because of this growth, there is still a very strong antibureaucratic sentiment in popular culture. People fear the anonymity of large organizations. They also worry that these organizations are inefficient, and that (coupled with anonymity) this inefficiency can breed corruption. This concern is amplified in the religious domain for another reason. Among other things, religion is supposed to be the last refuge of the individual, a place where bureaucratic norms have not yet penetrated. And this applies especially to religious organizations in the realm of care giving. Thus, it is common for people to prefer a personal request for religious giving than one coming from a bureaucracy. It is also common, especially for those who have become alienated from churches (Manny Rodriguez was an example) to express their alienation by saying they would prefer to give to individuals rather than to churches. Again, we may give in token amounts, especially if a poor person happens to amuse us or strokes our ego by

TABLE 8.3

Changes That Would Increase Giving

Question: "Would each of the following make you more likely to give money to a church, not make any difference, or make you less likely to give?"

| | Church Members Only: | | |
	More	*None*	*Less*
If the church was doing more to help the needy	65	29	3
If I had fewer economic needs myself	51	38	6
If I understood better what the church does with its money	45	47	3
If my family was benefiting more from the church's programs	35	53	7
If the church spoke out more on social justice	31	53	11
If the clergy were less materialistic	31	52	9
If the preacher gave better sermons	20	67	9
If the church was more liberal on sexual and moral issues	8	49	37
If the church took more stands on political issues	7	51	36
If the church emphasized giving money more than it does now	7	57	30

showing special appreciation, but we may be less willing to support the religious institutions that play a vital role in maintaining the sacred on a wider scale.

This last point suggests a fourth set of assumptions. As we saw in Chapter 7, understandings of poverty in the United States lead to an emphasis on charitable assistance for the needy much more than they do to economic reform movements or government welfare programs.

This concern for the needy then becomes one of the chief ways in which religious giving is, in turn, legitimated. Indeed, more people say they would increase their giving if religious organizations did more to help the needy than for any other reason. Most people think religious organizations already do a good job of assisting the needy, but they apparently want these organizations to do more and would give more generously to support such efforts.

Here again, there are several complex connections between our understandings of helping the needy and religious giving. One is that helping the needy is widely regarded as a religious virtue. As we saw in the last chapter, religiously oriented people tend to think about the problems of the needy and to acknowledge responsibility for helping the poor. We also saw, however, that there is a limit to how much people think the churches should be helping the needy. Appeals based on giving to help the needy, therefore, may have diminishing returns. Miriam Zellers, for example, says there is a danger in spending time on charitable causes, even within the church, rather than "working for God by winning people to the Lord." Still, helping the needy garners support across a wide spectrum of religious orientations—conservatives, moderates, and liberals alike. Giving money to help the needy is favored by all these groups because it is viewed as politically neutral and especially because it is not associated with political liberalism or with moral permissiveness. Thus, the religiously active are far less likely to say they would give more if their churches became more liberal on sexual issues or became more involved in politics than if the churches did more to help the needy.[15] Some people (Mike Kominski being one) favor giving money to churches to help the needy because they think political organizations and causes will just waste it, too. It may also be that encouraging churches to help the needy is a way in which some people—especially the nonreligious or the nominally religious—pass the buck: let those church people do it, don't ask us to pay more taxes to help the poor.

Finally, religious giving is also deeply influenced by assumptions about personal finances and, thus, by materialistic values and broader assumptions about money. Although it makes sense to say this, there has been considerable unwillingness on the part of religious leaders and in the public at large to acknowledge this fact. When religious giving is discussed, the issues that are generally emphasized are church programs themselves. For example, the annual fund-raising drive tells us why the preacher needs a raise or why the parking lot must be repaved or why a new VCR is needed, but it fails to consider the deep meanings that money and materialism convey in American culture. Accordingly, preachers blame themselves if giving goes down, and denominational leaders try to identify new programs that will appeal more to members or argue that better sermons would help a lot. The truth of the matter is, these strategies are not likely to increase religious giving substantially, at least if people's reactions themselves are believed. Only a third of church members say they would give more if the church's programs benefited their family more, only one in five would give more if the sermons were better, and in both cases some members say they would actually give *less*. What does make a considerable difference is if broader views of money are altered.

One of the key factors that most people say would increase their religious giving is if they had fewer financial needs themselves. It may seem trite to mention this factor, especially if the implication is that people must become wealthier to give more generously. We must remember, however, that our perceptions of financial needs are indeed *perceptions*. They are attitudes that reflect how we understand money and material goods more generally. We see a direct trade-off between our own expenditures and charitable giving. And, of course, at one level it is true that a dollar spent here cannot be spent there.[16] But it is curious that this trade-off is considered important by almost as many wealthier people as it is among poorer people.[17] In short, economic "needs" seem not to diminish with wealth.[18] So the way to increase giving is to alter how people perceive their economic needs, not to wait until people become rich.

The importance of taking attitudes into account is evident in another finding as well. What makes more of a difference in giving is simply how much people value money in the first place. Whether they have needs or not, those who value money less give more, and those who value it more give less.[19] This means that religious organizations concerned about charitable giving must also be concerned about understandings of money and materialism more generally, especially with addressing clearly what our economic needs should be, helping us to evaluate our expenditures, and fostering reflection on the meaning of money itself.[20] If only one person in six (as we saw in Chapter 5) has ever been taught that wanting a lot of money is wrong, it is little wonder that religious giving is not higher than it is.

Steve Young has thought about these issues a great deal. His words show clearly that the important consideration is not simply having enough money to give. Even those who do must strike an appropriate balance between what he calls "creeping consumption" and charitable behavior.

> It doesn't matter whether you make $100,000 or a million dollars a year, the system is going to cause you to consume 120 percent of it. Social climbing does it to you, TV and advertising do it, your family does, the tax system does. It's ugly. It stinks. So the question is, how do you cap your consumption? And then how much do you give to charity?

Volunteering in Religious Organizations

Giving of one's time is quite similar in many respects to the giving of money. We know from other research that the former is often deemed more worthy than the latter, apparently because it represents an investment of the self, rather than simply an easy way to pass off one's social obligations. As Mike Kominski says, "Giving from the heart means getting your hands dirty, not just writing a check." Volunteering—even in small amounts—is also a way of making ourselves feel better about who we are. It is, in this sense, subject to the same frameworks as religious giving, especially the assumption that it should be personal and effectively directed toward the needy. Those who give money are also more likely to give of their time, and vice versa, and religious volunteering is, of course, strongly influenced by the same measures of religious belief and involvement with which charitable giving is associated (see Table 8.4).[21] But if religious giving is influenced strongly by orientations toward money, then religious volunteering is more clearly shaped by attitudes toward work and levels of involvement in the workplace.

The most significant impact has probably come from the inclusion of women in the workforce. Throughout most of American history, women were expected to carry a large share of the responsibility for local church work and other community activities. The rationale was that men had fixed work schedules while women didn't, that women perhaps had a more nurturing temperament than men, and that in any case the sort of skills required (such as caring for the sick or preparing meals) were more properly in the female domain. Even today, women remain more actively involved in religious organizations and participate in services, classes, and fellowship groups more often than men. Gainful employment outside the home, however, has made it more difficult for women to find time to spend on church committees and related projects. Thus, while 37 percent of women with part-time employment say they have done volun-

TABLE 8.4

Volunteering in Religious Organizations

Percent who have done volunteer work at their church or synagogue in the past year:

Total labor force	28
Men working full-time	24
Men working part-time	25
Women working full-time	29
Women working part-time	37
Church or synagogue members	45
Attend services weekly	64
Attend services monthly	17
Attend less often	3
Protestants	33
Catholics	23
Conservatives	46
Moderates	30
Liberals	14
Fellowship group members	71
Nonmembers	17
Sunday school class members	68
Nonmembers	19
Heard stewardship sermon	63
Did not hear sermon	14

teer work at their church or synagogue, only 29 percent do so among those employed full-time. The latter are also more likely than the former to agree with the statement, "I'm too busy to do church work."[22]

Rachel Eisen illustrates how volunteer activities may have at one time substituted for the experience of pursuing a career. Before she became involved in her graphic design business, volunteering for temple activities was an important source of her personal identity. Now, even though her faith is still important, she has less time for these activities and they play a smaller part in sustaining her self-esteem. Steve Young illustrates the same process but in reverse. Although he is atypical (men with part-time jobs do not generally volunteer more than men with full-time jobs), having been able to retire early from his business has freed him considerably to work for his church.

The fact that spirituality is set apart from materialism, at least conceptually, is also significant to the meaning of religious volunteering.[23] Religious volunteering is a way of dramatizing one's commitment to values other than money and material possessions. Religious organizations may also be regarded as a haven from the workplace, a source of caring rather than cut-throat competition, and a way of realizing deeper dimensions of the human spirit than can be cultivated in a job. Volunteering in this realm can then be a way of escaping, doing something more worthwhile, helping people who really need it, or associating with people who share fundamental values and who enjoy being around one another. For this reason, people who do volunteer work in religious organizations often speak of the personal satisfaction that comes from these activities. Indeed, few of these activities can be considered truly altruistic or self-sacrificing, because the caregivers benefit from them as much as the recipients. Miriam Zellers, for example, says it is simply a matter of "experiencing joy" to do volunteer work at her church, and she admits she would quit if it became drudgery.

Yet it is also clear that religious volunteering is hard work. It can be a thankless task or more difficult to carry out than in the workplace, where material incentives can be used as leverage. Especially to recruit and organize other volunteers may involve, as Rachel Eisen observes, the "patience of a saint," or at least of someone who can always be grateful, even though the assistance given is fleeting and less than professional. Perhaps it is for this reason that religious volunteering is also positively associated with having thought more about the relationship between one's faith and one's work.[24] Especially if there is a trade-off between one's job and one's volunteering, mental and emotional effort is required to find an appropriate balance between the two.

Motivating Compassionate Behavior

Besides encouraging people to volunteer at churches and synagogues, religious commitment is also one of the leading sources of motivation for acts of caring and kindness of a wider variety. Previous research has shown that persons who attend religious services faithfully are much more likely than other people to be involved in community service projects and to donate time to other voluntary associations as well. These relationships persist even when other factors that might be associated with both attendance and volunteering (such as gender, age, and region of the country) are taken into account. The religiously involved are also more likely to value helping the needy and to put this value into practice by caring for the sick or providing comfort for the bereaved or lonely. There are, however, some areas of need to which religious commitment does not seem to extend, at least not in ways that differ from the caring shown by nonreligious people. Helping with emotional crises, stopping to give assistance to stranded motorists, or giving money to beggars, for example, are no more likely among the religiously involved than the uninvolved.[25] In the Economic Values Survey, it is clear that these patterns from previous research are again in evidence (see Table 8.5). Those who attend religious services regularly are more likely than the labor force as a whole to be

TABLE 8.5

Involvement in Volunteer Activities

	Total Labor Force	Weekly Churchgoers
Do you yourself happen to be involved in any charity or social service activities, such as helping the poor, the sick or the elderly? (percent yes)	25	39
Among those who said yes, percent who spend at least 5 hours a week on these activities	24	29
Percent who have done each in the past year:		
Visited someone in the hospital	73	80
Helped a relative or friend through a personal crisis	71	74
Donated time to a volunteer organization	35	48
Worked on a community service project	24	31
Given money to a beggar	41	40

involved in charitable and social service activities, more likely to devote greater numbers of hours to these activities each week, more
likely to have visited someone in the hospital, worked as volunteers,
and done community service projects, but no more likely to have
helped friends with personal crises or given money to a beggar.

Religious leaders can take some of the credit for these patterns. Active churchgoers are more likely to volunteer for a wide variety of
causes because these needs are brought to their attention in their Sunday school classes, fellowship groups, or on bulletin boards and in
church leaflets. Still, there must be a careful balance between activities that only maintain the religious organizations themselves and activities that help meet needs in the wider community. People need to
be encouraged to donate time and money to keep the churches and
synagogues solvent and to reach out beyond these organizations. If
giving and volunteering focuses too much on good feelings or benefit-
ing one's own family, then both of these larger needs may remain
unmet.

The impact of religious commitment on caring behavior appears to
be accomplished in two principal ways. Religious beliefs heighten the
importance of caring, and religious organizations help people put this
orientation into practice. The belief component is composed of mutually reinforcing assumptions about the existence of God, the love of
God, and biblical charges to believers to demonstrate God's love to
others. The sense of responsibility to God implied in teachings of the
calling and stewardship also appear to be part of this cluster. Data reveal that understandings of stewardship, exposure to stewardship sermons, a sense of being called, and thinking about responsibilities to
the poor, for example, are all positively associated with engaging in
charitable and social service activities (see Table 8.6). The organizational component helps reinforce motivation and provide information.
Reinforcement comes about through sermons, classes, and fellowship
groups that formally and informally encourage believers to put their
faith into practice. One of the most vivid indications of this role is that
people who claim to have a deep religious faith but who are not actively involved in a religious organization tend not to be engaged in
charitable activities, while those who claim the same level of faith and
are involved in a religious organization are much more likely to engage in charitable activities.[26] The informational role is quite straightforward: religious organizations tell people of opportunities to serve,
both within and beyond the congregation itself, and provide personal

TABLE 8.6

Correlates of Charitable Behavior

	Percent of Those Involved in Charitable Activities and Not Involved Who Responded as Indicated:	
	Involved	*Uninvolved*
Thought about relation to God a great deal	50	29
Thought a great deal about responsibility to the poor	33	14
Member of fellowship group	37	13
Heard stewardship sermon	44	20
Say making a lot of money is very important	35	51
Say materialism is extremely serious problem	35	26
Say money gives a good feeling about myself	75	76
Say living a comfortable life is very important	70	74
Say their work is very meaningful to them	48	34
Want more from life than just a good job and a comfortable lifestyle	35	25

contacts, committees, phone numbers, meeting space, transportation, or whatever it may take to help turn good intentions into action.

Mike Kominski vividly illustrates someone inspired by his religious beliefs to do volunteer work in the community. Unlike Steve Young and Rachel Eisen, whose volunteer work has taken place primarily under the auspices of their religious organizations, Mike's activities have extended well beyond either the Catholic church in which he was raised or the Pentecostal church he now attends. Yet the influence of religious belief and involvement has always remained strong. Many people survive near death experiences and do not interpret them in a way that leads to greater involvement in helping others. Mike Kominski's experience did so because his religious upbringing helped him understand it as a call from God to be of greater service. Living in a small town, he probably would have known about opportunities to serve anyway. But his religious involvement has at least sustained his motivation. Sometimes he becomes preoccupied with his work and his family. But then a sermon or a comment from one of the people at his church helps him remember his pledge to help others.

Mike Kominski also illustrates the importance of stories in turning religious sentiments into acts of kindness. Most people nowadays experience themselves, by their own accounts, at the center of a kind of vortex created by competing values, commitments, and motivations. They want to help others perhaps, but they also want to be successful, make a lot of money, and lead a comfortable existence. Even when they decide to do something helpful, they wonder whether they are doing it to serve someone else or because it will look good on their résumé and make them feel better about themselves. Mike Kominski admits his volunteer work makes him feel involved, as if he were important in the community. He also admits his good intentions leave him feeling tired after long meetings, and he asks himself why he bothers. But his near death story helps him organize all these conflicting orientations. While he recognizes his complex motives, this is a primordial experience in his life that he can look back on as a turning point. It provides a way of telling others (and himself) why he is doing what he does:

> People who knew me before know I'm a lot different now. I don't think my beliefs have changed so much, but I've gotten rid of a lot of junk, like wasting time, doing fruitless things, and not making every day count. I feel like I'm living on borrowed time. When you're at the edge of death, and you hear the doctors saying they don't know if you'll live, it really gets your attention. You'd always been too busy to tell people you loved 'em, or you couldn't call and check on somebody or do them a favor. It really shakes up your priorities. Now I've got a second chance. I'm grateful for it. I'm not going to squander it.

If religious commitment has a stronger impact on caring behavior than it does on aspects of economic behavior involving work and money, the reason is probably that acts of kindness are more easily turned into stories—narratives about special times and places, special needs, deeper motivations, turning points. They serve as epiphanies, much like miraculous answers to prayer, only perhaps more commonly, providing evidence that material pursuits are not the only important things in life. Being able to help others provides repeatable testimony that an individual is indeed a good and decent person, someone who respects higher values in life, rather than being a drone who does nothing but work and spend, spend and work.

What charitable behavior accomplishes, therefore, is not so much a complete transformation of an individual's values but (as Mike Kominski says) a reordering of one's priorities. And even that reordering may be minor rather than major. The quest for money in large quantities may be hard to reconcile with giving and volunteering, and indeed concerns about materialism in the society at large may be greater. But wanting a comfortable life and feeling good about having money may not conflict with giving and volunteering at all. Nor is it likely that work or a career will seem any less important. But all these pursuits may be relativized simply by the sense that there are also other important things in life (Table 8.6).

How Religious Organizations Help

I want to come back to the question of how telling stories about oneself as a caring person may make a difference to how an individual conceives of work, money, and materialism. Whether deeds of kindness transform the donors or not, there is nevertheless the question of whether they actually meet needs among their recipients. Who is helped? And are they helped materially? These are also important questions for understanding how religion interacts with the economic realm.

Because the Economic Values Study included only people who were working at least part-time, it does not provide as full a picture of who receives help from religious organizations as we would like. The unemployed, the retired, and the homeless would all be excluded. However, the study does provide the only national information available on *receiving* money from religious organizations. In the labor force as a whole, about 4 percent claimed to have received financial help from a religious organization during the past year. It is instructive to compare both the economic and the religious characteristics of these recipients with comparable members of the labor force who were not recipients (see Table 8.7).

The economic characteristics that set recipients apart from nonrecipients include lower family incomes; working in blue-collar, clerical, or sales occupations; unmarried persons; women working only part-time; parents who have children living with them at home; having been laid off in the past year; having taken a pay cut in the past year; being worried about paying bills; and having medical expenses to pay. All these characteristics indicate clearly that the recipients of financial help from religious organizations tend to be persons with above-average financial needs and with subnormal financial resources of their own.[27]

This profile is also revealing in one particular respect. The recipients of financial help from religious organizations fit precisely the profile of those who have been of greatest concern in studies of poverty and social welfare. Many of those presently on welfare, while employed sporadically or part-time, are women with small children heading single-parent households.[28] Because of divorce, abuse or abandonment by their husbands, or pregnancies outside of marriage, they have been unable to attain steady or more remunerative work, and with medical, housing, and child support costs to bear, their own resources are less than adequate. "They come knocking at the door with a rent bill they can't pay," says Steve Young, "and we'll give them $200 or $300 to help out, or maybe it's just some money to buy the kids a new pair of shoes. The need is there, but often we just aren't willing to see it." That religious organizations are partially supporting some of these families, therefore, is an important aspect of the overall provision of social welfare services.

The religious characteristics of these recipients are also revealing. The vast majority are church or synagogue members, most attend religious services faithfully, and a majority participate in fellowship or support groups.[29] When attendance is controlled, participation in fellowship groups still has a strong effect, apparently because people in these groups are more likely to make their financial needs public, either by discussing them with other members or by praying about them.[30] Thus, it seems clear, as Rachel Eisen observed, that for the religiously involved charity does indeed "begin at home." This also means relatively little of the financial support that religious organizations give to *individuals* actually extends beyond the confines of the

TABLE 8.7

Receiving Financial Assistance

	Percentage with Each of the Characteristics Listed Among Those Who Had, or Who Had Not, Received Financial Help from a Religious Organization in the Past Year	
	Recipients	*Nonrecipients*
Economic characteristics:		
In lower-income bracket	50	29
Blue-collar worker	46	42
Clerical/sales worker	26	16
Unmarried	30	22
Women working part-time	20	14
Have children at home	63	50
Laid off in past year	15	11
Pay cut in past year	25	13
Worried a lot about bills	45	27
Paying for medical expenses	53	29
Religious characteristics:		
Church/synagogue member	80	56
Attend weekly	72	30
In fellowship group	61	18
Received religious counseling	46	4

congregation itself (perhaps no more than one person in ten, judging from the proportion who say they seldom or never attend services). While this pattern leaves religious organizations open to criticism, it nevertheless has the positive consequence that recipients can also be given more than financial assistance alone. The large percentage who are in fellowship groups can receive emotional support, for example, and nearly as many, judging from the survey, have also received counseling from a religious organization.[31]

Emotional support may be a crucial element in getting people back on their feet. Steve Young says about 80 percent of the people he's helped financially are part of his church, but even the others he helps often need emotional support as much as anything else. He remembers one woman who received such support for about three years while she was getting a divorce.

> Some days she'd just come in and break down crying. So we tried to protect her and get her through the pain stage until she had an ability to make it on her own. Another guy, he lost his job, and we pretty much did the same thing.

Religious organizations also provide a great deal of assistance to the needy besides individual financial support. Informal voluntary services are one such form of assistance. These services, too, are more likely to be extended to fellow members than to nonmembers. But there is also clear evidence that infrequent attenders and nonmembers at least perceive of religious organizations and their members as potential sources of assistance. For example, another national survey (that included people not in the labor force) showed that even among persons who seldom or never attended religious services, more than half felt they could count on the members of a church or synagogue for assistance if a family member became ill or needed help.[32]

Besides supporting individuals directly, religious organizations also supply assistance indirectly through organized programs. The list of these services is certainly too long to enumerate fully but would include financial assistance or scholarships to low-income families who send their children to parochial schools (often a valuable resource in urban areas with decaying public school systems); financial support for paid professionals, such as hospital and prison chaplains, who provide technical advice as well as emotional support; funding for urban housing and community development programs; and free or at-cost use of facilities for nursery schools, breakfast programs, medical clinics, and employment counseling.

Certainly it is true that a substantial share of the money contributed to religious organizations goes for the support of these organizations themselves, including clergy salaries and the expense of maintaining a physical facility. But it has also been estimated that approximately half (46 percent) of donations to religious organizations are used to support activities other than religious ministry (or education), such as human services. About nine out of ten congregations report some kind of human service or welfare program, in fact. At least three-quarters are involved in international relief to some extent. And more than half help sponsor community development programs, hospital or nursing care, and other health-related programs.[33] Moreover, at least $8 billion annually is channeled by churches and synagogues to other organizations and individuals, such as denominational charities or community service agencies.

Ultimately, however, it is the individual recipients who matter the most to these programs. A number of the people we talked to mentioned how meaningful it had been to them to receive help from a religious organization. One man remembered that the priest had given him $400 at a time of desperate need. A family of refugees from East Asia were taken in by a local church. A young woman told how the church had found her a place to live during her divorce. And a young man described how the parish had helped him get an education. Many of these people, moreover, had themselves been inspired to help others as a result of these experiences. In the survey, 40 percent of those who had received help from a religious organization in the past year were currently engaged in charitable activities, and 75 percent made donations to charitable organizations.

The Cultural Cluster

The main conclusion of this chapter is that religious giving is part of a much larger cluster of beliefs and cultural assumptions and, for this reason, cannot be separated from how people think about their work, money, and materialism, any more than it can be cut off from beliefs about God, spirituality, and stewardship. This is because religious giving has important symbolic qualities. It dramatizes commitment and withdrawal, expenditure and sacrifice, what it means to be a spiritual person, and what a good religious organization should be. Were someone, say, a pastor or church planner, interested only in the question of financing religious organizations, therefore, that person would still need to understand more than programs, more than sermons, more than pledge drives and stewardship appeals. He or she would need to understand how the American public thinks about its money and its time and what constitutes worthy religious uses of these resources. I cannot emphasize this point enough, especially at a time when fund-raising efforts seem to focus increasingly on programmatic appeals, rather than considering the conflicting impulses and values that may motivate people to give or deter them from giving more.

A significant starting place is that most people believe religious or-ganizations use their resources wisely and effectively. It means that these organizations are deemed capable of conforming to the same logic of rationality that applies in the workplace and in the market. But there is also a healthy tension between religious organizations and these economic institutions. Some degree of inefficiency is expected, tolerated, and perhaps even desired as evidence that the spiritual realm has not become subject entirely to norms of economic rationali-ty. As always, there are costs and benefits associated with the ambiva-lence we feel toward religious organizations. The cost is that we may let this ambivalence excuse us from supporting them. The benefit is that we may blow the whistle when religious leaders abuse the trust placed in them. Moreover, different norms having to do with compas-sion, the personal touch, and spirituality itself are assumed to apply to religious giving and volunteering, not simply bottom-line efficiency. It is thus awkward at best to preserve the right mixture of responsibility, on the one hand, and of holding the dominant norms of economic ra-tionality in abeyance. Steve Young probably said it the best when he observed that the church must be wise, but in ways different from other social institutions.

Religious organizations are also placed in a bad spot by the some-what contradictory assumptions held by the American public concern-ing their material dimension. People want religious organizations to help those who do not have material abundance, to be less materialis-tic themselves, and to encourage others to abandon materialism. Thus, it bothers them when religious organizations seem to be materialistic or seem to emphasize money too much. This means that religious or-ganizations may have to find a way of appealing for money without ac-tually talking about it. "Helping the needy" seems to be an effective slogan because it takes material resources to do this and yet empha-sizes a worthy goal rather than the monetary means of achieving it. Helping the needy is perhaps an especially favored goal because it re-quires money, and yet it is a use that clearly extends beyond the salaries, buildings, and material accoutrements of religious organizations themselves.

Religious giving also stands in opposition to an emphasis on money in the lives of individual members. Those who give more to religious organizations value money less, and vice versa. At one level, this is quite understandable. Giving money away is the opposite of having it. But this relationship too is symbolic and therefore needs to be probed for its deeper meanings.

The starting place is actually the relationship between money and faith—and between spirituality and materialism—that we have examined in previous chapters. There, we saw considerable slippage in how religious admonitions against greed were actually applied. Americans are prone to argue that there is nothing wrong with having a lot of money. What counts is how a person thinks about money and perhaps even the uses to which it is put. One can even want it badly, recognize that having it is essential to one's identity, and say that one's feelings about oneself depend on it. Yet, a person must not become materialistic, meaning, not individualistic or selfish. Giving some small fraction of money away is thus an important gesture because it provides a token demonstration that one is not individualistic or selfish.

Another way of understanding what is going on here is to ask why most people give a little to religious organizations and other charities, rather than a lot more or, for that matter, none. To give nothing is an inadvertent symbolic gesture. It suggests one is indeed too materialistic (selfish) to part with anything. The only justification may be family needs (a form of charity that truly begins at home). But to give more than a little would serve no purpose. There is no objective standard suggesting that altruism must be demonstrated by an X percent contribution rather than a Y percent donation. More important, giving more is likely to run up against two other cultural hurdles. One is that religious organizations are asking for money, which annoys people and makes them think these organizations themselves are materialistic. The other is that feeling pressured destroys some of the spontaneity of giving and therefore diminishes the sense of moral worth people like to derive from giving "freely," as religious leaders are prone to emphasize.

To be sure, there are many "cultures" of religious giving rather than just one. Certainly Catholic teachings about alms may differ from Protestant fundamentalist views of freewill offerings and the like. In recent years, it has also been all too apparent that other subcultures were intervening in the logic of religious giving. Activists for conservative religious causes have sometimes withheld their donations from denominations they thought were too liberal, and liberal activists have done the same.

But the dominant conclusion that emerges from the survey and interview evidence we have considered in this chapter is that these subcultural differences may be less important than the more consensual understandings that influence thinking about religious giving across the board. When asked what would encourage them to give more (or less), religious liberals were more inclined than religious conservatives to give more if churches became more liberal on sexual issues. With this exception, however, there was striking agreement among conservatives, moderates, and liberals alike about what would and would not encourage more giving, just as there was among individuals as different in their religious beliefs as Steve Young, Rachel Eisen, and Mike Kominski. Across all groups, the important considerations were clearly what religious organizations were doing to help the needy, how well people felt they understood the uses to which their donations were being put, and how they perceived their own economic needs. In short, questions about money, materialism, and material need supplied the framework in which religious giving was understood, not a set of narrowly conceived theological orientations and certainly not a grab bag of political issues.

Giving of one's time is subject to many of the same considerations. It too represents a deeply symbolic activity whose meaning is conditioned by broader understandings. To give freely of one's time to a worthy cause becomes a source of good feelings about oneself. Such behavior also provides testimony that an individual isn't entirely selfish. Volunteering is, however, subject to somewhat greater cultural ambiguity than financial giving because of the ways in which work itself is understood. There may be a clear trade-off between buying a new pair of roller blades and putting a donation in the offering plate. One may seem worthier than the other. It may be much less clear that spending an evening on a church committee is any more worthy than working a double shift at the hospital. Is one more caring than the other? Difficult to say.

We come again, then, to caring for the needy and to the importance of being able to tell stories about such activities. Most people can argue in some general way that their regular work contributes to the betterment of the world. Yet few people can see that their work does this in any immediate or dramatic sense. They keep the computers going at a large investment bank and that in turn helps other people have jobs or pay their bills. But there is nothing very dramatic about any of this. Helping one's family, such as comforting a youngster whose feelings have been hurt, is a much more tangible way of helping out. And for this reason, many people value their family activities much more deeply than their work. Even family time, however, can be considered selfish if it does not do anything to benefit the wider community or those with serious needs. Thus helping the needy becomes an important way of dramatizing that one is a good and decent person.

It might then be argued that charitable behavior is actually the critical link between religious commitment and economic activities concerned with work and money. Helping the needy could be an object lesson for the helper, causing that person to devote less time to the workplace and becoming less attached to material possessions. It might even be argued that such activities play the key role in a way that stewardship sermons or abstract notions of responsibility to God do not because they involve the individual in concrete behavior. An alternative argument, though, would suggest that such activities are really nothing more than tokens. They provide easy ways to bracket work and money, putting them "in perspective," but not seriously limiting their appeal.

The truth of the matter appears to lie in the middle and indeed varies from person to person. There is some evidence that people who engage in religious giving, religious volunteering, or other charitable activities are less materialistic than others. But what this means exactly must be considered in the light of what we have learned in previous chapters. It does not mean that people are any less interested in money, have any fewer financial obligations, or are any less devoted to their work. Mostly, it is a gentle nudge, a reminder that there are other values in life, too, other needs, needy people who are not served by work and by money alone. In this sense, those inspired by religious convictions to help the needy want more out of life, rather than less. Unwilling to abandon their interest in work and money but wanting to be altruistic as well, they want it all.

From the standpoint of the recipients, none of this may matter very much. The important thing is whether some form of assistance becomes available at all. The evidence we have considered suggests that religious organizations are a significant source of assistance for people who clearly need this assistance. Just how significant it is depends on the question, in relation to what? It may represent only a fraction of what is channeled to the needy through government programs or an even smaller fraction of what might actually be needed. Yet it does make a difference. And to that degree, the understandings that generate this charitable behavior should also be taken seriously.

These understandings channel an otherwise vague sense of wanting to have a better world into voluntary assistance for the needy. They limit, as we saw in the last chapter, what it means to be a worthy recipient, and they direct attention more toward voluntary giving than support for economic restructuring through government policy. It may be possible to reshape these understandings so that they focus more on political reform, for instance, by speaking more forcefully about economic justice, rather than need alone. But to the extent that these understandings appear to be quite well institutionalized, it may also be worth attempting to work within them. They encourage people to help the needy through religious organizations and for religious reasons. If these organizations remain strong, such efforts are also likely to remain a significant feature of American life.

Chapter Nine

Considering the Future

Where do we go from here? American religion may be flourishing and, despite continuing worries and periodic setbacks, our economic system remains strong. But millions of people complain of job-related stress and burnout, millions feel they are working too many hours and need more time for themselves and to think about basic values, millions are overwhelmed with credit card debt and want more money to buy what the American Dream has promised them, millions fear that the nation has become too materialistic for its own good, and millions more suffer from chronic unemployment, poverty, and homelessness. Our faith helps us get through the day. Yet we suffer the anguish of overwork, of being caught up in a never-ending quest for material goods, and of wondering if we are doing the right things with our time and money. Does religion have a role to play? Are all these concerns to be solved through government programs and economic growth? Can anything be done at all?

The Role of Religious Organizations

Religion in America continues to be a vital repository of maxims about hard work, honesty, and the responsible uses of money. These maxims encourage those who think about them to value their work more, to derive greater personal satisfaction and meaning from it, to avoid bending the rules more often than they feel necessary, and to pursue material comforts without becoming obsessed with them. It is, we might say, in religion's interest to be relevant to the economic sphere in these ways. A faith that claims to have implications for all of human existence must apply itself even to the gritty world of work and money.[1]

Even if there were no need at all for economic behavior to be influenced by religion (say, if markets worked as well as some of their defenders think), it would still be likely to hear sermons about stewardship and to see books written about the theology of work. Chastising parishioners for being too materialistic is a way of getting their attention—and making them feel a bit uncomfortable—more so than preaching about the devil.

In more significant ways, organized religion is an important source of interpretation about things economic. One can imagine how different the books and articles written about economic scandals in the 1980s (RJR Nabisco, Lehman Brothers, Silverado, etc.) would have been if the notion of *greed* had somehow dropped out of the public vocabulary. And organized religion is, as we have seen, one of the sources that still prompts us to regard greed as a vice. Or the same might be said of long-running debates about the environment: impoverished without the language of stewardship. Such examples point to the importance of keeping certain vocabularies alive. Even if they do little to guide the private behavior of individuals, they offer a way of interpreting the meaning of public events.

For those who are deeply involved in religious communities, such discourse comes to the surface and provides a much clearer language for thinking about questions of work, money, and materialism. It may not prevent people of faith from behaving in ways that they—or others—might regard as being greedy, for example, deterring them from buying a wide-screen television set. Even in tight-knit groups, the authority of individual conscience is a cherished religious teaching. So one person may purchase a new toy in good conscience, while another decides not to. But communities of faith do provide all it takes, as a mystery writer might say, to "commit the crime" of behaving in ways different from the dictates of Madison Avenue: means, motive, and opportunity. The means may be little more than the evening a week that someone sets aside to attend a group, perhaps devoting a share of that time to helping the needy. The motive may be a biblical story about the threat of materialism. Opportunity can be created by the information networks implicit in such groups, for example, about a new book discussing faith and work or about a bill before Congress that has implications for the poor. The fact that a substantial minority of the population is involved in religious fellowship groups and attends religious services regularly, therefore, is a promising indication of the continuing ability of religious organizations to influence economic behavior.

Despite their limited effects on how we think about our work and money, religious organizations also play a continuing role in channeling time and money away from self-gratification—and the marketplace—toward uses that cannot so easily be justified in terms of self-interest (or readily priced). Besides the resources that people donate for maintaining religious programs themselves, a considerable investment is made in community programs of all kinds and in helping the needy. But there is no question that more could be done and that more needs to be done. Members of religious organizations claim they would give more generously if these organizations played a more active role in helping the needy. The leaders of these organizations might be well advised to take their members up on this claim.

One of the most serious barriers to religious organizations doing more is the temptation to treat economic matters as if they were the domain of someone else. Economists and business leaders have fostered the myth that only they can understand such issues. But religious organizations still have far richer languages in which to talk about greed than economists do. Biblical stories of caring for the needy remain richer and potentially more compelling than bottom-line analyses of social programs supplied by government officials. Most individuals make their financial decisions in a vacuum, worrying whether they are doing the right thing but acknowledging that they worry nevertheless. The minority who consult clergy on such matters is still larger than the number who seek professional advice from financial experts. This is a role that religious organizations might consider expanding.

The other barrier preventing religious organizations from making a difference in economic matters is speaking in such vague generalities that nobody is sure whether it even makes a difference to agree or disagree. If all that stewardship means is using your talents and doing something that makes you happy, what impact is this teaching likely to have on our behavior? As are most leaders of large organizations, clergy are averse to taking risks: they do not want to say anything that may stir up trouble, especially if it means losing the regular check of some generous donor. But stewardship, the calling, greed, materialism—these terms must all be defined if they are to mean anything. Clergy themselves need to define them. Clergy can also facilitate frank discussions in which parishioners are encouraged to define these terms for themselves and to consider personal applications of religious teachings about them.

For all its ups and downs, the American economy has been remarkably stable during the last half of the twentieth century. Religious organizations have not had to face the serious crises that an earlier generation experienced during the Great Depression or two global wars. Problems of materialism and poverty have become so familiar that they can be addressed from year to year without much new thinking at all. Perhaps this is why we so readily admit that greed is a sin but think little about changing our lifestyles. Yet, historical comparisons show that periods such as ours are often short-lived. Major shocks in economic circumstances occur with alarming frequency, and when they do, deep changes in religious life are often the result.

We, too, are facing increasingly uncertain times. Young people are having to make difficult choices about careers and to scale back expectations about wealth. Working couples with children may have already stretched their time and energy to the limit. Men and women who are approaching retirement are finding it harder to predict what their financial resources will be. In policy discussions, questions are being raised with increasing frequency about how to make the American worker work harder and ways to generate more tax revenues without destroying American competitiveness in the world market. Religious convictions that simply pat us on the back when we are feeling depressed may not be sufficient to carry us through these changing times. We may need to reflect more deeply on teachings about simplicity, moral restraint, sacrifice, and social justice. One task that religious organizations must accept in facing the future, therefore, is to think seriously about the implications of changing economic circumstances.

Schooling and the Soul

With a large portion of the public nearly illiterate on basic religious teachings, the prospect must also be faced of encouraging serious thought about the human side of economic behavior in other contexts. Public and private schools, colleges, and universities are the most likely setting. Encouraging thought is supposedly their forte, and they may be freer to do so than institutions such as business or government.

The problem is that schooling has long served primarily to prepare young people for survival in the marketplace, not to encourage wide-ranging thinking about its meaning and value in the first place. In recent years international competition has forced even greater attention to be paid to this dimension of schooling. Business leaders claim their firms cannot be competitive in the twenty-first century unless there is a vast pool of labor that knows how to read and write, solve algebraic equations, and design microchips. Eighth graders are subjected to increasing pressure to perform on standardized tests that measure these skills. They may long for the youthful innocence that once allowed them to dream of other aspirations.

But schooling has also been considered a place to attain wisdom about life and to prepare for it by thinking about fundamental values. Religion, once a common part of public-school instruction, has become a ticklish subject in recent decades because of concerns that public sponsorship of any particular creed or doctrine may endanger both the freedom of secular institutions and of religious expression at the same stroke. Nevertheless, there have also been growing efforts to teach about religion in schools, to permit religious organizations the right to use school facilities in the same way that secular groups do, and to include instruction in values as a more explicit part of higher education.

The implications of religious belief and practice for economic behavior need to be included in these educational efforts. Too often religion is taught in much the same way that it is practiced: as a matter of personal preference that has little to do with any community or any other aspect of life. Curricular specialization reinforces this tendency, encouraging religion to be considered in one course, science in another, economics in another. Thinking systematically about the relationships between faith and work or between spirituality and money can have a far more significant impact on personal life than keeping these issues sealed in their own separate compartments.

It may be especially difficult to guide thinking about moral restraint in economic matters because educators typically regard moral absolutes as impossibly arcane. Yet there is also a moral dimension to expressivist value orientations that needs to be considered more carefully. An emphasis on feelings can create an inner space in which reflection about appropriate courses of action can be considered. These feelings, in turn, need guidance by thoughtful consideration of the bases on which ethical decisions are made.

The Challenge of Gender

While it is important for religious and educational organizations to keep the relationships between basic human values and economic behavior at the forefront of their agendas, the specific content of these discussions must be informed by the challenges that arise from the wider society. Few of these challenges have been as notable in recent years as the changing character and definition of gender. Even more than for religion generally, where its implications are profound, gender has far-reaching consequences for the nexus between religion and economic behavior. The inclusion of large numbers of women in the labor force has been one of the most significant of these changes. Many of the concerns that have been voiced in recent years about overwork and job-related stress can be traced to the fact that a much larger share of overall household time is now devoted to the labor market than in most preceding periods. This means less time for activities such as child rearing, emotional repair work, and household maintenance. Perhaps as important as diminished time, however, is that schedules are more likely to be fixed by the workplace, thereby creating endless difficulties for dealing with household matters that cannot be so easily scheduled. To some extent, renewed interest in the emotional life, in time for reflection, and in thinking about basic values have all been forced into the public mind by these conflicts.

Changing gender roles in relation to the labor force have also subtly but profoundly altered the symbolic distinction between the material and the spiritual. For good or for ill, women often symbolized the spiritual to a greater extent than men, while masculinity and materialism were symbolically linked in the role of the male breadwinner. Practically speaking, a division of labor within the family often followed in which the emotional and spiritual nurturing of children fell to mothers, while fathers concerned themselves with work and money. With both mothers and fathers participating more actively in the workplace, rethinking of this division of labor has been inevitable.

Gender is also deeply implicated in the ways that charitable service to the needy is understood and provided. Although women continue to be more actively involved than men in churches and other voluntary organizations, this difference may well diminish over time. The fact that a large number of the needy are women heading single-parent households must also be taken into consideration as religious organizations attempt to address these needs. Changing definitions of work, including questions about the role of mothering as work, clearly need to be considered in the search to balance work-ethic and nurturing images of poverty and need.

The New Pluralism

In the past, American religion has been characterized by a high degree of pluralism, just as the society itself has been. Differences in denominations, nationality, and ethnic tradition have been vital to the ways in which religious communities sought to meet economic needs. The erosion (or blending) of many of these traditional distinctions has left religious organizations without the tight communal bonds on which some of these efforts were based. Mutual-benefit associations, guilds, and fraternal orders, for example, have given way to special-interest groups drawing individuals from many different backgrounds. Part of the challenge, then, is to create groups in which individuals can reconstruct some sense of sharing and belonging and, in these groups, to foster discussions of stewardship, workplace ethics, and norms for the use of money. But another challenge is to recognize the new pluralism that is currently reshaping American religion.

The source of this pluralism, like that of the past, is largely immigration. Latino, Asian, and Muslim populations in the United States have all increased dramatically in recent decades. Subdivisions among these populations, such as the differences between Cuban, Puerto Rican, and Mexican immigrants, or between Iranian and Pakistani Muslims, are also important. In many of these communities, a distinctive work ethic appears evident, and in some religious norms prescribe how investments should be made and promote self-help within the community.

Previous patterns suggest that such enclaves gradually assimilate into wider economic networks as their distinctive religious identities break down. Whether that pattern may again be repeated will depend to some extent on overall expansion in the economy. But pluralism has also influenced the character of American religion far beyond what the numeric size of such enclaves might indicate. In coming years, the relationships between religion and economic behavior will certainly be framed in dialogue between the established, largely white churches and synagogues of the middle class and the distinctive traditions of African Americans, Asians, Latinos, Muslims, and other groups.

The Centrality of Economic Responsibility

In the final analysis, the reason that religious beliefs and values remain crucial to any consideration of economic behavior is that the American public, individually and collectively, exercises control over a vast and disproportionate share of the world's economic resources. Although there are structural limitations built into the economic system itself, individual and collective decisions still make an enormous difference. By their own testimony at least, most Americans believe personal happiness depends to some extent on having money, most regard personal investments such as gaining an education or spending time working as determinants of how much or how little money they may have, most recognize some responsibility for caring for the needy, and most consider policy decisions concerning economic growth or social welfare an important determinant of national health as well. It may be that Americans think they are in control of economic decisions that are in fact beyond anyone's ability to manipulate, for example, when political leaders are blamed for a sluggish economy. Nevertheless, it is true that economic matters require a great deal of responsibility on the part of individuals.

It is thus of considerable public benefit to have religious traditions that encourage taking these responsibilities seriously. Organizations are, of course, structured to reward this orientation, requiring audits, expense reports, effective cost management, and so on. In personal life, some of the same incentives are present, for example, in penalizing individuals who pay their bills late or promoting those who work hard at their jobs. But there are enough uncertainties that economic responsibility cannot simply be taken for granted. Short-term benefits can be sought at the expense of long-term responsibility. Cynicism about the relationship between work and money can easily beset a society in which norms of professionalism have made it harder to calculate this connection precisely. Those with ample assets can squander their resources on personal gratification. And economic activities can be treated as a game in which the only rules are to win, no matter what the extrinsic costs may be.

But the concept of economic responsibility must also be weighed carefully. Enough has been written about the dour puritanism and the sober entrepreneurialism on which the nation was founded that many Americans are leery of counsel about economic responsibility. Too often responsibility has also been interpreted to mean looking out for Number One, period. Responsibility clearly depends on context. What may have been the responsible course of behavior in a nineteenth-century logging community is likely to need radical upgrading in an age of acid rain and depleted ozone.

Religious commitment can contribute valuably to the discussion of economic responsibility by enlarging the framework in which such determinations are made. A sense of calling can still provide reasons to be committed to helping the poor, even if the voice of God is faint, by placing work in a context other than the monthly paycheck. Stewardship can engender a desire to spend money in a way that helps the needy or that preserves the environment, even without requiring that all material pleasures be forgone. For these concepts to do more than simply legitimate the status quo, however, they must be part of both public and private debate.

The Public Debate

People of faith have played an increasingly active role in the public life of American society in recent years. Although many of the issues that have been debated have had economic implications, most of them have dealt with the so-called politics of morality—abortion, school prayer, pornography, homosexuality, and so on—rather than being focused primarily on economic policy. There are, nevertheless, some important lessons to be learned from this experience.

One is that public debate can easily become polarized, taking on an aura of antagonism that runs against the grain of religious teachings about fellowship and reconciliation. Another is that there is widespread public distrust about religious leaders playing too direct a role in politics. A concern for separation of church and state underlies some of this distrust. But it is also rooted in misgivings about politics more generally. Politics tends to be regarded as an arena of special interests distant from the concerns that ordinary people actually face;

hence, the language of morality has sometimes played better to arouse public sentiment than the language of politics.

Lessons of a more positive sort have also been learned. Public debate plays a valuable role in raising consciousness about the importance of particular issues. Journalism thrives on controversy. The more controversial an issue is, therefore, the more likely it is to be debated in the mass media. And the repetitious appearance of issues in these media can render them more amenable to discussion in other settings, such as classrooms, conferences, and churches. This means, of course, that public debate extends well beyond politics and politicians. Effective debate includes representatives of all major social institutions.

Clearly the time is ripe for serious public debate about economic issues. These issues are already in the newspapers and on television, but it is also becoming increasingly apparent that the terms of debate need to be broadened. Old slogans about social welfare or economic inclusion for the poor have ceased to appeal to the political conscience of middle-class Americans. The language of inflation, recession, taxes, and monetary policy, however, does not cover what needs to be said either.

Religious organizations can effectively build bridges between the narrower technical terms in which economic issues are often discussed and the questions about values and personal morality that have always been the special domain of faith traditions. Such bridges have been constructed around teachings concerning the poor or, on occasion, in denominational statements about economic justice or corporate responsibility. Too often, however, these statements are framed as matters of policy, leaving out the more personal dimensions of work and money that are of greatest concern to individuals. A more effective approach would be to recognize the systemic character of these issues; that is, the ways in which our personal lives and our well-being as a nation are connected. Public debate about economic issues will ring true, especially in religious communities, only if it draws on understandings deep with the traditions of the communities being addressed and if it challenges prevailing assumptions about work, money, and material possessions. These assumptions form a loosely coupled system. They cohere often by virtue of going unchallenged. Token behavior can thus satisfy an impulse, say, to be charitable without raising fundamental questions about the nature of materialism itself. The role of public debate is to engender discussion of these deeper connections.

Matters of Conscience

But ultimately these connections must be driven home at the level of conscience. It has become somewhat dated to speak of conscience, for too often this means an inner voice that no longer speaks with authority, if it speaks at all. Conscience must be shaped and reinforced; its voice must be supplied with a language. For economic behavior, that language must include more than abstractions about responsibility, stewardship, or economic justice.

Stories are especially helpful because they turn these abstractions into concrete examples. A story of greed can be a cautionary tale, warning against the dangers of excessive desires. By negative example, one learns models to avoid. Stories of caring or of devotion to meaningful work provide positive models to emulate.

The weakness of stories is that modern culture has instructed us well in the logic of self-interest. We know that stories can be self-justifying, and so a cautious response demands cynicism. Not knowing exactly how to make sense of a millionaire who sells his business to do church work, we can readily find ways to dismiss his example. Our conscience tells us that we too could be charitable if we had the luxury to do so.

Yet there is more to it than this. In contemplating others' stories, we recognize something in ourselves. We see that it is common for our conscience to speak to us with a mixed voice. We realize that others seldom have all the answers either. Their stories nevertheless suggest paths that we too may want to explore.

Advertisers and employers are all too ready to supply stories of their own. Their stories capture a piece of life, revealing why it is best to be loyal to the company or why brand X is better than brand Y. It takes more effort to create our own stories and bring in the more cumbersome questions of values and personal priorities. Part of exercising economic responsibility, therefore, is to be vigilant and pay attention to the larger questions. Surely this is the meaning of the religious teaching that counsels to whom much has been given, much will be required.

Beyond Conscience

What role, then, *should* spirituality play in guiding our work lives and how we handle our money? One vision—still shared by many religious leaders—is that the churches should play a heroic role. In this vision, the faithful stand in fundamental opposition to the world. Radically different lifestyles are the mark of the faithful. Indeed, the church transforms the world. Capitalism is replaced by a Judeo-Christian ethic, competition gives way to brotherly love, and self-interest fades in favor of communalism. Religious leaders work heroically on behalf of the poor and liberate the rest of us from social and spiritual bondage. Whatever the specific outcomes may be, this vision encourages the church to transform society into something quite different than it is now. An alternative vision calls the church to minister in much more modest ways. In this vision, spirituality should tickle people where they itch, rather than stir them up. Modest, realistic proposals should be made. The faithful should be accepted and affirmed. It is enough in this vision if people are encouraged to be even a little better than they might otherwise have been.

The heroic vision is, in my view, a fine vision that may inspire us from time to time but one that is fundamentally flawed. It does not affirm the realities of human life enough and it assumes either a use of political force that most of us would find terrifying or a sweeping change in consciousness that has no precedent in our history. The modest vision is equally flawed. It sells out too easily, risks nothing, and is an administrative convenience, rather than a moral vision that calls us to significant commitments.

There is a middle way. And it demands our attention if we are to save ourselves from the moral decay that goes with obsessive materialism and excessive secular work. This is the way of critical and collective resistance. We may not be able to effect sweeping changes in our society, but we can do more than simply affirm the way things are. We can do this by joining with others—in churches, synagogues, civic associations, and small groups—to reflect on our priorities, to talk about the difficulties we face in our work and in our spending, and to bring spiritual values to bear on these issues.

This is the only strategy that made a difference among the people we have considered in previous chapters. Those who were able to live their lives differently had found support for critical self-reflection and discussion of this kind. Recall Miriam Zellers. She found the strength to give up her job and follow her husband at a time when dominant social trends suggested doing just the opposite. She received support from her Bible study group and she has found new avenues of service open to her through her church. She does not believe, as she says, "that you always have to march to the beat of a different drummer from everyone else," but she does find it helpful to pray with other people about her work and her money and to consider their advice. Meeting with these people has helped her to think more deeply even about some of the assumptions she learned growing up in the church. Or recall Karen Kelsey. She found people her own age with whom to meet informally and discuss spirituality. When she decided to leave a high-stakes political career and become a clinical social worker, she was able to discuss her options with these people. John and Mary Phelps significantly reduce their consumer spending to help refugees. This commitment takes constant reinforcement from members of their parish. Mike Kominski comes home tired every night from driving his cement truck, but his church and civic association help him remain faithful to the pledge of helping others that he made after his motorcycle accident.

We may not agree with the decisions that any of these people made. The point is not that they were necessarily right in what they did but significantly guided by their spiritual commitments and thus by values that differed from the pressures they faced in the workplace and from the consumer culture in which we all live. They paused to think about their priorities, they put themselves among people who were doing the same thing, and as a result they made decisions that significantly altered their work and the ways they spent their money.

None of these people was able to escape the pressures of the marketplace entirely. Most continued to work outside the home and spent long hours at their work. None of them gave up the amenities of a middle-class lifestyle. They still went out to eat and probably bought more new clothes than they needed. We can criticize them for not doing more and we can see—as they also can see—that they were sometimes rationalizing. Yet their faith did make a concrete difference in their lives and in the lives of people around them. They stand out from many of the other people we talked to—and from the majority of those in our survey—who gave lip service to their faith but avoided thinking about its implications or let it make them feel better rather than challenging them to live any differently. Life was no less complex for those whose faith influenced them significantly; indeed, it was often more complex because they had to think consciously about their priorities rather than following the course of least resistance.

These people represent a vision of how religious faith can influence the disposition of our work and our money for the better. They were quite diverse in their backgrounds and in their religious orientations. They thought about religious teachings and read and discussed sacred texts. Some of them found clear guidance in these texts and in prayer; most found principles, values, and stories that called for reflection and application. These people banded together with other seekers who helped them think about their priorities and who reinforced alternative values and held each other accountable. They did not radically challenge social institutions, but they were generally aware that institutions are important and that individuals alone can seldom accomplish all that they wish. They dealt with the complex demands of their lives by simplifying their commitments, but also by discussing complexity itself. They found it necessary to keep their work in perspective, to think harder about ethical decisions than many of their co-workers, and to spend less money on themselves so that they could be of greater service to others.

Appendix A

Methodology

The research for this book was conducted in two phases. In the first phase in-depth interviews were conducted with 175 persons in a wide variety of occupations and from different regions of the country. These individuals were not selected through a random or systematic sampling plan. They were, however, selected according to a quota design that ensured a great deal of diversity. Approximately equal numbers of men and women were interviewed, and each gender category was further divided into approximately equal numbers of older and younger people. An attempt was made to interview approximately equal numbers of people in professional or managerial occupations and people in clerical, skilled, or semiskilled occupations, and within each broad stratum to include people from many different specific occupations. Because many of the questions focused on work, we conducted most of the interviews with men and women who were working full-time or part-time. To provide an alternative perspective, we conducted twenty-five of the interviews among men and women who were currently unemployed. We also sought to include a large number of different religious faiths and to include blacks, Hispanics, and Asians, as well as white Anglos. The interviews were conducted in cities, suburbs, and rural areas in various parts of the country, including Boston, Chicago, Minneapolis, Portland, San Francisco, Los Angeles, San Diego, Baton Rouge, Nashville, the District of Columbia, Philadelphia, Trenton, and New York. About a dozen different interviewers were involved, drawing on references from churches and synagogues, community organizations, colleges, neighbors, and friends to locate specific interviewees. Each interview lasted approximately two hours (some ranging up to five hours). Topics covered included personal backgrounds, parental backgrounds and childhood experiences, values, work experiences, attitudes toward money and material possessions, religious beliefs and involvements, participation in community organizations, and views on social issues. Each interview was tape-recorded and a verbatim transcript was produced of each tape. This process yielded approximately ten thousand pages of transcribed interviews. The smaller number of interviews featured in each chapter of this volume were chosen because of the diversity of religious and economic perspectives represented. These case studies are not necessarily representative of the larger number of interviews but do reveal both commonalities and the range of opinion in those interviews. The purpose of these case studies is not only to add a more personal or human dimension to the quantitative data but also to illustrate the language and arguments that lie behind some of the statistical patterns discussed.

The second phase of the project consisted of a survey of the U.S. labor force. The structured questions for the survey were written after a preliminary analysis of the in-depth interviews was made and following a thorough review of the published literature as well as some exploratory interviews with clergy. Nearly a hundred social scientists, historians, and students of American religion were also contacted to solicit ideas about general topics needing to be covered in the study. The survey was administered in February and March of 1992 to a sample of 2,013 persons who were currently working either full-time or part-time. The sample is intended to be representative of the active labor force age eighteen and over living in the continental United States. Compared with surveys aimed at representing the adult public, this survey intentionally omits students, retired persons, those doing unpaid household work or parenting, and persons currently unemployed. At the time of the survey, approximately 7 percent of the U.S. labor force was unemployed. The design is that of a replicated probability sample down to the block level in the case of urban areas, and to segments of townships in the case of rural areas. The sample design includes stratification by these seven size-of-community strata, using 1990 census data: (1) incorporated cities of population 1,000,000 and over; (2) incorporated cities of population 250,000 to 999,999;

(3) incorporated cities of population 50,000 to 249,999; (4) urbanized places not included in (1) through (3); (5) cities over 2,500 population outside of urbanized areas; (6) towns and villages of fewer than 2,500 population; and (7) rural places not included within town boundaries. Each of these strata are further stratified into four geographic regions: East, Midwest, South, and West. Within each city-sized regional stratum, the population is arrayed in geographic order and zoned into equal-sized groups of sampling units. Pairs of localities are selected in each zone, with probability of selection and each locality proportional to its population size in the most current U.S. census, producing two replicated samples of localities. Within each subdivision so selected for which block statistics are available, a sample of blocks or block clusters is drawn with probability of selection proportional to the number of dwelling units. In all other subdivisions or areas, blocks or segments are drawn at random or with equal probability. In each cluster of blocks and each segment so selected, a randomly selected starting point is designated on the interviewer's map of the area. Starting at this point, interviewers are required to follow a given direction in the selection of households until their assignment is completed. The sampling and field administration of the survey were subcontracted to the Gallup Organization.

The sample of completed interviews was weighted to bring the demographic characteristics of the final sample into alignment with the actual demographic characteristics of the continental U.S. adult labor force population. The weighting procedure used demographic and regional parameters from the U.S. Census Bureau's Current Population Survey as target parameters to bring the final sample of completed interviews into alignment with the regional distribution of population and the age, sex, education, and race distributions of the continental U.S. population of employed adults. The weighting variables have also been multiplied by a constant to ensure that the total number of weighted cases and the number of completed interviews (2,013) are the same. Table A.1 presents a comparison of percentages and numbers for the weighted and unweighted data for interviews completed. The table shows that the chief undersampling that occurred in the data collection process was among persons age 18–34 and in the West; conversely, oversampling occurred mainly among older persons. The undersampling of young people occurs mainly because persons in this category tend to be home less often on weekends when such surveys

TABLE A.1

Comparison of Weighted and Unweighted Data

	Unweighted		Weighted	
	%	N	%	N
Total labor force sample	100	2013	100	2013
Male	51	1023	54	1085
Female	49	990	46	928
Age 18–34	34	674	42	832
Age 35–49	40	808	38	774
Age 50 and over	26	526	20	407
High school or less	51	1032	51	1025
Some college	21	417	21	425
College graduate	28	563	28	563
East	25	505	24	473
Midwest	27	546	25	501
South	32	636	31	625
West	16	326	21	414
City size 1,000,000 plus	38	754	37	751
50,000 to 999,999	26	526	24	490
Less than 50,000	36	733	31	772
White	87	1751	86	1722
Nonwhite	13	262	14	291
Personal income $40,000+	17	350	18	365
$20,000 to $39,999	36	721	35	710
Less than $20,000	40	807	39	794

are typically conducted. The undersampling on the West Coast occurred because southern California was experiencing extreme flooding at the time the survey was administered. The weightings adjust the proportions to more nearly approximate their actual distribution in the U.S. population.

Although total numbers of weighted and unweighted cases are the same, the weighting procedure necessitates discrepancies between the two within the various subcategories being adjusted. Because of these

TABLE A.2

Recommended Allowance for Sampling Error
of a Percentage

In percentage points (at 95 in 100 confidence level)

	Sample Size				
	2,000	1,000	500	250	100
Percentages near 10	2	2	3	5	7
Percentages near 20	2	3	4	6	10
Percentages near 30	2	4	5	7	11
Percentages near 40	3	4	5	8	12
Percentages near 50	3	4	5	8	12
Percentages near 60	4	4	5	8	12
Percentages near 70	2	4	5	7	11
Percentages near 80	2	3	4	6	10
Percentages near 90	2	2	3	5	7

discrepancies, statistical measures of significance (such as Chi-square) are not always accurate. These inaccuracies are likely to be greatest when variables are being examined that may be systematically related to differences in age or region. In the text, percentages reported are based on weighted data because these have the greatest descriptive value. Relationships based on statistical inferences are based on unweighted data as these represent the actual number of interviews completed within various subgroups. In virtually all the statistical analyses, controls are also introduced for standard background factors such as age, gender, working full-time or part-time, income, and education.

In interpreting the survey results, one should bear in mind that all sample surveys are subject to sampling error, that is, the extent to which the results may differ from what would be obtained if the whole population had been interviewed. The size of such sampling errors depends largely on the number of interviews. Table A.2 may be used in estimating the sampling error of percentages reported herein. The computed allowances have taken into account the effect of the sample design upon sampling error. They may be interpreted as indicating the range (plus or minus the figure shown) within which the results of repeated samplings in the same time period could be expected to vary, 95 percent of the time, assuming the same sampling procedures, the same interviews, and the same questionnaire. The table would be used in the following manner: Say a reported percentage is 40 for a group that includes approximately 1,000 respondents. Go to row "percentages near 40" in the table and go across to the column headed "1,000." The number at this point is 4, which means that the 40 percent obtained in the sample is subject to a sampling error of plus or minus 4 points. Another way of saying it is that very probably (95 chances out of 100) the true figure would be somewhere between 36 and 44, with the most likely figure the 40 obtained. Many percentages presented in the text are based on the entire sample of labor force members. Thus, the column headed 2,000 gives a reasonable approximation of the sampling error to which these figures are subject. Other percentages and statistical relationships discussed in the text have been subjected to Chi-square or F-test measures of statistical significance. All relationships meeting a probability of .05 on these measures are considered statistically significant.

For bivariate relationships involving the entire sample or relationships involving no more than one control variable (such as gender or age), cross-tabular analysis was used with Chi-square as the preferred measure of statistical significance and gamma as a measure of the degree of statistical association for ordinal variables. Multivariate statistical analysis of the data generally involved discriminant function analysis. Discriminant analysis is an ideal method of analysis for data such as those obtained in the present study. It empirically differentiates among two or more groups in the data using multiple variables to differentiate among these groups. Another way to say this is that discriminant analysis allows us to make predictions about the likelihood of respondents' giving one answer to a question rather than a different answer on the basis of how respondents answer several other questions in the survey. As with all statistical procedures, certain assumptions are invoked when discriminant analysis is used. These are as follows: that no predictor variables can be linear combinations of each other, that the covariance matrices for each group must be approximately equal, and that each predictor variable must be measured at the interval level. In using discriminant analysis, we have avoided violating the first of these assumptions by a default in the selection of predictor variables (disallowing the simultaneous entry of variables that are very closely correlated). We have assessed the extent to which the second assumption may be violated by using the Box's *M* test. The third assumption is generally not met with any kind of survey data; however, we have, as in most multivariate applications, sought to minimize its importance by using binary ("dummy") predictor variables or items that at least involve ordinal levels of measurement. Researchers have generally found discriminant analysis to be a very robust procedure with regard to unequal covariance matrices and discrete data. We assessed the fitness of the various discriminant functions by testing their significance with a Chi-square statistic, by evaluating the Wilks' lambda statistic (an inverse measure of association), by examining the relative eigenvalues (indicating the proportion of explanation provided by one function relative to other functions), and by inspecting the squared canonical correlation. For each variable in the discriminant function, we assessed its relative strength by examining the standardized canonical discriminant function coefficients. A common rule of thumb is to treat any coefficient of .30 or higher as meaningful. We also checked the reliability of some of the most important findings by using multiple regression analysis and logistic regression analysis. To preserve readability, relatively simple percentage tables have been presented in the text; summaries of the results of multivariate statistical procedures have been reported in endnotes.

Table A.3 provides an overview of the religious composition of the U.S. labor force as determined by the Economic Values Survey. For purposes of comparison, the table also reports comparable figures taken from surveys representative of the entire adult population of the United States. (The figures shown for the entire adult population are taken from the author's 1989 survey of American values, reported in *Acts of Compassion*, in the case of church attendance and religious orientation, and from 1990 or 1991 Gallup polls in the case of membership, importance of religion, and religious preference; see George Gallup, Jr., *Religion in America, 1992* [Princeton: Gallup Institute, 1992].) Approximately a third of the labor force (as in the United States as a whole) attend religious services at least once a week. Another third attend anywhere from several times a year to several times a month. The remaining third attend only once a year or less. The content of these services varies enormously, of course. Some follow

TABLE A.3

Religious Composition of the U.S. Labor Force

	Labor Force	All Adults
Attendance at religious services:		
About once a week or more	33	33
At least several times a year	32	31
Once a year or less	34	34
Member of church or synagogue:		
Yes	58	68
No	42	32
Religious preference:		
Protestant	53	58
Roman Catholic	26	27
Jewish	3	2
Other	6	4
None	9	9
Importance of religion:		
Very important	41	58
Somewhat important	35	29
Not very important	23	13
Religious orientation:		
Conservative	20	26
Moderate	44	44
Liberal	30	23
Don't know	6	7

closely prescribed liturgies, others are free-form; some have lengthy sermons, others focus more on music; and so on. But the weekly service remains at the heart of virtually all congregations. Attendance is thus a sign of one's commitment, as well as a chance to be exposed to teachings on particular subjects.

Membership is another standard indicator of religious commitment. It means less than attendance, and its meaning has become more ambiguous in recent decades because membership criteria in many religious organizations have been relaxed. Whereas it was once necessary to be a member to receive communion, have one's children baptized, or vote in congregational elections, it has become increasingly common for congregations to permit fellow travelers to participate in these ways even if they are not members. As a result, the proportion of the total U.S. population who claim membership in any congregation has slipped somewhat, falling from 76 percent at the close of World War II to about 65 percent in recent polls. This figure is even lower in the labor force, probably because the labor force excludes retired people who are more likely to be members because they have lived longer in their communities. The labor force is also somewhat better educated and more geographically mobile than people who are not in it.

Religious preference has been a standard measure to which social researchers have given much attention. Initially the reason was that theories (such as Weber's theory about the Protestant work ethic) emphasized contrasts between Protestants and Catholics. In some studies this measure is also of interest because those who express no religious preference can be compared with those who do have a preference. Generally, though, religious preference has become less valuable for understanding differences in the American population. This is true even when information on specific Protestant denominations (Baptists, Presbyterians, and the like) is included. A great deal of research has shown that denominationalism is declining in significance. The distinctive beliefs of denominations have blended together as a result of ecumenism and a great deal of switching back and forth among members. And the social characteristics—differences in geographic region and social class—that once set denominations apart have also eroded. While most people still express a preference of one kind or another, it is thus less likely that these preferences will help very much in our understanding their behavior. In the text, I have examined the effects of religious preference, partly because there are some lingering differences between Protestants and Catholics in religious teachings, and partly because some other religious characteristics (congregation size, for example) vary across denomination. I have generally relegated these findings to notes, however, because they seldom prove to be statistically significant. Because of the small numbers of Jews in the sample, it has also been necessary to focus most of our discussion on Christians and other non-Jews.

How important religion is regarded in people's lives is a simple question that has been asked many times in public opinion polls. In Gallup studies, for instance, the proportions who say religion is very important to them personally generally range between 55 and 58 percent, down from approximately 75 percent in the 1950s. In the labor force, this proportion is lower, again because the labor force is younger and better educated on the whole than the entire population. I compare people in terms of how important religion is to them from time to time, especially when a simple measure like this is useful. For the most part, though, I use more refined indications of religious conviction.

Also shown in the table are the proportions of people who define themselves as religious conservatives, moderates, or liberals. Much attention has been given to the importance of these differences in recent studies of American religion. Indeed, there is strong evidence that religious conservatives are now more deeply divided from religious liberals than in the 1950s and 1960s. And this division may be more important for understanding many aspects of religious behavior than differences in denominational background. A conservative Baptist, for example, may have more in common with a conservative Catholic than with a liberal Baptist. At the same time, it is important not to overstate the distinction. Many people cling to the middle of the road, and on some issues even conservatives and liberals are in much agreement. The historical developments that have contributed to the division between religious conservatives and liberals have been discussed in some detail in my book *The Restructuring of American Religion*, as were the results of a major national study on this topic. Additional evidence and implications are considered in my book *The Struggle for America's Soul*, and more recently in *Acts of Compassion*. A rather large literature has emerged, much of it in my view either overstating or dismissing the importance of the conflicts between religious conservatives and liberals. In the present study I have used the same question as in my previous research, which asks respondents to summarize their own religious orientation along a six-point scale ranging from "very conservative" to "very liberal." The figures in the table represent the two scores at either end of the scale and the two in the middle. I have classified the two middle scores as "moderates" to emphasize that they take a less extreme position than those to their left or right. It is also important to recognize, though, that the left or right leaning of this group is also sometimes significant. Compared with the research I did in the mid-1980s using this question, the present results suggest a continuation, if not a deepening, of the division between liberals and conservatives. Fewer now than then are unwilling or unable to place themselves on the continuum at all, and more place themselves at the extremes than in the middle. The most significant difference between the labor force and the general population is that more of the former are religious liberals, and more of the latter are religious conservatives.

These are the standard measures. But they provide only a minimal indication of the religious complexity of the American labor force. In the text I probe this complexity in much greater detail. Rather than simply examining church attendance, I examine whether people claim to have heard certain kinds of sermons. I consider whether deeper levels of involvement, such as participation in Sunday school classes and fellowship groups, makes more of a difference to economic behavior than sheer attendance at services. I also compare people in terms of how much they think about certain issues, their views of the Bible and of ethics, their levels of giving, and a variety of other beliefs and activities.

Appendix B

The Economic Values Survey

(U.S. Labor Force Sample)

101. Are you currently working full time, part time, going to school, keeping house, or what?

    1 Working full time (ASK Q. 102)
    2 Working part time (ASK Q. 102)
    3 Unemployed, laid off, looking for work (TERMINATE)
    4 Retired (TERMINATE)
    5 In school (TERMINATE)
    6 Keeping house (TERMINATE)
    7 Other (TERMINATE)
    8 Don't know, refused (TERMINATE)

102. IF WORKING, FULL OR PART TIME: How many hours did you work last week, at all jobs?

    1 00–09 hours
    2 10–19 hours
    3 20–29 hours
    4 30–39 hours
    5 40–49 hours
    6 50–59 hours
    7 60–69 hours
    8 70–79 hours
    9 80 or more hours
    10 Don't know, refused

103. Please tell me which of these categories on this card most nearly describes the kind of work that you do. Just call off the number, please.

    1 Professional worker
    2 Works at skilled trade/craft
    3 Semiskilled worker
    4 Manager/executive/official in business
    5 Runs own business with 2 or more employees
    6 Farm owner or farm manager
    7 Clerical worker
    8 Sales worker
    9 Manufacturer's representative
    10 Service worker
    11 Laboring worker
    12 Farm laborer/helper
    13 Other
    14 Can't say

104. Are you self-employed or do you work for someone else?

    1 Self-employed
    2 Work for someone else
    3 Don't know, refused

105. Which of the categories on this card best describes the kind of organization you work for?

    1 A for-profit organization, such as a business
    2 A private, nonprofit organization, such as a community center or church
    3 A tax-supported organization, such as a government agency or a school

4 (Other)
5 Don't know, refused

106. About how many people are employed at the place where you work?

    1 Nobody else but me
    2 Fewer than 5 people
    3 5–9 people
    4 10–19 people
    5 20–49 people
    6 50–99 people
    7 100–499 people
    8 500–999 people
    9 1000 or more people
    10 Don't know, refused

107. In a typical day, about how many people do you work closely with in your job?

    1 0 (Nobody else)
    2 1 (One other person)
    3 2 to 5 people
    4 6 to 10 people
    5 11 to 20 people
    6 More than 20 people
    7 Don't know, refused

108. In your work, do you have a lot of control over each of the following, or not?

		YES	NO	DK
a	Organizing your daily schedule	1	2	3
b	Setting long-range objectives	1	2	3
c	Making major day-to-day decisions	1	2	3
d	Deciding how many hours to work	1	2	3
e	Allocating tasks to other people	1	2	3

109. How much does your work vary from day to day—a great deal, a fair amount, some, or only a little?

    1 A great deal
    2 A fair amount
    3 Some
    4 Only a little
    5 Don't know, refused

110. On this card are some reasons people give for getting into their present line of work. Which ones were the most important for you?

		MENTIONED	NOT MENTIONED
a	The opportunity to use my talents	1	2
b	Wanting to grow as a person	1	2
c	The challenge it presented me	1	2
d	Knowing people in this line of work	1	2
e	Freedom to make my own decisions	1	2

		MENTIONED	NOT MENTIONED
f	Flexible hours	1	2
g	The money	1	2
h	Circumstances just led me to it	1	2
i	The chance to become successful	1	2
j	Parent or relative in this line of work	1	2

111. Which one was the most important reason of all?

    1 The opportunity to use my talents
    2 Wanting to grow as a person
    3 The challenge it presented me
    4 Knowing people in this line of work
    5 Freedom to make my own decisions
    6 Flexible hours
    7 The money
    8 Circumstances just led me to it
    9 The chance to become successful
    10 Parent or relative in this line of work

112. How many different lines of work have you been in—not counting jobs while you were growing up?

    1 Only one
    2 Two
    3 Three
    4 Four
    5 Five
    6 Six
    7 Seven
    8 Eight or more
    9 Don't know, refused

113. Using the responses on this card, how well would you say each of the following phrases describes your present work—very well (V), fairly well (F), not very well (N), or not at all (A)?

		V	F	N	A	DK
a	Provides a lot of variety	1	2	3	4	5
b	Is often boring	1	2	3	4	5
c	People at work care about me personally	1	2	3	4	5
d	I work in a huge bureaucracy	1	2	3	4	5
e	It drains me emotionally	1	2	3	4	5
f	It is mentally stimulating	1	2	3	4	5
g	Good opportunity to advance	1	2	3	4	5
h	It suits my personality	1	2	3	4	5
i	It physically exhausts me	1	2	3	4	5
j	There is a lot of pressure	1	2	3	4	5
k	It is very competitive	1	2	3	4	5
l	I have a lot of freedom	1	2	3	4	5
m	It pays very well	1	2	3	4	5

114. On a scale where "10" means extremely satisfied and "0" means extremely dissatisfied, how satisfied are you with your work?

Dissatisfied   Satisfied
   0 1 2 3 4 5 6 7 8 9 10   11 DK

115. Thinking specifically about job-related stress, how often do you use these measures to relieve feelings of stress from your job—Never (N), rarely (R), sometimes (S), or often (O)?

		N	R	S	O	DK
a	Come home and watch TV	1	2	3	4	5
b	Talk with close friends	1	2	3	4	5
c	Get some physical exercise	1	2	3	4	5
d	Discuss it with your spouse	1	2	3	4	5
e	Pray or meditate	1	2	3	4	5
f	Drink alcoholic beverages	1	2	3	4	5
g	Work on a hobby	1	2	3	4	5
h	Go shopping	1	2	3	4	5
i	Take a few days off	1	2	3	4	5
j	See a therapist	1	2	3	4	5
k	Talk to a member of the clergy	1	2	3	4	5
l	Keep it to yourself	1	2	3	4	5
m	Attend a support group	1	2	3	4	5

116. Most days, when you get home from work, how much energy do you have left for other things—a lot, a little, hardly any, or none?

   1 A lot
   2 A little
   3 Hardly any
   4 None
   5 Don't know, refused

117. In the past year, which of these have you experienced in your work?

		MENTIONED	NOT MENTIONED
a	Being laid off	1	2
b	Taking a cut in pay	1	2
c	Feeling seriously burned out	1	2
d	Having to do something you thought was unethical	1	2
e	Seeing something you thought was illegal	1	2
f	Feeling your work was compromising your values	1	2
g	Being reprimanded	1	2
h	Wondering if you were in the right line of work	1	2
i	Felt that you were being sexually harassed	1	2
j	Felt that you were being discriminated against	1	2
k	Having an argument with your boss	1	2
l	Having to do things that were against your better judgment	1	2

118. In general, how often are you bothered by stress in your job situation?

   1 Almost every day
   2 Several days a week

3 Once or twice a week
4 Less than once a week
5 Never
6 Don't know, refused

119. Which of these, if any, is currently a source of stress in your work?

		MENTIONED	NOT MENTIONED
a	Conflict with co-workers	1	2
b	An unsupportive boss	1	2
c	Working too many hours	1	2
d	Having to meet deadlines	1	2
e	Not enough time for my family	1	2
f	Having to make decisions	1	2
g	Feeling "burned out"	1	2
h	Not being paid well enough	1	2
i	Needing more time for myself	1	2
j	Feeling my work doesn't count	1	2
k	Wanting other things in life	1	2
l	Doing too many different things	1	2
m	An unpleasant work environment	1	2
n	Bureaucracy and red tape	1	2

120. How much does each of the following motivate you to work hard and do your work really well—would you say it motivates you a great deal (G), a little (L), or none (N)?

		G	L	N	DK
a	Praise from your boss	1	2	3	4
b	Competition	1	2	3	4
c	Trying to fulfill your own potential	1	2	3	4
d	A supportive working environment	1	2	3	4
e	Fear of losing your job	1	2	3	4
f	Being paid more money	1	2	3	4
g	Knowing you've helped someone	1	2	3	4
h	The hope of a promotion or award	1	2	3	4
i	Doing it to benefit your family	1	2	3	4

121. In your line of work, do people who work the hardest generally get paid the best, or isn't that the way it is?

1 Generally get paid the best
2 Isn't the way it is
3 Other
4 Don't know, refused

122. Suppose you had a tough decision to make at work. Would each of these be a major consideration (MAJ) for you, a minor consideration (MIN), or not a consideration (NOT)?

		MAJ	MIN	NOT	DK
a	What you thought was morally right	1	2	3	4
b	What would benefit you the most	1	2	3	4
c	How your family would react	1	2	3	4
d	Whether you would feel good about it	1	2	3	4
e	What would benefit other people the most	1	2	3	4

		MAJ	MIN	NOT	DK
f	Trying to obey God	1	2	3	4
g	What would benefit your company/employer	1	2	3	4

123. Now, which one would you give the most weight to of all?

1 What you thought was morally right
2 What would benefit you the most
3 How your family would react
4 Whether you would feel good about it
5 What would benefit other people the most
6 Trying to obey God
7 What would benefit your company or employer
8 Don't know, refused

124. How much do you admire people in each of the following kinds of work—would you say a lot (AL), some (S), only a little (OL), or none at all (NAA)?

		AL	S	OL	NAA	DK
a	Clergy	1	2	3	4	5
b	Nurses	1	2	3	4	5
c	Stock brokers	1	2	3	4	5
d	Business managers	1	2	3	4	5
e	Teachers	1	2	3	4	5
f	Therapists	1	2	3	4	5
g	Housewives	1	2	3	4	5

125. How important is each of the following to your basic sense of worth as a person—absolutely essential (AE), very important (VI), somewhat important (SI), or not very important (NVI)?

		AE	VI	SI	NVI	DK
a	Your family	1	2	3	4	5
b	Your community	1	2	3	4	5
c	Your work	1	2	3	4	5
d	Your hobbies or leisure activities	1	2	3	4	5
e	Your moral standards	1	2	3	4	5
f	Taking care of yourself	1	2	3	4	5
g	Helping people in need	1	2	3	4	5
h	Living a comfortable life	1	2	3	4	5
i	Paying attention to your feelings	1	2	3	4	5
j	Your relation to God	1	2	3	4	5
k	Making a lot of money	1	2	3	4	5
l	Being able to do what you want to	1	2	3	4	5
m	Being successful	1	2	3	4	5

126 On the whole, how happy are you—very happy, fairly happy, or not very happy?

1 Very happy
2 Fairly happy
3 Not very happy
4 Don't know, refused

127 Thinking back to your childhood, how happy were you then—would you say very happy, fairly happy, or not very happy?

1 Very happy
2 Fairly happy
3 Not very happy
4 Don't know, refused

128. Do you agree strongly (AS), agree somewhat (A), disagree somewhat (D), or disagree strongly (DS) with each of the following statements?

		AS	A	D	DS	DK
a	Getting in touch with your inner feelings is more important than doing well in your job	1	2	3	4	5
b	I need a lot of time to be quiet and reflect on things	1	2	3	4	5
c	Working on my emotional life takes priority over other things	1	2	3	4	5
d	Exploring my inner self is one of my main priorities	1	2	3	4	5
e	I believe in following a strict set of moral rules	1	2	3	4	5
f	My feelings are my best guide when I'm making a decision	1	2	3	4	5
g	Certain values must be regarded as absolutes	1	2	3	4	5

129. In your work, have you done each of the following any time during the past month?

		YES	NO	DK
a	Arrived later than you're supposed to	1	2	3
b	Bent the rules in dealing with someone	1	2	3
c	Covered for someone who had made a mistake	1	2	3
d	Not asked questions about something you suspected was wrong	1	2	3
e	Saw other people doing things that might be unethical	1	2	3
f	Used office equipment for personal uses	1	2	3
g	Charged for expenses that might not be legitimate	1	2	3
h	Blown the whistle on someone for wrongdoing	1	2	3
i	Taken time off from work that you shouldn't	1	2	3
j	Bent the truth a bit in what you told people	1	2	3

130. If you saw something at work that you thought was ethically wrong, would you be most likely to. . .

1 Figure it's not appropriate to say something
2 Figure that people probably had their reasons for doing what they did
3 Say something if you felt like it at the moment, or
4 Tell them you thought what they were doing was wrong
5 Don't know, refused

131. Which one of the statements on this card is the best definition of ethics?

1 Always trying to be honest
2 Being able to decide what's right or wrong
3 Doing your best

4 Behaving in a responsible way, or
5 Feeling good about what you do
6 (Other)
7 (Don't know, refused)

132. Does ethics, in your view, mean. . .

   1 Something that applies in the same way to everybody, no matter what the situation, or
   2 Something that varies depending on the circumstances you are in
   3 Don't know, refused

133. Do you mostly agree strongly (A) or mostly disagree (D) with each of the following statements?

		A	D	DK
a	Being ethical will pay off economically	1	2	3
b	It is OK to bend the rules sometimes at work	1	2	3
c	I always behave ethically in my work	1	2	3
d	You just have to do what feels right and hope for the best	1	2	3
e	As far as ethics is concerned, no organization is perfect	1	2	3
f	I feel responsible to make sure others I work with behave ethically	1	2	3

134 Here are two statements about income taxes. Which one better expresses your own view?

   1 In filing your income tax returns, you should follow the rules very carefully and pay exactly what you owe
   2 There are a lot of "gray areas" on income tax returns, and you are better off fudging some of them than being completely honest about everything
   3 Other
   4 Don't know, refused

135. Have you ever received some kind of training in ethics, such as taking a course in it, either as part of your work or outside of your work?

   1 Yes, as part of my work
   2 Yes, outside of my work
   3 Yes (both or unspecified)
   4 No
   5 Don't know, refused

136. If you were facing an important ethical dilemma at work, how likely would you be to do each of the following—very likely (VL), fairly likely (FL), fairly unlikely (FU), or very unlikely (VU)?

		VL	FL	FU	VU	DK
a	Talk with your boss or someone else higher in the organization	1	2	3	4	5
b	Talk to fellow employees	1	2	3	4	5
c	Make the decision mainly by paying attention to your own feelings	1	2	3	4	5
d	Seek advice from a member of the clergy	1	2	3	4	5
e	Try not to burden your family with it	1	2	3	4	5
f	Read things to see what other people had done in the same situation	1	2	3	4	5

137. When you were growing up, how often did your parents discuss family finances in your presence—frequently, once in awhile, or never?

    1 Frequently
    2 Once in awhile
    3 Never
    4 Don't know, refused

138. As a child, how clear were you about how your parents made decisions about money—very clear, somewhat clear, somewhat unclear, or very unclear?

    1 Very clear
    2 Somewhat clear
    3 Somewhat unclear
    4 Very unclear
    5 Don't know, refused

139. When you were growing up, were your parents. . .

    1 Very well off financially
    2 Fairly comfortable financially
    3 A little squeezed financially
    4 Fairly hard up financially
    5 Don't know, refused

140. As far as you know, did the Great Depression in the 1930s affect your parents or grandparents a lot, only a little, or not at all?

    1 A lot
    2 Only a little
    3 Not at all
    4 Don't know, refused

141. In the past year, how often have you discussed each of the following with people outside your immediate family — never (N), hardly ever (H), fairly often (F), or quite often (Q)?

		N	H	F	Q	DK
a	Your salary or income	1	2	3	4	5
b	Your family budget	1	2	3	4	5
c	How much you pay for major purchases	1	2	3	4	5
d	Worries you might have about money	1	2	3	4	5
e	How much you spend on routine things	1	2	3	4	5
f	How much you gave to charities	1	2	3	4	5

142. In the past year how often have you discussed your personal finances with each of the following—never (N), hardly ever (HE), fairly often (FO), or quite often (QO)?

		N	HE	FO	QO	DK
a	People at work	1	2	3	4	5
b	A member of the clergy	1	2	3	4	5
c	A therapist or counselor	1	2	3	4	5
d	A financial expert	1	2	3	4	5
e	Members of your church/synagogue	1	2	3	4	5
f	Your friends	1	2	3	4	5

143. How many of your close friends have told you how much money they make—would you say all of them, most of them, only a few of them, or none of them?

    1 All of them
    2 Most of them
    3 Only a few of them
    4 None of them
    5 Don't know, refused

144. In handling your personal finances, do you. . .

    1 Follow a strict, itemized budget
    2 Follow a budget that provides general guidelines
    3 Have a budget, but not follow it very closely
    4 Don't have a budget
    5 Don't know, refused

145. What grade would you give yourself for the way you handle your money—an A, B, C, D, or F?

    1 A
    2 B
    3 C
    4 D
    5 F
    6 Don't know, refused

146. Here are some statements about gifts and loans. Does each one describe you very well (V), fairly well (F), not very well (N), or not at all (A)?

		V	F	N	A	DK
a	I'd rather give something I made than something I've bought	1	2	3	4	5
b	I prefer not to loan money to relatives or friends	1	2	3	4	5
c	I prefer to give gifts that are practical, rather than something just for fun	1	2	3	4	5
d	Giving gifts is an important link between me and my family and friends	1	2	3	4	5
e	I like to give gifts that are really unusual	1	2	3	4	5

147. Do you give money to any charitable organizations?

    1 Yes (ASK Q. 148)
    2 No (SKIP TO Q. 149)
    3 Don't know, refused (SKIP TO Q. 149)

148. IF YES: Do you generally. . .

    1 Give on a regular, planned basis
    2 Give when you happen to feel there is a need
    3 Other
    4 Don't know, refused

149. In the past year has each of the following bothered you a lot (LOT), bothered you a little (LIT), or not bothered you (NOT)?

		LOT	LIT	NOT	DK
a	Worrying about how you were going to pay your bills	1	2	3	4
b	Feeling anxious about purchases or other decisions about money	1	2	3	4
c	Feeling guilty about the things you were spending money on	1	2	3	4
d	Wishing you had more money than you do	1	2	3	4
e	Not feeling good about yourself	1	2	3	4

150. Are you currently facing any of the concerns listed on this card?

		MENTIONED	NOT MENTIONED
a	Saving for children to go to college	1	2
b	Paying for medical expenses	1	2
c	Saving for retirement	1	2
d	Saving to buy a house	1	2
e	Paying off college loans	1	2
f	Meeting high mortgage payments	1	2
g	Needing to buy a new car	1	2
h	Paying off credit card debts	1	2
i	Helping other relatives meet financial obligations	1	2
j	Paying alimony or child support	1	2

151. In general, do you think wealthy people are...

1 Happier than other people
2 Just as happy as other people
3 Not as happy as other people
4 Don't know, refused

152. In your job, how close is the relationship between how hard you work and how much money you make? Would you say...

1 Very close
2 Fairly close
3 Not very close
4 Not at all close
5 Don't know, refused

153. In order to have a lot more money than you have now, how willing would you be to do each of the following—would you say very willing (VW), fairly willing (FW), fairly unwilling (FU), or very unwilling (VU)?

		VW	FW	FU	VU	DK
a	Work longer hours each week	1	2	3	4	5
b	Take a high-pressure job	1	2	3	4	5
c	Take a job that was less interesting but paid better	1	2	3	4	5
d	Move to a different part of the country	1	2	3	4	5
e	Start your own business	1	2	3	4	5

		VW	FW	FU	VU	DK
f	Get more education	1	2	3	4	5
g	Play the lottery	1	2	3	4	5
h	Not have children	1	2	3	4	5

154. Were you ever taught that it is wrong to want a lot of money?

    1 Yes
    2 No
    3 Don't know, refused

155. On this scale, where "10" means you admire someone a lot, and "0" means you do not admire them at all, how much do you admire each of the following?

a	People who do not have to work hard because they have a lot of money	0 1 2 3 4 5 6 7 8 9 10
b	People who have a lot of money and still work hard	0 1 2 3 4 5 6 7 8 9 10
c.	People who take a lower-paying job to help others	0 1 2 3 4 5 6 7 8 9 10
d	People who inherit large sums of money	0 1 2 3 4 5 6 7 8 9 10
e	People who make a lot of money by working hard	0 1 2 3 4 5 6 7 8 9 10
f	People who work hard but never make much money	0 1 2 3 4 5 6 7 8 9 10
g	People who spend a lot of money traveling	0 1 2 3 4 5 6 7 8 9 10
h	People who give a lot of money to charitable causes	0 1 2 3 4 5 6 7 8 9 10

156. Suppose you were thinking about buying a new car. Would each of these be a question you would think about a lot (LOT), a little (LIT), or not think about (NOT)?

		LOT	LIT	NOT	DK
a	Will it get good mileage?	1	2	3	4
b	Which dealer will give me the best deal?	1	2	3	4
c	Which make do I like best?	1	2	3	4
d	How does having a car fit into my basic values?	1	2	3	4
e	Are automobiles consistent with protecting the planet?	1	2	3	4

157. Would you agree strongly (AS), agree somewhat (A), disagree somewhat (D), or disagree strongly (DS) with each of these statements?

		AS	A	D	DS	DK
a	Money is the root of all evil	1	2	3	4	5
b	Our society is much too materialistic	1	2	3	4	5
c	Children today are always wanting too many material things	1	2	3	4	5
d	Advertising is corrupting our basic values	1	2	3	4	5
e	Having money means having more freedom	1	2	3	4	5
f	Having money is often a burden	1	2	3	4	5
g	Money is one thing, morals and values are completely separate	1	2	3	4	5
h	Having money gives me a good feeling about myself	1	2	3	4	5
i	Parents should not talk about finances in front of children	1	2	3	4	5

158. If there was less emphasis on money, do you think our society would be. . .

    1 A lot better off
    2 Somewhat better off
    3 No better off and no worse off
    4 Somewhat worse off
    5 A lot worse off
    6 Don't know, refused

159. How much control do you feel you have over each of the following—a lot (LOT), a little (LIT), or hardly any (HA)?

		LOT	LIT	HA	DK
a	Your own attitudes toward money	1	2	3	4
b	How much you spend each month	1	2	3	4
c	How much you earn each month	1	2	3	4
d	How much you think about money	1	2	3	4
e	What you spend your money on	1	2	3	4
f	How members of your family spend money	1	2	3	4

160. How important is each of the following to you—absolutely essential (AE), very important (VI), fairly important (FI), not very important (NVI), or not at all important (NAA)?

		AE	VI	FI	NVI	NAA	DK
a	Having a beautiful home, a new car, and other nice things	1	2	3	4	5	6
b	Being able to travel for pleasure and see interesting things	1	2	3	4	5	6
c	Building up enough investments for your retirement	1	2	3	4	5	6
d	Having a high-paying job	1	2	3	4	5	6
e	Wearing nice clothes	1	2	3	4	5	6
	Eating out at nice restaurants	1	2	3	4	5	6

161. In round numbers, how much did you earn from your job last year—in 1991—before taxes or other deductions?

    01 Less than $10,000
    02 $10,000–$19,999
    03 $20,000–$29,999
    04 $30,000–$39,999
    05 $40,000–$49,999
    06 $50,000–$59,999
    07 $60,000–$69,999
    08 $70,000–$79,999
    09 $80,000–$89,999
    10 $90,000–$99,999
    11 $100,000–$109,999
    12 $110,000–$119,999
    13 $120,000–$129,999
    14 $130,000–$139,999
    15 $140,000–$149,999
    16 $150,000–$159,999
    17 $160,000–$169,999
    18 $170,000–$179,999

19 $180,000 or more
20 Don't know, refused

162. What was your total family income, from all sources, last year—in 1991—before taxes?

01 Less than $10,000
02 $10,000–$19,999
03 $20,000–$29,999
04 $30,000–$39,999
05 $40,000–$49,999
06 $50,000–$59,999
07 $60,000–$69,999
08 $70,000–$79,999
09 $80,000–$89,999
10 $90,000–$99,999
11 $100,000–$109,999
12 $110,000–$119,999
13 $120,000–$129,999
14 $130,000–$139,999
15 $140,000–$149,999
16 $150,000–$159,999
17 $160,000–$169,999
18 $170,000–$179,999
19 $180,000 or more
20 Don't know, refused

163. Which people on this card know what your income is?

		MENTIONED	NOT MENTIONED
a	Your spouse	1	2
b	Your parents	1	2
c	Your children	1	2
d	Your closest friends	1	2
e	A sister or brother	1	2
f	Your coworkers	1	2

Now, on another topic. . .

164. Are you currently married, widowed, divorced, separated, or have you never been married?

1 Married (ASK Q. 165)
2 Widowed (SKIP TO Q. 173)
3 Divorced (SKIP TO Q. 173)
4 Separated (SKIP TO Q. 173)
5 Never married (SKIP TO Q. 173)
6 Don't know, refused (SKIP TO Q. 173)

IF RESPONDENT IS CURRENTLY MARRIED, ASK Q. 165; OTHERS, SKIP TO Q. 173.

165. Last week was your (wife/husband) working full time, part time, going to school, keeping house, or what?

1 Working full time (ASK Q. 166)
2 Working part time (ASK Q. 166)

3 With a job, but not at work because of temporary illness, vacation, or strike (ASK Q. 166)
4 Unemployed, laid off, looking for work (SKIP TO Q. 169)
5 Retired (SKIP TO Q. 169)
6 In school (SKIP TO Q. 169)
7 Keeping house   (SKIP TO Q. 169)
8 Other (SKIP TO Q. 169)
9 Don't know, refused (SKIP TO Q. 169)

166. IF WORKING, FULL OR PART TIME: How many hours did (he/she) work last week, at all jobs?

0   00–09 hours
1   10–19 hours
2   20–29 hours
3   30–39 hours
4   40–49 hours
5   50–59 hours
6   60–69 hours
7   70–79 hours
8   80 or more hours
9   Don't know, refused

167. IF WITH A JOB, BUT NOT AT WORK: How many hours a week does (he/she) usually work, at all jobs?

0   00–09 hours
1   10–19 hours
2   20–29 hours
3   30–39 hours
4   40–49 hours
5   50–59 hours
6   60–69 hours
7   70–79 hours
8   80 or more hours
9   Don't know, refused

168. Please tell me which of these categories on this card most nearly describes the kind of work (he/she) does.

1 Professional worker
2 Works at skilled trade/craft
3 Semiskilled worker
4 Manager/executive/official in business
5 Runs own business with 2 or more employees
6 Farm owner or farm manager
7 Clerical worker
8 Sales worker
9 Manufacturer's representative
10 Service worker
11 Laboring worker
12 Farm laborer/helper
13 Other
14 Can't say

169. Do you and your spouse generally think the same way about money, or do you differ in how you think about money?

    1 Think the same way
    2 Differ in how we think about money
    3 Other
    4 Don't know, refused

170. Compared with your spouse, are you more careful about spending money, less careful about spending money, or about the same?

    1 More careful about spending money
    2 Less careful about spending money
    3 About the same
    4 Don't know, refused

171. When you and your spouse have arguments, how often is money one of the issues—would you say it often is, sometimes is, seldom is, or never is?

    1 Often is
    2 Sometimes is
    3 Seldom is
    4 Never is
    5 Don't know, refused

172. Who would you say does most of the housework—you, your spouse, or both equally?

    1 You
    2 Your spouse
    3 Both equally
    4 Don't know, refused

173. ASK EVERYONE: How many children have you ever had? (Include all that were born alive, including any from a previous marriage.)

    1 None (SKIP TO Q. 178)
    2 One
    3 Two
    4 Three
    5 Four
    6 Five
    7 Six
    8 Seven
    9 Eight or more
    10 Don't know, refused

174. IF ANY CHILDREN: How many of these children are currently living with you in your home?

    1 None
    2 One
    3 Two
    4 Three
    5 Four
    6 Five

7 Six
8 Seven
9 Eight or more
10 Don't know, refused

175. IF ANY CHILDREN: How many of these children are currently age 6 or younger?

1 None
2 One
3 Two
4 Three
5 Four
6 Five
7 Six
8 Seven
9 Eight or more
10 Don't know, refused

176. IF ANY CHILDREN: For emotional support, do your children come more to you, your spouse, or to both equally?

1 You
2 Your spouse
3 Both equally
4 Don't know, refused

177. IF ANY CHILDREN: How sure are you about what to teach your children? Would you say you are. . .

1 Very sure
2 Somewhat sure
3 Somewhat unsure
4 Very unsure
5 Don't know, refused

178. ASK EVERYONE: How do you feel, in general, about the way children are being raised in our society? Do you feel our nation is doing. . .

1 An excellent job
2 A good job
3 A fair job
4   A poor job, or
5 A very poor job
6 Don't know, refused

179. How seriously, if at all, does your work life conflict with your family life? Would you say. . .

1 Very seriously
2 Seriously
3 Somewhat
4 Hardly any
5 None
6 Don't know, refused

180. In relating your work life to your family life, has each of the following been a very big issue (VBI), a big issue (BI), a small issue (SI), or not an issue (NAI) for you?

		VBI	BI	SI	NAI	DK
a	Arranging child care	1	2	3	4	5
b	Getting household chores done	1	2	3	4	5
c	Finding time for yourself	1	2	3	4	5
d	Having to bring work home with you	1	2	3	4	5
e	Your spouse being too busy	1	2	3	4	5
f	Caring for elderly relatives	1	2	3	4	5
g	Family members not appreciating your work	1	2	3	4	5

181. Would you agree strongly (AS), agree somewhat (A), disagree somewhat (D), or disagree strongly (DS) with each of the following statements?

		AS	A	D	DS	DK
a	My work is helping to make the world a better place	1	2	3	4	5
b	Even if I had enough money, I would still work	1	2	3	4	5
c	I feel good about the work I do	1	2	3	4	5
d	My family and friends respect the kind of work I do	1	2	3	4	5
e	My family is the main reason I work hard	1	2	3	4	5
f	My family comes first; my work second	1	2	3	4	5
g	When things are bad at work, I'm cranky with my family	1	2	3	4	5
h	When things are bad at home, I don't do as well at my job	1	2	3	4	5
i	I can be myself easier at home than at work	1	2	3	4	5

182. Because of your obligations to your family—spouse, children, parents, or other relatives—have you ever done any of the following?

		YES	NO	DK
a	Taken a job you wouldn't otherwise have taken	1	2	3
b	Turned down a job you might have otherwise accepted	1	2	3
c	Refused a promotion that would have added to your job pressures	1	2	3
d	Worked part time instead of full time	1	2	3
e	Taken a secure job instead of a higher-paying job	1	2	3
f	Refused to work overtime	1	2	3
g	Refused to travel or be away from home	1	2	3
h	Taken on additional work in order to pay for things	1	2	3

183. How well does each of the following statements describe you—very well (V), fairly well (F), not very well (N), or not at all (NA)?

		V	F	N	NA	DK
a	I'm working harder than I did 5 years ago	1	2	3	4	5
b	I have more money than I did 5 years ago	1	2	3	4	5
c	I wish I could work fewer hours than I do	1	2	3	4	5
d	I think a lot about money and finances	1	2	3	4	5
e	I should get more sleep than I do	1	2	3	4	5
f	I seldom get enough time for myself	1	2	3	4	5
g	My work is very meaningful to me	1	2	3	4	5
h	I sometimes feel burned out in my job	1	2	3	4	5

i	I wish I had more money than I do	1	2	3	4	5
j	I have a lot of financial obligations	1	2	3	4	5
k	I wish I had more time for my family	1	2	3	4	5
l	I need more time to think about the really basic issues in life	1	2	3	4	5
m	I want more from life than just a good job and a comfortable lifestyle	1	2	3	4	5
n	I'd like to spend more time exploring spiritual issues	1	2	3	4	5
o	I worry about meeting my financial obligations	1	2	3	4	5
p	I'm working myself to death	1	2	3	4	5
q	I'm under a lot of pressure	1	2	3	4	5
r	I think a lot about my values and priorities in life	1	2	3	4	5

Now, on a different topic. . .

184. How often, if at all, do you attend religious services?

    1 More than once a week
    2 About once a week
    3 Several times a month
    4 About once a month
    5 Several times a year
    6 Once a year or less
    7 Never (SKIP TO Q. 186)
    8 Don't know, refused

185. When you attend religious services, how important is each of the following to you—very important (V), fairly important (F), not very important (N), or not at all important (A)?

		V	F	N	A	DK
a	The opportunity to give back some of the money God has given you	1	2	3	4	5
b	Sermons that inspire you to work hard and be responsible	1	2	3	4	5
c	Being with different people than the ones you work with	1	2	3	4	5
d	Time to think about things other than your work	1	2	3	4	5
e	An escape from daily cares and responsibilities	1	2	3	4	5
f	A feeling of comfort	1	2	3	4	5
g	Getting divine guidance in making decisions	1	2	3	4	5
h	Just knowing the people there care about you	1	2	3	4	5

186. Are you currently a member of a church or synagogue?

    1 Yes (Ask Q. 187)
    2 No (Go to Q. 190)
    3 Don't know, refused

187. How many people belong to this church or synagogue? Would you say...

    1 Fewer than 100
    2 100 to less than 200
    3 200 to less than 300

4 300 to less than 500
5 500 to less than 1,000
6 1,000 or more
7 Don't know, refused

188. Of your closest friends, how many would you say attend this congregation?

1 None
2 One or two
3 Three to five
4 More than five
5 Don't know, refused

189. How much money did you give last year to religious organizations of all kinds? (RECORD DOLLAR AMOUNT)

$__ __, __ __ __ .00

190. What is your religious preference?

1 Protestant (ASK Q. 191)
2 Catholic
3 Jewish
4 Eastern Orthodox
5 Other
6 Mormon   GO TO Q. 192
7 Moslem
8 Hindu
9 None
10 Don't know, refused

191. What specific denomination or faith is that?

01 Church of Jesus Christ of Latter-Day Saints (Mormon)
    Baptists:
02 Southern Baptist Convention
03 American Baptist Convention
04 National Baptist Convention of America
05 National Baptist Convention, USA
06 Other Baptist (specified)
07 Baptist, don't know which denomination
08 Episcopalian
    Lutheran
09 Evangelical Lutheran Church in America
10 Missouri Synod Lutheran
11 Other Lutheran (specified)
12 Lutheran, don't know which denomination
    Methodist
13 United Methodist Church
14 A.M.E. Zion Church
15 A.M.E. Church
16 Other Methodist (specified)
17 Methodist, don't know which denomination
18 Presbyterian
19 Presbyterian Church (USA)

20 Presbyterian Church in America
21 Other Presbyterian (specified)
22 Presbyterian, don't know which denomination
23 United Church of Christ (or Congregationalist or Evangelical and Reformed)
24 Christian Church (Disciples of Christ)
25 Church of the Nazarene
26 Assemblies of God
27 Pentecostal
28 Fundamentalist
29 Nondenominational or independent church
30 Other Protestant (specified)
31 Protestant, unspecified

192. How important would you say religion is in your own life...

1 Very important
2 Somewhat important
3 Not very important
4 Don't know, refused

193. How important would you say religion was in your family while you were growing up. . .

1 Very important
2 Somewhat important
3 Not very important
4 Don't know, refused

194. When you were a child, did your parents do any of the things on this card?

		YES	NO	DK
a	Say grace at meals	1	2	3
b	Pray about financial decisions	1	2	3
c	Read the Bible at home	1	2	3
d	Have family devotions	1	2	3
e	Read Bible stories to you	1	2	3
f	Send you to Sunday School	1	2	3

195. In the past year, how much have you thought about each of the following—a great deal (G), a fair amount (F), a little (L), or hardly any (A)?

		G	F	L	A	DK
a	Your relationship to God	1	2	3	4	5
b	What the Bible teaches about money	1	2	3	4	5
c	How to link your faith more directly to your work	1	2	3	4	5
d	The connection between religious values and your personal finances	1	2	3	4	5
e	The differences between spiritual growth and material possessions	1	2	3	4	5
f	What the Bible teaches about work	1	2	3	4	5
g	Your responsibility to the poor	1	2	3	4	5

196. In your opinion, is each of the following statements about the Bible true (T) or false (F)?

		T	F	DK
a	The Bible is the inspired word of God	1	2	3
b	Everything in the Bible should be taken literally, word for word	1	2	3

		T	F	DK
c	The Bible may contain historical or scientific errors	1	2	3
d	According to the Bible, Jesus was born in Jerusalem	1	2	3
e	The book of Acts is in the Old Testament	1	2	3
f	The Bible is a detailed book of rules that Christians should try to follow	1	2	3

197. Which activities on this card have you done within the past year?

		DONE	NOT DONE
a	Regularly attended an adult Sunday school class	1	2
b	Participated regularly in a fellowship or support group	1	2
c	Prayed about money matters	1	2
d	Heard a sermon about personal finances	1	2
e	Talked about your work with a member of the clergy	1	2
f	Thanked God for a financial blessing	1	2
g	Heard a sermon on stewardship	1	2
h	Participated in a religious retreat	1	2
i	Heard a sermon that inspired you to work harder	1	2
j	Discussed your faith with someone at work	1	2
k	Participated in a religious group that met in the workplace	1	2
l	Received counseling from a religious organization	1	2
m	Received financial help from a religious organization	1	2

198. Do you mostly agree (A) or mostly disagree (D) with each statement on this card?

		A	D	DK
a	The Bible contains valuable teachings about the use of money	1	2	3
b	I feel God has called me to the particular line of work I am in	1	2	3
c	God wants me to have the kind of job that will make me happy	1	2	3
d	God doesn't care how I use my money	1	2	3
e	I should give God a percentage of the money I earn	1	2	3
f	People who work hard are more pleasing to God than people who are lazy	1	2	3
g	It is morally wrong to have a lot of nice things when others are starving	1	2	3
h	Riches get in the way of our truly knowing God	1	2	3
i	The poor are closer to God than rich people are	1	2	3
j	Being greedy is a sin against God	1	2	3
k	Praying in the morning helps me have a better day at work	1	2	3

199. In deciding what kind of work to go into, did your religious values influence your decision? Would you say. . .

1 Yes, definitely
2 Yes, maybe
3 No
4 Don't know, refused

200. Which statement on this card comes closest to your own view?

1 God wants us to work at whatever makes us happiest
2 God wants us to find work that best suits our individual talents
3 God wants us to do something with our lives that will be useful to the world
4 God doesn't really care what kind of work we do

5 Other
6 Don't know, refused

201. Would you say each of these statements is mostly true (T) or mostly false (F)?

		T	F	DK
a	Members of the clergy have very little understanding what it is like in the real workaday world	1	2	3
b	Churches are too eager to get your time and money	1	2	3
c	The clergy are doing God's work more than any of the rest of us are	1	2	3
d	Clergy think church work is more important than the real work we do	1	2	3
e	Clergy are a good source of advice when you are having at work	1	2	3
f	Clergy are mostly opposed to women having jobs outside problems the home	1	2	3
g	Clergy are good to go to when you need emotional support	1	2	3
h	Churches do a good job of helping people who are in financial need	1	2	3

202. On a scale from 1 to 6, where "1" is "very conservative" and "6" is "very liberal," where would you place yourself in terms of your religious views?

Very conservative	Very liberal	DK
1 2 3 4 5 6		0

203. Using the same scale, how would you define your political views, where "1" is "very conservative" and "6" is "very liberal"?

Very conservative	Very liberal	DK
1 2 3 4 5 6		0

204. Would you like to see churches and synagogues emphasize each of the following a lot more (LM), somewhat more (SM), somewhat less (SL), or a lot less (LL)?

		LM	SM	SL	LL	DK
a	Encourage people to be less materialistic	1	2	3	4	5
b	Make sermons more relevant to the problems people face in their work	1	2	3	4	5
c	Help people facing career changes	1	2	3	4	5
d	Be supportive to working women	1	2	3	4	5
e	Provide job training, housing, and other services for the poor	1	2	3	4	5
f	Encourage people to give more time and money to religious programs	1	2	3	4	5
g	Speak out on ethical problems in business	1	2	3	4	5

205. Which one of these would be the best definition of stewardship?

1 Giving a certain percentage of your money to the church
2 Using your individual talents in a responsible way
3 Taking good care of our planet, or
4 Remembering that God made everything

5 Other
6 Don't know, refused

206. Is the idea of stewardship. . .

1 Very meaningful to you
2 Fairly meaningful to you
3 Not very meaningful to you
4 Not at all meaningful to you
5 Don't know, refused

207. Do you mostly agree (A) or mostly disagree (D) with each of these statements?

		A	D	DK
a	Churches generally use the money they get wisely and responsibly	1	2	3
b	Giving money to churches is more important than giving it to other organizations	1	2	3
c	It annoys me when churches ask me to give money	1	2	3
d	I'd rather give money to a needy family than to a church	1	2	3
e	I'm more likely to give money to a church if someone I know personally asks me	1	2	3
f	I'm too busy to do church work	1	2	3

208. Would each of the following make you more likely to give money to a church (M), not make any difference (N), or make you less likely to give (L)?

		M	N	L	DK
a	If the church were more liberal on sexual and moral issues	1	2	3	4
b	If my family were benefiting more from the church's programs	1	2	3	4
c	If the preacher gave better sermons	1	2	3	4
d	If the church emphasized giving money more than it does now	1	2	3	4
e	If the church took more stands on political issues	1	2	3	4
f	If the church were doing more to help the needy	1	2	3	4
g	If the church spoke out more on social justice	1	2	3	4
h	If the clergy were less materialistic	1	2	3	4
i	If I had fewer economic needs myself	1	2	3	4
j	If I understood better what the church does with its money	1	2	3	4

Now, on a different topic. . .

209. How many years have you lived in your present community?

1 Less than one
2 One to less than two
3 Two to less than three
4 Three to less than five
5 Five to less than ten
6 Ten or more
7 Don't know, refused

210. Do you. . .

    1 Know people better at work than in your neighborhood
    2 Know people in your neighborhood better than at work
    3 Know people in both places about equally
    4 Or not know people at either place
    5 Don't know, refused

211. Are you currently involved in any small group that meets regularly and provides support or caring for those who participate in it?

    1 Yes
    2 No
    3 Don't know, refused

212. How serious a problem do you think each of the following is in our society—extremely serious (ES), serious (S), a small problem (SP), or not a problem (NP)?

		ES	S	SP	NP	DK
a	Individualism	1	2	3	4	5
b	Materialism	1	2	3	4	5
c	The breakdown of community	1	2	3	4	5
d	Moral corruption	1	2	3	4	5
e	Selfishness	1	2	3	4	5
f	The breakdown of families	1	2	3	4	5
g	People turning away from God	1	2	3	4	5
h	Corruption in business	1	2	3	4	5
i	The condition of the poor	1	2	3	4	5
j	Political corruption	1	2	3	4	5
k	People working too hard	1	2	3	4	5
l	People not being in touch with their feelings	1	2	3	4	5
m	Too much emphasis on money	1	2	3	4	5
n	Problems in our schools	1	2	3	4	5

213. Do you yourself happen to be involved in any charity or social service activities, such as helping the poor, the sick or the elderly?

    1 Yes (ASK Q. 214)
    2 No (SKIP TO Q. 215)
    3 Don't know, refused (SKIP TO Q. 215)

214. IF YES: About how many hours a week do you spend on these activities?

    1 Less than one hour a week
    2 One hour to less than two hours
    3 Two hours to less than five hours
    4 Five hours to less than ten hours
    5 Ten hours to less than twenty hours
    6 Twenty hours or more
    7 Don't know, refused

215. In the past year, have you. . .

		YES	NO	DK
a	Visited someone in the hospital	1	2	3
b	Helped someone through an emotional crisis	1	2	3

		YES	NO	DK
c	Donated time to a volunteer organization	1	2	3
d	Worked on a community service project	1	2	3
e	Done volunteer work at your church or synagogue	1	2	3
f	Given money to a beggar	1	2	3

216. To help the needy in our society, do you think each of the following would help a lot (LOT), help a little (LIT), or not help (NOT)?

		LOT	LIT	NOT	DK
a	If more people gave a few hours a week to doing volunteer work	1	2	3	4
b	Spending more money on government social welfare services	1	2	3	4
c	If everyone just worked harder at their own jobs	1	2	3	4
d	Getting businesses to take a more responsible role in their communities	1	2	3	4
e	If more people took an active role in their churches	1	2	3	4
f	Policies to promote faster economic growth	1	2	3	4

217. On the whole, do you think our economic system is. . .

1 The best system we could possibly have
2 Basically OK, but in need of some tinkering
3 In need of some fundamental changes
4 Needing to be replaced by a different system
5 Other
6 Don't know, refused

218. Which of the statements on this card best describes your own opinion?

1 It is quite possible to make many significant changes in our economic system
2 It is possible to make a few significant changes in our economic system
3 Economic forces are pretty much beyond our control
4 Don't know, refused

219. How well do you feel you understand how our economic system works?

1 Very well
2 Fairly well
3 Not very well
4 Not at all well
5 Don't know, refused

220. Do you think each of the following has too much influence in shaping our nation's goals and values (TM), about the right amount of influence (RA), or too little influence (TL)?

		TM	RA	TL	DK
a	Television	1	2	3	4
b	Politicians	1	2	3	4
c	Large corporations	1	2	3	4
d	Small businesses	1	2	3	4
e	Churches	1	2	3	4
f	Nonprofit organizations	1	2	3	4
g	Scientists	1	2	3	4

		TM	RA	TL	DK
h	Working people	1	2	3	4
i	School teachers	1	2	3	4

221. On the whole, how do you feel about the future of our country—very optimistic, fairly optimistic, fairly pessimistic, or very pessimistic?

    1 Very optimistic
    2 Fairly optimistic
    3 Fairly pessimistic
    4 Very pessimistic

222. How interested are you in each of the following—very interested (VI), fairly interested (FI), or not very interested (NVI)?

		VI	FI	NVI	DK
a	Environmental issues	1	2	3	4
b	Local news	1	2	3	4
c	National politics	1	2	3	4
d	Problems of addiction	1	2	3	4
e	The issue of abortion	1	2	3	4
f	Helping reduce crime	1	2	3	4
g	Helping improve the schools	1	2	3	4
h	Doing well in your job	1	2	3	4
i	International affairs	1	2	3	4
j	Thinking about basic values	1	2	3	4

And now, just a few questions so that my office will have some information about the background of each respondent.

223. In politics, as of today, do you consider yourself a Republican, a Democrat, or an Independent?

    1 Republican (GO TO Q. 225)
    2 Democrat (GO TO Q. 225)
    3 Independent (ASK Q. 224)
    4 Other party (GO TO Q. 225)

224. As of today, would you say you lean more to the Democratic party or to the Republican Party?

    1 Democratic
    2 Republican
    3 Don't know

225. We are interested in finding out how often people are at home to watch TV or to listen to the radio. Would you mind telling me whether or not you happened to be at home yesterday (last night, last Saturday, last Sunday) at this particular time?

    1 Yes, at home
    2 No, not at home

226. How about the day (night, Saturday, Sunday) before at this time?

    1 Yes, at home
    2 No, not at home

227. And how about the day (night, Saturday, Sunday) before that at this time?

    1 Yes, at home
    2 No, not at home

228. What is your position in this household?

    1 Male head of household
    2 Female head of household/wife of head of household
    3 Son of head of household
    4 Daughter of head of household
    5 Father of head of household
    6 Mother of head of household
    7 Other male
    8 Other female

229. Who in your family is the most responsible for making the decisions about how to handle your family's savings and investments?

    1 Respondent mainly
    2 Both respondent and spouse equally
    3 Both respondent and parent(s) equally
    4 Both respondent and other persons equally
    5 Respondent's spouse mainly
    6 Respondent's parent mainly
    7 Other person mainly

230. Do you own or rent your home?

    1 Own
    2 Rent
    3 Other arrangement

231. What was the last grade or class you completed in school?

    1 None, or grades 1–4
    2 Grades 5, 6, or 7
    3 Grade 8
    4 High school incomplete, grades 9–11
    5 High school graduate, grade 12
    6 Technical, trade or business
    7 College, university, incomplete
    8 College, university, graduate

232. And what is your age? (Record actual age: __ __)

233. Are you, or is your husband/wife, a member of a labor union?

    1 Yes, respondent is
    2 Yes, spouse is
    3 Yes, both are
    4 Neither are

234. Are you yourself of Hispanic origin or descent, such as Mexican, Puerto Rican, Cuban, or other Spanish background?

    1 Yes
    2 No
    3 Don't know

235. Check whether:

    1 White man
    2 White woman
    3 Black man
    4 Black woman
    5 Other man (specify)
    6 Other woman (specify)

Notes

Chapter Two. Our Moment in History

1. *The Republic*, Book IX.
2. Sigmund Freud, *Collected Papers*, vol. 2 (New York: Basic Books, 1959), p. 351.
3. Clifford Geertz, *The Interpretation of Cultures* (New York: Basic Books, 1973), chap. 4.
4. John Lynch, *Spain Under the Habsburgs*, vol. 1, *Empire and Absolutism, 1530–1780* (Oxford: Oxford University Press, 1964); J. H. Parry, *The Spanish Theory of Empire in the Sixteenth Century* (Cambridge: Cambridge University Press, 1940); and J. A. Fernandez-Santamaria, *The State, War, and Peace: Spanish Political Thought in the Renaissance, 1515–1559* (Cambridge: Cambridge University Press, 1977).
5. Geertz, *The Interpretation of Cultures,* chap. 5.
6. Max Weber, *Ancient Judaism* (New York: Free Press, 1952), especially chaps. 6 through 10.
7. Robert Darnton, *The Great Cat Massacre and Other Episodes in French Cultural History* (New York: Basic Books, 1984), chap. 2.
8. Bronislaw Malinowski, *Argonauts of the Western Pacific* (London: Routledge, 1922).
9. William A. Christian, Jr., *Local Religion in Sixteenth-Century Spain* (Princeton: Princeton University Press, 1981); Janusz Tazbir, "The Cult of St. Isidore the Farmer in Europe," in *Poland at the 14th International Congress of Historical Sciences in San Francisco* (Warsaw: Polish Academy of Sciences, Institute of History, 1975).
10. Max Weber, *The Sociology of Religion* (Boston: Beacon Press, 1963), chap. 9.
11. Daniel Bell, *The Coming of Post-Industrial Society: A Venture in Social Fore-*

casting (New York: Basic Books, 1973), remains a useful introduction to the main issues. See also Norman Birnbaum, *The Crisis of Industrial Society* (New York: Oxford University Press, 1969), and Talcott Parsons, "Religion in Post-Industrial America: The Problem of Secularization," *Social Research* 41 (1974): 193–225. Much of the literature on professionalization, the "new class," and phases of economic development cited in subsequent chapters is also relevant to the argument about postindustrial society.

12. *The Apologia of Robert Keayne: The Last Will and Testament of Me, Robert Keayne, All of It Written with My Own Hands and Began by Me, Mo: 6: I: 1653, Commonly Called August, The Self Portrait of a Puritan Merchant,* edited by Bernard Bailyn (Gloucester, Mass.: Peter Smith, 1970). The case of Robert Keayne is well known because of his own writing, but it should not necessarily be regarded as a typical or recurrent episode in Puritan history.

13. These characteristics of mercantilism are culled from a wide variety of sources, including Immanuel Wallerstein, *The Modern World-System*, vol. 2, *Mercantilism and the Consolidation of the European World-Economy, 1600–1750* (New York: Academic Press, 1980); Marc Raeff, "The Well-Ordered Police State and the Development of Modernity in Seventeenth- and Eighteenth-Century Europe: An Attempt at a Comparative Approach," *American Historical Review* 80 (1975): 1225–54; Gustav Schmoller, *The Mercantile System and Its Historical Significance* (New York: Macmillan, 1896); Eli F. Hecksher, *Mercantilism,* 2 vols. (New York: Macmillan, 1955); and Charles Wilson, *Mercantilism* (London: Routledge, 1958).

14. Religious influences in Puritan Boston were limited in other ways. Merchants influenced the clergy enough to encourage them, implicitly at least, to address issues that would not interfere with their business operations. Sermons delivered in Boston in the 1630s and 1640s in fact lead one to conclude that other topics were addressed far more frequently than economic matters. These were already a domain over which the clergy had only limited influence. Indeed, clergy sometimes found themselves at odds both with the merchants and colonial officials. Moreover, clergy themselves faced serious economic needs. The diaries of clergy reveal that they were far from uninterested in their own salaries, houses, libraries, and other amenities. In short, they lived with the desires and temptations of the period as much as anyone else. Too, drunkenness and sloth may have been widespread among the common people. It was difficult for the churches to impose their disciplined moral and spiritual norms on everyone. In theory, these norms applied equally. But the social mechanisms to enforce them were lacking.

15. On Franklin, see especially Paul Leicester Ford, *The Many-Sided Franklin* (New York: Century, 1899); Phillips Russell, *Benjamin Franklin: The First Civilized American* (New York: Brentano's, 1927); Verner W. Crane, *Benjamin Franklin and a Rising People* (Boston: Little, Brown, 1954); Charles L. Sanford, *Benjamin Franklin and the American Character* (Boston: D.C. Heath, 1955); and Peter Baida, *Poor Richard's Legacy: American Business*

Values from Benjamin Franklin to Donald Trump (New York: William Morrow, 1990).

16. See such historical studies as Barry Levy, *Quakers and the American Family: British Settlement in the Delaware Valley* (New York: Oxford University Press, 1988), and John Brooke, *The Heart of the Commonwealth: Society and Political Culture in Central Massachusetts, 1713–1861* (New York: Cambridge University Press, 1989). There is some evidence, at least during the early decades of industrialization, that an ascetic religious ethic may have contributed to upward mobility among the working classes. A study of the relationship between evangelical religion and economic behavior in antebellum Philadelphia, for example, shows that evangelical males experienced greater occupational mobility than nonevangelicals, especially moving into roles as master craftsmen and small retailers, apparently as a result of religious teachings encouraging them to work hard, save their money, avoid the consumption of alcohol, and provide for their families. See Bruce Laurie, *Working People of Philadelphia, 1800–1850* (Philadelphia: Temple University Press, 1980). But religion did not simply propel individuals into new positions of economic prominence. Just as in the case of Franklin, there was often a tension between economic behavior and other personal pursuits. For many immigrants, religious orientations encouraged loyalty to tradition, to other languages and other ways of life, than those that were becoming prevalent in the new cities or on the expanding American frontier. Working-class families may have found Sunday church services the bright spot in their week, but these services may not have elevated them economically or helped them put food on the table. See Herbert Gutman, *Work, Culture, and Society in Industrializing America: Essays in American Working-Class and Social History* (New York: Knopf, 1976). Most treatments of the relationships between religion and economic behavior during the period of advanced industrialization—say, from about 1850 through the end of World War I—emphasize the extent to which religious arguments were turned into the service of shopkeepers, mill owners, and industrialists. Evangelical revivals, it has been argued, were promoted by elites to discipline their workforces and help them adapt to the regimented lifestyles required by industrialization. Methodism, for example, appears to have spread especially rapidly in areas where agriculture and manufacturing were drawing people into the marketplace, undercutting their ties to ethnic and family groups, and forcing them to be more self-reliant. The disciplined, individualistic approach to piety championed by the Methodists apparently rang true to people in such circumstances. Others have argued that industrialists themselves legitimated their new power in local communities by bankrolling churches and fostering relief programs for the poor. Some instances have been found in which religious sects, rivalries among Protestant denominations, and conflicts between Catholics and Protestants may have made it harder for trade unions to organize or for workers with common economic grievances to cooperate with one

another. Historians of this era differ over the underlying motives propelling new conceptions of the relationships between faith and economic life. One interpretation, often rooted in Marxist theory, draws the cynical conclusion that elites consciously exploited religious organizations for their own economic benefit. A more common interpretation holds that industrialists and shopkeepers were sincere in their religious convictions but championed beliefs that often had the unexpected consequence of legitimating their privileged status and of maintaining the working class in a more subordinate role. A few historical studies also point to the positive good that may have resulted from religious beliefs, such as efforts to oppose economic exploitation, build settlement houses, pass child labor laws, and expand educational opportunities.

17. Several useful studies that provide historical insight into the dilemmas of modernity in this period include Michael Cassity, *Defending a Way of Life: An American Community in the Nineteenth Century* (Albany, N.Y.: State University of New York Press, 1989); David Thelen, *Paths of Resistance: Tradition and Dignity in Industrializing Missouri* (New York: Oxford University Press, 1986); and Robert Wiebe, *The Search for Order, 1877–1920* (New York: Hill and Wang, 1967).

18. Mary Ryan, *Cradle of the Middle Class: The Family in Oneida County, New York, 1790–1865* (New York: Cambridge University Press, 1981).

19. See, for example, Thomas Cochran, *Railroad Leaders, 1845–1890: The Business Mind in Action* (Cambridge, Mass.: Harvard University Press, 1953).

20. Robert B. Reich, "Reclaiming Our Edge," *Working Woman* (September 1993): 46.

21. This separation can be traced to early-eighteenth-century Europe, where it appears to have been encouraged by the simultaneous growth of cities, political bureaucracies, and large-scale industry and commerce. The growing anonymity of urban life permitted individuals to develop more complex, multiple selves but in the process made these selves less stable and more problematic to maintain. Mechanisms have also emerged in modern societies to deal with these problems (one thinks of therapies and self-help methods, for example). Generally speaking, so much of the theoretical literature has stressed the disjuncture between public and private that care needs to be exercised in thinking through the specific empirical ramifications of this distinction.

Chapter Three. Faith and Work

1. Stephen Hart and David Krueger, "Faith and Work: Challenges for Congregations," *Christian Century* (July 15–22, 1992): 683–85.

2. Juliet B. Schor, *The Overworked American: The Unexpected Decline of Leisure* (New York: Basic Books, 1991), p. 29.

3. Economic Values Survey. See the appendix on Methodology for a description of this study. Results reported in the text are from a question that read,

"How well does each of the following statements describe you—very well, fairly well, not very well, or not at all?" Sixty-six percent said the statement "I'm working harder than I did 5 years ago" described them very well or fairly well; 52 percent said this for the statement "I wish I could work fewer hours than I do."

4. Ibid. Other studies also reveal that a substantial number of people work more than the standard forty-hour week. In a Harris survey, for example, professionals, people with incomes over $50,000, and those termed "baby boomers" worked an average of 52 hours a week, and among small business-people 57 hours. These figures are reported in Benjamin K. Hunnicutt, "No Time for God or Family," *Wall Street Journal,* January 4, 1990, p. A12. Results of a 1991 Gallup survey, though reported in less detail, also indicate that many Americans work more than the standard forty-hour week. Thirty-nine percent reported they work more than 45 hours in a typical week; one person in eight works more than 60 hours a week; Larry Hugick and Jennifer Leonard, "Job Dissatisfaction Grows; `Moonlighting' on the Rise," *The Gallup Poll,* September 2, 1991, p. 10.

5. Schor, *The Overworked American*, p. 25.

6. M. L. DeFleur, "Children's Knowledge of Occupational Roles and Prestige: Preliminary Report," *Psychological Reports* 13 (1963): 760; S. L. O'Bryant, M. E. Durrett, and J. W. Pennebaker, "Sex Differences in Knowledge of Occupational Dimensions Across Four Age Levels," *Sex Roles* 6 (1980): 331–37.

7. Economic Values Survey. The figures for wondering if they were in the right line of work and feeling seriously burned out are the proportion of people in the labor force who say they have experienced these problems within the past year.

8. Ibid.

9. Although many substantive definitions of work appear in the published literature, the perspective that work cannot be defined in terms of intrinsic characteristics but must be considered a cultural construct is the necessary starting point for any social scientific discussion of the subject; see especially the useful conceptual and historical survey of the cultural meanings of work in Keith Grint, *The Sociology of Work: An Introduction* (Cambridge: Polity Press, 1991), chap. 1.

10. Richard Hall, *The Dimensions of Work* (Beverly Hills, Calif.: Sage, 1986), p. 13, defines work as "the effort or activity of an individual performed for the purpose of providing goods or services of value to others; it is also considered to be work performed by the individual." Since what is "of value" depends on cultural assumptions, this definition also stresses the culturally constructed character of work. It may be objected, however, that "of value to others" is neither a clear nor necessary characteristic of work.

11. Adrian Furnham, *The Protestant Work Ethic: The Psychology of Work-Related Beliefs and Behaviours* (London: Routledge, 1990), p. 144.

12. In the Economic Values Survey, 40 percent of married women said they did

most of the housework, while 45 percent of the married men said their spouse did. See also Arlie Hochschild, *The Second Shift: Working Parents and the Revolution at Home* (New York: Viking, 1989); and Sarah Fenstermaker Berk, *The Gender Factory: The Apportionment of Work in American Households* (New York: Plenum, 1985).

13. Sharon Toffey Shepela and Ann T. Viviano, "Some Psychological Factors Affecting Job Segregation and Wages," in *Comparable Worth and Wage Discrimination: Technical Possibilities and Political Realities*, edited by Helen Remick (Philadelphia: Temple University Press, 1984), pp. 47–58; Donald J. Treiman and Heidi I. Hartmann, *Women, Work and Wages: Equal Pay for Jobs of Equal Value* (Washington, D.C.: National Academy Press, 1981).

14. Some evidence, however, suggests that marital status has a significant confounding effect on these relationships; see Bredley R. Hertel, "Gender, Religious Identity, and Work Force Participation," *Journal for the Scientific Study of Religion* 27 (1988): 574–92.

15. The most useful theological discussion I have found is that of Miroslav Volf, *Work in the Spirit: Toward a Theology of Work* (New York: Oxford University Press, 1991); other helpful discussions include John C. Haughey, *Converting Nine to Five: A Spirituality of Daily Work* (New York: Crossroad, 1989); John A. Bernbaum and Simon M. Steer, *Why Work? Careers and Employment in Biblical Perspective* (Grand Rapids, Mich.: Baker Book House, 1986); and Graham Tucker, *The Faith-Work Connection: A Practical Application of Christian Values in the Workplace* (Toronto: Anglican Book Centre, 1987).

16. Volf, *Work in the Spirit*, pp. 14–16.

17. Daniel Bell, *The Coming of Post-industrial Society* (New York: Basic Books, 1973); B. Bruce-Briggs, ed., *The New Class?* (New Brunswick, N.J.: Transaction, 1979).

18. Much of this literature is discussed in James Davison Hunter, *American Evangelicalism: Conservative Religion and the Quandary of Modernity* (New Brunswick, N.J.: Rutgers University Press, 1983); and James Davison Hunter, *Evangelicalism: The Coming Generation* (Chicago: University of Chicago Press, 1987).

19. In the Economic Values Survey, for example, 76 percent of weekly churchgoers said they admired teachers a lot, compared with 67 percent of those who seldom attended religious services. The relationship for admiring nurses was about the same magnitude, as was also the case for admiring therapists. The relationship between church attendance and admiring housewives was somewhat stronger, and for admiring clergy, quite strong. The possibility that church attendance is simply associated with higher admiration scores in general, however, is indicated by the fact that there was also a slight relationship with admiring business managers.

20. Robert Wuthnow, *Acts of Compassion: Caring for Others and Helping Ourselves* (Princeton: Princeton University Press, 1991).

21. Using dummy variables for particular occupational categories, and control-

ling for gender, age, education, and being employed full or part time, the likelihood of being employed in a profession is not significantly associated with church attendance, church membership, or denomination (dummy variables for Protestant, Catholic, Presbyterian, and Baptist); being employed as a business executive or manager, net of these other factors, turns out to be somewhat *positively* associated with church attendance and with being a Catholic or Protestant rather than choosing some other religious preference; blue-collar employment is not significantly related to any of these religious variables; nor are service occupations.

22. Net of other factors, Catholics are somewhat more likely to be self-employed, and churchgoers are significantly more likely to be employed in the nonprofit sector.

23. Robert Wuthnow, *The Restructuring of American Religion: Society and Faith Since World War II* (Princeton: Princeton University Press, 1988); James A. Riccio, "Religious Affiliation and Socioeconomic Achievement," in *The Religious Dimension: New Directions in Quantitative Research*, edited by Robert Wuthnow (New York: Academic Press, 1979), pp. 199–228.

24. Andrew M. Greeley, *The American Catholic: A Social Portrait* (New York: Basic Books, 1977).

25. Wuthnow, *The Restructuring of American Religion*; Wuthnow, *The Struggle for America's Soul: Evangelicals, Liberals, and Secularism* (Grand Rapids, Mich.: Eerdmans, 1989).

26. Wuthnow, *Acts of Compassion*. The 1989 survey conducted for this study showed weaker relationships between education and religious orientation than the 1984 survey conducted for *The Restructuring of American Religion*.

27. In the Economic Values Survey, 18 percent of professionals identified themselves as religious conservatives, as did 15 percent of semiprofessionals (clerical and sales workers); in comparison, 26 percent of managers did so, as did 22 percent of blue-collar workers. Among professionals, 40 percent claimed to be religious liberals, compared with 31 percent of managers, 32 percent of semiprofessionals, and 24 percent of blue-collar workers.

28. When asked, "How well would you say each of the following phrases describes your present work?" the proportions answering "very well" or "fairly well" to each of the following among the total labor force and among weekly churchgoers, respectively, were "there is a lot of pressure" (56 and 55), "it is very competitive" (49 and 48), "it physically exhausts me" (41 and 41), "it drains me emotionally (33 and 32), and "is often boring" (26 and 20). None of these relationships was significant either in multivariate models controlling for age, gender, and education.

29. Wuthnow, *Struggle for America's Soul*, chap. 7.

30. Bill Fogelman, "Eroding the Idea of Vocation," *Laynet* 3 (Fall 1992): 14.

31. Tucker, *The Faith-Work Connection*, p. 2.

32. Sebastian de Grazia, *Of Time, Work and Leisure* (New York: Twentieth Century Fund, 1962), chaps. 1 and 2.

33. Multivariate analysis of the relationships between saying that work is essential to one's identity and various measures of religious commitment, based on comparisons of stepwise discriminant analyses and logit regression analyses, reveals that the value of work is significantly higher among persons who consider religion important in their lives, and (with the importance of religion taken into account) among persons who think a great deal about the relationship between their faith and their work or about what the Bible teaches concerning work. These relationships hold when respondents' age, occupation (professional or managerial vs. other occupations), and level of employment (full time or part time) are controlled. Additional models were tested in which gender and education were also controlled, but these variables were not significantly related to the dependent variable. Church attendance and church membership were not significant, but this appears to be because the importance of religion captures the same variations. Dummy variables for Protestantism, Catholicism, and religious conservatism were included in the models as controls, but did not have significant effects.

34. The same analyses were performed on level of interest in doing well at one's job as for saying that work was essential to one's sense of personal worth. The same religious variables proved to be statistically significant, again controlling for age, occupation, and level of employment. The coefficients were, however, somewhat weaker in these models.

35. Respondents who said they worked fifty or more hours a week were compared with respondents who said they worked fewer hours each week. Professionals and managers, full-time workers, older people, and men were more likely to work longer hours. The importance of religion and how much people had thought about faith and work or the Bible and work were statistically significant, controlling for these other variables, but the coefficients fell below commonly accepted levels and added nothing to the overall amount of explained variance in the models.

36. In the Economic Values Survey, 74 percent of weekly churchgoers agreed with the statement, "My family is the main reason I work hard," compared with 63 percent of those who seldom attended religious services; 88 percent of the former agreed that "my family comes first, my work comes second," compared with 78 percent of the latter.

37. Results of a multivariate analysis that included controls for full- or part-time employment, age, education, and gender.

38. Joanne Miller, "Jobs and Work," in *Handbook of Sociology*, edited by Neil J. Smelser (Beverly Hills, Calif.: Sage, 1988), pp. 327–60.

39. Victor H. Vroom, *Work and Motivation* (New York: Wiley, 1964), chaps. 5 and 6.

40. Donald J. Vredenburgh and John E. Sheridan, "Individual and Occupational Determinants of Life Satisfaction and Alienation," *Human Relations* 32 (1979): 1023–38; Fern K. Willits and Donald M. Crider, "Religion and Well-Being: Men and Women in the Middle Years," *Review of Religious Research* 29 (1988): 281–94.

41. Christopher G. Ellison, "Religious Involvement and Subjective Well-Being," *Journal of Health and Social Behavior* 32 (1991): 80–99; Kimberley Reed, "Strength of Religious Affiliation and Life Satisfaction," *Sociological Analysis* 52 (1991): 205–10.

42. Multivariate analysis controlling for full- or part-time employment, age, gender, and education shows that church attendance is associated with a lower likelihood of having an argument with the boss, being laid off, having to go against one's judgment, being reprimanded, and taking a cut in pay; in discriminant models, all these coefficients, however, fall below the customary level of .30; none of the other items in Table 3.4 is significant. From a different set of questions, church attendance was associated negatively with having conflict with one's boss but positively with stress from the work environment and from value conflicts; it was unrelated with factors such as pay concerns, deadlines, redtape, and pressure.

43. This conclusion is drawn from examining multivariate models, using discriminant analysis, in which age, occupation, level of employment, gender, and education were controlled, and in which various religious items were introduced as predictor variables.

44. One of the most intriguing results from my analysis of the Economic Values Survey data is that the relationships between religious factors and job satisfaction are significantly reduced when level of happiness with life in general is controlled. This control, however, does not reduce the relationships between job satisfaction and background factors such as age, occupation, or amount of employment. Judging also from which religious variables seem to have the greatest effect on job satisfaction, we note that what appears to be going on is the following: involvement in a religious community (as measured by participation in religious services and having close friends in one's congregation) reinforces a positive orientation toward life, and this orientation in turn explains why such people express higher levels of job satisfaction.

45. The distinction between religious-specific behavior and religious-related behavior is especially evident in multivariate models: controlling for full- or part-time employment, age, gender, and education, and examining all the various modes of coping with stress simultaneously, we observe that church attendance is significantly related to prayer and meditation and seeking advice from clergy, but (with the exception of a negative relationship with drinking alcohol) is not significantly related with any of the other coping activities.

46. Among persons attending religious services every week, 41 percent said they pray or meditate to relieve feelings of stress from their job (compared with 9 percent of those attending seldom or never), and 7 percent say they talk to a member of the clergy (compared with 1 percent of the other group). The regular attenders were 9 points more likely to discuss stress with their spouses than the infrequent attenders, 5 points less likely to come home and watch television, 11 points less likely to keep it to themselves, 3 points more likely to talk with friends, and 4 points less likely to drink alcohol.

47. Burnout is more common among full-time workers, professionals and managers, and women in the labor force. Taking account of these factors, we note that it is less common among those who attend religious services regularly and have more friends in their congregations. This variable was also one of the few work-related variables that was significantly related to how much one thinks about one's relationship to God and how often one prays. In other words, it appears to be influenced more by devotional activities than job satisfaction is.

48. Max Weber, *The Protestant Ethic and the Spirit of Capitalism* (New York: Scribner's, 1958).

49. Kurt Samuelsson, *Religion and Economic Action: A Critique of Max Weber* (New York: Harper & Row, 1957); and see the overviews of literature on the Protestant ethic thesis in S. N. Eisenstadt, ed., *The Protestant Ethic and Modernization* (New York: Basic Books, 1968); Robert W. Green, ed., *Protestantism, Capitalism and Social Science* (Lexington, Mass.: Heath, 1973); Roger O'Toole, *Religion: Classic Sociological Approaches* (Toronto: McGraw-Hill Ryerson, 1984); and Benjamin Nelson, "Weber's Protestant Ethic: Its Origins, Wanderings and Foreseeable Futures," in *Beyond the Classics?*, edited by Charles Y. Glock and Phillip E. Hammond (New York: Harper, 1973), pp. 71–130.

50. The strongest correlates of feeling called are the overall importance attached to religion, how much one has thought about the relationship between faith and work or the Bible and work, and whether religious values influenced one's choice of work; these relationships pertain when age, occupation, full- or part-time employment, gender, education, church attendance, and denomination are controlled.

51. These relationships hold in multivariate models that examine the relationships between the calling item and all the reasons given for choosing one's line of work simultaneously.

52. Multivariate models examining these motivational statements simultaneously and controlling for age, gender, and professional or managerial occupation also sustain these results.

53. All of the results pertaining to the calling also appear in the data when the question about religious values influencing one's choice of work is substituted.

54. Results of a discriminant model including both items.

55. Based on multivariate models that include standard background characteristics as controls.

56. These results pertain specifically to the calling, which produces significant effects even when the importance of religion, religious orientation, church attendance, and denomination are controlled. Thinking a lot about the relationship between one's faith and work also produces similar results.

57. These conclusions are based on multivariate analyses in which age, occupation, full- or part-time employment, gender, and education are controlled.

58. The correlates of workplace religious groups are much like those of dis-

cussing faith at work, with the exception that workplace groups tend to distinguish Protestants from Catholics and conservatives from moderates, taking levels of religiosity into account. Workplace groups also appear to be more strongly associated with drawing connections between one's faith and work than are mere discussions of faith in the workplace.

59. See Doug Hill in Chapter 5.

60. Frederick Winslow Taylor, *Scientific Management: Comprising Shop Management, The Principles of Scientific Management, Testimony Before the Special House Committee* (New York: Harper & Row, 1946).

Chapter Four. Ethics in the Workplace

1. Albert Bergesen and Mark Warr, "A Crisis in the Moral Order: The Effects of Watergate upon Confidence in Social Institutions," in *The Religious Dimension: New Directions in Quantitative Research*, edited by Robert Wuthnow (New York: Academic Press, 1979), pp. 277–98; and Jeffrey C. Alexander, *Action and Its Environments: Toward a New Synthesis* (New York: Columbia University Press, 1988), chap. 5.

2. Although the periodical literature on these various scandals is extensive, an especially helpful overview is Steven V. Roberts and Gary Cohen, "Villains of the S&L Crisis," *U.S. News and World Report*, October 1, 1990, pp. 53–59; a useful overview of a more theoretical nature is that of John Makin, "Business Ethics," *Public Opinion* (November/December 1986): 4–6. Case studies of particular companies also provide lively reading on this subject; for example, Bryan Burrough and John Helyar, *Barbarians at the Gate* (New York: Harper & Row, 1989); Hope Lampert, *True Greed* (New York: New American Library, 1989); Michael M. Thomas, *Hanover Place* (New York: Warner Books, 1989); and John Taylor, *Circus of Ambition* (New York: Warner Books, 1989).

3. A survey conducted by the Gallup Organization and reported in the *Wall Street Journal*, October 31, 1983, p. 33.

4. Stephen Koepp, "Having It All, Then Throwing It All Away," *Time*, May 25, 1987, p. 23.

5. Conducted by the Josephson Institute for the Advancement of Ethics and reported by the Associated Press in "Bedrock Values Crumbling," *Trenton Times*, October 11, 1990, p. C3.

6. *The Gallup Poll*, September 20, 1981; August 15, 1985; and November 16, 1988. In the 1988 study, for example, 16 percent of the public rated the honesty and ethical standards of business executives high or very high, while 25 percent rated them as low or very low. Pharmacists, clergy, college teachers, and medical doctors received the highest ratings; real estate agents, stockbrokers, insurance salesmen, and car salesmen received the lowest.

7. A national survey conducted for me by the Gallup Organization in 1989 as part of my research on altruism and individualism.

8. "Ethics are Nice," *Wall Street Journal*, September 8, 1987, p. 1.

9. "Ethical Dilemmas," *Wall Street Journal*, June 9, 1987, p. 1.

10. "Ethics in American Business: A Special Report," unpublished report based on a study by Touche Ross & Company, 1983.

11. I refer readers, for an example, to the excellent treatment of ethics in Jeffrey Stout, *Ethics After Babel: The Languages of Morals and Their Discontents* (Boston: Beacon, 1988).

12. An excellent example is J. Philip Wogaman, *Economics and Ethics: A Christian Inquiry* (Philadelphia: Fortress Press, 1986), who states forthrightly that "ethics is often presented and understood too narrowly" (p. 5).

13. As evidence, with age, education, and occupation controlled, defining ethics as honesty was associated only with a lower likelihood of bending the truth among all the activities shown in Table 4.1.

14. Specifically, 48 percent said ethics, in their view, meant "something that applies in the same way to everybody, no matter what the situation," and 48 percent said it meant "something that varies depending on the circumstances you are in" (4 percent were undecided). The former were significantly less likely to have bent the rules, bent the truth, covered for someone else, and ignored others' wrongdoing.

15. This definition of ethics does better at predicting lower likelihoods of bending the rules, charging illegitimate expenses, taking illegitimate time off, misusing office equipment, and bending the truth, but all of these relationships are weak.

16. Robert Nisbet, "Individual Ethics," *Public Opinion* (November/December 1986): 7–8.

17. John P. Alston, "Review of the Polls: Attitudes Toward Extramarital and Homosexual Relations," *Journal for the Scientific Study of Religion* 13 (1974): 479–81; David F. Greenberg and Marcia H. Bystryn, "Christian Intolerance of Homosexuality," *American Journal of Sociology* 88 (1982): 515–48; Joseph E. Faulkner and Gordon F. DeJong, "A Note on Religiosity and Moral Behavior of a Sample of College Students," *Social Compass* 15 (1968): 37–44.

18. Dr. Mary B. Van Leeuwen, Calvin College, personal correspondence.

19. Graham Tucker, *The Faith-Work Connection: A Practical Application of Christian Values in the Workplace* (Toronto: Anglican Book Centre, 1987); Myron Rush, *Lord of the Marketplace* (Wheaton, Ill.: Victor Books, 1986), chap. 6.

20. Multivariate analysis, controlling for age, gender, full- and part-time work, and occupation, yields positive relationships between the importance of religion and not arriving late, not misusing office equipment, not bending the truth, not taking illegitimate time off, not arriving late, and not bending the rules; all but the last are relatively weak. Church attendance produces similar results.

21. I am grateful to John Boli for encouraging me to think about the extent to which ethics has become institutionalized; on the broader argument, see especially George M. Thomas, John W. Meyer, Francisco O. Ramirez, and

John Boli, *Institutional Structure: Constituting State, Society, and the Individual* (Beverly Hills, Calif.: Sage, 1987); and John W. Meyer and W. Richard Scott, *Organizational Environments: Ritual and Rationality* (Beverly Hills, Calif.: Sage, 1983).

22. Barbara Ley Toffler, *Tough Choices: Managers Talk Ethics* (New York: Wiley, 1986), p. 26, makes a similar observation: "The values and operating style of an organization (`the culture') have a potent effect on what managers identify as ethical concerns in their work and on how they go about handling those concerns."

23. Albert O. Hirschman, *The Passions and the Interests: Political Arguments for Capitalism Before Its Triumph* (Princeton: Princeton University Press, 1977); Milton L. Myers, *The Soul of Modern Economic Man: Ideas of Self-Interest, Thomas Hobbes to Adam Smith* (Chicago: University of Chicago Press, 1983).

24. "Ethics Pay," *Wall Street Journal*, December 29, 1987, p. 1.

25. Many people told us they would exit the system if they were asked to do something they felt was unethical, but whether this might simply be the easy way out remained an open question. One man, for example, had quit two jobs (one in a tuna cannery and one as an inspector in a sneaker factory) because he felt shoddy products were being passed along to consumers. In his exit interview he explained why, but the personnel department simply responded, "well, that's not my business."

26. On the definition of value orientations and their relationship to evaluative or moral action, see especially Talcott Parsons and Edward A. Shils, *Toward a General Theory of Action: Theoretical Foundations for the Social Sciences* (New York: Harper & Row, 1951), chap. 3.

27. Max Weber, *The Sociology of Religion* (Boston: Beacon, 1963).

28. Discourse and legitimation are emphasized in Peter L. Berger and Thomas Luckmann, *The Social Construction of Reality: A Treatise in the Sociology of Knowledge* (Garden City, N.Y.: Doubleday, 1966), chap. 2.

29. Background on the historical and philosophical roots of these value orientations is provided in my book *The Consciousness Reformation* (Berkeley and Los Angeles: University of California Press, 1976); and in Steven M. Tipton, *Getting Saved from the Sixties: Moral Meaning in Conversion and Cultural Change* (Berkeley and Los Angeles: University of California Press, 1982).

30. Tipton, *Getting Saved from the Sixties*, p. 7.

31. My discussion of individualistic utilitarianism follows that of Robert N. Bellah et al., *Habits of the Heart: Individualism and Commitment in American Life* (Berkeley and Los Angeles: University of California Press, 1985). I reverse the order of the two words to better distinguish this kind of self-interest from corporate utilitarianism.

32. Tipton, Bellah, and others generally do not distinguish corporate utilitarianism as a special type of ethical reasoning because their discussions go beyond the workplace.

33. William H. Whyte, Jr., *The Organization Man* (Garden City, N.Y.: Doubleday, 1956), p. 6.

34. Alasdair MacIntyre, *After Virtue*, 2d ed. (Notre Dame: University of Notre Dame Press, 1984), pp. 11–12; Alasdair MacIntyre, *A Short History of Ethics* (New York: Macmillan, 1966), pp. 249–52.

35. On the philosophical bases of emotivism, see G. E. Moore, *Principia Ethica* (Cambridge: Cambridge University Press, 1903).

36. Kenneth Blanchard and Norman Vincent Peale, *The Power of Ethical Management* (New York: William Morrow, 1988), p. 24.

37. For example, Bernard Williams, *Problems of the Self* (Cambridge: Cambridge University Press, 1973), p. 226, writes of the "woodenness" associated with Kant's objections, especially if they lead to the view that "if you can't do a good turn to everybody in a certain situation, you shouldn't do it to anybody."

38. See the discussion of "expressive individualism" in Bellah et al., *Habits of the Heart*, chap. 2.

39. For a wide-ranging discussion of the historical conditions giving rise to the present emphasis on "expressivism," see Charles Taylor, *Sources of the Self: The Making of the Modern Identity* (Cambridge, Mass.: Harvard University Press, 1989).

40. Doug Sherman and William Hendricks, *Keeping Your Ethical Edge Sharp* (Colorado Springs: NavPress, 1990), p. 15.

41. Allan Gibbard, *Wise Choices, Apt Feelings: A Theory of Normative Judgment* (Cambridge, Mass.: Harvard University Press, 1990), especially chaps. 3 and 7.

42. Thomas Nagel, *The Possibility of Altruism* (Princeton: Princeton University Press, 1970), p. 1. Useful discussions of altruism that also include summaries of empirical studies of the subject include C. Daniel Batson, "Prosocial Motivation: Is It Ever Truly Altruistic?" *Advances in Experimental Social Psychology* 20 (1987): 65–122; C. Daniel Batson, Michelle H. Bolen, Julie A. Cross, and Helen E. Neuringer-Benefiel, "Where Is the Altruism in the Altruistic Personality?" *Journal of Personality and Social Psychology* 50 (1986): 212–20; and Kristen R. Monroe, Michael C. Barton, and Ute Klingemann, "Altruism and the Theory of Rational Action: Rescuers of Jews in Nazi Europe," *Ethics* 101 (1990): 103–22.

43. Nagel, *The Possibility of Altruism*; Russell Hardin, *Morality Within the Limits of Reason* (Chicago: University of Chicago Press, 1988).

44. Nel Noddings, *Caring: A Feminine Approach to Ethics and Moral Education* (Berkeley and Los Angeles: University of California Press, 1984).

45. Tipton, *Getting Saved from the Sixties*, pp. 4–5.

46. Taylor, *Sources of the Self*, chap. 15.

47. Tipton, *Getting Saved from the Sixties*, p. 3, writes, "Biblical morality . . . asserts that there are features of an act itself (being commanded by God), besides the good or bad consequences it produces, that make it right."

48. James M. Gustafson, *Can Ethics Be Christian?* (Chicago: University of Chicago Press, 1975), especially chaps. 4 and 5.

49. For a parallel discussion of "moral assumptions" among teenagers, see Robert Coles, *Girl Scouts Survey on the Beliefs and Moral Values of Ameri-*

ca's Children (New York: Girl Scouts of the United States of America, 1990). Using somewhat different categories and questions, this report estimates that 25 percent of American teenagers are "civic humanists" who try to serve the common good (altruists), 20 percent are "conventionalists" who do what authority figures tell them to do (similar to corporate utilitarians), 18 percent are "expressivists" (emotivists), 16 percent are "theists," and 10 percent are "utilitarians." I am grateful to James Davison Hunter, the architect of this report, for bringing these findings to my attention. Dr. Hunter is conducting further research on the moral assumptions of children and teenagers.

50. Results drawn from using the "give most weight to" responses were validated with multivariate models in which the "major consideration" responses to all the value orientation questions were introduced simultaneously. These models support the conclusions summarized in the text and, if anything, suggest stronger relationships.

51. The *Girl Scouts Survey* referred to earlier found significant differences among teenagers adopting different moral assumptions in activities such as cheating on exams, condoning premarital sexual relations, and engaging in underage drinking of alcohol.

52. With age, education, and full- or part-time work controlled, and using the measures for value orientations that allowed for multiple responses (as "major considerations"), we see that *disagreeing* that bending the rules at work is okay was very strongly associated with theistic moralism, moderately associated with moral absolutism, moderately associated with corporate utilitarianism, and negatively associated with individualistic utilitarianism and emotivism (it was unrelated to altruism).

53. See my book, *Sharing the Journey: Support Groups and America's New Quest for Community* (New York: Free Press, 1994).

54. This question was asked in 1989 as part of a national survey I commissioned for the Gallup Organization in conjunction with the writing of *Acts of Compassion: Caring for Others and Helping Ourselves* (Princeton: Princeton University Press, 1991).

55. This response was positively associated with both individualistic and corporate utilitarianism as measured by the value orientation questions; as other results indicate, the former especially appears to be associated with *higher* levels of ethically questionable behavior.

Chapter Five. Orientations Toward Money

1. Religious teachings about money are discussed in David S. Noss and John B. Noss, *Man's Religions*, 7th ed. (New York: Macmillan, 1984); Maria Leach and Jerome Fried, eds., *Standard Dictionary of Folklore, Mythology, and Legend* (New York: Harper & Row, 1972); Lewis Hyde, *The Gift: Imagination and the Erotic Life of Property* (New York: Vintage, 1983); Jacques Ellul, *Money and Power* (Downers Grove, Ill.: Inter-Varsity Press, 1984); and

Jacob Needleman, *Money and the Meaning of Life* (New York: Doubleday, 1992). On concepts of money among native peoples of North America, see Thomas Buckley, "The One Who Flies All Around the World," *Parabola* 16 (1991): 4–9.

2. For an overview of recent academic literature on money, see Viviana A. Zelizer, "The Social Meaning of Money: ˋSpecial Monies,'" *American Journal of Sociology* 95 (1989): 342–77. Zelizer demonstrates that Karl Marx, Émile Durkheim, and Max Weber, among the founding generation of sociologists, all recognized that monetary exchange was one of the characteristics that most clearly distinguished modern from premodern societies. It was Georg Simmel, however, who devoted the most sustained attention to the subject and who argued that money was completely indifferent with respect to human values (Georg Simmel, *The Philosophy of Money*, trans. by Tom Bottomore and David Frisby [London: Routledge, 1978], originally published in 1900). For Simmel, money was a means of attaining values, but it did not determine which values should be pursued. One person might pay ten dollars for X and another person ten dollars for Y. The difference between X and Y had nothing to do with the money itself. Simmel also emphasized the divisibility of money, arguing that it was thus the most subject of any commodity to quantification. Money, he argued, could be understood strictly in quantitative terms, rather than having to take quality (or values) into account. One could ask simply "how much," leaving aside questions about what, how, or why. Other social scientists have disagreed with Simmel's overall perspective but still arrived at largely the same conclusions about money. For example, Marx's criticisms of the emphasis on money in capitalist societies were rooted partly in an assumption that money drove out other values (Karl Marx, *Capital*, vol. 1, edited by Friedrich Engels [New York: International, 1984], originally published in 1867). Once money became the primary medium of exchange, Marx argued, people were likely to think more in terms of quantities and prices than in terms of anything else. Money, he feared, would also make everything alike, or at least substitutable. Thus, X and Y might be rooted in very different value systems, but pricing them would tend to reduce both to a kind of utilitarian standard. In American sociology, Talcott Parsons saw money more in symbolic than in materialistic terms. Yet Parsons also regarded money as a special kind of symbol. It was a universal means of exchange, a way of signifying economic value. Thus Parsons tended to place money in an entirely different category of analysis than he did values and other kinds of symbols (see especially Talcott Parsons and Neil J. Smelser, *Economy and Society* [New York: Free Press, 1956]).

3. In recent years, social scientists have begun to challenge the earlier notions of money. Viviana Zelizer has shown, for example, that money is not value-free but subject to social processes that give it distinctive meanings. These meanings, moreover, vary from one social setting to another. In some pre-

modern societies, the stones or shells that served as money were classified some as female and others male. In modern societies, Zelizer shows, money is still subject to gender definitions. Pin money or an allowance, for instance, may be under the jurisdiction of women and subject to quite different rules than money identified as a salary or a paycheck. Marcia Millman has also stressed the social meanings of money, showing that "cold cash" actually becomes a hotly contested subject when it is considered in the real-life context of families (*Cold Cash and Warm Hearts* [New York: Free Press, 1990]). Husbands and wives, she observes, argue about it, frequently attach highly different values to the same amounts of dollars, worry about the spending habits of their children, take each other to court, and apply fundamentally nonmonetary standards to the ways in which they give gifts or make out wills. In fairness to the earlier work, it should be noted that recent studies do not basically modify the claim that money is a quantifiable, impersonal medium of economic exchange, or that it is generally associated with prices, utilities, and market transactions. The recent work does, however, pick up an aspect of the earlier work that tends to be neglected in purely economic treatments of money, namely, that money has *meaning* and thus must be understood in the context of other values and beliefs. A suggestive study in the social-psychological literature is Paul F. Wernimont and Susan Fitzpatrick, "The Meaning of Money," *Journal of Applied Psychology* 50 (1972): 218–26. Their research uses factor-analysis techniques to isolate orientations from attitude questions, including some that parallel themes in my chapter, such as belief that money is evil and belief that money is unimportant. See also Adrian Furnham, "Many Sides of the Coin: The Psychology of Money Usage," *Personality and Individual Differences* 5 (1984): 95–103.

4. These conclusions are drawn from stepwise discriminant analyses of the three dependent variables shown in Table 5.1, with gender, age, income, and education as controls, and with church membership, church attendance, denomination, importance of religion, and religious orientation introduced simultaneously.

5. With the same models as indicated in the previous note, variables were introduced separately for each of the additional religious factors mentioned in the text.

6. Thinking about one's relationship to God was actually one of the more strongly related variables, but this may partly be a function of its being worded similarly to the question about thinking about the Bible and money; still, it was strongly related to agreeing that the Bible contains valuable teachings about money as well.

7. Stewardship sermons can be about topics other than finances, as discussed elsewhere in the chapter; one indication of this is that their effect on people's thinking a lot about religious values and personal finances is statistically weaker than is the effect of sermons specifically concerned with personal finances.

8. The measure of childhood religious exposure was whether one's parents read the Bible at home while the person was growing up, one of several such measures included in the survey, including attendance at services and saying table grace, all of which were highly related to one another.

9. My reference is to the idea of "plausibility structures" developed in Peter L. Berger, *The Sacred Canopy* (Garden City, N.Y.: Doubleday, 1966). In fairness, Berger does not diminish the importance of beliefs but in stressing their dependence on informal friendships and conversations leaves room for a kind of sociometric reductionism; discussed in Wuthnow, *Rediscovering the Sacred: Perspectives on Religion in Contemporary Society* (Grand Rapids, Mich.: Eerdmans, 1992), chap. 1.

10. The relationship was significantly stronger for thinking about religious values and personal finances than for thinking about the Bible and money, possibly because such groups (even Bible study groups) tend to focus on personal applications, or possibly because support groups may include discussions of faith or spirituality without actually discussing the Bible.

11. Solomon Schimmel, *The Seven Deadly Sins: Jewish, Christian, and Classical Reflections on Human Nature* (New York: Free Press, 1992), p. 166.

12. J. Arthur Baird, *The Greed Syndrome: An Ethical Sickness in American Capitalism* (Akron: Hampshire Books, 1989), provides one example.

13. The 79 percent of weekly church attenders who say "I wish I had more money than I do" describes them very well or fairly well is only slightly lower than the 84 percent in the labor force overall who give these responses.

14. Multivariate analysis showed that saying religion was important had the strongest net effect on believing greed to be a sin, while church attendance, sermons, and fellowship groups had weak or insignificant effects. Having been taught that money was wrong was associated with having been reared by parents who read the Bible at home and with thinking about one's relationship to God, but not with church attendance, sermons, or fellowship groups.

15. These relationships are statistically significant, controlling for age, gender, education, working full- or part-time, and family income, and are sustained when church attendance is taken into account, as well as in models that also include importance of religion and religious orientation. Several additional nuances are worth noting: although sermons on stewardship are negatively associated with valuing money, sermons on personal finances are not (perhaps because such sermons can also be about ways in which to gain money through spirituality); although thinking a lot about one's relationship to God is negatively associated with valuing money, simply valuing one's relationship with God a great deal is not (does this mean that spirituality must be active?); hearing stewardship sermons and agreeing that the Bible contains important teachings about money largely "explain away" the residual effects of church attendance (i.e. church attendance appears to make a difference only if it actually exposes people to specific instruction about money); religiosity

as a child has no continuing impact on how much or how little people value money as adults.

16. Results based on multivariate analysis in which a number of background variables and self-rated religiosity were also controlled. The lottery question was more significantly associated with church membership than with frequency of attendance.

17. Agreeing that riches get in the way of knowing God, while limited to a minority of weekly churchgoers, is nevertheless influenced positively by most measures of religious involvement, controlling for various background characteristics. In addition to church attendance, other factors that make a difference include hearing sermons on personal finances and stewardship, participating in a fellowship group, thinking about the connections between the Bible and money, and childhood religiosity.

18. When church attendance, importance of religion, and religious orientation (conservative or liberal) are examined simultaneously (taking into account age, gender, education, and family income), church attendance is positively associated with admiration on three of the statements, negatively associated with one, and not associated with four. Importance of religion is positively associated with three and not associated with the other five. Religious conservatism is negatively associated with one, positively associated with four (but weakly with three of the four), and unrelated to three.

19. The role of the work ethic in legitimating wealth is indicated by the fact that multivariate models in which all the items shown in the table are used to predict personal emphasis on work and personal emphasis on money show that emphasis on work is most strongly associated with the item about admiring rich people who still work hard, while emphasis on money is most strongly associated with admiring people who make a lot of money by working hard.

20. Karl Marx, "Contribution to the Critique of Hegel's Philosophy of Right," reprinted in *Marx and Engels on Religion*, edited by Reinhold Niebuhr (New York: Schocken, 1964), p. 42.

21. Charles Y. Glock and Rodney Stark, *Religion and Society in Tension* (Chicago: Rand McNally, 1965).

22. In addition to the personal stories about money being associated with unhappiness that our interviewees told us, we also found ample evidence of such anecdotes in published form. John Jacob Astor, for example, is alleged to have said that "money brings me nothing but a certain dull anxiety," and J. Paul Getty remarked that he "would gladly give all my millions for just one lasting marital success." These quotes are taken from Joseph Epstein, *Ambition: The Secret Passion* (Chicago: Ivan R. Dee, 1980), p. 113, who adds, "The need to believe that money does not bring happiness—that quite the reverse is true—runs very strong. And why not? It is so very solacing."

23. Some empirical evidence from surveys suggests that happiness and income are not correlated, or are so very weakly; see Angus Campbell, *The Sense of*

Well-Being in America (New York: McGraw-Hill, 1981); in the labor force survey there was a significant but weak relationship.

24. Some early evidence to this effect was presented in Joseph Luft, "Monetary Value and the Perception of Persons," *Journal of Social Psychology* 46 (1957): 245–51.

25. For example, among persons who said they were bothered a lot by being anxious about their purchases or money decisions, 65 percent said they were bothered at least a little by not feeling good about themselves; among those bothered a little about money decisions, 43 percent gave this response, and among those not bothered by money decisions, only 15 percent did.

26. In the labor force study, 56 percent of respondents with personal incomes above $40,000 said they were very happy, compared with 45 percent of respondents with personal incomes under $20,000; conversely, 7 percent of the latter but only 1 percent of the former described themselves as not very happy.

27. Kent Yamanchi and Donald Templer, "The Development of a Money Attitude Scale," *Journal of Personality Assessment* 46 (1982): 522–28. This research found widespread anxiety about money and showed that this anxiety did not diminish at higher levels of income.

28. Adrian Furnham and Alan Lewis, *The Economic Mind* (New York: St Martin's, 1986), p. 110, express the same point this way: "Money may make one less worried about some things but more worried about others."

29. These results are based on discriminant analyses with age, gender, education, and family income controlled, and with the effects of church attendance, importance of religion, religious orientation, and denomination examined simultaneously. In these models, church attendance was actually *positively* associated with feeling anxious, guilt, and wishing for more money. Adding other, more specific religious variables into the models showed that belief in biblical inspiration also had positive effects on anxiety and guilt. In contrast, negative effects were associated with thinking a lot about one's relationship to God, having heard a sermon on stewardship in the past year, having friends in one's congregation, and participating in a fellowship group.

30. Thirty-five percent of people surveyed in the labor force study agreed that "parents should not talk about finances in front of children" and when asked how clear they were as children about how their own parents made financial decisions, only 19 percent said "very clear," while 33 percent said "somewhat clear," 22 percent said "somewhat unclear," 20 percent said "very unclear," and 7 percent were unsure.

31. The proportions in the labor force who said they remembered their parents arguing about money were as follows: frequently, 19 percent; once in a while, 40 percent; and never, 33 percent. That such arguments may be on the rise is suggested by the fact that 22 percent of respondents ages 18 to 34 replied "frequently," compared with only 13 percent of respondents age 50 or over.

32. Although numerous reasons can be adduced to suggest why it may be useful to discourage frank discussions of money, research among children reveals a great deal of confusion on the subject—confusion that could presumably be mitigated by more explicit conversation; see Hans G. Furth, *The World of Grown-Ups: Children's Conceptions of Society* (New York: Elsevier, 1980), chap. 5. Other studies of children's understandings of money are reviewed in Furnham and Lewis, *The Economic Mind*, chap. 3. These authors cite only two studies that have examined the relationships between parental behavior and children's, noting that both show significant effects. It also seems evident, however, that research and advice manuals alike consider allowances to be the decisive factor, rather than considering the importance of role modeling and discussions.

33. Other data that reveal Americans' reluctance to discuss money is presented in Carin Rubenstein, "Money and Self-Esteem, Relationships, Secrecy, Envy, Satisfaction," *Psychology Today* 15 (May 1981): 29–44.

34. Based on discriminant models in which distinctions between members or nonmembers, or between weekly and less frequent attenders, were predicted using all the items simultaneously about financial topics that had been discussed outside the immediate family.

35. Controlling for level of church attendance, having heard a stewardship sermon is statistically related to attaching greater meaning to the idea of stewardship, but the relationship is weak (about the same as that of thinking about one's relationship to God in general or being in a fellowship group).

36. As elsewhere in the chapter, the conclusions summarized in the text are based on discriminant models in which age, gender, education, and family income are controlled, in which church attendance, importance of religion, religious orientation, church membership, and denomination are introduced simultaneously, and in which additional models include one of the following specific religion variables: belief in biblical inspiration, belief in biblical literalism, hearing a sermon on money, hearing a sermon on stewardship, thinking a lot about one's relationship to God, having friends in the congregation, participating in a fellowship group, or being raised by parents who read the Bible at home.

37. The percentages who said they would think a lot about "are automobiles consistent with protecting the planet" were 25 percent among those who said stewardship was very meaningful to them, 20 percent among those who said it was fairly meaningful, and 17 percent among those who said it was not very meaningful. About 40 percent in each category said they would think a little about this issue. It is perhaps notable that among those who say stewardship is very meaningful, 35 percent still say they would not think at all about this issue.

38. Barbara Ehrenreich, *The Worst Years of Our Lives: Irreverent Notes from a Decade of Greed* (New York: Pantheon, 1990), p. 3.

Chapter Six. The Meaning of Materialism

1. Karl Marx and Friedrich Engels, *The German Ideology* (New York: International Publishers, 1947); *Marx and Engels on Religion*, edited by Reinhold Niebuhr (New York: Schocken, 1964); useful secondary sources include Henri Lefebvre, *The Sociology of Marx* (New York: Vintage, 1968), especially chap. 3; Martin Seliger, *The Marxist Conception of Ideology: A Critical Essay* (Cambridge: Cambridge University Press, 1977); Bruce Mazlish, *The Meaning of Karl Marx* (Oxford: Oxford University Press, 1984), especially chap. 7; Neil J. Smelser, "Introduction," pp. i–xxxviii in *Karl Marx on Society and Social Change*, edited by Neil J. Smelser (Chicago: University of Chicago Press, 1973); and Robert Tucker, *Philosophy and Myth in Karl Marx*, 2d ed. (Cambridge: Cambridge University Press, 1972), especially chap. 9; and on religion, Bryan S. Turner, *Religion and Social Theory* (London: Heinemann, 1983), especially chap. 3; and Norman Birnbaum, "Beyond Marx in the Sociology of Religion?" pp. 3–70 in *Beyond the Classics? Essays in the Scientific Study of Religion*, edited by Charles Y. Glock and Phillip E. Hammond (New York: Harper & Row, 1973).

2. Mary Douglas has herself addressed the connection between materialism and symbolic boundaries in a complementary way but has focused on the ways in which consumption patterns dramatize symbolic boundaries, rather than on the ways in which symbolic boundaries demarcating materialism may influence consumption habits or other activities; see Mary Douglas and Baron Isherwood, *The World of Goods* (New York: Basic Books, 1979); since Veblen's coinage of the phrase "conspicuous consumption," the symbolic aspects of material culture have been much discussed; Thorstein Veblen, *The Theory of the Leisure Class: An Economic Study of Institutions* (New York: New American Library, 1912).

3. The approach taken in Chapter 6 to the meanings of materialism draws heavily on structuralist anthropology, perhaps most notably associated with the work of Claude Lévi-Strauss, which emphasizes that cultural patterns cannot be understood either as random constellations of beliefs or as value complexes that might have the sort of logical consistency for which a philosopher would look (see Claude Lévi-Strauss, *Structural Anthropology* [New York: Basic Books, 1963], and Edmund Leach, *Claude Levi-Strauss* [London: Penguin, 1974]). This work suggests that cultural patterns must be understood in terms of an underlying structure; that is, an arrangement among symbols that creates boundaries, demarcations, connections, and parallel constructions. There is also a long tradition in cultural studies that emphasizes the importance of implicit classification schemes, the ways in which conceptual categories are demarcated, and the power these categories may exercise in our public and private lives. The anthropologist Mary Douglas, for example, has taken up the idea of looking at symbolic boundaries (without borrowing other Lévi-Straussian arguments) to show that boundaries be-

tween groups carry enormous importance, and that they are often symbolized through the physical body and in ritual acts performed upon the body (Mary Douglas, *Purity and Danger: An Analysis of Concepts of Pollution and Taboo* [London: Penguin, 1966]; also relevant is Mary Douglas, *Natural Symbols* (New York: Vintage, 1970); her disagreements with Lévi-Strauss are presented in "The Meaning of Myth, with Special Reference to `La Geste d'Asdiwal,'" pp. 49–70 in *The Structural Study of Myth and Totemism*, edited by Edmund Leach (London: Tavistock, 1967). I follow the "structural approach" discussed in my book *Meaning and Moral Order: Explorations in Cultural Analysis* (Berkeley and Los Angeles: University of California Press, 1987). In the simplest terms, this approach emphasizes that we create order in our everyday experience by drawing distinctions between pairs of symbols. The idea of "night," for example, is essential to our understanding of "day." And because each is essential to the other, we set them apart. Even though as much as a quarter of any twenty-four-hour day may be neither or both (the twilight time surrounding sunrise and sunset), we tend to think of day and night as discrete categories (on this point, see Albert Bergesen's discussion and extension of Mary Douglas's ideas in Robert Wuthnow, James Davison Hunter, Albert Bergesen, and Edith Kurzweil, *Cultural Analysis: The Work of Peter L. Berger, Mary Douglas, Michel Foucault, and Jürgen Habermas* (London: Routledge, 1984), chap. 3. Furthermore, having distinguished the two, we also use these categories to help us understand a wide variety of other ideas and activities. Storytellers, for instance, conjure up images of evil by turning the "bad guys" loose at night or by having them operate in dark rooms. For a more general discussion, see Eviatar Zerubavel, *The Fine Line: Making Distinctions in Everyday Life* (New York: Free Press, 1991).

4. It would be easy, of course, to overstate this case. My point here is that social theory, as does popular discourse, depends on the meanings implied in paired concepts. Thus, contemporary discussions of the sacred are inevitably influenced by an implicit comparison with the presumed "profanity" of everyday life, or in other contexts, by an assumption about the secularity of political institutions. Pitting spirituality against materialism thus provides a way of altering familiar perspectives.

5. Examined in my book, *Acts of Compassion: Caring for Others and Helping Ourselves* (Princeton: Princeton University Press, 1991); this present discussion is an extension of that study's interest in the cultural construction and resolution of paradox.

6. I offer this caveat especially to students, who, in my experience, can be avid seekers of hypocrisy in matters religious but reluctant scholars in pursuing ideas that may go beyond ad hominem explanations.

7. For more discussion of the meanings of the material world and of materialism in Judeo-Christian teachings, see the essays in my edited volume, *Rethinking Materialism: The Spiritual Dimension of Economic Behavior* (Grand Rapids, Mich.: Eerdmans, 1995).

8. George Gallup, Jr., *Religion in America: 1992* (Princeton: George H. Gallup International Institute, 1992).

9. In the labor force survey, 50 percent of Catholics said "the clergy are doing God's work more than any of the rest of us are" was a true statement, compared with 39 percent of Protestants.

10. In theology and in the social sciences the idea of symbolically constructed realities, providing possibilities for "multiplex" layers of meaning, has also been profoundly influential. The contrast between multiplex realities and dualistic religious systems is usefully described in Robert N. Bellah, *Beyond Belief: Essays on Religion in a Post-Traditional World* (New York: Harper & Row, 1970), chap. 2.

11. Among persons who had thought a great deal about what the Bible teaches concerning money, for example, 88 percent had thought at least a fair amount about the differences between spiritual growth and material possessions, while this proportion dropped to 23 percent among those who had thought little or hardly any about biblical teachings on money.

12. Results based on multivariate models in which gender, age, education, occupation, and family income are controlled. The relationship between thinking about this difference and church attendance can largely be "explained away" by controlling for amount of thinking about one's relationship to God, suggesting that thinking about spirituality and material possessions in particular is rooted more in a thoughtful approach to one's religious life than to participation merely in a religious subculture. Apart from this factor, the strongest relationships, controlling for church attendance, were with agreeing that riches get in the way of knowing God, and claiming the idea of stewardship was very meaningful; both these relationships suggest that thinking about spirituality and material possessions actually does involve thinking about the ways in which the two are distinct, yet related.

13. Controls for gender, age, education, occupation, and family income were included. The negative relationship between the dependent variable and church attendance was largely accounted for when thinking about one's relationship with God was added, supporting the claim that this item is accepted more through tacit assent than through thoughtful analysis. The relationship with biblical literalism was the strongest of any of the variables examined and persisted when biblical inspiration and church attendance were controlled. The positive association with saying riches get in the way of knowing God was also relatively strong.

14. With gender, age, education, occupation, family income, and church attendance controlled, valuing feelings and saying that one's emotional life is important and that exploring one's inner self is important were positively associated with both dependent variables; and emphasizing feelings more than one's job and needing time to reflect on one's life were positively associated with thinking about differences between spirituality and material possessions.

15. It is worth noting that these three ways of understanding the spiritual and

the material bring us back to an issue with which Max Weber became preoccupied in his studies of religion and economic behavior. Understanding the two to be fundamentally in tension, Weber was interested in the ways in which this tension might be resolved *rationally*. See especially Max Weber, *Economy and Society*, 2 vols., edited by Guenther Roth (Berkeley and Los Angeles: University of California Press, 1978), pp. 63–90 and 576–600; the issue of alternative modes of rational resolution is also taken up in Talcott Parsons, *The Structure of Social Action*, vol. 2 (New York: Free Press, 1937), and in Peter L. Berger, *The Sacred Canopy* (Garden City, N.Y.: Doubleday, 1966), chap. 3. In Weber's terms, the dualism illustrated by Warren Means emphasizes nonrationality (the unpredictable and inexplicable character of the miraculous). Gene Atwood's dualism, in contrast, illustrates a more rational mode of reconciliation in that a systematic arrangement of priorities (means and ends) is emphasized. Karen Kelsey is closer to what Weber characterized as a mystical or pietistic understanding. Her thinking is dominated by rationality to the extent that it emphasizes growth and the proper allocation of time, and yet its emphasis on feelings also limits the extent to which behavior can be subjected to rationality. Conceiving of prayer as a kind of ritual activity, we can also see that this boundary is dramatized by the movement of requests or goods from one realm to the other. What Weber adds is a way to think about how much or how little distance is implied in the boundary. Where the distance is great (Warren Means), there is still a conceptual tension or contrast implied, but for all practical purposes the distance itself obviates any need to reconcile the two realms systematically. Where the distance is small (Gene Atwood), the tension becomes more acute, necessitating greater effort to coordinate the two realms. Moreover, when both realms are, in a Weberian sense, understood rationally (that is, to have a cognitively understandable order), then effort is required to arrive at consistent relationships between the two. In contrast, where this form of rationality is not held to apply as clearly (Karen Kelsey), it becomes possible to deny that answers can be (or have been) achieved and to regard the relationships as a matter of intuitive trial-and-error experimentation.

16. The strongest of these relationships are between church attendance and saying materialism is a problem and saying that advertising is corrupting our values; the weakest, with saying that children are too materialistic.

17. Believing that materialism and too much emphasis on money were serious problems was most strongly associated with thinking a lot about the differences between spiritual growth and material possessions; saying that children were too materialistic showed the weakest relationship. The money versus morals item was most strongly associated with agreeing that the society is too materialistic and that money is the root of all evil, and least strongly associated with the view that less emphasis on money would make the society a lot better.

18. Alan MacFarlane, *The Culture of Capitalism* (London: Basil Blackwell,

1987), chap. 5, argues that capitalism is the reason evil has disappeared in modern societies, a development he regards as enormously consequential; if so, the displacement of evil onto the idea of materialism (largely without benefit of Marx) may be one of the more paradoxical features of capitalist culture.

19. The claim that materialism serves as a generalized symbol of evil, or more precisely of social ills, receives support by two findings from detailed analysis of the survey data. One is that the more seriously materialism was perceived to be a social problem, the more likely it was for other problems also to be identified; thus, out of a list of fourteen such problems, the median number identified as at least "serious" by people who thought materialism was an extremely serious problem was nine, compared with four among those who thought materialism was serious, and two among those who thought it was either a small problem or not a problem. (Of those who regarded it as extremely serious, fewer than 1 percent failed to identify at least one other problem as being serious.) The other finding is that a factor analysis (varimax rotation) of the fourteen items revealed that materialism defined the most important of three distinct factors (had the strongest item-to-factor coefficient), and that six other items also loaded highly on this factor (it accounted for 38 percent of the variance, compared with 10 and 7 percent, respectively, by the remaining two factors).

20. The conclusion here is drawn from multivariate models in which those who said materialism (or money emphasis) was an extremely serious problem were distinguished from those who said it was less of a problem, when we used as simultaneously predictor variables all the other problems identified in Table 6.1, and in separate models only nine of the items that seemed most likely to be associated. Although there is some response bias due to the adjacent ordering of some items in the interview, this bias is minimized by the fact that the entire list was rotated at random and by virtue of having two different dependent variables. In the nine-variable models, individualism, selfishness, and the breakdown of community were significantly associated with both dependent variables; in the full models, selfishness was with both, but individualism and breakdown of community only with materialism. Except for the association of the two dependent variables with each other, none of the other items was significantly associated with both of the dependent variables. (In models in which only one item was introduced at a time, more of the items were associated with the materialism item than when all the items were introduced simultaneously.)

21. A way of substantiating this claim statistically is to examine the relationship between a measure of religious involvement (such as church attendance) and saying that materialism is a serious social problem (this relationship is strongly positive), and then introduce being concerned about selfishness (or individualism or the breakdown of community) as a control in the model: when this is done, the control eliminates the zero-order effect of church attendance.

22. Controlling for background factors such as age, education, gender, and income, being concerned about materialism was negatively associated with wanting nice things, traveling for pleasure, and wanting nice clothes. Multivariate analysis involving all the items reveals that the desire for a beautiful home and to travel remained negatively associated with perceiving materialism as a serious problem, but wanting nice clothes and eating out were not.

23. Desiring to travel is negatively associated with both church attendance and valuing one's relationship to God, controlling for other variables; having a beautiful home and eating at nice restaurants are only weakly associated with church attendance and unrelated to valuing one's link with God; and wearing nice clothes is unrelated to both.

24. We shall consider these misgivings again in Chapter 8; here, it is worth noting that 48 percent of those who thought churches are too eager for money said they would give more if religious organizations emphasized giving more, while 70 percent did so among those who did not feel churches are too eager for money.

Chapter Seven. The Poor and Economic Justice

1. Stephen Hart, *What Does the Lord Require? How American Christians Think about Economic Justice* (New York: Oxford University Press, 1992), p. 4.

2. Craig Gay, *With Liberty and Justice for Whom? The Recent Evangelical Debate Over Capitalism* (Grand Rapids, Mich.: Eerdmans, 1991); Gene Burns, *Frontiers of Catholicism* (Berkeley and Los Angeles: University of California Press, 1992). Both books provide valuable complementary reading to the present chapter.

3. These relationships are sustained when other background factors are taken into account. Indeed, the relationships between gender and responsibility appear to be largely attributable to the fact that women are more likely to attend religious services regularly than men. And with religious services controlled, younger people are actually somewhat *more* likely to think about responsibility to the poor than older people.

4. Taking into account attendance at religious services, the relationship between religious conservatism and thinking about responsibility to the poor remains statistically significant but is too weak to be considered substantively important. Yet, with attendance controlled, biblical literalism and belief in biblical inspiration both remain positively associated with thinking about responsibility to the poor, and of the two, biblical literalism is the more strongly associated (both in separate models and when the two items are examined simultaneously).

5. A multivariate model predicting differences between those who think a great deal about their responsibility to the poor and those who think about it less often, taking into account a standard list of background variables, shows that thinking about one's relationship to God is a very strong predictor, and that

it remains strong when level of attendance at religious services is also included; indeed, it reduces the effect of attendance by about two-thirds.

6. In similar models, the effects of the items about stewardship are generally weaker than that of thinking about one's relationship to God, what the Bible teaches about money, or about how to relate religious values more closely with personal finances, but clearly are influenced less by similarities of question wording. The stewardship items reduce the effect of religious attendance by about a third, while the items about religion and money reduce it by about two-thirds.

7. In other words, the sign of the coefficient for the effect of having friends in one's congregation on thinking about responsibility *reverses* when attendance is controlled. That *thoughtfulness* is the key factor, rather than friendship, is suggested by the fact that the effects of being in a Sunday school class or a fellowship group remain positive.

8. Without church attendance in the model, agreeing with this statement is related at a moderately strong level with thinking about responsibility to the poor; with attendance in the model, this relationship remains statistically significant but is weaker than any of the other relationships discussed in the text.

9. This finding appears to be consistent with other research that has found a correlation between the Protestant work ethic and attitudes toward the poor; for example, A. MacDonald, "Correlates of the Ethics of Personal Conscience and the Ethics of Social Responsibility," *Journal of Consulting and Clinical Psychology* 37 (1971): 443, and A. MacDonald, "More on the Protestant Ethic," *Journal of Consulting and Clinical Psychology* 39 (1972): 116–122.

10. Conclusions based on multivariate models in which age, gender, education, occupation, and income are controlled; saying that stewardship is a meaningful idea has a positive effect in the models even with level of religious attendance controlled; simply having heard a stewardship sermon in the past year was not significant in the models; Sunday school attendance and participation in fellowship groups had a significant effect on admiring the poor but not on believing their condition was extremely serious.

11. Donal Dorr, *Option for the Poor: A Hundred Years of Vatican Social Teaching* (Dublin: Gill and Macmillan, 1983), p. 6.

12. Multivariate analysis revealed that educational differences largely explained away the effects of family income, race, and age.

13. The proportions who agree are 26 percent among Catholics, compared with 21 percent among Protestants; 31 percent of blacks agree, compared with 19 percent of whites; 25 percent of low-income people (bottom third) agree, compared with 14 percent of upper-income people (top third); 26 percent of weekly religious attenders agree, compared with 15 percent of infrequent attenders.

14. Banker Harold Bentley's remarks about the poor offer a clear illustration of

the individual attributes that may be credited with making people poor: "We had a gal, one of our tellers at work, she'd worked for us about ten years and her husband had just gone to pot. He was drinking and gambling and just wasting money and he led her all the way through bankruptcy. And we knew that they were having a hard time for Christmas, so we took up a collection. A few of us got together and we raised, I think, $600 in about three days. We knew we could give it to her, but we didn't want him to get at it. So, we went and bought a gift certificate. Another gal, we knew she was having a hard time and we bought all their Christmas presents. A lot of times it's divorce. One was a lady had a problem with her husband, he was in the military and he was accused of molesting the daughter, so he was separated, so it just caused havoc in the family. And he was being held outside of the home. They were in base housing and she was working for us, so we decided we could help her out for Christmas to make it easier for the kids. She didn't have much money. She was only working part-time and then full-time. The other gal, her husband had pretty much drained all their money and was more interested in going hunting and fishing and playing around with his money with the gambling than he was taking care of the two kids."

15. These images of the poor have been widely discussed in so-called just world theories and in attribution studies; see especially Joe R. Feagin, *Subordinating the Poor* (Englewood Cliffs, N.J.: Prentice-Hall, 1975), and Patricia Gurin, "Expectancy Theory in the Study of Poverty," *Journal of Social Issues* 26 (1970): 83–104. Some of this literature suggests that religious beliefs reinforce individualistic or blame-the-victim images of the poor, but social class and education appear to be even more important factors, and cross-national research shows these images are by no means limited to the United States.

16. Belief that many changes are possible is more common among older than younger people, and among the better educated, those with higher incomes, and those working in professional or managerial occupations. Controlling for these differences, there are no significant effects due to attendance at religious services, but those who have heard sermons on stewardship and say the idea of it is meaningful are more likely than others to believe changes are possible. Women and men did not differ on this item, but people living on the West Coast were more likely than average to believe changes possible, while East Coast residents were less likely. Residents of large cities were significantly less likely to think changes possible than residents of smaller towns and rural areas, and blacks were less optimistic than whites about making changes. Substantively, these results indicate strongly that the disadvantaged are far less likely to think economic changes are possible than those who are already in advantaged social strata.

17. Women and better-educated people are more likely than average to say the economic system needs fundamental change or replacing; there is no relationship between these views and frequency of church attendance; by a margin of 9 percent to 5 percent, religious conservatives are more likely than

religious liberals to choose the "best system we could possibly have" response, but none of the other responses differ between the two groups; those who attend Sunday school classes or fellowship groups, and who are more exposed to thinking about stewardship, are slightly less likely than others to believe fundamental changes are needed, but these differences amount only to several percentage points.

18. His full statement is as follows: "I'm talking from a scriptural point of view, and from the point where I believe God has created mankind to fit into this design. I think men should be leaders. I think men should be providers. I think women should be those who encourage emotionally, strengthen the bonds at home, build up, strengthen the leaders, the men. That's not happening today. And I think a fall-out from that is broken relationships, so many single parents, single mothers. Trying to go out and try and make a living. Can hardly make ends meet. And with these kids, because men have walked out on them. Men have not taken their responsibility in that regard. And oftentimes I think men are shrinking back because women are surging ahead in being assertive. And I think men feel threatened and belittled when women become assertive, and it threatens their positions. And so I think our whole society is being turned on its head because of that. We're not following the, I think, the God-given guidelines for roles and responsibilities. I think because of that we have a lot of inequity in society."

19. Results of a nationwide New York Times/CBS News Poll conducted May 6–8, 1992; reported in Robin Toner, "Politics of Welfare: Focusing on the Problems," *New York Times*, July 5, 1992, p. 1.

20. A different way of saying this is that there is a thirty-one point spread on the volunteer item between those who have thought a great deal and those who have thought only a little about responsibilities to the poor; in contrast, there is only a nine-point spread on the government item.

21. Standard demographic factors were associated with these various proposals. Women were more likely than men to express confidence in volunteer efforts, church activity, and government programs, while men were more likely than women to favor economic growth. The better educated were more likely than the less educated to favor volunteer activity and business involvement but less likely to favor hard work and church activity. With these factors and age, income, and occupation controlled, church attendance was positively associated with volunteer work and church activity, negatively associated with government programs, and unrelated to the other items. In addition, religious conservatism was related with a lack of confidence in government programs (and largely explained away the relationship with church attendance). Stewardship sermon exposure and saying stewardship was a meaningful idea were positively associated with confidence in volunteer efforts and church activity, negatively associated with government programs, and unrelated to most of the other items.

22. Doug Hill observes, for example, "Oftentimes some people are doing won-

derful jobs and it seems like at times are not being compensated for the work that they do, whereas other people do work which is fairly menial, and oftentimes their compensation seems to be a lot greater."

23. The negative relationship between church attendance and saying churches should emphasize programs for the poor a lot more takes on additional significance in view of the fact that there were positive relationships between church attendance and supporting a lot more emphasis on most other activities, including one's dealing with the relationship between faith and economic life, for example, "encouraging people to be less materialistic."

Chapter Eight. Charitable Behavior

1. Alexis de Tocqueville, *Democracy in America*, 2 vols. (New York: Vintage, 1945 [originally published in 1835]).

2. Brian O'Connell, editor, *America's Voluntary Spirit* (New York: Foundation Center, 1983); Robert H. Bremner, *American Philanthropy*, 2d ed. (Chicago: University of Chicago Press, 1988).

3. Virginia A. Hodgkinson, *Giving and Volunteering in the United States* (Washington, D.C.: Independent Sector, 1990); Walter Powell, editor, *The Nonprofit Sector: A Research Handbook* (New Haven: Yale University Press, 1987).

4. Estelle James, editor, *The Nonprofit Sector in International Perspective: Studies in Comparative Culture and Policy* (New York: Oxford University Press, 1989); Robert Wuthnow, editor, *Between States and Markets: The Voluntary Sector in Comparative Perspective* (Princeton: Princeton University Press, 1991).

5. The possible exception is Israel, but strict comparisons are impossible because of different reporting schemes, variations in the definition of charities and nonprofit organizations, and variations in pass-through programs involving government and business; for a discussion, see Wuthnow, *Between States and Markets*.

6. According to *Giving USA* (New York: AAFRC, 1992), total charitable giving for the year ending December 31, 1991, amounted to $124.8 billion, with religion accounting for $67.6 billion, or 54.2 percent of the total. Eighty percent of all giving was from individuals.

7. Hodgkinson, *Giving and Volunteering*, p. 26.

8. These relationships also remain strong when standard demographic characteristics, including family income, are controlled. Age, education, and family income have significant effects on the likelihood of giving at least $500 a year to religious organizations; controlling for these differences, race and gender do not. Of religious variables, church attendance has the strongest effect, followed by having heard a stewardship sermon, participation in Sunday school classes, and membership in a fellowship group; other variables generally have only a weak effect when church attendance is controlled.

9. Virginia A. Hodgkinson, Murray S. Weitzman, and Arthur D. Kirsch, "From Commitment to Action: How Religious Involvement Affects Giving and Volunteering," pp. 93-114 in *Faith and Philanthropy in America*, edited by Robert Wuthnow and Virginia A. Hodgkinson (San Francisco: Jossey Bass, 1990); see also chapters on blacks and Jews in this volume; and Wuthnow, *Acts of Compassion: Caring for Others and Helping Ourselves* (Princeton: Princeton University Press, 1991).

10. The proportions who have given $500 or more in the past year for each of the following are as follows: thought about what the Bible teaches about money a great deal, 33 percent; a fair amount, 29 percent; little or hardly any, 21 percent. Thought about responsibility to the poor a great deal, 36 percent; a fair amount, 25 percent; little or hardly any, 17 percent. Thought about faith and work a great deal, 35 percent; a fair amount, 28 percent; little or hardly any, 19 percent. Experienced a calling, yes, 30 percent; no, 22 percent. Idea of stewardship is very meaningful, 35 percent; fairly meaningful, 24 percent; not very or not at all meaningful, 14 percent. Multivariate statistics indicate that the items dealing specifically with monetary issues and religion indeed have stronger effects on religious giving than items dealing with work or with general religiosity.

11. Using the labor force data, ordinary least squares multiple regression models (in which demographic and income factors are controlled) reveal that the average increment in religious giving to be gained from church members increasing their attendance at religious services either from yearly to monthly or from monthly to weekly is $456 annually; that the increment expected from members also becoming regular participants in a Sunday school class is $1,319 annually; from becoming a member of a fellowship group, $762 annually; and from hearing a sermon about personal finances, $537. Monetary values (expected increments in annual religious giving) can be associated with other factors as well: getting people to think more about the relationship between their faith and finances ($324), their responsibility to the poor ($148), and being thankful for financial blessings ($233). Caution is advised in interpreting such results, however, because of assumptions about linearity and the normal distribution of variables that are not adequately met.

12. In another national survey, three people in four agreed that charities often fatten the pocketbooks of their administrators; Wuthnow, *Acts of Compassion;* shortly after the Economic Values Survey was conducted in 1992, widespread public attention was drawn to allegations that William Aramony, head of United Way, had been one such administrator.

13. Among those who disagreed that churches use their money wisely, only 13 percent had given $500 or more in the past year, compared with 26 percent of those who agreed with the statement.

14. The relationship between feeling annoyed and giving less is evident in the fact that 12 percent of those who said they were annoyed by church requests for money gave $500 or more, compared with 27 percent of those who were

not annoyed; whether one causes the other, or is merely an after-the-fact rationalization, cannot be determined from such data.

15. Catholics differ from Protestants mostly in saying they would give more if the church were more liberal on sexual and moral issues.

16. Studies of charitable giving have generally documented relationships between levels of disposable family income and levels of giving, and have sometimes shown the negative effects of recessions as well. The Economic Values Survey, in addition to revealing an effect of family income on giving, also found some traces of broader economic conditions. The 10 percent who had been laid off within the past year, for example, were only half as likely to have given $500 or more to religious organizations than those who had not been laid off. About one person in seven also claimed to have sustained a pay cut in the past year. But these people were almost as likely to have given $500 or more as people who had not experienced a pay cut.

17. Among individuals with incomes in the top third of the sample, 41 percent said they would give more if they had fewer economic needs themselves, compared with 51 percent of individuals in the bottom third.

18. The data on perceived financial obligations by level of income are presented in Chapter 4.

19. The proportions who give at least $500 a year to religious organizations is 17 percent among those who say making a lot of money is absolutely essential to them, 18 percent among those who say it is very important, and 31 percent among those who say it is fairly important or not very important.

20. Several other values were also negatively related to religious giving: living a comfortable life, being successful, having a beautiful home and other nice things, having a high-paying job, wearing expensive clothing, and eating at nice restaurants.

21. A comparison of multivariate models with religious volunteering as the dependent variable and with religious giving as the dependent variable reveals that the two are associated almost identically with other measures of religious belief and involvement. Controlling for attendance at religious services, participating in Sunday school classes is one of the strongest predictors of religious volunteering. Participating in a fellowship group is actually the strongest predictor of religious volunteering, and makes more of a difference to volunteering than it does to giving. Having friends in the congregation is also more closely associated with volunteering than with giving, as might be expected. Stewardship sermons have an equivalent effect on volunteering as on giving. Relatively speaking, it appears that volunteering is more decisively affected by other measures of congregational *participation* than by religious beliefs or lifestyle characteristics.

22. The percentages are 39 percent among women employed full-time and 33 percent among women employed part-time. The *perception* of being too busy is also one of the strongest predictors of not doing religious volunteer work.

23. Valuing money is in fact negatively associated with religious volunteering, just as it is with religious giving. Values that are *positively* associated with religious volunteering include family, community, helping the needy, and one's relationship with God. Other values that are negatively associated with religious volunteering include personal freedom, being successful, having a beautiful home and other nice things, traveling for pleasure, a high-paying job, wearing expensive clothes, and eating at nice restaurants.

24. Among those who have thought a great deal about linking their faith and their work, 63 percent have done volunteer work at their church or synagogue in the past year, compared with 41 percent of those who have thought about this link a fair amount, and only 16 percent of those who have thought about it little or hardly any.

25. Wuthnow, *Acts of Compassion*.

26. Ibid. The earlier results are also evident in the Economic Values Survey data. Respondents who attended religious services at least several times a year and were also involved in either a Sunday school class or a fellowship group were compared with respondents who attended religious services at least several times a year but were not involved in a class or group. Among the former there was a strong relationship between how important respondents said religion was to them and their likelihood of being involved in charitable or social service activities; among the latter, there was no relationship. Probably the reason is that group involvement puts people in direct contact with others, makes their faith public, and suggests specific opportunities for charitable behavior. In this, charitable behavior seems to be different from many of the other effects of religious participation on values and attitudes. On most items having to do with work, money, and thinking about the relationship of faith to work and money, subjective religiosity is as strongly related to these items among the marginally involved as it is among the actively involved. This is true even of religious giving. The implications of this finding should not be overstated, but they do cast some doubt on sociological arguments about the role of so-called plausibility structures in reinforcing subjective beliefs. The relationships between religiosity and many aspects of work and money perhaps do not depend heavily on such plausibility structures because (1) these relationships are not discussed explicitly in many religious settings, or (2) these relationships are rather widely (if not deeply) institutionalized in public religious and moral discourse.

27. Because only 4 percent of the total sample had received financial support, statistical significance is reached only when these differences are quite large. Multivariate statistical analysis of the main demographic variables indicates that income, race, and part- or full-time employment remain significant when age, occupation, education, and gender are controlled.

28. Figures compiled by the House Ways and Means Committee in 1992 indicated that 30 percent of people going on welfare were unmarried women with children, and another 45 percent were recently divorced or separated; "Life of Quiet Poverty," *New York Times*, July 7, 1992, p. A16.

29. Other religious characteristics suggest that recipients are distributed fairly broadly within the religiously involved population; for example, 26 percent of recipients defined themselves as religious conservatives and 28 percent as religious liberals, percentages that were nearly the same as in the labor force as a whole. Because religious liberals generally show lower levels of involvement on other religious measures, these figures actually suggest that liberal churches may be doing a somewhat better job of supporting the financially needy, other things being equal, than conservative churches.

30. Participation in fellowship groups "explains" about two-thirds of the relationship between attendance at religious services and receiving financial help. Substantively, this means that fellowship groups are the place, more than religious services, where such needs come to be identified. The fact that praying about money and discussing finances with members of a church or synagogue are strongly related to receiving financial help is also significant. These relationships point to the importance of group settings in which the broader taboo in American culture against discussing money can be overcome.

31. Controlling for income and part- or full-time employment, receiving financial assistance remains strongly associated with attendance at religious services; when participation in fellowship groups is added to the model, the effect of group participation is also significant and strong; it accounts for about two-thirds of the initial effect of attendance. Substantively, these results suggest that participation in fellowship groups is probably how potential recipients are identified and supported. These models also support the conclusion that religious conservatism or liberalism among recipients is not a factor.

32. The exact figure was 54 percent; the survey was conducted in 1989 as part of my study of volunteer activity in the United States; described in Wuthnow, *Acts of Compassion.*

33. Hodgkinson et al., "From Commitment to Action," p. 96.

Chapter Nine. Considering the Future

1. Social scientists have often appealed to religious leaders to be interested in social and economic issues because of their gravity; I am simply suggesting here that it is also in the interest of religious leaders themselves to address such issues, rather than handing them over to secular leaders.

Selected Bibliography

Auletta, Ken. *Greed and Glory on Wall Street: The Fall of the House of Lehman*. New York: Random House, 1986.

Baida, Peter. *Poor Richard's Legacy: American Business Values from Benjamin Franklin to Donald Trump*. New York: William Morrow, 1990.

Bailyn, Bernard, ed. *The Apologia of Robert Keayne: The Last Will and Testament of Me, Robert Keayne, All of It Written with My Own Hands and Began by Me, Mo: 6: I: 1653, Commonly Called August, The Self Portrait of a Puritan Merchant*. Gloucester, Mass.: Peter Smith, 1970.

Baird, J. Arthur. *The Greed Syndrome: An Ethical Sickness in American Capitalism*. Akron: Hampshire Books, 1989.

Beckford, James A. *Religion and Advanced Industrial Society*. London: Unwin Hyman, 1989.

Bell, Daniel. *The Coming of Post-Industrial Society: A Venture in Social Forecasting*. New York: Basic Books, 1973.

Bellah, Robert N. *Beyond Belief: Essays on Religion in a Post-Traditional World*. New York: Harper & Row, 1970.

Bellah, Robert N., Richard Madsen, William M. Sullivan, Ann Swidler, and Steven M. Tipton. *Habits of the Heart: Individualism and Commitment in American Life*. Berkeley and Los Angeles: University of California Press, 1985.

Berger, Peter L. *The Sacred Canopy: Elements of a Sociological Theory of Religion*. Garden City, N.Y.: Doubleday, 1966.

——. *A Far Glory: The Quest for Faith in an Age of Credulity*. New York: Free Press, 1992.

Berger, Peter L. and Thomas Luckmann. *The Social Construction of Reality: A Treatise in the Sociology of Knowledge*. Garden City, N.Y.: Doubleday, 1966.

Birnbaum, Norman. *The Crisis of Industrial Society*. New York: Oxford University Press, 1989.

349

Blanchard, Kenneth and Norman Vincent Peale. *The Power of Ethical Management*. New York: William Morrow, 1988.

Bremner, Robert H. *American Philanthropy*, 2d ed. Chicago: University of Chicago Press, 1988.

Brooke, John. *The Heart of the Commonwealth: Society and Political Culture in Central Massachusetts, 1713–1861*. New York: Cambridge University Press, 1989.

Buckley, Thomas. "The One Who Flies All Around the World." *Parabola* 16 (1991): 4–9.

Burns, Gene. *Frontiers of Catholicism*. Berkeley and Los Angeles: University of California Press, 1992.

Campbell, Angus. *The Sense of Well-Being in America*. New York: McGraw-Hill, 1981.

Caplow, Theodore, Howard M. Bahr, and Bruce A. Chadwick. *All Faithful People: Change and Continuity in Middletown's Religion*. Minneapolis: University of Minnesota Press, 1983.

Cassity, Michael. *Defending a Way of Life: An American Community in the Nineteenth Century*. Albany: State University of New York Press, 1989.

Cochran, Thomas. *Railroad Leaders, 1845–1890: The Business Mind in Action*. Cambridge, Mass.: Harvard University Press, 1953.

Coles, Robert. *A Spectacle Unto the World: The Catholic Worker Movement*. New York: Viking, 1973.

———. *The Call of Stories: Teaching and the Moral Imagination*. Boston: Houghton Mifflin, 1989.

Crane, Verner W. *Benjamin Franklin and a Rising People*. Boston: Little, Brown, 1954.

Dobbelaere, Karel. "Secularization: A Multi-Dimensional Concept." *Current Sociology* 29 (1981): 1–215.

Dorr, Donal. *Option for the Poor: A Hundred Years of Vatican Social Teaching*. Dublin: Gill and Macmillan, 1983.

Douglas, Mary. *Purity and Danger: An Analysis of Concepts of Pollution and Taboo*. London: Penguin, 1966.

———. "The Effects of Modernization on Religious Change," pp. 25–43 in *Religion and America: Spirituality in a Secular Age*, edited by May Douglas and Steven M. Tipton. Boston: Beacon, 1983.

Douglas, Mary and Baron Isherwood. *The World of Goods*. New York: Basic Books, 1979.

Ehrenreich, Barbara. *The Worst Years of Our Lives: Irreverent Notes from a Decade of Greed*. New York: Pantheon, 1990.

Ellul, Jacques. *Money and Power*. Downers Grove, Ill.: Inter-Varsity Press, 1984.

Ellsberg, Robert, editor. *By Little and By Little: The Selected Writings of Dorothy Day*. New York: Knopf, 1983.

Epstein, Joseph. *Ambition: The Secret Passion*. Chicago: Ivan R. Dee, 1980.

Feagin, Joe R. *Subordinating the Poor*. Englewood Cliffs, N.J.: Prentice-Hall, 1975.

Ford, Paul Leicester. *The Many-Sided Franklin*. New York: Century, 1899.

Foucault, Michel. *The Archeology of Knowledge*. New York: Random House, 1972.

Friedman, Milton. *Essays in Positive Economics*. Chicago: University of Chicago Press, 1953.

Furnham, Adrian. "Many Sides of the Coin: The Psychology of Money Usage." *Personality and Individual Differences* 5 (1984): 95–103.

———. *The Protestant Work Ethic: The Psychology of Work-Related Beliefs and Behaviours*. London: Routledge, 1990.

Furnham, Adrian and Alan Lewis. *The Economic Mind: The Social Psychology of Economic Behavior*. New York: St. Martins Press, 1986.

Furth, Hans G. *The World of Grown-Ups: Children's Conceptions of Society*. New York: Elsevier, 1980.

Gay, Craig. *With Liberty and Justice for Whom? The Recent Evangelical Debate Over Capitalism*. Grand Rapids, Mich.: Eerdmans, 1991.

Geertz, Clifford. *The Interpretation of Cultures*. New York: Basic Books, 1973.

Gibbard, Allan. *Wise Choices, Apt Feelings: A Theory of Normative Judgment*. Cambridge, Mass.: Harvard University Press, 1990.

Glock, Charles Y. and Rodney Stark. *Religion and Society in Tension*. Chicago: Rand McNally, 1965.

Greeley, Andrew M. *Crisis in the Church*. Chicago: Thomas More Press, 1979.

Greeley, Andrew M. *Social Change in American Religion*. Cambridge, Mass.: Harvard University Press, 1990.

Gustafson, James M. *Can Ethics Be Christian?* Chicago: University of Chicago Press, 1975.

Gutman, Herbert. *Work, Culture, and Society in Industrializing America: Essays in American Working-Class and Social History*. New York: Knopf, 1976.

Hart, Stephen. *What Does the Lord Require? How American Christians Think about Economic Justice*. New York: Oxford University Press, 1992.

Hecksher, Eli F. *Mercantilism*, 2 vols. New York: Macmillan, 1955.

Hirschman, Albert O. *The Passions and the Interests: Political Arguments for Capitalism Before Its Triumph*. Princeton: Princeton University Press, 1977.

Hodgkinson, Virginia A. *Giving and Volunteering in the United States*. Washington, D.C.: Independent Sector, 1990.

Hyde, Lewis. *The Gift: Imagination and the Erotic Life of Property*. New York: Vintage, 1983.

James, Estelle, editor. *The Nonprofit Sector in International Perspective: Studies in Comparative Culture and Policy*. New York: Oxford University Press, 1989.

Kekes, John. *Moral Tradition and Individuality*. Princeton: Princeton University Press, 1989.

Keller, Rosemary Skinner. *Calling and Career: Vocational Journey in the American Experience*. Louisville: Westminster/John Knox, 1994.

Lampert, Hope. *True Greed: What Really Happened in the Battle for RJR Nabisco*. New York: New American Library, 1990.

Lane, Robert E. *The Market Experience*. Cambridge: Cambridge University Press, 1991.

Laurie, Bruce. *Working People of Philadelphia, 1800–1850*. Philadelphia: Temple University Press, 1980.

Levy, Barry. *Quakers and the American Family: British Settlement in the Delaware Valley*. New York: Oxford University Press, 1988.

Luckmann, Thomas. *The Invisible Religion: The Transformation of Symbols in Industrial Society*. New York: Macmillan, 1967.

Luft, Joseph. "Monetary Value and the Perception of Persons." *Journal of Social Psychology* 46 (1957): 245–51.

Luhman, Niklas. "The Individuality of the Individual: Historical Meanings and Contemporary Problems," pp. 313–28 in *Reconstructing Individualism: Autonomy, Individuality, and the Self in Western Thought*, edited by Thomas C. Heller, Morton Sosna, and David E. Wellbery. Stanford: Stanford University Press, 1986.

MacFarlane, Alan. *The Culture of Capitalism*. London: Basil Blackwell, 1987.

Machlup, Fritz. *Methodology of Economics and Other Social Sciences*. New York: Academic Press, 1978.

MacIntyre, Alasdair. *A Short History of Ethics*. New York: Macmillan, 1966.

———. *After Virtue*, 2d ed. Notre Dame, Ind.: University of Notre Dame Press, 1984.

Malinowski, Bronislaw. *Argonauts of the Western Pacific*. London: Routledge, 1922.

Martin, David. *A General Theory of Secularization*. New York: Harper & Row, 1978.

Marx, Karl and Friedrich Engels. *The German Ideology*. New York: International Publishers, 1947.

Meyer, John W. and W. Richard Scott. *Organizational Environments: Ritual and Rationality*. Beverly Hills, Calif.: Sage, 1983.

Miller, William D. *Dorothy Day: A Biography*. San Francisco: Harper & Row, 1982.

Moore, G. E. *Principia Ethica*. Cambridge: Cambridge University Press, 1903.

Myers, Milton L. *The Soul of Modern Economic Man: Ideas of Self-Interest, Thomas Hobbes to Adam Smith*. Chicago: University of Chicago Press, 1983.

Nagel, Thomas. *The Possibility of Altruism*. Princeton: Princeton University Press, 1970.

Needleman, Jacob. *Money and the Meaning of Life*. New York: Doubleday, 1992.

Niebuhr, Reinhold, editor. *Marx and Engels on Religion*. New York: Schocken, 1964.

Nisbet, Robert. "Individual Ethics." *Public Opinion* (November/December, 1986): 7–8.

Noddings, Nel. *Caring: A Feminine Approach to Ethics and Moral Education*. Berkeley and Los Angeles: University of California Press, 1984.

O'Connell, Brian, editor. *America's Voluntary Spirit*. New York: Foundation Center, 1983.

Parry, J. and M. Bloch, editors. *Money and the Morality of Exchange*. Cambridge: Cambridge University Press, 1989.

Parsons, Talcott. *The Structure of Social Action*, 2 vols. New York: Free Press, 1937.

———. *Sociological Theory*. New York: Free Press, 1967.

———. "Religion in Post-Industrial Society: The Problem of Secularization." *Social Research* 41 (1974): 193–225.

Parsons, Talcott and Edward Shils. *Toward a General Theory of Action: Theoretical Foundations for the Social Sciences*. New York: Harper & Row, 1951.

Powell, Walter, editor. *The Nonprofit Sector: A Research Handbook*. New Haven: Yale University Press, 1987.

Raeff, Marc. "The Well-Ordered Police State and the Development of Modernity in Seventeenth- and Eighteenth-Century Europe: An Attempt at a Comparative Approach." *American Historical Review* 80 (1975): 1225–54.

Rubenstein, Carin. "Money and Self-Esteem, Relationships, Secrecy, Envy, Satisfaction." *Psychology Today* 15 (May 1981): 29–44.

Rush, Myron. *Lord of the Marketplace*. Wheaton, Ill.: Victor Books, 1986.

Russell, Phillips. *Benjamin Franklin: The First Civilized American*. New York: Brentano's, 1927.

Ryan, Mary. *Cradle of the Middle Class: The Family in Oneida County, New York, 1790–1865*. New York: Cambridge University Press, 1981.

Samuelsson, Kurt. *Religion and Economic Action: A Critique of Max Weber*. New York: Harper & Row, 1957.

Sanford, Charles L. *Benjamin Franklin and the American Character*. Boston: D.C. Heath, 1955.

Saussure, Ferdinand de. *Course in General Linguistics*. New York: McGraw-Hill, 1959.

Schimmel, Solomon. *The Seven Deadly Sins: Jewish, Christian, and Classical Reflections on Human Nature*. New York: Free Press, 1992.

Schmoller, Gustav. *The Mercantile System and Its Historical Significance*. New York: Macmillan, 1896.

Schor, Juliet B. *The Overworked American: The Unexpected Decline of Leisure*. New York: Basic Books, 1991.

Sen, Amartya. "Rational Fools: A Critique of the Behavioral Foundations of Economic Theory." *Philosophy and Public Affairs* 6 (1977): 317–44.

Sherman, Doug and William Hendricks. *Keeping Your Ethical Edge Sharp*. Colorado Springs: NavPress, 1990.

Sterngold, James. *Burning Down the House: How Greed, Deceit, and Bitter Revenge Destroyed E. F. Hutton.* New York: Summit Books, 1990.

Taylor, Charles. *Sources of the Self: The Making of the Modern Identity*. Cambridge, Mass.: Harvard University Press, 1989.

Thelen, David. *Paths of Resistance: Tradition and Dignity in Industrializing Missouri*. New York: Oxford University Press, 1986.

Thomas, George M., John W. Meyer, Francisco O. Ramirez, and John Boli. *Institutional*

Structure: Constituting State, Society, and the Individual. Beverly Hills, Calif.: Sage, 1987.

Tipton, Steven M. *Getting Saved from the Sixties: Moral Meaning in Conversion and Cultural Change*. Berkeley and Los Angeles: University of California Press, 1982.

Tocqueville, Alexis de. *Democracy in America*, 2 vols. New York: Vintage, 1945.

Toffler, Barbara Ley. *Tough Choices: Managers Talk Ethics*. New York: Wiley, 1986.

Tucker, Graham. *The Faith-Work Connection: A Practical Application of Christian Values in the Workplace*. Toronto: Anglican Book Centre, 1987.

Veblen, Thorstein. *The Theory of the Leisure Class: An Economic Study of Institutions*. New York: New American Library, 1912.

Wallerstein, Immanual. *The Modern World-System*, vol. 2, *Mercantilism and the Consolidation of the European World-Economy, 1600–1750*. New York: Academic Press, 1980.

Warner, R. Stephen. "Work in Progress Toward a New Paradigm for the Sociological Study of Religion in the United States." *American Journal of Sociology* 98 (1993); 1044–93.

Weber, Max. *Ancient Judaism*. New York: Free Press, 1952.

Weber, Max. *The Protestant Ethic and the Spirit of Capitalism*. New York: Scribner's, 1958.

Weber, Max. *The Sociology of Religion*. Boston: Beacon Press, 1963.

Wernimont, Paul F. and Susan Fitzpatrick. "The Meaning of Money." *Journal of Applied Psychology* 50 (1972): 218–26.

Whyte, Jr., William H. *The Organization Man*. Garden City, N.Y.: Doubleday, 1956.

Wiebe, Robert. *The Search for Order, 1877–1920*. New York: Hill and Wang, 1967.

Williams, Bernard. *Problems of the Self*. Cambridge: Cambridge University Press, 1973.

Wilson, Bryan. *Religion in Secular Society: A Sociological Comment*. Baltimore: Penguin, 1963.

Wilson, Charles. *Mercantilism*. London: Routledge, 1958.

Wogaman, J. Philip. *Economics and Ethics: A Christian Inquiry*. Philadelphia: Fortress Press, 1986.

Wuthnow, Robert. *The Consciousness Reformation*. Berkeley and Los Angeles: University of California Press, 1976.

———. *Meaning and Moral Order: Explorations in Cultural Analysis*. Berkeley and Los Angeles: University of California Press, 1987.

———. *The Restructuring of American Religion: Society and Faith Since World War II*. Princeton: Princeton University Press, 1988.

———. *The Struggle for America's Soul: Evangelicals, Liberals, and Secularism*. Grand Rapids, Mich.: Eerdmans, 1989.

———. *Acts of Compassion: Caring for Others and Helping Ourselves*. Princeton:

Princeton University Press, 1991.

―――. *Christianity in the 21st Century: Reflections on the Challenges Ahead.* New York: Oxford University Press, 1993.

―――, editor. *Between States and Markets: The Voluntary Sector in Comparative Perspective.* Princeton: Princeton University Press, 1991.

Wuthnow, Robert and Virginia A. Hodgkinson, editors. *Faith and Philanthropy in America.* San Francisco: Jossey-Bass, 1990.

Yamanchi, Kent and Donald Templer. "The Development of a Money Attitude Scale." *Journal of Personality Assessment* 46 (1982): 522–28.

Zerubavel, Eviatar. *Hidden Rhythms: Schedules and Calendars in Social Life.* Berkeley: University of California Press, 1981.

―――. *The Fine Line: Making Distinctions in Everyday Life.* New York: Free Press, 1991.

Zuckerman, Michael. "Holy Wars, Civil Wars: Religion and Economics in Nineteenth-Century America." *Prospects* 16 (1991): 205–40.

Index